THE KILLING FIELDS

DIANA WASHINGTON VALDEZ

Copyright ©, 2005, 2006, 2020 by Diana Washington Valdez

All rights reserved, including the right of reproduction in whole or in part or in any form without written permission except in the case of brief quotations in critical articles and reviews.

The Killing Fields: Harvest of Women

Published by Peace at the Border
Peace at the Border Film Productions
1700 Northside Drive
Suite A7 PMB 2395
Atlanta, Georgia 30318
www.borderechoes.com

Book Editor: Robert Locke

Photography Coordinator: Leonel Monroy

The Killing Fields: Harvest of Women, First Edition in English, 2006 by Peace at the Border (978-0-6151-4008-7).

ISBN – 13: 978-0-9777992-2-0
ISBN: 978-0-9777992-2-0

Comments

"Diana Washington Valdez has done an outstanding job of investigative reporting on a social issue that just won't go away. Young working-class women in Juarez, Mexico, have been the victims of unspeakable violence, rape and murder, over a period of many years. What initially seemed to be a matter of police incompetence has evolved into a national disgrace. Ms. Washington Valdez has shown the way, and highlighted the problem with cold, hard facts learned at considerable personal risk. All that is needed now is the political will to seriously follow up on her good work."

Gordon F. Ellison, Retired
Federal Bureau of Investigation
Special Agent and Legal Attaché

"[This book] awakens in all of us the stark reality of the vulnerability of women in the border city of Ciudad Juarez, Mexico. Mexican governmental indifference toward its working-class women population is shown at its highest forms, clearly depicting these women as second class citizens in a city where the rich, the politicians, and the well-connected have it all, while the rest of its citizenry live in squalor, fear, and an overall sense of total frustration. Diana Washington Valdez has done a superb job in exposing these realities."

George A. McNenney, Retired
United States Customs Service
Special Agent in Charge

"The book is a powerful and blunt document, important for its clear lines of investigation: two or more serial killers, low-level drug dealers, two gangs, a group of powerful men, and copycats. In addition, it presents a previously unexplored line of investigation that points to an analysis of femicides as messages directed at U.S. and Mexican economic interests, be they bilateral anti-drug projects or trade accords."

Marisa Belausteguigoitia
Mexico National Autonomous University
Gender Studies Program, Mexico City

"This book is very good. It is remarkable for its references to powerful people, such as the "narco juniors," and how they may have disposed of our daughters' bodies. I read it slowly because I want to understand everything that has happened."

Paula Flores González
Mother of Sagrario González Flores

"I am convinced that the book contains much truth. My other daughter wanted to read it, too."

Bertha Marquez
Mother of Adriana Torres Marquez

"Many things about the book impressed me, such as the allegations that people in the drug trade are involved in the murders. There are many truths here, and I would like for this journalist to continue her research .... I hope that it will help us to someday find out who killed our daughters and for the whole truth to come out."

Ramona Morales
Mother of Silvia Morales

"In her book, Washington Valdez gives a detailed and chronological account of how these murders in the border town progressed. (She) acknowledges that these women are victims of a corrupt society that existed in this part of Mexico before the murders began."

"Journalist Diana Washington Valdez investigates the sexual homicides of women in the Mexican town of Juarez. This heartbreaking expose implicates high-level police and well-known citizens in the unsolved murders."

Carmen Ospina
Criticas Magazine

"I admire the efforts by human rights activists around the world and fellow artists like Salma Hayek, Eve Ensler, Jane Fonda, Sally Field, Gloria Steinem and journalist Diana Washington Valdez. I am deeply honored to join them to continue the work on this very important issue." – *Amnesty International news release.* [Amnesty International awarded Jennifer Lopez the Artists for Amnesty Award for producing *Bordertown*, a movie about the Juarez femicides that was presented at the 2007 Berlin International Film Festival.]

Amnesty International/Jennifer Lopez

THE KILLING FIELDS

Harvest of Women

by

Diana Washington Valdez

Peace at the Border
Atlanta, Georgia

More about the topics in this book @

The film "Border Echoes (Ecos de una frontera)," Lorena Mendez-Quiroga, available now on DVD, www.bordDark Suns on iTunes (apple.com)erechoes.com

The podcast "Forgotten: Women of Juarez," Oz Woloshyn & Monica Ortiz-Uribe, Forgotten: Women of Juárez | iHeartRadio

The film "Dark Suns/Soles Negros/Soleils Noirs," Julien Elie, Dark Suns on iTunes (apple.com)

Author's blog Diana Washington Valdez

INTRODUCTION

This book by border journalist Diana Washington Valdez reminds us that justice has not prevailed for the families of hundreds of girls and women who were brutally murdered and disappeared in Ciudad Juarez, Mexico, across the border from El Paso, Texas. *Harvest of Women: Safari in Mexico* will make your heart stop and your mind question why the atrocities that began twelve years ago continue to this day. The cold facts will direct you to the same conclusion – that it is only a matter of time before the drug cartel crosses the Rio Grande and these heinous crimes begin to occur on the U.S. side of the border. This thoroughly researched book, with its disturbing findings, is an excellent source of information for people who want to be genuinely informed about this tragic human rights issue. It should be required reading for students of Border Studies. The concerns over what was taking place in our neighbor city prompted the Legislature to address the matter. As a result, I introduced a resolution during the 78th Texas Legislature requesting that the FBI be directly involved in assisting the Mexican authorities in their investigations into the murders. Texas Governor Rick Perry signed House Concurrent Resolution 59 on June 22, 2003.

State Representative Norma Chávez

Texas House of Representatives, District 76 El Paso, Texas

For J.C. Emmnuel,

and for all the stars

whose lights were dimmed.

Contents

Introduction i
Prologue: Deaths that cry out 1

PART I 7

1. Border Safari 9
2. Near Cartel Ranch 15
3. Lomas de Poleo, 1996 21
4. Atrocities 29
5. Sagrario's Death 38
6. The Gringo 47
7. Cristo Negro 51
8. Death of a Lawyer 61
9. The Cotton Field Murders 67
10. The Crime Scene 75

PART II 83

11. The Drug Cartel 85
12. Amado's Cartel 91
13. Heidi and Isabel 99
14. The Cartel Wars 110
15. The police cartel 118
16. Terror with a badge 123
17. Police blotter 132
18. Sharif the Egyptian 148
19. Investigations on trial 158
20. Escaped killer 168

PART III 185

21 The FBI: Plaza Sweep 187
22. Mexico's dirty war 197
23. The FBI and femicides.. 213
24. Botched operation 226
25. Modus operandi... 237
26. Operation Sagrario 246
27. Mexico's secret files 254
28. Pacts of Power 261
29. Chihuahua City 266
30. The Femicides Spread 275

PART IV 287

31. The Politicians.. 289
32. The Pact... 301
EPILOGUE 311
Photographs... 316
Glossary 338
Notes 339
Bibliography 360
Appendix 377
About the Author 402
About Peace at the Border 403
Index 404

Prologue

Deaths That Cry Out

It was the brutality with which they killed the young women that first caught my attention. That winter's day of 1999, I stayed up into the early morning hours reading narratives that described death after horrible death. Despite what the Mexican authorities said, the murders were not normal. And they were many.

Dating back to 1993, girls in their adolescent and teenage years suffered unspeakable atrocities, including gang rape and mutilation. Between 1993 and 2005, approximately 470 girls and women died violently in Juarez, Mexico – far more than the 379 deaths the Mexican Federal Attorney General reported for that period. They were killed in various ways: strangled, stabbed, bludgeoned, shot to death. Dozens more are missing.

Janeth Fierro, one of the early victims, was only twelve years old in 1994 when she was abducted. The authorities recovered her strangled body and determined she had been raped. In September 1995, the body of Silvia Rivera Morales, a seventeen year-old student, was dumped in Lote Bravo, an area just south of the Juarez International Airport.

Her right breast was severed, and her left breast mauled by human teeth. That was the year authorities discovered the bodies of several other young women in the same site. All of them were killed with the same ferocity.

Seventeen-year-old Sagragrio Gonzalez Flores disappeared in April of 1998, after finishing her shift at a maquiladora. Later, someone passing by a grassy patch in another part of Juarez saw her body and called the police. The site was about ten miles east of her assembly plant, where hundreds of men and women turned out electronics components by the thousands.

She, too, had been raped, stabbed, and strangled. In 1996, more bodies were discovered in the northwest desert region known as Lomas de Poleo. During a visit to Juarez in 1999, FBI profilers analyzed the Mexican case files for Lote Bravo and Lomas de Poleo. The FBI sent the experts a month after U.S. President Bill Clinton and Mexican President Ernesto Zedillo met in Merida, Mexico.

Five years later, two new presidents, Vicente Fox and George W. Bush, also discussed the Juarez murders. According to Mexican authorities, a mysterious triangle was etched on the backs of several of the victims with a knife or other sharp instrument. A triangle is associated with ultra-right-wing groups, with secret societies, and Nazis. It is also a symbol and map associated with the alliance of drug-traffickers in the "Gold Triangle" states of Chihuahua, Durango and Sinaloa.

The accounts I read that night in 1999 were disturbing. Although not all the murders were related, almost all of them involved extreme violence. The victims also shared striking similarities. It was apparent that the crimes involved a selection process and highly organized abductions. Young women were disappearing in the city's downtown without anyone seeing or hearing anything.

At first, it seemed as though the systematic slayings were the work of depraved criminals with police protection and ties to the underworld. There were indications of that. As this investigation continued, it became evident that far more sinister factors were behind this harvest of death.

Time revealed that some of the killers were powerful men with links to the highest levels of the Mexican government. Police officials who knew they were preying on young women from poor families did nothing to stop them. Dr. Rita Laura Segato, a social anthropologist, said such cabals and their accomplices act as fraternities that use deaths "to mark their territory and seal their pacts of silence." Dr. Julia Monarrez Fragoso, a sociologist in Juarez, referred to the deaths as *femicides* – gender murders. Serial killers, vicious gangs and drug dealers also were getting away with the murders of women in Juarez.

The crime wave that transformed Mexico's largest border city into a global symbol for women's murders did not occur overnight. The unsolved slayings and disappearances had their roots in Mexico's "dirty war," and in alliances with drug cartels that gave rise to extensive networks of corrupt business leaders, soldiers, police, and government officials.

Powerful drug lords and their protectors bribed and intimidated those involved in the investigations. Under pressure to solve the crimes, authorities jailed numerous men who were framed or tortured until they confessed to several of the murders.

The authorities had no scientific proof against any of the suspects in four of the most notorious multiple homicide cases. Because of the impunity that prevailed in Juarez, similar murders and disappearances spread to other places, including the Chihuahua state capital.

In 2003, Cynthia Kiecker, an American citizen from Minnesota, and her husband, Ulises Perzabal, were accused of killing one of the young femicide victims of Chihuahua City. The U.S. State Department was convinced the couple had been tortured into confessing to the girl's murder.

The rampant violence perpetrated by the Carrillo Fuentes drug cartel, which ravaged and terrorized Juarez during this period, served to cloak powerful people who used the slayings to protect their economic interests. A group of men known as "juniors" (slang for the children of wealthy families) also was involved in several of the murders, and for many years, these people remained in the background.

Slowly, however, the veil was pulled back, and it shook them. "The juniors are worried," a source cautioned. "They don't want their names divulged." A concerned government source warned that a Mexican official had launched "Operation Disappearance," to silence a Mexico City journalist Sergio Gonzalez Rodriguez who was also investigating the murders. The official hatched the plan after an influential citizen complained that we were getting too close.

In late 2003, *La Jornada* published an abstract of this book manuscript, and several Mexican police sent a message that I should cease my investigation. Several collaborators and I began to receive telephone calls with strange background noises, including that of an electric saw and a child's voice crying, "Mommy, no!" A U.S. federal officer in El Paso, Texas, received similar messages. Investigators traced the calls back to Mexico. An American woman from El Paso who appeared in a British documentary about the murders received threats, too.

Since the beginning, threats and intimidation became a part of this odyssey. In Juarez, experts have come and gone. And nothing changes. Mexico's government has refused to permit the FBI, which previously provided important leads, to investigate the murders directly. Amnesty International, the Inter-American Commission on Human Rights and the United Nations registered protests with the Mexican government for failing to stop the murders.

Periodic pronouncements by Mexican officials that they solved the crimes bewildered the families of victims who still seek justice. In some cases, the government offered the families compensation in exchange for their silence.

Mexican lawyers Mario Escobedo Anaya and Sergio Dante Almaraz, who defended two men accused unjustly of murdering eight women in 2001, were gunned down in the streets of Juarez.

Although their deaths occurred four years apart, the brazen attacks served notice to everyone involved in this issue.

Juarez is not some dusty border town. It is Mexico's largest border city with nearly two million souls and about 300 assembly plants known as *maquiladoras*, most of them owned by Fortune 500 companies. People work and carry out the normal activities of life. Yet, high-order criminals also operate in the city, and they appear to have free rein.

Heavily armed commandos roam the streets, abducting and executing people in broad daylight. The police never arrest anyone for those brazen crimes. While police look the other way, U.S. corporations go about their business, ignoring the atrocities. Even the Mexican federal government seems powerless to do anything.

The explanation for all this terror would come years later, after that winter's night in 1999. It involved a pact that destined people in the border city to unspeakable violence and horror. It condemned women to fear for their lives.

The pattern of brutal murders of women has spread to other parts of Mexico and Central America. The deaths are occurring where crime lords from Colombia to the U.S.-Mexican border are fighting over coveted corridors of drug, arms, and human-trafficking. Juarez is but one such corridor, albeit an important one.

In February 2006, the Mexican Federal Attorney General's Office released its report on the issue of the Juarez women's murders. The 420-page report said the crimes were vastly exaggerated, there were no serial murders, family violence was the primary cause for them, and most of the slayings were solved.

Human rights groups viewed the report as a whitewash. Without international intervention, the next decade may prove deadlier than the first for the women of Juarez. This book was written because lives are at stake.

PART I

*"He uncovers the deeps out of darkness
and brings deep darkness to light."*

Job 12:22

1.

BORDER SAFARI

CIUDAD JUAREZ–Olga Alicia Carrillo Perez was the center of her mother Irma's world. She was twenty years old when she vanished the evening of August 10, 1995, in downtown Juarez. She had been working at a shoe store and saving money to go to college. Her body was found a month later. Intrigue shrouded her disappearance and death. The authorities charged an Egyptian national, Abdel Latif Sharif Sharif, with the murder, but Perez was not satisfied that the real killer was in jail.

"Anita," a friend of her daughter, was among the last people to see the young woman alive that evening in August. On the day that Carrillo disappeared, Anita had given her a ride to the National Action Party (PAN) headquarters on Avenida 16 de Septiembre and Cinco de Mayo in Juarez. The political party had just come into power in Juarez and Chihuahua after decades of control by the Institutional Revolutionary Party's corrupt hierarchy, and Olga was active in the PAN's youth group.

Riding on the people's hopes for change, the PAN's Francisco Barrio was elected governor of Chihuahua, Francisco Molina Ruiz was appointed state attorney general, and Ramon Galindo became mayor of Juarez. The PAN held all the top state and city law enforcement posts. The party's success came just as the rising numbers of women killed and disappeared began to alarm the border community. That August 10th, Carrillo's plans had included a 7:30 p.m. youth meeting at the PAN's headquarters. After she failed to come home, her mothers and other relatives and friends began a desperate search. They made fliers with her picture and affixed them to poles and walls around the city. They talked to anyone she might have encountered that day, from co-workers and supervisors to bus drivers.

Galindo, the city's incoming mayor, had arranged for the PAN youth group to go on a retreat in the Chihuahua Sierra. After Carrillo was reported missing, Galindo forbade the young members from assisting in efforts to find her.

Perez said she sensed something was terribly wrong the day her daughter did not come home. At the time, Irma was seeking extra work to help her daughter afford the college she had set her heart on attending.

Carrillo's body was found later in Lote Bravo, a parcel at the south end of the city where the bodies of other teenage girls and young women were discovered in 1995. The grisly find shook the community. The medical examiner's office said the girl's right breast was severed and her left breast was literally bitten off. She had been stabbed repeatedly, her neck was broken, and there were signs she had been raped. Authorities said the other victims found in the same patch of desert exhibited similar injuries.

The details of Carrillo's death, of the unspeakable brutality she had endured, filled her mother with rage. Perez said the authorities told her at first that the body they recovered was her daughter. "But later they told me that she was among the victims of Lomas de Poleo, and not among the ones who were found in Lote Bravo." Such confusion reigned throughout the investigations of the Juarez women's murders.

"I can't cry anymore," Perez said. "I am all cried out, but the pain never goes away. How can anyone kill a young girl in this manner? It isn't right. What they did to my Olga just isn't right."

When I first met her, Perez was living in the same home she had shared with her daughter in one of the older neighborhoods of central Juarez. For a living, she cooked and sold hamburgers and soft drinks from a stand in front of her house. She lived less than two miles from the border, and the skyscrapers of downtown El Paso, Texas, were visible from her street. She supplemented her income by selling used clothing and working part time as a housekeeper in Juarez and El Paso.

Perez was a tough-talking woman whose crude street language barely masked the pain and anger that smoldered within her. She said again that she was not satisfied the body she signed for was really her daughter's. A Juarez academic who was able to see the girl's case file said a DNA test arranged by a Texas university confirmed her identity. Yet, Perez remained unconvinced.

"How can it be her when all they gave me was a bag of bones? They told me, 'This is your daughter,'" Perez said. "She wasn't dead that long for her body to be so decomposed. To this day, I believe the authorities have hidden a lot of things from me about my daughter's death."

In a later interview, Perez wept as she related an encounter with a young woman who bore a striking resemblance to her daughter.

"The other day, I met someone down the street who looked so much like my Olga that I asked her to stop by my house and see my daughter's portrait on the living room wall. She was amazed at how much she looked like her. I hugged her, imagining it was Olga Alicia."

Perez said Rogelio Loya, a Juarez city official and member of the PAN, was the only person of note who offered to assist in finding her daughter. He persuaded the police to go out and look for the missing girl. But his help did not last long.

"His family asked that we no longer call him because he received death threats for wanting to help us. To this day, I don't know why he was threatened," Irma said. "He didn't say anything to me. Rogelio's mother was very upset when she called and begged us to let him be."

Eight years later, in 2003, Loya served on the Juarez city council under Mayor Jesus Alfredo Delgado. Irma thought about approaching him, but hesitated. He never contacted her again.

Like other young women her age, Carrillo dreamed of a storybook romance with a handsome suitor. Her mother said she had a crush on Luis Arenal, a city councilman and rising star in the Juarez PAN's youth organization. Carrillo dated Arenal for a couple of weeks, but he broke her heart when he called off the relationship.

Police questioned the young political leader because he was among the last to see Carrillo alive at the party's August 10 youth meeting. Authorities did not charge him with wrongdoing and dismissed him as a suspect.

Espionage

In 1999, I called Perez to go over some details of my previous interviews with her. There was noisy static on the telephone, and it seemed to grow louder the longer we talked. The call ended abruptly, at the very moment I asked her to spell Luis Arenal's name. I was unable to reach Perez by telephone for the next three days, and she was unable to call out from her home for about a week.

The significance of the obvious telephone intercept had less to do with Arenal than with the fact that four years after Carrillo's death, someone was still monitoring the mother's contacts with outsiders. In Mexico, it was not uncommon for third parties to eavesdrop on and even record telephone conversations. Government and organized crime operatives do it, and no one bothers with a court order. Sometimes, it is so blatant you can hear an unmistakable beep every 15 seconds, inserted when unsophisticated equipment is used to record telephone conversations.

After that experience, and for Perez's safety, I felt it was prudent to conduct any further conversations with her about the case in person.

In *Drugs and Democracy in Latin America*, authors Laurie Freeman and Jorge Luis Sierra said that Mexico's military had the resources and ability to conduct espionage throughout the state of Chihuahua. According to their report, the military's mission was to use any means available to obtain information about armed groups, criminal gangs and various other organizations, as well as to monitor subversive activities, political propaganda, the unjustified presence of foreigners, and the proselytizing by priests or leaders of religious sects, environmentalists and others. The authors cited a 2000 document from Mexico's National Defense Secretary, "General Order of the 33rd Infantry Battalion," which, in effect, gave the military free rein to conduct political espionage. Residents of Mexico often were aware that they should not discuss sensitive issues over the telephone. They also knew that anything the government deemed suspicious became a target for monitoring. What they did not know was who ordered the monitoring, or for what purpose. A Mexican army source said later that military intelligence officials were appalled by the rising violence against women in Juarez, "but they were not permitted to intervene or disclose what they knew."

A caretaker at the PAN headquarters said he last saw Carrillo walking behind the party's building after she left the youth meeting. However, he refused to say if he noticed anything unusual that night. A canal runs behind the PAN building. An alley and a building used by the PAN for training sessions are on the north side of the canal. Perez said the political party shut down the auxiliary building after Carrillo's body was found.

A few feet from the PAN offices, on the corner of Ignacio Zaragoza and Cinco de Mayo, is the Instituto de Estudios Computacionales, a private school that offers computer classes and operates an open high school. In December 2003, two teenage girls accused a man of luring them to the school and raping them there. The year before, several missing or dead girls from Juarez and Chihuahua City were linked to other computer schools, which recruited young men and women in both cities.

A shoddy investigation

The PAN caretaker was not the only person too fearful to talk about Carrillo's case, and no one seemed to know with certainty how or whether she left the premises alive. Carrillo's former supervisor, "Anita," who had dropped her off at the PAN meeting, refused to say anything else.

To Perez's consternation, Anita withheld the identity of an important older man, possibly a lawyer, who made a habit of stopping by to talk to Carrillo at the El Vaquero shoe store where she and Anita worked. Perez said Anita was seized by fear.

Carrillo also worked at a lawyer's office in central Juarez, but Perez said the man who visited her daughter at the shoe store was not from that law firm. Ironically, Carrillo already had notified the shoe store on 1610 Avenida Tecnologico that she was quitting. She went to work on the day of her disappearance because the store had asked her to help out one last time.

Perez insists she practically had to drag police to the shoe store to interview Olga's former co-workers. "They, the police agents, tried on some boots at the shoe store and joked around with the store employees. As far as I'm concerned, that was the extent of their investigation," Perez said. "At first, they told me Sharif had killed my daughter. Later, the police said that Sharif had paid the Rebeldes (Rebels) gang to kill her.

"What hurt us, the families, most of all is how the police tried to smear the reputations of our girls. They told the news media that they led double lives. They said they were loose girls or prostitutes. I know my daughter, and she was none of these things."

2.

NEAR CARTEL RANCH

The authorities said Silvia Elena Rivera Morales was found in Lote Bravo in 1995 near Olga Alicia Carrillo's body.

Her mother, Ramona Morales, told her story at the 2003 "Maquiladora Murders" conference at the University of California at Los Angeles.

Professor Alicia Gaspar de Alba organized the event, which Amnesty International co-sponsored. It brought together hundreds of academics, activists, journalists, and mothers of victims to discuss the border city's deadly years. Conference workers said actor Nicolas Cage and other Hollywood celebrities donated money to help cover expenses for the mothers to attend.

Morales said her daughter was seen alive for the last time on July 11, 1995, when she was on her way to the Iberoamericana Preparatory School. Just like Carrillo, Rivera had been strangled, raped and mutilated. Her body was discovered on September 2, 1995. Her right breast was severed, her left breast torn off by human teeth.

Ramona Morales said her husband, Angel Rivera, lost the will to live after learning the gruesome details of his daughter's death. "He's the one who identified her body. I believe he died from overwhelmingly grief," she said.

Silvia Rivera was a typical teenager who liked to have fun. She was very close to her family, especially her mother. "She and some of the other girls from the neighborhood liked to go dancing at a place called La Cueva (the cave), Ramona Morales said. "It was a dance hall that was inside the Zaragoza dairy property and not too far from the house."

The mother also said her daughter was a big fan of Selena, the *Tejano* music singer. Selena performed one of her last concerts in El Paso, Texas, before her fan club president killed her on March 31, 1995. Rivera cried inconsolably when she heard the shocking news. Jennifer Lopez portrayed the star-crossed singer in the movie "Selena," the picture that advanced the music star's cinema career. Ten years after Rivera's death, Jennifer Lopez returned to the border, this time to star in "Bordertown," a film about the women's murders in Juarez.

Another mother at the UCLA conference was Norma Andrade, a Juarez elementary school teacher who became a widow in much the same way as Ramona Morales. Her seventeen-year-old daughter, Lilia Alejandra Garcia Andrade, was abducted and murdered in 2001.

I met Garcia's father before he contracted cancer, the disease that ended his life two years after his daughter's death. Before Jose Garcia died, the family could barely afford pain medication for him.

Mexico's *machismo* culture

The two women's husbands were raised in Mexico's *machista* culture, steeped in its requirement to prove one's manhood at any cost. In extreme cases, *machismo* manifests itself in domestic violence, and in the attitude of police who belittle reports of sexual assaults or family violence.

These two fathers felt they had somehow failed to protect their daughters and blamed themselves for their deaths. A third man, the father of a 1998 victim, confided that he stopped having intimate relations with his wife after his daughter was killed. He could not overcome the sense that he had failed his wife as well.

In 1995, Adriana Torres Marquez was barely fifteen when she was murdered with the same savagery as the others. She was reported missing six months before her body was found off the highway to Casas Grandes, near Granja Santa Elena, in south Juarez. The semi-rural neighborhood is located near a now notorious ranch where FBI and Mexican federal agents unearthed the bodies of five men during the 1999 "Plaza Sweep" investigation.

The teenager's mother, Bertha Marquez, said the girl was seen alive on May 8 in front of a Tres Hermanos shoe store on Vicente Guerrero, across from the Roman Catholic cathedral in the city's downtown. According to various sources, several of the victims were last seen going to or from one of the shoe stores or had worked there.

An autopsy determined that Torres' neck was broken as she was being strangled. Forensic experts said other victims also had broken necks. They speculated the attackers did this for sexual reasons. It involved breaking the neck at a certain point of the vertebrae, experts explained. This same type of neck injury was reported in victims whose bodies were found as late as 2003.

Ten years after Torres' murder, I ran into her mother at a Burlington Coat Factory store in El Paso, Texas. Over the years, I had not seen Bertha Marquez at many of the public events with other victims' families. "I never joined any of the advocacy groups that marched in the streets or went to see officials like the president to demand justice. In my heart, I knew from the beginning that the authorities were never going to do anything to solve my daughter's murder," she said with a tragic resignation.

At that moment, neither she nor I knew why that was the case. The answer came much later.

Questions about body's identity

Authorities also attributed the 1995 death of Elizabeth Castro Garcia to Abdel Latif Sharif Sharif. A friend of hers said she last saw the seventeen-year-old at the corner of Juarez Avenue and Vicente Guerrero in downtown Juarez. Castro attended an ITEC computer school on Francisco Villa, a street adjacent to railroad tracks and parallel to Juarez Avenue.

Her family reported her missing on August 14. Her body was found on August 19, near the kilometer 20 marker of the Casas Grandes highway in south Juarez.

A pattern was beginning to emerge. Castro, Torres, and other girls were vanishing in broad daylight in the most densely populated part of the city. Most of the disappearances were taking place on weekdays and in the afternoon. The girls disappeared in the course of normal activities. They were on their way to work or school, to meet friends or to run errands.

More police patrol the downtown sector than any other part of Juarez. Yet, when these girls vanished, nobody saw or heard anything. Most of the downtown places linked to the girls are only fifteen minutes by foot from the Paso del Norte International Bridge that separates Juarez and El Paso, a short walk to one of the safest cities in the United States.

Dr. Irma Rodriguez Galarza, a forensic specialist for the Chihuahua State Attorney General's office, concluded that some of the young women who were mutilated were tortured while they were alive.

"Their injuries were not post-mortem wounds," she said. For several years, Rodriguez, an expert in her field with two published textbooks, worked to reconstruct the remains of unknown victims who authorities hoped might someday be identified.

Two years before her own daughter was killed, Rodriguez had a long list of victims awaiting identification. The list included forty-two women and seventy men. These figures often were left out of the total number of victims the authorities referred to publicly.

On occasion, Chihuahua State Governor Patricio Martinez said "a bag of bones" was all the previous administration of Governor Francisco Barrio left behind for his staff to work with. I asked Rodriguez whether it was possible that the unidentified remains dated back as far as the 1980s or earlier.

"No," she replied. All the remains in the inventory were recovered between 1995 and 1996, during the peak of the killing frenzy. She said the remains were tagged as homicide victims, but little else was known about them. Given conditions in the Chihuahua State Attorney General's office, it is unlikely the identities of most of these 112 men and women will ever be known.

Danger in downtown

Juarez Avenue is lined with shops and bars that cater mostly to tourists. Americans walk across the border at the Paso del Norte International Bridge. They come from El Paso to buy souvenirs, medications, and liquor.

At night, especially on weekends, the zone turns into party central for hundreds of U.S. teenagers who flock to the strip because of Mexico's lower drinking age. After guzzling two-for-one beers, they take over the avenue's nightlife. The Kentucky Club, a classic bar, has been a popular watering hole for generations.

In 1998, on orders from a drug dealer in El Paso, alleged Juarez city police picked up three young men from El Paso at the Kentucky Club, whisking them away to the unknown. Their families never saw them again. During the same period that women were being killed with impunity, hundreds of men disappeared from Juarez in the same manner as these El Paso residents, taken away by armed men wearing police uniforms and badges. Between 800 and 1,000 men are estimated to have vanished from the border city between 1993 and 2005

A couple of blocks south of the Kentucky Club is the Noa Noa nightclub, a literal shrine to singer-composer Juan Gabriel. The title of one of his early hits is "Noa Noa." The native of Michoacán state grew up in Juarez and became an international star. To soften the negative publicity created by the women's deaths; Juan Gabriel gave a free outdoor concert in 1999 on Juarez Avenue. Fifteen thousand people showed up.

Another club, frequented mostly by locals, is located at the south end of Juarez Avenue, before Avenida 16 de Septiembre. There, the Sinoalense Club swings to the sounds of live *banda, cumbia* and *norteña* music. Passersby are lured into the place by the sultry Latin music that spills into the night. Men and women maquiladora workers stop in for a drink or a dance after a long workday at one of the hundreds of the city's foreign-owned plants.

Across the street from the club is the Glamour cosmetology school, where Juanita Sandoval once worked. Sandoval was found dead on February 17, 2003, in a place called "Cristo Negro". The authorities said two bodies were recovered from the site that day. But neighbors and a Juarez news photographer claim they saw police remove three bodies.

Around the corner from the cosmetology school is another Tres Hermanos shoe store, in the same vicinity where another victim was last seen alive before she, too, disappeared.

The ITEC computer school that Castro attended is around the corner from the shoe store. On the same square block, bounded by the streets of Juarez Avenue, 16 de Septiembre, Francisco Villa and Abraham Gonzalez, was a business that an intelligence report said may have been linked to the disappearances of young women.

The downtown entertainment center extends to the red light district, which begins at Mariscal, the first street west of Juarez Avenue. Even with police looking on, street vendors openly hawk marijuana and cocaine. During an excursion to accompany a Canadian journalist through the district, one of the hawkers who worked the sidewalks kept pestering us to buy cocaine.

Jim Conley, a former editor at the *El Paso Times*, said some taxi drivers let their American customers know that they can get anything they want in Juarez, "including sex with underage girls." Such clandestine activities occur in the back rooms of certain bars and brothels in "la Mariscal." The cab drivers know all the places.

The systematic abductions and slayings of young women that brought worldwide notoriety to Juarez were occurring right here, in front of everybody.

Hardrick Crawford Jr., a former special agent in charge of the FBI division in El Paso, thought so, too. One day, while still with the FBI, he and another agent were returning to El Paso from a meeting with Mexican officials when they found themselves at the corner of Francisco Villa and Juarez Avenue. The agent who accompanied Crawford told him they were in the same spot where some of the victims were last seen alive.

Crawford looked about the busy intersection and said, "The killer is right here. He's here somewhere."

3.

LOMAS DE POLEO, 1996

Vicky Caraveo belongs to the city's affluent elite. She founded an advocacy group called *Mujeres por Juarez* (Women for Juarez).

In Mexico, it is rare for a woman of her socio-economic status to become a social activist rubbing shoulders with the underclass. She began making headlines when she protested electric rate hikes in the early 1990s. She felt the increases were exorbitant and fleeced poor people. Today, she continues that protest by practicing frugality with the electricity in her home. One evening, it was so dark inside her large home in the Club Campestre neighborhood that I wished I had taken a candle to read my notes. "I know I can afford to pay for it," Caraveo said, "but that's not the point."

Another consumer cause she took up stemmed from widespread complaints by Juarez residents who alleged that propane gas companies were cheating them. Residents claimed they paid for a full tank of gas but often got one that was less than full. "I went to one of the Zaragozas (who wields influence in the gas industry) to complain about all this, hoping they might do something to help. But the only response I got was, 'We are a business," Caraveo said.

In 2004, *Norte de Ciudad Juarez* newspaper published a quarter-page ad titled "TOMZA and the new special prosecutor for the Juarez case." The ad, as well as a couple of news stories, alleged that a member of the powerful and extensive Zaragoza clan misled consumers by allegedly providing gas tanks that were not filled to levels required by government standards.

The ad, signed by Fernando Martinez Cortes of Mexico City, also alleged that TOMZA's workers in Guatemala were familiar with complaints about the gas tanks, and news stories in Guatemala alleged that the company also faced worker complaints in that country. The ad also called on Mexican authorities to investigate what one of the Zaragozas might know about the women's crimes.

Several Juarez business associations responded immediately with their own ad, and vigorously defended the executive as an honorable man.

About this time, a source in the Center for Research and National Security (CISEN), the CIA's equivalent in Mexico, said an official in that agency whose initials are "J.A." was transferred from his post after he started to look into the allegations. The source said a high-level official in the Vicente Fox administration ordered an end to the investigation. *Reforma* journalist Sergio Gonzalez Rodriguez received the same information.

Neither the Juarez businessman the ad mentioned, nor Carolina Diaz, a spokesperson for the president's office, responded to questions about the allegations.

The business class

I once asked Caraveo why the wealthy business leaders of Juarez did not join forces to stop the women's murders. Her uncle, Eloy Vallina, a powerful developer with important political connections, could serve as a catalyst for such a movement within the business class.

A. Jaime Bermudez, another powerhouse, is a former Juarez mayor and a former national director of Petroleos Mexicanos (PEMEX), the country's national oil company. He is credited with being the architect of the 1965 Border Industrialization Program, which brought hundreds of maquiladoras to Mexico. The program was part of Mexico's border-revitalization plan that replaced the old Bracero program for Mexican migrant workers. Mexico's population was growing, and the country needed jobs. U.S. corporations needed cheaper labor.

With their collective influence, surely the *empresarios* could put an end to the horrible crimes.

I will never forget Caraveo's embarrassed explanation. She hung her head and paused briefly, then said, "They don't care about poor women." Her reply stunned me. It had not occurred to me that not everyone cared.

I marveled that border business leaders would not be interested in protecting the pool of young working women who helped them to become fabulously wealthy. The underlying message was: These women are disposable.

The passionate activist, granddaughter of a Mexican army general, led a privileged life and had no need to get involved in an issue that had dragged some into disgrace and others to their death.

The tall *norteña* woman with green eyes provoked controversy when Governor Patricio Martinez appointed her to head the Chihuahua State Women's Institute. Other activists felt she had sold out to the government. But then, Caraveo never cared about what others thought of her.

Tableau

Through the group she founded, Caraveo came to know women who lived in Anapra, Felipe Angeles and Lomas de Poleo, some of the poorest neighborhoods, where several of the victims, dead and missing, had their homes.

In a move instigated by feuding politicians, hundreds of squatters came to settle in the late 1990s in the newly developed parts of Lomas de Poleo. Other residents had settled into the older parts of the desert neighborhood nearly thirty years ago. They were hardy pioneers who built precarious homes out of wooden crates, abandoned box springs and materials that others had discarded in nearby arroyos.

In 1996, Caraveo and a group of community volunteers conducted a sweep in an undeveloped part of Lomas de Poleo. By the end of 2003, Caraveo or members of her group had taken part in twenty-seven such searches.

This time, they were looking for eighteen-year-old Guadalupe del Rio Vazquez, who disappeared without a trace in 1996. The young woman lived in Felipe Angeles, a poor neighborhood that stares directly across the Rio Grande at the campus of the University of Texas at El Paso.

As they were combing the desert, the search party came across an intriguing artifact: a wooden plank about five feet high and two feet wide containing some remarkable artwork.

The board was discovered in a shack in the middle of the desert. Inside the concrete-block building, the searchers saw what looked like dried bloodstains on the cement floor. They also found women's underwear and other articles of clothing. Outside the shack, which had two doors and two windows, was a large mound of human hair.

There were no furniture or lighting or plumbing fixtures in the building. "The place (except for the blood stains) was spic and span, clean," Caraveo said. "The wooden board was leaning against one of the walls. We all looked at it."

It was the only piece of wood like it in the area. It had pencil drawings of nude women, soldiers, the Juarez mountain range, desert cactus and some plants believed to depict marijuana. It had drawings of the ace of spades, a Star of David and numerous Nazi swastikas.

Ten women were drawn on both sides of the board. All but one of them were nude. The most prominent features were their eyes, pubic area, breasts, and hair that was shaded in with a pencil. The artist did not draw details of their hands and feet.

The soldiers were in two squads of four to five each. Juarez maintains a motorized infantry battalion in the south end of the city, next to the Cereso prison.

"It was getting late," Caraveo said, "and after we found the pantyhose there, we didn't want to stick around any longer and decided to leave. One of the men helped us load the board, which was heavy, onto the back of a pickup truck." The group packed the other items inside a plastic bag.

Once back in the city, Caraveo contacted Jorge Lopez Molinar, the state deputy attorney general for the Juarez region, to notify him of what they had found. He did not show up, but at his request, Caraveo and the others handed over the items to one of his subordinates. The authorities told Caraveo that they would sort through them and have experts analyze the drawings.

"Later on, they told us the stains inside the building were pigeon blood," Caraveo said.

The Mexican press published pictures of the board and reported the discovery. But six years later, when foreign journalists asked to see it, the authorities told them it never existed. In retrospect, Caraveo said, "I should never have given it to them. It's gone forever now."

The board and its drawings could have been the work of an imaginative artist or was left behind by someone who wanted to provide clues. A victim could have made the sketches before she was killed. The authorities' denial of its existence fueled suspicions that there was something to hide. The drawings suggested the soldiers escorted drug and human and or sex-traffickers in the desert. Missing hands and feet in the drawings indicated the women were tied and could not escape.

When he died after an illness in December 2005, Jorge Lopez Molinar took many secrets to his grave concerning the Juarez femicides. He served six years as the top state law-enforcement official in Juarez during Governor Francisco Barrio's administration. A Mexican federal official who investigated the women's murders during the 1990s said Lopez Molinar supervised police who were implicated in several of the killings, but he opted to shield them or to look the other way.

During another desert sweep to look for victims, a volunteer searcher wandered into an unfamiliar area near Lomas de Poleo. The person stumbled onto a ranch that was wholly out of place in the middle of the desert. It was luxurious, with palm trees, a swimming pool, green grass, and an airstrip. Another member of the search party found the lost volunteer and warned her never to go near that place again. The group reported finding the ranch, but for authorities, it was nothing but a mirage. The people who worked at a nearby ranch in the desert, however, did not imagine the bodies they would discover in Lomas de Poleo.

Shocking desert deaths

Eight more bodies of girls, ranging in ages from fifteen to twenty years old, were found in an undeveloped part of Lomas de Poleo. Like the victims of Lote Bravo in 1995, the authorities said they were strangled, stabbed, and mutilated.

Police reported finding the first group of bodies in Lomas de Poleo in March 1996. They found the rest nearby the following month. Police said one of the victim's hands were tied with her shoelaces. This killer's signature was also found on several of the eight bodies discovered in 2001 in a cotton field inside the city.

According to a 1998 Chihuahua State government document, Rosario Garcia Leal, 17, was among the 1996 Lomas de Poleo victims. The report described the items that were near or on her body. They included a blue sweater with the maroon letter "R," brown pants, a green headband, a card from someone named "Hector," a black watch with a Philips factory logo, a gold-colored band, a set of earrings in the shape of black leaves, a ring with a silver-colored heart and a Philips factory smock. Inside the smock's pockets, police found two identification cards bearing Garcia's photograph.

Documents related to the case said a man who worked for rancher Jose Pasillas Martinez was the first to come across her body. Pasillas, the document said, called one of the *bandas civiles* groups for help. These groups consist of volunteers who communicate with CB radios. They had ample experience searching the city's desert edges for bodies. This time, the group called the authorities, and state investigators rushed to the site.

In a photograph of the crime scene, the slain teenage girl is laying on her stomach. Her head rests on her right arm, her left arm flexed at the elbow with the hand touching her right arm. Her dark hair is off her back. She is wearing a white bra that was pulled above the breasts. A pair of white underpants was left on her right thigh, and she wore a pair of white, ankle-length socks.

The report said the medical examiner's staff found sperm in her vagina. Strangulation was the cause of death. Her body was less decomposed than the others that were found at Lomas de Poleo. Her death was estimated to have occurred seventy-two hours earlier. If the semen was saved, it was never mentioned again. It did not match samples taken from any of the suspects who were accused in the murders.

The other victims authorities identified with Rosario Garcia Leal on April 7, 1996, in the part of Lomas de Poleo known as Ejido Lopez Mateos, were "Veronica" Castro Pando, 18, and Irma Perez's daughter,

Olga Alicia Carrillo Perez, 20. Other reports, however, list Carrillo as one of the Lote Bravo victims of 1995.

The site at Lomas de Poleo where the bodies were found is about 2.5 kilometers south of the Pistola Dam near Anapra. Hernan Rivera Rodriguez, chief of Averiguaciones Previas, the Chihuahua State office that processes all criminal complaints, signed off on the autopsy reports for the Lomas de Poleo victims.

Years later, a special federal prosecutor included Rivera among a long list of state officials and investigators who allegedly mishandled the early investigations. Rivera, who had worked for Lopez Molinar, surfaced in 2005 as a spokesman for a Mexican congresswoman whose husband was killed execution style in Juarez that year. The circumstances of the shooting remain unclear, and no arrests were reported.

On March 29, 1996, Veronica Castro's sister, Maria del Consuelo Castro Pando, went to ask state police if she could enter the morgue to see if her missing sister was among the bodies. The family told police that Veronica Castro was last seen March 4, 1996, heading to her job at the Essex assembly plant. An official report states that the sister said descriptions of clothes found at the site matched what her sister was wearing when she disappeared.

The statement also alleges that Castro's mother and sister said Veronica Castro frequented dance clubs on Segundo de Ugarte in downtown Juarez. Authorities had linked the clubs to Egyptian national Abdel Latif Sharif Sharif and to the "Rebeldes" gang. The girl's family later denied ever making such statements about her.

Castro also was the niece of Felipe Pando, a retired police official, who provided information in 1999 about a Mexican serial killer arrested in connection with alleged serial slayings in Juarez in the 1980s. The killer, who escaped from custody, remains at large.

In 2001, Juarez city officials had asked Felipe Pando to assist with a parallel investigation of eight bodies discovered in 2001 in a cotton field. At the time, Jose Reyes Ferriz, a member of the Institutional Revolutionary Party (PRI), was interim mayor, and Armando Prieto was his police chief.

In Mexico, state police have primary jurisdiction in murder cases, and they had handled all investigations of the Juarez women's murders. For the shadow investigation, Pando rounded up several old-timers who were familiar with case files from their days on the police force. A source familiar with the operation said their efforts were frustrated because criminal records of some of the people they considered potential suspects were missing from the police archives.

Nothing came of the city's parallel inquiry into the 2001 murders, which officials did not make public. The only whiff of it came when a political operative scolded Pando for nosing around in state homicide cases. Pando worked briefly for the interim city government's internal affairs division.

In 1996, officials charged the "Rebeldes" gang and Sharif with Veronica Castro's murder. But years later, Pando was still having second thoughts about who had killed his niece.

In another tragic twist, another of the former policeman's nieces, Airis Estrella Pando, was brutally murdered in May of 2005. The little girl's body was left inside a trash container filled with cement near the "Caballito" (Little Horse) mountain.

The desert mountain's nickname comes from the stick figure of a white horse that is painted on its southern side. Drug investigators said pilots flying drug-laden airplanes used the horse figure as a reference point to land at one of the clandestine airstrips in the area. According to locals, the drug cartel and other criminal elements tossed bodies inside caves in the mountains.

"The men who killed little Airis intended to dispose of her body in one of those caves, but it got dark that day before they could get to the Caballito mountain," said a source who also alleged that several people were involved in the girl's murder.

The public outcry over her death, and over the separate slaying of another young girl that month, prompted Chihuahua State officials to ask the FBI in El Paso to help with the crime scene investigation.

After that, Chihuahua State police arrested two men in Airis Pando's death and charged them with the heinous crime. Mexican officials congratulated themselves on the results they said stemmed from "a scientific investigation."

4.

Atrocities

In the middle of the 1990s, Juarez was scarred by widespread fear and relentless violence. A new criminal order seemed to invite ever more shocking atrocities. The blood thirst was unquenchable, and murder took on a surreal quality. It was as if Juarez had been invaded by the death squads of South America's former dictatorships.

Yet life went on. Maquiladoras kept churning out components, and tourists kept crossing the border to drink a Corona and buy trinkets at the mercado. Parents dropped off their children at school, workers went to their jobs, and the universities handed out degrees.

Four sets of multiple homicides of women occurred between 1993 and 2003. The bodies of eight murdered women were found in Lote Bravo in 1995; nine in Lomas de Poleo in 1996; eight in an inner-city parcel that was part cotton field in 2001; and six in Cristo Negro in 2003. Between these bursts of high-profile slayings, other isolated and suspiciously similar murders took place.

These bodies were scattered across Juarez, usually off one of the main thoroughfares. The Mexican press often referred to such deaths as "sacrifices," particularly when the victim was female.

For a journalist from the United States, it seemed an unusual term to apply to homicide victims. The word invokes the notion of ritual, conjuring images of ancient Aztecs sacrificing humans to appease their gods. Eventually, the cultural gap narrowed for me. In light of what was happening in Juarez, the use of the word "sacrifice" made perfect sense.

During the deadly years, from 1993 to 2005, the authorities found that most of the victims were Mexican nationals. They were natives of Juarez, or residents of the country's interior who had moved to the border in search of jobs. They came from cities and from farm and ranching communities.

They came from places like Coahuila, Durango, Zacatecas, Sinaloa, Guanajuato, Oaxaca, Mexico State, Veracruz, Chiapas, and Mexico City. Many sought jobs in the maquiladoras, and others hoped to cross the border into *El Norte*.

U.S. and Mexico border wages

Although they were glad to find work, the new arrivals soon found that their salaries barely covered necessities. In 2003, the average wage at the Juarez assembly plants was $3 to $4 a day, exactly what it had been in 1988, when I worked at one as part of an assignment for the *El Paso Times*. U.S. corporations own most of the plants in Juarez, and the work is often tiring and tedious. Young men and women make up the majority of the workforce.

With the permission of parents, people as young as fourteen can legally work at the plants. And it was not unusual for maquiladoras in the city to hire thirteen-year-olds with fake birth certificates. To make ends meet, entire families often work at the plants, pooling their resources to pay for housing, utilities, groceries, and other living expenses.

The biggest difference between both sides of the border is that in Mexico a maquiladora worker can make $4 a day, while the legal minimum wage on the U.S. side is $5.15 an hour. That difference is a matter of economic survival. It is the reason so many immigrants risk their lives to enter the United States illegally.

The hugely disparate economies generate a constant tension at the border.

The El Paso Interreligious Sponsoring Organization, a faith-based advocacy group, dismisses the notion that families who earn U.S. minimum wage have it made. For years, EPISO has lobbied for a "living wage" of at least $7.50 an hour for a family of four.

That is on the U.S. side of the border. On the Mexican side, organizations such as the Maquiladora Association oppose attempts to raise wages at the assembly plants. A former director of the association once claimed that Mexico's economy would collapse if foreign-owned plants were forced to raise wages.

Another economic dynamic that threatens Mexican citizens is the periodic devaluation of the peso. In 1994, Mexico suffered one of its worst economic setbacks when its currency lost two-thirds of its value against the dollar. The devaluation, which many Mexicans suspect former presidents set off intentionally, virtually wiped out the middle class.

But the cheaper peso also allowed maquiladoras to expand.

That was good for Mexico, since some of the plants were already moving to China or Central America in pursuit of still-cheaper labor.

During boom periods, maquiladoras would contract with labor brokers to recruit employees by the busloads from southern states like Veracruz, a tropical paradise without enough jobs for its residents. The occasional economic downturns also have left thousands of Juarez residents unemployed and stranded at the border.

Life on the border

U.S. and Mexican immigration officials have long known the border is a magnet that draws people from many different places. Not all of the Chihuahua State murder victims were from Mexico. Several came from the Netherlands, Honduras, El Salvador, Brazil, and Guatemala.

Over the years, several U.S. citizens and legal residents also met with violent deaths in Juarez. Because they were from outside the border city, the Mexican press did not report much about them beyond when and how they died. Mark Leoni, a U.S. consular official formerly assigned to Juarez, said before he was transferred to Washington, D.C., that Mexican officials usually informed his office of drug-related deaths and disappearances of U.S. citizens. But he was genuinely surprised to learn that U.S. citizens were among the murdered women of Juarez.

Citizens or legal residents of the United States included sisters Victoria Parker Hopkins Barragan, 27, and Rita Pearl Parker Hopkins, 35, El Paso, 1996; Donna Striplin Boggs, 28, Albuquerque, New México, 1994; Laura Inere, 27, 1995; Cynthia Portillo González, 26, El Paso, 2002; Rosa Arellanes García, 24, El Paso, 1997; Blanca Estela Vázquez, 43, 1996; Ignacia Soto, 22, Fabens, Texas, 1995; Gloria Olivas Morales de Ríos, 28, El Paso, 1995; Deissy Salcido Rueda, 26, El Paso, 2002; Teresa Herrera Rey, 26, El Paso, 1997; Miriam Sáenz Rivera, 14, El Paso, 2002; Leticia Alvidrez Carrera, 27, El Paso, 2002; Maria Tullius, 22, El Paso, 2003; and Carolina Carrera Aceves, 30, El Paso, 2002.

Donna Striplin Boggs was found stabbed to death on the banks of the Rio Grande across the border from the Asarco copper smelter in El Paso. Her case is unsolved. The body of Blanca Estela Vazquez was found in Lote Bravo. Ignacia Soto was stabbed to death. Gloria Olivas, who was abducted with Walter Rios and Alejandro Fuentes, was strangled. Laura Inere, a U.S. citizen who lived in Juarez, was shot several times in a cemetery on Dec. 25, 1995; a policeman linked to drug-trafficking was implicated.

As the years wore on, more women were being killed by gunfire than in the past, an indication that gangs and drugs were at work. Knives or other sharp instruments also were popular with the killers, followed by large rocks and other blunt objects.

While about a third of the homicides appeared to be sex murders, domestic and crime-related violence, such as gang battles and robberies, were responsible for the rest. The drug trade is why more women are dying from gunfire than in the past.

Most people unfamiliar with the U.S.-Mexican border are not aware of the constant flow of people traveling back and forth between the two nations. Each country has its own laws, constitution, and system of justice. Immigration laws are different, too. Anyone can enter Mexico at the border without having to present a passport or visa. To enter the United States, a citizen of another country must present a passport and visa, or a U.S. border-crossing card commonly referred to as a "laser visa." The U.S. Consulate in Juarez, one of the busiest consulates in the world, issues thousands of laser visas each year.

The main factor in determining whether to grant such a visa is income. The applicant must prove he or she has a steady job and is not likely to use the visa to stay permanently in the United States.

The American Consulate also issues student visas to those who attend colleges in El Paso, Texas, and other nearby schools. Students cross the border daily to attend classes.

Many maquiladora managers and administrators live in El Paso and commute to assembly plants in Juarez. Some doctors, lawyers and police who work in Juarez buy homes and live in El Paso. Many residents have relatives on both sides of the border and cross on the weekends to visit them. Juarez residents with laser visas or passports and tourist visas travel to the U.S. side to shop, have dinner or attend concerts and theaters.

Daily border life also includes those who come to the border without proper immigration documents. They cross over with hired human smugglers when the U.S. Border Patrol is not watching or try on their own to evade the sensors and patrols.

Since 1993, officials have enforced "Operation Hold the Line," a U.S. policy that altered border life dramatically. It led to the deaths of hundreds driven to try their luck crossing into dangerous deserts along the border. But, based on the estimates of officials and others, "Hold the Line" did not end illegal immigration.

Mark Lambie, a photographer for the *El Paso Times*, was with me in 2005 when we spotted a group of illegal immigrants below the Paso del Norte International Bridge. We were at the middle of the bridge, near the official boundary, when we saw a "coyote," or smuggler, lead six men and women across the Rio Grande, a concrete canal, through the bottom of a chain link fence and over to the rail yards in El Paso.

It was 2:30 in the afternoon, and we could see a Border Patrol vehicle parked about a quarter mile east of the bridge. A man at the top of the bridge, a few feet from us, whistled and used hand signals to guide the "coyote" beneath the bridge while keeping an eye on the Border Patrol car.

Lambie photographed the activity crossing as the smuggler cursed and yelled at us.

We were waiting on a Mexican immigration official who was returning from the U.S. side of the international bridge. In her arms, the official carried a Mexican toddler that the U.S. authorities had turned over to her. The boy was separated from his mother after Border Patrol agents caught a group of undocumented immigrants on the U.S. side of the border. That, too, is part of daily life on the border.

Violence in Juarez

The Pan American Health Organization (PAHO), a part of the World Health Organization, has a field office in El Paso. According to one of its annual mortality reports, PAHO reported that homicide was the second leading cause of death of young women in Juarez. Between 1995 and 1997, 124 women died of homicides in Juarez, compared to thirty-six in Tijuana and thirteen in Matamoros.

The population at that time of the three cities was 1.2 million in Juarez, 1.1 million in Tijuana and 420,000 in Matamoros. By the end of 2005, after another period of explosive growth, Juarez had added more than 300,000 more residents. Despite official statements to the contrary, violence against women had increased disproportionately in Juarez.

Although the string of disturbing murders did not begin in 1993, there is consensus that the number of women's murders from all causes soared during the 1990s. In the past, Chihuahua State used to report women's murders for INEGI, the federal statistics center, under a miscellaneous crimes classification. In its 1998 report, Mexico's National Commission on Human Rights recommended that the state change its methods for reporting the crimes.

The commission also recommended sanctioning state officials who oversaw the investigations. This was not done. The 1998 report was the first Mexican government document to address the problems associated with the Chihuahua State murder investigations in a credible manner. Other equally significant documents are Amnesty International's 2003 report on the crimes and the 2003 report by the United Nations Office Against Crime and Drugs.

Because reliable statistics were hard to come by in Mexico, Dr. Cheryl Howard, a sociologist at the University of Texas at El Paso, relied on death certificates to determine how many Juarez women were homicide victims. PAHO used a similar methodology. Howard, a respected professor, has lived on the border for many years. Like countless others, she was shocked and intrigued by the deaths across the border.

Through her research, Howard found that women's murder rates were considerably higher for Juarez than for Tijuana and Matamoros. Amnesty International found that the rate of slain women in Juarez had risen from one in ten for every man killed in the 1980s to six in ten in the 1990s, a four-fold increase. The report also criticized Mexican authorities for their unwillingness to recognize a "pattern of gender violence," and accused them of responding to the issue with a policy of disinformation.

Asma Jahangir, a special rapporteur for the United Nations, visited Juarez in 1999 in response to the insistent pleas of families and activists. During her visit, she talked to relatives of victims, to representatives of maquiladoras and to government officials.

She also met with state Special Prosecutor Suly Ponce and criticized Mexican officials for blaming the victims for their deaths. In her writings and press conferences, Jahangir described the Mexican officials in charge of the investigations as "arrogant." She said she felt they viewed the victims as people of little value.

Her words seemed harsh, but they reflected what many in Juarez thought about their authorities. Chihuahua Governor Patricio Martinez publicly referred to Amnesty International's 2003 report on the murders with a profanity. An FBI official said that, based on the agency's experience, most of the Chihuahua State officials they met tended to treat the murders as an "annoyance" rather than as a serious matter for law enforcement.

The Inter-American Commission of Human Rights, which also investigated the crimes, said in its report that something "unusual" was happening in Juarez. Everyone else could see it – except for the Mexican officials. Tijuana and Matamoros, two other border cities similar to Juarez, also have floating populations, maquiladoras and drug-trafficking. But Juarez was setting the record for violence against girls and women.

It is ironic that this was taking place next door to the First World, to the foremost democratic republic on the globe. Despite the objective findings of PAHO and academics like Howard and Dr. Julia Monarrez Fragoso, Chihuahua State authorities continued to minimize the problem. They attacked their critics and accused journalists and human rights activists of exaggerating.

Business emperors

The silence of the Mexican state's movers and shakers was as disturbing as the efforts of officials to crush their critics. When it came to the women's murders, the notable elites abstained from publicly condemning the brutal slayings. Besides Jaime Bermúdez and Eloy Vallina, the elite also included Federico de la Vega, Manuel Sotelo, Miguel Fernández, Teófilo Borunda, Pedro Zaragoza, Enrique Terrazas, Tomas Zaragoza, Valentín Fuentes and Rómulo Escobar, among others.

Mexico's business elites are called *empresarios*, a word that sounds like "emperor," which is how they are viewed. The business emperors in the border state of Chihuahua benefited directly or indirectly from the labor of young women. They own the industrial parks that lease buildings to maquiladoras, they produce materials for housing, and they produce and sell consumer products that all families in Juarez purchase.

In July of 2003, federal officials met in the border city to announce an integrated security plan for Juarez. Interior Secretary Santiago Creel, a member of Vicente Fox's Cabinet, was the highest-ranking official in attendance. Business executive Angelica Fuentes was called on to represent the city's business class for the announcement of the government's plan to protect the women of Juarez.

Victims' families who attended the meeting were dismayed that Fuentes spoke mostly about the economy. In 2004, Fuentes hired a prominent Mexican communicator to help counter the negative publicity the border city had received around the world. It appeared the elite's response to the women's murders was reduced to spin and damage control.

During an interview at his Juarez law office, Nahum Najera Castro made a remarkable statement. Between October 1998 and March 1999, Najera served as the state deputy attorney general for the Juarez zone. His post was the equivalent of a district attorney. "Officials lack the will, the capacity and the honesty to solve the crimes," he said. It was the most honest assessment ever spoken by a Mexican official.

5.

Sagrario's Death

Sagrario Gonzalez Flores came to Juarez from her native state of Durango to join relatives who had found jobs at the city's assembly plants. The teenager went to work for a General Electric maquiladora. One day, Sagrario left the plant in mid-afternoon at the end of her shift. The seventeen-year-old with an angelic face was going home. Hers was a humble house in Lomas de Poleo at the eastern edge of the city.

The entire family had pitched in to build it. The teenager's mother, Paula Flores, said her daughter wanted to take guitar lessons so she could help cheer up the Sunday Mass at the Catholic Church she attended. She sang in the church choir. The Gonzalez family was close knit and held to old-fashioned values. The parents taught Gonzalez and her siblings to respect their elders, to do their chores without complaint and to hold God in high esteem.

Perhaps what set the Gonzalezes apart was just how normal they were. There was nothing dysfunctional about this family. At the end of a hard day's work, loving parents, brothers, and sisters would welcome Sagrario Gonzalez home. She had that to look forward to each day. The family also stood apart in this punishing desert, where crushing poverty and despair had engulfed many of their neighbors.

The teenager's father Jesus Gonzalez was determined to keep the family intact and focused on their dreams. He and his wife had agreed early on that their children would get an education. Together, they were designing a future filled with promise.

A fine, white dust

Lomas de Poleo looks whitewashed. A fine white powder leaves a permanent film on everything it touches. The wind that always blows, lightly at times and heavily at others, spreads it across the desert. The dust coats your mouth, hair, and skin. Vicky Caraveo, a longtime Juarez community activist, insists the place is not healthy. Several women who lived there have died of cancer, and she suspects something in the environment is responsible.

A few of the older homes in Lomas de Poleo are made of cinder blocks. In newer parts, homes are built on what activists said is an old landfill with a thin layer of dirt on top. Some homes are made of wooden pallets discarded by the city's assembly plants. Others are precariously assembled from old mattresses and bedsprings and roofed cardboard. Hand-sewn curtains that hardly slow the wind and rain often serve as doors. Dirt floors are common.

Skinny dogs roam the rough streets, sniffing for rare scraps, while children wearing that thin white coat of dust dart in and out of their yards. The young ones have managed to turn the desolate shantytown into a vast playground.

This was Sagrario's neighborhood, a place for the hardiest of pioneers. In the distance, the tower of the old Asarco copper smelter is visible from its perch on the El Paso side of the Rio Grande. During the 1970s, health officials blamed the smelter for high levels of lead found in the bloodstreams of children who lived in its shadow, in a workers' community called Smeltertown. It was a major health scandal, and families were relocated to other parts of El Paso.

Caraveo said Juarez also has a hydrofluoric acid plant, a potentially disastrous health hazard for the border, thanks to the late Carlos Hank Gonzalez. She said the powerful Mexican politician was responsible for ensuring that a foreign company received a permit to build the plant in the southern edge of Juarez.

The acid is highly toxic, and the potential for a deadly leak constantly worries officials on both sides of the border. Rail cars carry the acid across the border, through the densely populated centers of Juarez and

El Paso. The plant has changed owners several times since it began producing the corrosive substance.

Sagrario disappears

The day she disappeared, Sagrario Gonzalez left the plant at the Bermudez Industrial Park to head back to Lomas de Poleo, toward the eastern end of the city. She had to catch two buses to get home. Each day, tens of thousands of Juarez residents use the bus to get to and from work or school.

After a seven-mile trip, Gonzalez's first bus would drop her off in downtown Juarez. Then she would catch the bus to Lomas de Poleo, about eight miles away over winding streets and unpaved roads. Other riders left the same bus at Felipe Angeles and Anapra, two poor neighborhoods along the route.

The teenager and several of her relatives had been working the night shift. Then Gonzalez was switched to days, with her shift ending at 3 p.m. Although she was able to leave the plant earlier in the day, she no longer had relatives who could escort her home.

There was plenty of light left in the day when Gonzalez vanished on April 16, 1998. Her killer or killers snatched the young woman on her way home.

Over the years, Lomas de Poleo has served as a graveyard for other girls and young women. Many of them were last seen alive in the city's bustling downtown or had to pass through there to catch the bus.

When it was apparent that Gonzalez might be in trouble, friends and relatives mobilized quickly and began their search. Like others before and after them, they printed fliers with a picture of the girl and posted them around the city. They talked with anyone who might have seen her on that fateful day. Her mother, Paula Flores could not sleep and would not rest until they found her.

Then, a man the family knew suggested they search the western end of the city, in an area known as Valle de Juarez. Twelve days later, passersby stumbled on Gonzalez's body in the part of Valle de Juarez called

Loma Blanca. According to Dr. Irma Rodriguez Galarza, a former Chihuahua State forensic official, the girl was stabbed numerous times and strangled.

Paula Flores shared a poignant story about her daughter, an anecdote that is also mentioned in *El Silencio que la voz de todas quiebra*, a book that contains touching portrayals of some of the young Juarez victims. She said her daughter kept a pair of pet parrots named "Mary" and "Luis." "Mary" died the day Sagrario failed to come home. The second parrot, "Luis," flew away into the mountains on April 28, the day before the girl's body was found.

Increasingly frustrated at the investigation's lack of progress, Guillermina Gonzalez, Sagrario's sister, helped launch Voces sin Eco (Voices without Echo), a group that demanded justice for her sister and the other victims. Olga Carrillo's mother, Irma Perez, and the families of other victims were members.

The group struggled to stay afloat. Irma Perez said they had no budget and "sometimes our members couldn't make the meetings because they didn't have the money for bus fare," about 25 cents at the time. Poverty was a powerful enemy.

The group became known for painting black crosses on pink squares throughout the city. A new cross was painted each time another girl or woman was killed. The heartrending image became an enduring symbol for their cause. A member of Justicia por Nuestras Hijas (Justice for Our Daughters) explained that black stood for death and pink for the promise of life and youth.

Guillermina Gonzalez said the group was attacked constantly by government operatives, and it became increasingly difficult to sustain the organization.

In the face of such adversities, Voces sin Echo was put on hold for several years.

It was around this time that the group met Brian Barger, a journalist who has worked for CNN and the *Washington Post*. Moved by what he found in Juarez, Barger became instrumental in the founding of Casa Amiga, the city's first rape crisis center.

In 2004, on the sixth anniversary of Sagrario Gonzalez's death, some of the group's former members decided to paint new crosses and freshen up old ones that had faded. They were joined by Caraveo and members of Amigos de las Mujeres de Juarez, a U.S. advocacy group based in Las Cruces, New Mexico.

That same week, human remains were discovered at a site south of Juarez. The area, adjacent to the San Valentin Ranch, is used by off-road racers, and several of them came across the body.

Amazingly, Samira Itzaguirre and one of her radio show co-hosts had to help police find the remains after a listener who saw the body tipped off the radio station. On their first trip to the site, police found nothing. Authorities said the remains were those of an unidentified man, but the people who made the discovery said they saw women's clothing with the body.

In June of 2004, Paula Flores, still without assurance that Gonzalez's body was properly identified, shared the following letter she wrote to her daughter:

Sagrario,

If by some miracle of God you are still alive and this notebook finds its way to you, and I am no longer living, I want you to know that for me you were never dead and you were always on my mind and in my heart. You are worth more than all the money in the world, and you are a treasure to all of us. I would like to say more to you, but perhaps God will permit me to tell you this in person someday. I miss you very much, my princess. Your mother who loves and remembers you every second of her life.

Paula Flores

In February 2005, the family witnessed the detentions of suspects in Gonzalez's death. Police detained Jose Luis Hernandez Flores (no relation to the victim's family) and said they were looking for as many as three others, including a man identified as Manuel "Chivero" Gatica. He had disappeared from Juarez for a couple of years and, had it not been for the family notifying police of his whereabouts, would have escaped.

Police alleged that Gatica smuggled people across the border, and that he and Hernandez may be connected to the death of a cab driver whose corpse was found near Gonzalez's body.

Reportedly, Gonzalez had spurned one of the suspects when he asked her for a date. Hernandez claimed that Gatica paid him $500 to help abduct the girl. The investigation ended with the arrest of Hernandez.

A year later, tragedy once again struck the Gonzalez household. Mexican authorities reported that Sagrario's father, Jesus Gonzalez, 53, had died in a murder-suicide. The other victim, whom police said he allegedly shot before turning the gun on himself, was thirty-three-year-old Rosalba Salinas Segura. They were found July 15, 2006, inside a home in Anapra, ironically, on a street called Isla del Sacrificio (Island of Sacrifice). Children who heard the shots were the first to enter the cardboard shack and see the bodies.

Trails of death

In 1999, fourteen-year-old Nancy Villalba was sexually assaulted and left for dead. She survived and identified her attacker as Jesus "Tolteca" Guardado Marquez, 27, a contract bus driver for the U.S.-owned maquiladora that employed her. Police alleged Guardado was part of a criminal band of bus drivers they nicknamed the "Toltecas." Guardado said he confessed to several crimes because he was tortured, and his family was threatened. Chihuahua State authorities used Villalba's case as a jumping-off point to solve the murders of seven women killed between June 1998 and March 1999.

They were Brenda Méndez Vázquez, 14; Maria Mendoza Arias, 28; Celia Gómez de la Cruz, 14; Rosalbi López Espinoza, 25; Irma Rosales Lozano, 13; Elena García Alvarado, 35; and an unidentified girl about fourteen to sixteen years old. The victims included a dancer, students, and assembly-plant workers.

Unlike other victims, whose bodies had been found in clusters in Lomas de Poleo and Lote Bravo, the bodies of these girls and women were scattered across Juarez. Several were found at the south end of the city near the Cereso prison, the Chihuahua State police academy, the Mexican army post, the PEMEX sports field, the Cerro Bola foothills, and a large ranch linked to the Juarez drug cartel. Other bodies were found near Zaragoza, at the northeast edge of Juarez.

The authorities attributed the latest deaths to Abdel Latif Sharif Sharif and the "Toltecas" bus drivers. It was the second time Sharif was charged with being the intellectual author of multiple murders. While the accused men denied the allegations, their indictments provided a brief victory for Governor Patricio Martinez, who had promised during his election campaign to make Juarez safe again for women. Martinez had complained that the Francisco Barrio administration had left him with nothing to work with but "a bag of bones" and case files in complete disarray.

With the arrests and charges against these men, Martinez in 1999 proclaimed, "This nightmare is over. It is finished." But he was wrong. Before his six-year administration ended, he would see two more spectacular multiple-homicide cases. Talk around the governor's office began to echo the same thing former Governor Francisco Barrio's staff had suspected, that bodies were "planted" to hurt them politically.

Cases grow cold

Guadalupe Estrada Salas, a maquiladora worker, was only sixteen years old when she was killed in 1993. Officials said her body was too decomposed to determine whether she had been raped. A Chihuahua State government report, which reporters nicknamed *el Libro Rojo* (the Red Book), said a manager at the Bravo Electrosistemas maquiladora that employed her was the last person at the company to see her alive. Authorities who questioned him said he could account for his whereabouts during the time the girl was missing. The manager admitted being friendly with the girl and that he sometimes gave her rides in his car.

The investigation, like so many others, is pending.

The file for Sandra Vasquez Juarez, who worked at a Zenith plant, is also collecting dust. Her case illustrates the jurisdictional challenges the border poses for both countries.

Vasquez's body was found floating on the U.S. side of the Rio Grande on July 10, 1996. The El Paso County Medical Examiner's office conducted the autopsy and concluded that she died of "manual strangulation." Because the El Paso police believed the murder took place in Mexico, they passed the case to their counterparts in Juarez.

The "Red Book" also mentions the brutal slaying of Silvia Laguna Cruz, a sixteen-year-old who also worked at a maquiladora. She was last seen alive in 1998, while on her way to the North American Data Processors plant.

Her body was found about a hundred yards south of Zaragoza Boulevard in East-Central Juarez. The authorities said she was raped and stabbed twenty times. The police report also said her killer or killers "sadistically nailed an object to her chest."

Robert Ressler suspects serial killers

The similarities of the victims and how they were killed suggested that one or more serial killers were at work. Former FBI profiler Robert Ressler, who coined the term "serial killer," traveled to Juarez in 1998 at the invitation of the Chihuahua State government. He theorized then that some of the murders were serial in nature. The international expert and author said someone was preying on young women in the border city.

Although the maquiladoras employ thousands of women, not all of the Juarez victims worked in one. Dr. Julia Monarrez Fragoso, a researcher at the Colegio de la Frontera (COLEF), found after an exhaustive study that about a fifth of them had worked at one of the assembly plants. The others were students, dancers, homemakers, business owners, and a couple of prostitutes. This is the world in which the murders occur.

Given the city's demographics, Monarrez said, young women from low-income families are likely to end up working at maquiladoras. Dr. Cheryl Howard adds that young women with limited economic prospects are more likely to become involved with men who are drug dealers. At the same time, young men in search of work are drawn to the drug trade, which actively recruits desperate people to transport, distribute and sell marijuana, cocaine, and heroin.

Felix Gonzalez, a veteran Juarez journalist, said police have told him they rarely investigate homicides. "The cops say they make up things they put in the files so they can clear a case and move on to the next one. Some files contain fictitious entries, such as a boyfriend that doesn't exist being the main suspect and things like that."

Howard said, "The unpunished crimes have been sending the message that it is all right to kill women."

6.

The Gringo

Mario Mercuri and Vanesa Robles, a couple of journalists from Guadalajara, were with me in Juarez in 2002 when another colleague called. Felix Gonzalez, at the time an editor with *El Mexicano* newspaper, spoke excitedly over the telephone.

He said his paper might have come across the man who was killing the women of Juarez and invited me to his office to look at some materials. Mercuri and Robles were in town researching the crimes, so I invited them to come along.

It was late at night when Mercuri and I rushed over to meet Gonzalez, who by then had pulled out several boxes of papers, letters, notebooks, albums, and photographs. They belonged to an elderly American who had not returned to his Juarez apartment in a couple of months. The landlord, assuming his tenant would not be returning, had cleared out the apartment. But some of the things he gathered had aroused the landlord's suspicion, and he took the old man's belongings to *El Mexicano*.

Gonzalez said the newspaper notified the authorities, "but they're not in any hurry to take a look, and just maybe the *gringo* is the killer." The three of us sat down and pored through the man's notebooks, photographs, and correspondence.

It seems the man, in his late 60s, was on some kind of Viagra adventure. Based on notes and receipts, he purchased the drug regularly and had sex with numerous prostitutes. He kept detailed notes about his prolific trysts, complete with photographs and details about his sexual partners. For instance, he described one woman as having a good figure but being poor in bed. His album also included a picture of another woman who lived with him for a short time.

On the surface, it did not appear that our mystery man was a serial killer. He probably did not return from his last visit to the United States because he became ill or died.

But the episode brought up something that had not been considered before – the grave vulnerability of women who worked in the city's sex industry.

Several Juarez barmaids in the downtown sector freely admitted that they made extra money by sleeping with customers, a dangerous activity given current conditions. The old American happened to write that some of his sex partners were drug addicts who had died after overdosing.

"You'd be surprised," Gonzalez said. "There are *many* girls that die like this." But their deaths rarely make headlines. They are the city's invisible victims. A drug overdose can also mask a homicide.

The deaths of a couple of women whose bodies showed signs of violence were ruled drug overdoses. On September 23, 2002, such a victim was found in the San Lorenzo colonia near the Manuel Sotelo border trucking company and the *Norte de Ciudad Juarez* newspaper building. The new Chihuahua Women's Institute was announced that day.

The unfortunate woman was Erica Perez Escobedo, 29, who was found partially nude with the strap of her purse wrapped around her neck. State officials, who said her death was due to an overdose, rationalized that the case should not be investigated as a murder because drug intoxication was the principal cause of death. Criminologist Oscar Maynez and others in the community were skeptical of the medical examiner's ruling.

In 2004, Erica Perez's mother, Elia Escobedo, attended a forum on the Juarez women's murders. It was the week that Dr. Rita Laura Segato, a university professor in Brazil, presented her analysis of the murders. Elia Escobedo's mother said one of the things that concerned her most was how the authorities had disparaged her deceased daughter's reputation, a common complaint among families of victims. The family proved later that Perez, a maquiladora worker, did not abuse drugs and her drug tests at work showed she was clean.

State police raid bars

In March of 2004, state officials targeted prostitutes during police raids at bars in the city's red light district. Police said the operation was propelled by the discovery of yet another woman's body in the Cristo Negro area earlier that month.

Guadalupe Morfin Otero, the federal commissioner appointed by President Fox to develop a plan to end the violence against women in the border city, was moved to write a poem about the woman's death. Morfin, a published author, read the poem aloud during one of our interviews.

Chihuahua State officials said they ordered the raids in the red light district to gather information about Rebeca Contreras Mancha's death. They claimed Contreras was a prostitute who worked for drug dealers, and that her death was revenge for some breach on her part. The officials also said they wanted to protect the prostitutes by registering them.

But it is unlikely that officials were genuinely concerned about these most marginalized of women. They never cracked down on the pimps, some who are drug dealers, and who recruit, drug, and compel women to serve in the sex trade. They also did not go after the police that collected fees from the prostitutes to allow them to work.

Nevertheless, the ad hoc registration gave officials the opportunity to create an updated list of the women.

Vanessa Johnson, director of the nonprofit FEMAP Foundation in El Paso, said the organization estimates that 3,000 or more women (and a few men) work as prostitutes in Juarez. Adair Margo, a FEMAP founder, said the organization has helped some of these women to make the transition into regular jobs or to become legitimately self-employed. The foundation helps the women through business micro-loans, training, and scholarships for vocational schools.

Margo, who operates an art gallery in El Paso, said the Juarez women's murders came up during a discussion with George W. Bush while he was governor of Texas. She said First Lady Laura Bush and Texas first lady Anita Perry (Governor Rick Perry's wife) visited Juarez and were informed about the murders.

"It is like a sore that has been left to fester for a long time," said Margo, who was chairperson for the committee that raised money for the Bush re-election campaign in Texas. She also worked closely with Juarez philanthropist Guadalupe de la Vega on various FEMAP projects.

The black hole

Antonio Medina is the president of a business association that represents nightclub owners in Juarez. He amply described what amounts to a black hole for women in Juarez. After entering it, they can disappear and no one would ever know if they moved, died, or were recruited to work in another city.

Medina said he and other old-timers lament the kind of changes that have transformed the red light district into a dangerous place for women:

"Organized crime has bought many of the downtown nightclubs, and it's to the point that we don't know any more who the real owners are. Prostitution used to be regulated, and it was a far different story than it is today. Before, everyone knew who the girls were and where they lived. Now, they have girls who use assumed names, and no one knows where to find their families when something happens to them. In the old days, it would not even occur to anyone to kill these women. The authorities could find out immediately who a girl was with last, and they would be all over him."

7.

CRISTO NEGRO

Ed Vulliamy, a reporter for the *London Observer*, and Allison Forbes, a reporter at the *El Paso Times*, were in Juarez when they came across several people who said they had reported the discovery of three women's bodies in January 2003 and were surprised that the Juarez newspapers and television stations had not reported it.

Vulliamy, Forbes and I later returned to Juarez to ask the witnesses to show us where they had found the bodies. Without hesitating, one of them led us to an area in upper Lomas de Poleo, past a security guard station at the entrance of a sprawling ranch and straight to a desert brush area.

A bright plastic bag tied to a bush marked the spot, but the wind and shifting sands had erased any evidence of the violence. The man who led us there, and whose name is omitted for his safety, described the bodies and their clothes. He said one of them had short hair and a small ring in a pierced eyebrow.

A security guard riding an all-terrain vehicle greeted our escort in a friendly manner. The ATM had a sticker for Radio Magia Digital, and we were told that the ranch belonged to Boone Menchaca, a businessman who owned several radio stations in Juarez and El Paso. The witness even gave us the numbers of the city police vehicles that came to cordon off the area, and the name of the funeral home that transported the bodies from the site.

Questioned about these events, city police gave three different explanations for the witness accounts. First, the Juarez city police went to cordon off the area for the state police investigators. Second, officials said city police started to cordon off the site but left because it became too dark to work.

The third response was: "You'd better talk to the state police because they handle all the homicide investigations." Angela Talavera, the state special prosecutor for the women's murders, adamantly denied that state police were hiding the discovery of three bodies.

Chihuahua State authorities, at least according to statements to the press, had re-established working ties with the FBI in El Paso, so it seemed reasonable that the U.S. agency might be informed about the murders. FBI Special Agent Art Werge, the Bureau's press liaison, agreed to look into it.

He called back later to say Mexican officials told the FBI they had found a woman's body, but not three. The Mexican officials also said they were withholding the information to avoid jeopardizing their investigation. It was not clear when and where the body was found.

Manuel Esparza Navarrete, a state official who responded to the FBI's query, told a Juarez reporter that he could not lie to the FBI when he admitted that Chihuahua State police had found a woman's body but were keeping it under wraps.

If the Chihuahua State officials were holding back on something as serious as a homicide, then what else could they be hiding and why? After the *El Paso Times* and the *London Observer* reported the incident, *Norte de Ciudad Juarez* newspaper published the same story after its reporters located other people who corroborated the account about the three bodies. The following month, on February 17, 2003, several women's bodies were found a couple of miles east of the Lomas de Poleo area we had visited. The site, which is inside a gravel pit operated by a cooperative, is in a site called Cristo Negro (the Black Christ) because of a special cross a Juarez family had installed nearby. State authorities said they recovered three bodies that day, but a *Norte* photographer who lingered at the site reported seeing a fourth cadaver that caught the eye of alert neighbors. Chihuahua State officials denied that they found more than three bodies that day.

Later, Mexican federal investigator Rolando Alvarado confirmed that a total of six victims were associated with the 2002-2003 Cristo Negro cases. They were identified as Esmeralda Juarez Alarcon, Violeta Alvidrez Barrios, Juanita Sandoval Reyna, Gloria Rivas Martinez, Teresa Lopez, and a sixth person presumed to be Maria Isabel Mejia Sapien.

It was eerie. The girls worked or went to school in the same downtown Juarez area where previous victims were last seen alive. Sandoval, 17, worked at and attended the Glamour beauty school on Juarez Avenue; Rivas, 15, worked at the Estrella store on Avenida 16 de Septiembre near the cathedral; Mejia, 18, worked at the other Estrella store on the same street but two blocks east.

Alvidrez, 18, went to the nearby Allende Preparatory School on Avenida Vicente Guerrero and worked at the Venusa maquiladora; Juarez, 17, worked in the Mercado Carranza selling women's clothing and attended an ECCO computer school about half a block from her workplace. A second ECCO computer school was located on Avenida 16 de Septiembre, near one of the Estrella stores.

Berenice Ramos Monarrez, one of the eight November 2001 victims, also attended the Allende Preparatory School.

Once they became involved in the state investigations, Mexican federal investigators decided to look into two cases they suspected had ties to organized crime. The cases included a total of fourteen victims, the eight whose bodies were found in a cotton field in 2001, and the six bodies recovered in Cristo Negro between October 2002 and February 2003. But three years later, the federal investigators returned the fourteen cases to the state authorities without action.

Handing out fliers

During a binational march to protest the murders in 2003, Violeta Alvidrez's mother, Emilia Barrios, passed out fliers of her missing daughter in downtown Juarez. Allison Forbes showed me the flier with a picture of the young girl. Later that same month, Alvidrez's body was found in the Cristo Negro area. This was the new graveyard for young women.

One fact was inescapable: the murder victims from Lote Bravo, Lomas de Poleo, the cotton field, and Cristo Negro bore striking similarities. They were young and came from poor families. Some had been tied, and their bodies were nude or partially nude. They were raped and strangled.

Some of the girls had the "same look," including a slight hair curl on their forehead, as though someone were selecting girls who fit a particular profile. They were slender and attractive.

Other coincidences soon surfaced. Elizabeth Castro, the 1995 teenaged victim that Sharif was accused of killing, was a friend of Mayela Gonzalez, sister of Claudia Ivette Gonzalez, who officials say was among the eight victims found in the cotton field in November 2001. Mayela Gonzalez and Castro lived near each other. Castro attended the ITEC computer school on Francisco Villa, which is near the downtown schools and places where future victims worked and had their classes.

A triangle on her back

The state police file for Elizabeth Castro says she had a triangle carved on her back, a mark the killer or killers also left on several of the previous Juarez victims. But Chihuahua State authorities held firm. They said the deaths were not related. They also said all, but the six Cristo Negro murders had been solved.

The same month that police reported finding three Cristo Negro victims, a young girl who had been missing for several days was found dead in an area near the Ferrocarril Mexicano (FERROMEX) railroad tracks and the Chihuahua State deputy attorney general's office complex.

Little Berenice Delgado Rodriguez, who was only six years old, was abducted by a stranger near her home. Her killer or killers raped her, and then stabbed her five times. The medical examiner said she died from a stab wound to the heart.

Hitting bottom

After receiving that news, I hit bottom emotionally. I sat in a daze at my desk in the newsroom. Then I sent a message to Metro Editor Armando Durazo, telling him I could no longer report on the Juarez murders. I told him I could not write about one more death. He understood.

Eventually, though, the moment passed, and I learned later that some colleagues had reported similar experiences. We were being affected in different ways. Several collaborators, including activists and academics, confided that they were depressed or had nightmares.

Canadian criminologist Candice Skrapec, who examined nearly 200 of the Juarez murder files, said she believed more than one serial killer was at work in Juarez, and that one of them was targeting incredibly young girls. "I'm sure that if they solve one of these (child-murder) cases, they will solve the rest," she said. Little Berenice's brutal death remains unsolved.

Edgar Fernandez Jurado, a man with alleged ties to the drug cartel, was arrested in January 2002, charged in the savage sexual assault of an adolescent boy. He was arrested as a result of public pressure, but police did not investigate his past for possible connections to other crimes.

People in the village east of Juarez, where Fernandez lived and where the attack occurred, claimed police had protected him because of his links to powerful drug dealers. As the grisly murders continued, there remained one constant: Authorities showed no apparent willingness to conduct a serious investigation.

Mysterious bodies

A couple of months before the bodies of eight young women were found in a cotton field in November 2001, three people I know made a disturbing discovery at the Juarez city morgue. They went to look at the body of a recent homicide victim in hopes of helping a family locate a missing relative.

The victim was not the person they sought. But, before they left, a morgue assistant offered to show them a new part of the facility, which had modern refrigeration units required to preserve bodies.

Inside, two of the three visitors found themselves standing before a table, staring at the bodies of nine young women. They were stacked one on top of the other. A numbered tag was attached to each body.

"We were told that the bodies were there because no one had come to the morgue to identify them," said one of the visitors. "They were so well preserved that pictures of their faces could be taken and published so that their families could identify them."

One of the three people who saw the bodies was a Mexican law-enforcement official. Publicly, the authorities denied these bodies existed. We began to speculate that these bodies, at least eight of the nine, could have been among those that ended up a few months later in the cotton field across from the Maquiladora Association. Who were the victims in the morgue? And, what became of the bodies?

Land disputes

A Juarez reporter said other sources at the state police complex alleged privately that the eight bodies that were found in November 2001 were found behind a grocery store and moved later to the cotton field parcel. Authorities denied the rumor. People who live near the cotton field reported seeing several police vehicles parked there shortly before the bodies were discovered. Given the context of these crimes, it is within the realm of the possible that bodies, after discovery, were moved to less controversial sites.

After the federal government got involved in the investigations, federal police were posted at the cotton field parcel around the clock for more than two years. Anyone who entered the parcel, including activists and journalists, had to show an identification card and state the purpose of their visit. The federal officers photographed visitors and wrote down the license plate numbers of their vehicles.

The explanation given for this exceptional security was that criminals are known to return to the scene of their crimes. It was the only vacant parcel or crime scene in Juarez that received such attention.

The graveyards

The bodies of women have been tossed in groups on or near the city's disputed lands, including Lote Bravo, Lomas de Poleo, and land adjacent to Cristo Negro.

During the 1990s, political operatives sent squatters to occupy land in exchange for their votes during elections. The squatters settled on parts of Lote Bravo and Lomas de Poleo. In 2003, a brigade of city police was ordered to dislodge hundreds of families from Lote Bravo. They did so with much fanfare and violence. Many of the squatters set their shacks afire rather than watch them sold off for parts.

According to a 1998 report on the Juarez murders by the Mexican National Commission of Human Rights, several powerful families owned land in Lote Bravo and Lomas de Poleo. Sections of Lote Bravo at the time were owned by Jose A. Padilla Rodriguez; INFONAVIT (a government housing program); Desarollo de Chihuahua Corporation; the City of Juarez;

Amparo Rodriguez Douglas de Padilla; Sergio Bermudez Espinoza; and Alicia Quevedo Verdes.

The report said the Lote Bravo tract extended north to Sucesion Enrique C. Creel and Simon Rodriguez, south to the Ejido Zaragoza Extension, east to Simon Rodriguez and west to the Panamerican Highway. Much of Lote Bravo was developed after the grisly discovery of eight bodies in 1995.

During Francisco Barrio's administration, the city expropriated Lote Bravo to accommodate rapid urban growth. The landowners fought this for years but could not prevail against the government's power of eminent domain.

The report also said that at the time of the murders, the late Pedro Zaragoza Vizcarra was the owner of record of Lomas de Poleo. The tract extended north to the Rio Grande, south to Sucesion Leandro Valle, west to Puerto Anapra and east to Geronimo Villegas.

Between 2003 and 2005, tensions between residents of Upper Lomas de Poleo and the Zaragoza family had escalated to a dangerous level. Residents said a turning point came when Zaragoza security guards cut off electricity to their homes and allegedly threatened the people who refused to move off the land.

In September of 2004, residents of the neighborhood complained to the Roman Catholic bishop of Juarez that Zaragoza guards allegedly had destroyed their makeshift chapel. Then things quieted down for a bit. The residents rebuilt their chapel, and the bishop conducted a Mass there.

But the following year a resident was killed in a scuffle, allegedly with the security guards. Activists from Juarez, Mexico City and the United States tried to help the residents stay on the land.

Paula Flores, mother of 1998 victim Sagrario Gonzalez Flores, was among many who advocated for the residents who were under attack. The residents claimed the land was federal property that belonged to "the nation" of Mexico.

Three years before the land dispute, I had called a telephone number for one of the Zaragoza families in Juarez. A woman answered and identified herself as Mrs. Pedro Zaragoza. I asked her if the family had ever experienced any problems because of the bodies found in Lomas de Poleo in 1996.

She responded that they had many problems because people were squatting on their land. She said it was not right that they were there. She ended our brief conversation by saying, "None of this better be published." The Zaragoza family is extensive, and some of its members have owned many kinds of businesses.

Some of the Zaragozas are related to the Fuentes family, another large clan with major businesses and land holdings. Several of the families have relatives or associates who own transnational corporations and have holdings in Mexico's interior and in Spain and Guatemala.

According to a U.S. Customs Service investigative report, some Fuentes family members were suspected of drug smuggling. In 1997, *Insight Magazine* and CBS TV's *60 Minutes* reported on drug-trafficking allegations involving gas trucks belonging to a Tomas Zaragoza company. The owners denied any wrongdoing.

In 1991, Baldomero Fuentes, a resident of Juarez and El Paso, was sentenced by a Juarez court to one year's probation for possession of cocaine. *Insight* also reported that Baldomero Fuentes and the late Rafael Aguilar were founders of the original Juarez drug cartel in the 1980s.

Aguilar, who also lived in Juarez and El Paso, married one of the Zaragoza women. In the border region, people still speak with awe of the powerful Zaragoza and Fuentes families.

Two years ago, a truck driver in El Paso said he was sitting at the Sunland Park Racetrack and Casino in Sunland Park, New Mexico, when he was approached by a man who introduced himself as one of the Zaragoza's representatives. The truck driver said the man offered him a lucrative job hauling legitimate cargo and "an occasional load of drugs." It is important to note that U.S. and Mexican law enforcement officials have mentioned only a couple of members of the Zaragoza and Fuentes families in connection with suspicious activities. Mexican officials consider the rest to be legitimate businesspeople. The families tend to shun the news media, but through spokespersons they have denied any wrongdoing.

In 1999, alleged squatters also confronted property owners, among them Jaime Bermudez Cuaron, over disputed land in northwest Juarez near Cristo Negro, Anapra, and Lomas de Poleo. The Bermudez family and a man named Jose Ochoa Rodriguez were involved in a legal dispute over the fifty hectares. According to an account in *Norte de Ciudad Juarez*, guards armed with assault rifles sought to remove the squatters, who complained to reporters that seemingly "all of Juarez belongs to Bermudez." The same had been said of other notable men in the state of Chihuahua.

The bodies are planted

According to Juarez property records, the parcel where the eight bodies were found in November 2001 belonged at the time to a relative of former Governor Francisco Barrio.

In 2001, the body of Lilia Alejandra Garcia Andrade, 17, was found on a parcel that belonged to former Chihuahua Governor Teofilo Borunda. The former governor sent a bulldozer to clear overgrown brush from the parcel after police removed the body, and after complaints that the tall brush made it an ideal place to hide bodies. Borunda's land was located on one of the city's main thoroughfares, the Panamerican Highway.

It was also across the street from a major shopping center and from the city's first Walmart store. The politicians might be correct to suspect that the bodies of murdered young women were left intentionally in politically embarrassing locations.

The killers are organized

In some of the cases, autopsies and other information indicated victims were held captive for days or weeks before they were killed. However, their bodies were not always found right away. In the case of the eight bodies discovered in 2001, medical examiners determined that one of the victims had been dead for about eight months before her body was found, while the most recent victim had been dead about three weeks. Another victim was reported missing in 2000.

Authorities could never explain the time gap, which means the bodies probably were stored somewhere before someone decided it was time to dump them. There was talk of freeze burns on the skin of one or two of the eight 2001 cottonfield victims, suggesting they were kept post-mortem in a refrigerated facility.

These are crimes involving abduction, rape, torture, murder and the storage and transportation of bodies. Only a highly organized group could carry out crimes of such complexity and magnitude.

This sinister group, which likely includes police, has operated undetected for years. The killers may have planted bodies in certain places to make a political statement, to send a message to the community, to embarrass or harm unwitting landowners or to communicate with each other through a macabre code. It is a modus operandi that speaks of money and power. There must be money enough to finance complex logistics and to buy the silence of co-conspirators.

Gradually, sources in police, business and political circles confirmed that a corrupt network of law-enforcement officials, politicians, business leaders and drug traffickers had made it possible for some men to turn the murder of women in Juarez into a sport. The sources alleged the corruption that protected them reached the highest levels of the government.

8.

Death of a Lawyer

On the night of February 5, 2002, Mario Escobedo Anaya left the law office he shared with his father on Avenida Constitucion. He got into his pickup truck and headed to a store parking lot on Zaragoza Boulevard. He had an appointment to review bond arrangements for the mother of an escaped convict nicknamed "Venado" (the Deer).

She had been jailed on suspicion of harboring her son. Authorities said Francisco Estrada, the suspect's real name, had killed a policeman after his flight from the state prison in Chihuahua City. He had originally been arrested in February 2001 on drug charges.

The young lawyer was also defending one of the two bus drivers accused of raping and murdering eight women whose bodies were discovered in a cotton field in November 2001. As he turned into the parking lot that February night, Escobedo Anaya noticed that someone was following him. Mario Escobedo and his father, Mario Escobedo Salazar, also an attorney, and Sergio "Dante" Almaraz Mora, a lawyer who represented the second accused bus driver, were in the process of tearing apart the official case against their clients.

The news media frequently carried accounts of flaws the defense lawyers pointed out in the government's investigation. The attorneys also received death threats. The anonymous callers warned them to back off. Escobedo Anaya suspected that the people trailing him planned to corner him. His departure from the store parking lot immediately became a high-speed chase through the streets of Juarez, mostly along Municipio Libre. A desperate Escobedo Anaya called his father on the cell phone he held with one hand while maneuvering the speeding truck with the other.

"Help me!" he yelled at his father.

The elder Escobedo tried to calm his son. Within moments, he was in his own car, rushing frantically to catch up with the son. Moments later, after more short and frantic calls, the father heard a loud noise over the cell phone and lost contact with his son.

When Escobedo Salazar arrived, about three minutes after the young lawyer's final call, he realized that had just heard the sound of his son's truck crashing. The father saw police surround the scene of the crash. They said his son had died in the wreck, and they told him to stand back. But the wreck did not kill young Escobedo Anaya. He died from a gunshot wound to the head.

In January 2002, weeks before the lawyer's death, a crew from ABC TV's *Downtown 20/20* interviewed the three Juarez defense lawyers. Other U.S. and Mexican journalists were present at the law office when the ABC TV team led by John Quiñones arrived. The reporters also interviewed the wives of the two bus drivers accused in the eight deaths. Hardrick Crawford Jr., the special agent in charge of the FBI office in El Paso, and former Chihuahua State forensics chief Oscar Maynez Grijalva also were interviewed for the *20/20* segment.

The report on the Juarez women's murders aired January 31, 2002. Less than a week later, Escobedo Anaya was shot to death by Mexican state police. At first, Chihuahua State authorities said state police officers killed the lawyer because they mistook him for "Venado," the fugitive. A short time later, authorities said the lawyer fired his gun at police, who were forced to return fire in self-defense.

Much later, an eyewitness stepped forward to reveal a vastly different version of the events that unfolded that night. He was a taco vendor who had hesitated to make a statement against the police because he was afraid. The witness said that after the lawyer's truck crashed, the police officers who were chasing him got out of their vehicles. He said one of them, state Commander Alejandro Castro Valles, jumped onto the back of Escobedo Anaya's truck, broke the back window with his gun, and shot the injured lawyer at close range. The judge who handled the complaint against the police was unwilling to accept the witness account. The authorities exonerated the state policemen involved in the chase that ended with the lawyer's death.

Police implicated

Norte de Ciudad Juarez published remarkable photographs showing that the bullet holes in one of the unmarked police vehicles involved in the pursuit did not exist the night Escobedo Anaya was killed. The bullet holes appeared later, apparently planted to support the policemen's claims of self-defense. *Norte* took the first photograph of the police vehicle without bullet holes the night of the killing. The second photograph of the same vehicle with bullet holes was taken later at the police impound lot.

But there was much more to the young lawyer's death. U.S. and Mexican intelligence sources alleged that drug lord Vicente Carrillo Fuentes previously had dispatched "Venado" to assassinate Chihuahua Governor Patricio Martinez. A previous attempt to kill Martinez on January 17, 2001, in Chihuahua City had failed, and the cartel allegedly sent "Venado" to finish the job.

It was not clear whether Escobedo Anaya knew this when he set out that fatal night to make the bond arrangements for the fugitive suspect's mother.

According to the intelligence sources, one of the places where the fugitive hid out after the lawyer's death was at a cousin's home in El Paso County. The *El Paso Times* reported that Mexican police captured him in November of 2002 during one of his return trips to Mexico.

In Chihuahua City, a reporter asked Estrada (Venado), before he was locked up, whether it was true that he was involved in a plot against the governor. He did not flinch at the question and denied the allegation as coolly as if someone were asking if he liked coffee better than tea.

Chihuahua State authorities tried to evade the issue all together. Later, in response to questions about the allegations, one of the governor's press officers in Chihuahua City simply said that "Venado" did not fit the profile of someone who might be part of an assassination plot.

The Chihuahua State authorities charged state Police Officer Victoria Loya in the attempt to kill the governor. Carlos Acosta Valenzuela, a lawyer who initially represented her, said the ballistics did not add up. Even if she had fired the shot that nearly killed the governor, he asserted that someone else in the governor's palace also fired a gun.

At one time, the same Chihuahua City lawyer who represented Loya considered defending Sharif, but he changed his mind after learning that it would have to be on a contingency basis. In October 2005, *El Mexicano* reported that during one of his trips to Juarez, Acosta committed suicide with a handgun.

Alejandro Castro Valles, the state police commander who mortally wounded Mario Escobedo Anaya, also lived in El Paso. U.S. law-enforcement officers quietly tried to find Castro Valles in connection with other matters. The commander reportedly wanted to buy a home in El Paso and was in the process of getting his immigration papers in order. However, the heat over young Escobedo Anaya's death was so intense that he and the other officers left the area for a time.

Castro Valles is the son of Fermin Robledo, a well-known television news host for Channel 44 in Juarez, which is owned by Arnoldo Cabada, a prominent businessman. Luis Cabada, a translator for the FBI in El Paso, is a relative of the Mexican TV station owner.

Advocacy groups were concerned that FBI employees had family ties to people in Mexico, and that was enough to dissuade some of them from visiting the Bureau's office in El Paso. They reasoned that information given to the FBI could end up in the wrong hands. In fact, that actually occurred later with an FBI translator from Chihuahua state. Because of family ties, even within a regional population of nearly two million souls, the border can be a small world.

Chihuahua officials said publicly that the state police officers under public attack were welcomed at any time to return to their jobs.

In late 2003, Castro Valles and his assistant, Jaime Gurrola, who also participated in the pursuit of Mario Escobedo Anaya, turned up in Mexico City, where they worked as administrators for the Mexican federal Controller's Office, which investigates official corruption. They were hired when Francisco Barrio, the nation's anti-corruption czar under Vicente Fox and former governor of Chihuahua State, was the cabinet secretary overseeing the office. Once again, it was *Norte de Ciudad Juarez* that broke the news.

Eduardo Romero, named federal controller after Barrio resigned to run for Congress, had Castro Valles and Gurrola fired shortly after their backgrounds were made public. Their dismissals occurred after federal Commissioner Guadalupe Morfin Otero paid Romero a visit to discuss the Juarez community's concerns about the two former state police officers. Interestingly, Castro Valles and Gurrola had served under officials of the National Action Party and of its rival organization, the Institutional Revolutionary Party. Political party affiliation seemed to make no difference.

One of the most poignant scenes from this era was the sight of Mario Escobedo Salazar and his fellow lawyers carrying his son's casket to the front door of the Chihuahua State Deputy Attorney General's office in Juarez. They had joined the throngs of Juarez citizens who had been demanding justice from their officials for years. Instead of justice, they would come to experience the same bitter impotence the families of the slain young women had lived with for so long.

I saw Mario Escobedo Anaya a couple of days before his death. I had gone to his law office to pick up some documents from his father related to the two accused bus drivers. Escobedo Anaya was standing outside the building talking with several friends.

The ruddy-faced young lawyer smiled and shook my hand when I greeted him. That is how I remember him, a friendly man with a ready smile.

Bus driver suspect dies in jail

In February of 2003, a year after Escobedo Anaya's death, Gustavo Gonzalez Meza, the bus driver suspect he and his father were defending, died in the Chihuahua City state prison under suspicious circumstances. Under the law, suspects in the Juarez murders were supposed to be tried and jailed in the same city.

State officials, however, transferred all the high-profile suspects to Chihuahua City, about 250 miles south of the border. In part due to Morfin's intervention, on February 20, 2002, state officials acceded and sent Garcia's fellow accused, Victor Javier "Cerillo" Garcia Uribe, back to the prison in Juarez.

Escobedo Anaya's death three months after the discovery of the eight young women's bodies in 2001 climaxed an extensive campaign of intimidation against the activists and victims' families who clamored for truth. The community viewed the slain lawyer as a martyr for the cause, and his numbing death galvanized many people into action.

Protests against the Chihuahua State government soon echoed around the world. Some were convinced the state had killed the lawyer in reprisal for his vigorous defense against an apparent injustice. But instead of frightening people into silence, his death had the opposite effect. The worst thing that could happen – death at the hands of officials – had just occurred.

New activists like Marisela Ortiz, a Juarez schoolteacher, and advocates from the United States rose to the occasion. By the end of 2003, the activists had taken the message about the Juarez women's murders to an international arena.

The Inter-American Commission on Human Rights in Washington, D.C., Amnesty International of London, the United Nations and Mexico's National Commission of Human Rights are some of the organizations that came to the border city at the insistent requests of activists and victims' families. Other advocates, north of the border and in other countries, worked to get their governments involved.

9.

THE COTTON FIELD MURDERS

Arturo Gonzalez Rascon, a grandfatherly man who tended to eloquence at times, was the Chihuahua State attorney general. On November 10, 2001, a Sunday, he called a news conference to make an important announcement. We knew it would be about the eight bodies found in the cotton field, but we were totally unprepared for what occurred.

The state official announced that teenager Laura Berenice Ramos and seven other girls were raped and strangled by two bus drivers who confessed to the crimes. He said both men also confessed to dumping the eight bodies in the parcel at Ejercito Nacional and Paseo de la Victoria.

Down the hallway, a desperate Miriam Garcia, wife of Victor Javier Garcia Uribe, one of the accused bus drivers, and his lawyer, Sergio Dante Almaraz, claimed that police who wore Halloween masks had abducted the suspects from their homes and tortured them into confessing. They told reporters that the two men had nothing to do with the crimes.

Sergio Gonzalez Rodriguez, an author and journalist for *Reforma* newspaper in Mexico City, flew to Juarez soon after receiving the news about the bodies. We went to the press conference and watched, incredulous, at what unfolded that day. State authorities had solved a complex multiple homicide case in only two days.

It was a bloody month

November 2001 was a bloody month for Juarez. Besides the discovery of the eight bodies, a woman who worked as a dancer at the Medusa's nightclub was found dead in a room at the Motel Royal on Tecnologico

Avenue (also known as the Panamerican Highway). And then four young men were abducted, tortured, and murdered after leaving the Hooligans nightclub, on the same street as the Motel Royal.

The club and the hotel are about two miles west of the cotton field. Sources alleged that police and a relative of drug lord Amado Carrillo Fuentes were implicated in the four men's deaths, but no one was ever arrested. The Motel Royal is across the street from the vacant lot where the body of seventeen-year-old Lilia Alejandra Garcia's body was found on February 21, 2001. Death seemed to permeate Juarez.

The parcel where the eight bodies were discovered on November 6 and 7, 2001, is on the corner of a busy intersection and across the street from the Association of Maquiladoras, a business organization that represents the city's assembly plants.

That section of Paseo de la Victoria Street is named after A. Jaime Bermudez, the Juarez founder of the assembly plant industry. Maquiladoras employ thousands of young women in border cities like Tijuana, Matamoros, and Juarez. The maquiladoras and the drug trade are the twin engines that drive the Juarez economy.

The grisly graveyard, which is part cotton field, is surrounded by a new housing development for low-to middle-income families, by the former Jaime Bermudez Ranch and by the exclusive Mision de Los Lagos country club development.

Further west along Ejercito Nacional, one of the main streets that border the parcel, is a highly commercialized neighborhood that could pass for just about any in the United States, with its Walmart, modern shopping centers, convenience stores, restaurants, car repair shops, gymnasiums, and nightclubs.

It was one of the most unlikely places to leave bodies. It was as if they were left there specifically for someone to find.

Skrapec: Brazen killers

People on foot often took shortcuts through the large corner parcel. Others pulled up in vehicles and illegally dumped trash into one of the two ditches there. On November 6, 2001, a passerby alerted police after he spotted a body in an irrigation ditch that cuts across the cotton field. The eight bodies were in various stages of decomposition. The youngest victim was probably fourteen years old.

Investigators and experts from the state forensics staff were called to the field. Cadets from the Chihuahua State Police Academy were sent to help search for human remains. Dr. Irma Rodriguez Galarza, one of the experts combing the area, left abruptly because her son, who was in a Chihuahua City hospital, developed complications after surgery.

Four months earlier, Dr. Rodriguez had identified her own daughter's body in the city morgue. She had vowed then that she would never again work with bodies. "I was still hurting, but I couldn't say no. I set aside my emotions and my own turmoil over my daughter's unsolved murder to help," she said before leaving the cotton field to attend to her son.

Canadian criminologist Candice Skrapec, who inspected the cotton field later, said the killer or killers were incredibly brazen to have tossed the bodies there. Was it a message? Were the killers mocking the authorities? Were they boasting of their power?

This case, more than any other, would symbolize everything that was wrong with the investigations into the murders that had plagued the city since 1993. Over the years, the cases were characterized by a lack of true investigation, a disregard for victims and their families, the arrests of suspects whose guilt was doubtful, intimidation and threats against advocacy groups, and the official bungling and corruption that permitted the slayings to continue.

On its face, the case also presented an unparalleled opportunity to get to the bottom of the murders.

Counting the deaths

According to my research, an estimated 470 girls and women had been killed in Juarez between 1993 and 2005. Of these, about a third were sex-murder victims, an estimate that Dr. Julia Monarrez Fragoso agreed with. It was much more difficult to arrive at an accurate number of missing women.

Although authorities went to great lengths to distinguish between sex-murder victims and other homicide victims, in many cases it was impossible from skeletal remains to tell whether a victim was raped before she was killed. Besides, it did not matter. Sex was not the motive for the notorious murders. In the case of rape, experts know that sex is not the motive. Rape is committed to express power or dominion over the victim. Many women's murders, regardless of the motive, were unpunished crimes, and that made their deaths an issue of justice.

In August 2003, Amnesty International released a report on the women's murders titled "Intolerable Killings: Ten Years of Abductions and Murders in Ciudad Juarez and Chihuahua." Amnesty included in its count the murders of Chihuahua City, for a grand total then of "approximately 370" deaths, including 137 that involved sexual assault.

The Chihuahua State Women's Institute headed by Vicky Caraveo came up with 321 total murders for the same period, including ninety sex-murders. The institute's report was based on an audit of newspaper articles and other information made available to Caraveo's office.

The government accepted the state institute's report as the first official statistic of its kind for the women's murders, which were now being referred to as "femicides." Before then, the officially reported number of victims fluctuated wildly. In early 2003, the Chihuahua State Attorney General's Office, which is responsible for overseeing the investigations, was reporting "about 280 murders."

Mexican federal Attorney General Rafael Macedo de la Concha's office in Mexico City quoted a figure of 258 deaths, and the Mexican National Commission of Human Rights, under Jose Luis Soberanes, cited 248 cases in its reports. De la Concha's office said its figure came from the state, and the National Human Rights Commission said 248 was actually the number of victims' families that its staff had managed to interview.

Arriving at the true number of victims, or as close to it as possible, was one of the major challenges of my investigation. To reduce the number of victims, as the authorities had done casually over the years, would be to commit a further injustice to the slain women and their families.

Maynez: Something is wrong

Juarez had become a city that people around the world associated with the murders of women. With the latest multiple-homicide case, Mexican authorities finally had an opportunity to change that. At least three of the deaths appeared to be recent, and there was a strong potential to recover workable evidence.

It was highly likely in such an urban location that someone saw or heard something that might provide the needed break. That possibility faded quickly. Oscar Maynez Grijalva, the state forensics chief, had just started his scientific investigation when he learned that higher-ups in the Chihuahua State Attorney General's Office already had two suspects in custody.

The buzz in the state office was that the governor had ordered his staff to solve the murders by Monday or heads would roll. Mothers with missing daughters, who heard the news on television, mustered their courage and went to the morgue. Irma Monreal, the mother of a missing fifteen-year-old, Esmeralda Herrera Monreal, was among them. Officials at first refused to let the mothers see the bodies.

Maynez felt the developments were coming far too fast. While the forensics staff was painstakingly combing the area for evidence, another official sent earth-moving equipment to start digging large holes in the parcel, presumably to help find bodies. The work stopped after Maynez explained the folly of using heavy machinery to unearth human remains. Such equipment could destroy or bury evidence.

Years before, when Maynez held a different post in the Chihuahua State Attorney General's Office, he warned officials in writing about the possibility that a serial killer was at work. His superiors, including state law enforcement officials Javier Benavides, Jorge Ostos, and the late Jorge Lopez Molinar, brushed him off. "One of them even cursed at me and told me to get my report away from him," Maynez recalled. One of the men said he recalled Maynez but not his report, while the other two claimed they did not remember Maynez at all.

The clean-cut criminologist and academic, educated in Mexico and the United States, was shocked this time when Chihuahua State police asked his staff to help plant evidence against the two bus drivers accused in the eight murders.

Maynez said he and his team had thoroughly checked the van that police said the two suspects allegedly used to abduct the women. His staff applied Luminol to the vehicle to detect even very faint blood residue. "It was clean," Maynez said.

And before he could get DNA test results back to confirm the identities of the victims, state Attorney General Gonzalez Rascon had read off their names at the November 10 press conference.

He said the victims were Claudia Ivette González, 20; Verónica Martínez Hernández, 19; Esmeralda Herrera Monreal, 15; Laura Berenice[DWV1] Ramos, 17; Mayra J. Reyes Solís, 17; Maria Acosta Ramírez, 19; Guadalupe Luna de la Rosa, 20; and Barbara Martínez Ramos, 20.

The official insisted the bus drivers had provided police with the full names of the victims, a claim that left many skeptical. But as far as officials were concerned, the murders were solved.

They also ordered field investigators back to their offices. The investigation was over.

"Something smells," Maynez concluded.

Evidence left behind

Time would show that the idealistic Maynez was not far off the mark. The results of the DNA tests, which a Mexican federal congressman made public months later, would cast doubt on the identities of the eight victims.

Shortly after authorities reopened the parcel to the public, another journalist and I went to inspect the site. Pieces of yellow and red police tape were flapping in the wind that day. Skillfully placed wooden stakes, with white string that formed long rectangles and the labels indicating where each body was found, were all that remained of the field investigation.

The first three bodies were found on November 6 in a ditch that runs parallel to the cotton field. Five more bodies were found the next day at the other end of the parcel, inside another ditch and under heaps of trash.

One of the bodies was left next to a tree with mistletoe that grew along an irrigation ditch that was used to feed water to the cotton plants. Was it a coincidence or a twisted gesture that led the killer or killers to place a body next to the mistletoe?

About four feet from the spot, outside the ditch, several of us found a large mound of long, reddish-brown human hair and a bone fragment. We photographed the items and, in case they were evidence, we dropped them off at the Chihuahua State forensics office.

Families react

Irma Monreal's daughter was on the official list of victims. The mother, a maquiladora worker, blamed herself for her daughter's death because she had moved her family from Zacatecas to Juarez.

"I didn't see much of a future for me or my family by continuing to work on farms in Zacatecas, and I decided to move to the border where we could at least find jobs at the maquiladoras," she said.

Monreal became worried when her fifteen-year-old daughter, Esmeralda Herrera, failed to come home in the afternoon from her part-time job as a housekeeper. She and her other children set out to look for the girl after police refused to dispatch a search patrol.

Monreal was at work in the Dutch-owned Philips plant when a co-worker told her that a television station had just reported the discovery of several women's bodies. She left immediately for the state Attorney General's Office and the morgue.

"When I got there, I inquired with one of the state police officers, and he told me to pick up a newspaper if I wanted to know what was going on," she said. "I got hold of a newspaper and went back to see if I could find out if my missing daughter was among the latest serial murder victims. A different police officer who was there told me I shouldn't believe everything I read."

The authorities had not notified the families of the young victims they identified at the press conference. Most of the families heard it from the news media. The mothers, sisters, fathers, brothers, and other relatives of missing women streamed into the state police offices to find out whatever they could.

Some were shown clothing worn by the victims, but not the bodies. Benita Monarrez, mother of Laura Berenice Ramos Monarrez, said she never got to see the actual body "because they told me I wouldn't be able to handle it." Monarrez was not the only mother who wondered later whether the body she signed for was really her daughter.

Massive candlelight vigil

During their morning radio show, Samira Itzaguirre and her fellow hosts voiced outrage over the latest deaths. This was the third time in less than a decade that the city had awakened to such a shocking discovery. Multiple bodies were found at Lote Bravo in 1995 and in Lomas de Poleo in 1996. In between, other brutally murdered victims were found in the outskirts of the city, on city streets and in motels. And each time, the authorities were adamant that there was no connection.

Itzaguirre, wanting to dignify the memory of the victims, invited the community to join a vigil where the eight bodies were found. She set a goal of 10,000 candles. An estimated 25,000 people showed up on December 16, 2001, with candles for the vigil.

The radio personality's talent for mobilizing the community and her penchant for questioning official accounts caught the attention of state authorities. She and her fellow radio-show announcers paid a heavy price for giving airtime to the accused bus drivers' wives and their defense lawyers. The radio station canceled their program, other local media outlets blacklisted them, and Itzaguirre became the target of a smear campaign.

According to a receipt, government funds were used to pay for a newspaper ad that attacked Itzaguirre. "The worst part," Itzaguirre said, "was when a strange man showed up at my little girl's school and showed her a picture of me. It was a warning that they would go after my family next."

Shortly after that, several unidentified women from the upper class provided funds for an expensive safety campaign called "Ponte Viva" (Be Alert) aimed at young women in Juarez. Many people criticized the multimedia publicity campaign because its message placed the burden of safety on women, rather than on the authorities charged with their protection.

10.

THE CRIME SCENE

Two U.S. advocacy groups helped to organize a new sweep of the cotton field parcel on February 24, 2002. They came at the request of families who were told their daughters or sisters were among the eight bodies that were found there. I went to cover the sweep with Linda Stelter, a photographer for the *El Paso Times*. Victor Muñoz, a member of the Coalition Against Family Violence on the Border, and Cynthia Bejarano, a criminal justice professor at New Mexico State University, were among the people we met that day.

Some of the mothers of victims showed up, along with several Juarez city police officers who were sent to keep an eye on things. The search party also included "bandas civiles" (CB radio) volunteers, who found women's clothing, such as shoes and underwear, and mounds of hair on the other side of the Ejercito Nacional underpass.

There was room enough in the underpass, actually a concrete drain under the roadway, for several people to hide. The most dramatic find that day was twenty-year-old Claudia Ivette Gonzalez's missing overalls. Her mother, Josefina Gonzalez, gasped when a young boy showed her the beige overalls. He had found them inside a yellow plastic bag, from a Soriana grocery store, by the ditch in the cotton field. She grabbed the clothing and held it as though she were embracing her daughter.

The searchers had decided to give the families a chance to pick out any items they recognized. But the city police officers had a different idea and called the state police. State investigators rushed to the site and took custody of the items. The families never got an opportunity to inspect them.

The next day, state police ordered a formal sweep of the area and reported finding Ivette Gonzalez's Lear Corporation employee badge. Maynez said there was no way his staff could have overlooked all those items during the initial investigation in November. "We conducted a thorough search and photographed the sites. There was nothing before where these items were found." There seemed to be no explanation except that someone, the killers, or their accomplices, had returned to the site to get rid of the girl's overalls and employee badge.

Lear was soundly criticized after it was revealed that Claudia Ivette Gonzalez had disappeared after the maquiladora turned her away from work because she was two minutes late. Company officials said she had been late several times, and it was standard procedure to turn away tardy employees. Those two minutes apparently cost the young woman her life. With the latest developments, the families of victims and others began to suspect the possibility that a cover-up was at work.

"Someone rich and powerful has to be involved. Only someone like that can keep getting away with this," said Claudia Ivette's mother, Josefina Gonzales. Chihuahua State Attorney General Arturo Gonzalez Rascon defended what he characterized as a "professional investigation."

Border cargo: March 2002

A collarbone fragment was in the glove compartment of my car, inside a clear plastic package from the Chihuahua State Attorney General's Office labeled "evidence." I was driving over the International Bridge of the Americas, heading back to El Paso from Juarez, and worried that U.S. inspectors would question or seize the packet.

That would require explaining that I was part of a relay team that was transporting the three-inch remnant of a homicide victim to a laboratory in California. The laboratory's DNA test would prove whether it belonged to seventeen-year-old Laura Berenice Ramos Monarrez, one of the eight victims whose bodies were found in the cotton field in 2001.

The results would also tell us whether Mexican officials, who had pronounced the multiple-homicide case solved, really knew who she was. Or, worse, whether they had lied about her identity. It was precious cargo, and it was crucial to get it across the U.S. border because the rest of the body had been cremated. Fortunately, none of the U.S. bridge officials decided to check inside my sedan. They looked in the trunk and under the hood, the new procedure since the federal agencies went on heightened alert in the wake of the September 11, 2001, terrorist attacks.

The intense inspections meant having to wait from two to three hours to cross the El Paso-Juarez bridges, a trip that used to take ten to twenty minutes. In this region, the only terrorists that border residents know of are the drug dealers who exact revenge for lost drug loads, corrupt police who use their badges to kidnap or eliminate rivals, and the monsters who systematically kidnapped, raped and killed girls and young women across the border from El Paso.

When I got back to El Paso that evening, I examined the bone closely. Based on what I knew about the crimes, I did not want to imagine how the girl might have died, whoever she was. The next day, I called Azul Luna, who had flown back to Los Angeles after conducting several interviews in Juarez for a media project.

She was glad that I had gotten the bone across the border. "They decided to go through my entire luggage at the airport this time," said Azul, an artist who was filming a documentary about the murders. "I don't know what I would have done or what would have happened if they had found it in my suitcase."

I photographed the bone fragment, wrapped it carefully, and mailed it to California. Then I talked to Lorena Mendez-Quiroga about the arrangements she was making for the tests. It would cost $4,000 to have the bone tested against the mother's DNA sample. For the price, a world-class laboratory was going to do the DNA analysis. The California laboratory said it received the bone on June 6, 2002 from Justice for the Women of Juarez: "This item consisted of a five and a half inch long curvy clavicle bone with no adhering tissue. The bone appeared to be clean and in good condition. Approximately 0.79 grams of bone was drilled and extracted for its DNA content. The extract was quantified, amplified for mitochondrial DNA markers, and subjected to mitochondrial DNA sequencing."

None of us had that kind of money, but Mendez-Quiroga and her associates stood a better chance of raising it in the United States than the mother could in Mexico. Although the results could not be used in a Mexican court, they would provide one of the few truths Benita Monarrez would have about her daughter's fate. The Chihuahua State authorities had told her that her daughter was among the eight victims who were found in November 2001.

Other DNA tests

According to a document provided in 2002 by Mexican federal Congressman David Torres Rodriguez, the DNA test from the Mexican federal government's laboratory in Mexico City for Laura Berenice Ramos proved negative. It was not a match. In fact, the Mexican DNA tests could not confirm the identities of seven of the eight cotton field victims. The confusing reports threw the mothers of the victims into an emotional tailspin.

Later, the California lab requested another sample from Monarrez. I contacted her and she made the trip to El Paso. A medical technician in El Paso volunteered to draw her blood. He had a hard time finding a good enough vein for the blood sample, but after much prodding and poking, he managed to extract enough blood for the test.

"I always have this problem because my veins are very small," Monarrez remarked. She also provided several of her hairs with roots intact.

The lab received the blood and hairs and ran the tests, but it would not disclose the results until the bill was paid in full. Finally, in 2003, the lab confirmed a positive match. The bone fragment belonged to Laura Berenice Ramos. For reasons unknown to me, the decision was made to disclose the results later during Univision's *Cristina* television show, with the mother present.

They marched for life

In February of 2003, the same month lawyer Mario Escobedo Anaya was killed, a coalition of advocates called Mujeres de Negro (Women in Black) took to the streets with a dramatic and emotional march that began in Chihuahua City and ended 250 miles later at the Paso del Norte International Bridge. Long black dresses and pink hats became the trademarks of the women who refused to let Chihuahua State's slain daughters be forgotten. They were like mothers in perpetual mourning.

When the "Exodus for Life" contingent reached the Juarez city limits, a group of political thugs greeted the marchers. The "anti-demonstrators" shoved and pushed the women. Among those who were knocked down in the scuffle were Vicky Caraveo and Guadalupe de la Vega, the prominent Juarez philanthropist. Several men who accompanied the women intervened. They created a physical wedge between the two groups, and that permitted the marchers to continue into Juarez without further problems. The tactic also diffused the conflict.

As the throng reached Avenida 16 de Septiembre, I saw Professor Julia Monarrez Fragoso in front of the Borunda Park. She was an academic at the Colegio de la Frontera (COLEF) in Juarez who had conducted extensive research on the murders. Dr. Monarrez was a woman of great courage and integrity, and never hesitated to challenge official accounts with her carefully researched facts and figures.

The crowd of marchers swelled to thousands as they walked down Triunfo de la Republica, a two-way street that turns into the one-way Avenida 16 de Septiembre, one of the main thoroughfares. The protesters alternated between short songs in memory of the victims and chants that defied Governor Patricio Martinez's alleged attempts to stop the procession. Had Martinez been astute, he would have led the protest. Instead, people from his political party tried to hinder it. De la Vega said the governor had asked her to use her influence to stop the march, "but I told him I could not do that because I was one of the organizers."

Samira Itzaguirre, the Juarez radio show host, was at the front of the line. The threats and harassment over her involvement in the issue had forced her to consider seeking political asylum in the United States.

I stood on one side of Juarez Avenue as the marchers turned from Avenida 16 de Septiembre and were about to reach the end of the road at the border.

"It's enough to make you cry," said an elderly woman who watched the solemn parade.

The cross at the border

When the protesters arrived at the end of the road, several of them climbed off a truck that had transported a large and impressive cross from Chihuahua City. They hooked up power tools and began to install it at the foot of the international bridge. The wooden cross was attached to a large metal panel, about 12 feet high, and which glistened with metal spikes.

A sign at the top of the cross proclaimed "Ni Una Mas" (Not one more). Other ornaments, including a plastic torso of a woman at the bottom of the cross, gave the new border fixture an eerily abstract quality. Tags with the names of victims, some labeled "unknown," were affixed to the metal spikes.

Mexican bridge officials and armed police officers wrote down the names of the speakers. They asked people in the crowd questions about the leaders. Because of their connections, the organizers had obtained permission from federal officials to install the cross and block bridge traffic for several hours.

Using a bullhorn, Itzaguirre challenged anyone to take down the cross and told a cheering crowd: "If they take it down, we'll be right back and put up a bigger one in its place."

The Chihuahua City pilgrims said several men from their city who were temporarily out of work wanted to contribute in some way to the protest. One of them, Jaime Garcia Chavez, had come up with the idea for the cross. With a deep sense of purpose, he and the others got to work, using their skills and tools to fashion the cross out of whatever scrap materials they could find.

Every day, after that march, hundreds of thousands of travelers who crossed the border would see their striking handiwork. Through media images and the internet, people around the world saw the cross, too, a constant reminder of injustice.

The Women in Black had another important message to deliver that day. They said young women in Chihuahua City were being killed and disappeared in the same manner as the victims of Juarez. U.S. journalist Kent Paterson, another collaborator, said similar murders of women also were occurring in other parts of Mexico. And in Guatemala, a country that once was a part of Mexico, the slaughter of hundreds of women was just beginning.

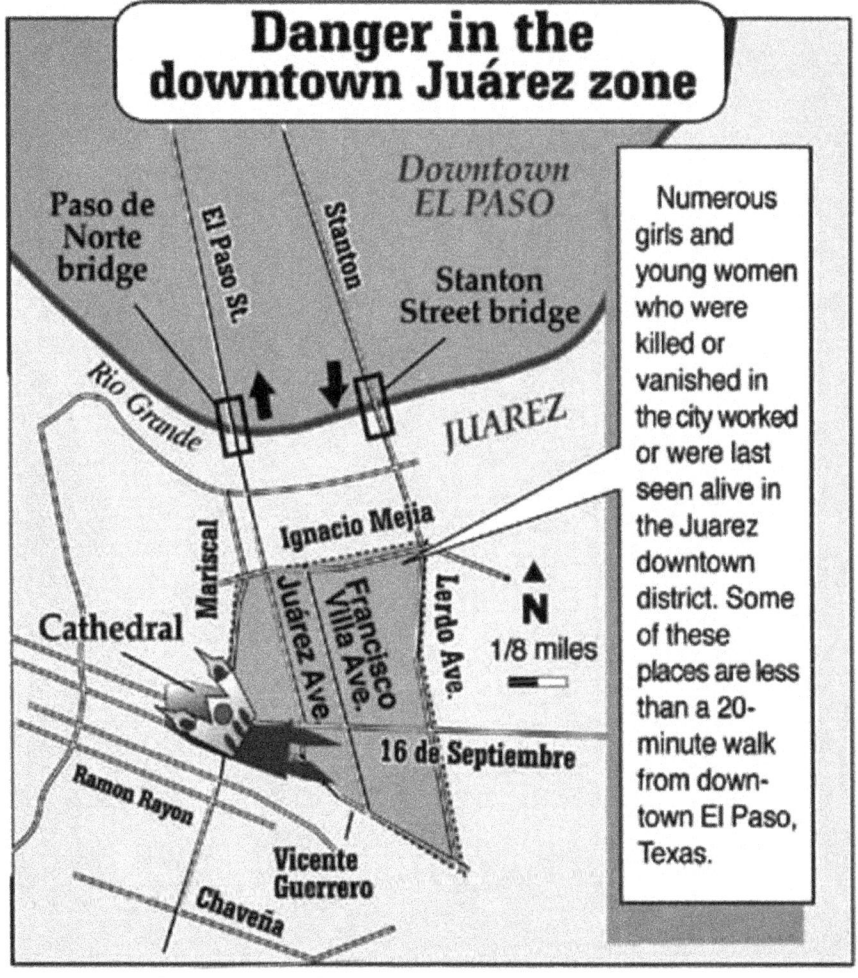

PART II

Every truth passes through three stages before it is recognized. In the first it is ridiculed, in the second it is opposed, in the third it is regarded as self-evident.

Arthur Schopenhauer

11.

The Drug Cartel

The Juarez drug cartel was the single factor most responsible for pushing Juarez into one of the darkest and most violent chapters of its history. The women's murders cannot be understood outside this context. The crimes were not isolated incidents. Under the brothers Amado and Vicente Carrillo Fuentes, both from the drug-cradle state of Sinaloa, the cartel's corrupting influence and its terrorist rule set the tone for the border during the 1990s.

After wresting control of the Chihuahua State *plaza* (drug corridor), they transformed the drug trade into a mega-corporation with assets in the billions of dollars. Anti-drug officials in Mexico and the United States blamed the syndicate for hundreds of unsolved disappearances and deaths. Police do not investigate the human carnage left in its wake. And that is how the cartel manages to turn each of its murders and kidnappings into a mystery.

Patricia

Patricia Garibay is a petite woman with green eyes who lives in the United States. This day, she stared at the Juarez Mountains across the border from El Paso. "Where are you?" she asked. She meant her brother, Jorge Garibay. In January of 1998, several alleged Mexican police officers yanked him and two friends, Matthew Baca and Eddie Barragan of El Paso, from the Kentucky Club on Juarez Avenue.

No one ever saw them again. Police at all levels in Juarez denied having anything to do with their detention, despite the fact that dozens of people witnessed the police abductions in broad daylight. The club is only a couple of blocks from the Paso del Norte International Bridge.

"Jorge had left the drug-trafficking business. He became a Christian and was going to start his own church," said Patricia Garibay. "Then someone who was trying to break into the business begged him to put him in touch with some key people. He did not want to do it, but that was Jorge, always willing to help someone. That's what happened."

Garibay was close to her brother. Both were insomniacs who enjoyed working or socializing during hours when most people are asleep. Both got involved with the drug trade in different ways. Her brother spent several years as a trafficker before giving up those ways.

Patricia Garibay said she had an eight-year romance with Rafael Aguilar Guajardo, a former federal police official and a founder of the Juarez drug cartel before the Carrillo Fuentes organization took over. "Rafael was the love of my life," she said.

During the summer of 2001, Patricia drove her sedan across the border at Fabens, Texas, to a site just south of the Rio Grande. She was pursuing a lead from someone who said her missing brother was buried in a particular farm tract. She was told the bodies of Matthew Baca and Eddie Barragan might be there, too.

She went with a friend, and they began to dig in several places. Garibay said the area known as El Millon, where the farm tract was located, was in the heart of drug-trafficking country. Major drug lords were reputed to own ranches there.

El Millon, which means the Million in English, is a small agricultural community where many people reportedly work for the cartel in some capacity. The site she was led to was about 200 feet from the road. It was a blistering hot summer day in August. She and her friend tensed up each time a passing truck or car slowed down.

It was hard not to notice two women with shovels turning dirt near a parked car with Texas plates. They dug in the white sandy soil covered with desert brush. Exhausted and dehydrated, they finally gave up.

When they tried to leave, Garibay's car became stuck in the sand, and they had to walk down the road to find help. Five men who were drinking beer outside a ranch house offered their help. The men used their truck and a chain to pull the sedan out of the sand, while the two women with shovels dug dirt away from the tires.

One of the men remarked, "It's awfully convenient that you happen to have shovels in the trunk of your car." Lest the suspicious strangers started to ask more questions, the two women ignored the remark.

Later, Garibay's friend became extremely irate when she learned that the clue they were chasing that day came from a clairvoyant consulted by Henry Barragan, Eddie's father.

The elder Barragan, a convicted drug dealer, had inspired the reckless excursion he was too fearful to carry out himself. Although Garibay did not find her brother that day, she kept looking for him for a very long time. Later, U.S. federal agents said Jose "Pepe" Cruz, a convicted drug dealer who is serving a fifty-year sentence in a U.S. federal prison, holds the key for solving the Barragan, Garibay, and Baca cases. But he is not talking.

Circle of friends

In 1996, the bodies of two El Paso sisters, Victoria Parker Hopkins, 35, and Rita Parker Hopkins, 37, were found in the sandy terrain of Valle de Juarez, on the eastern outskirts of the Juarez city limits. It was not far from El Millon. The El Paso detectives who looked into their disappearance surmised that someone lured the women to Juarez from their home in El Paso.

Once there, each woman was shot in the head multiple times. In a photograph from their case file, one of the sisters appears to be dressed in fancy pajamas and looks as if she is merely resting. A pool of blood surrounds the upper half of her body.

Mexican authorities said their deaths were related to the drug trade, which was the death knell for any further investigation. In Juarez, suggesting that a death was associated with the cartel, whether true or not, accomplished several things. It stigmatized the victims and made human rights groups reluctant to push for answers to their deaths. And it guaranteed impunity for the killers. It is rare for Mexican investigators assigned to drug murders to solve a case.

Up to a point, the El Paso police investigated the deaths of the Parker sisters. El Paso detectives said they had linked the women socially to Eddie Barragan. Subsequently, two El Paso cousins Richard and Ruben Lopez were convicted in Mexico in the slayings of the Parker sisters. FBI investigators helped bring the case to a close. Witnesses said the sisters were killed because they were suspected of snitching on the Lopezes, but it turned out they were instead the victims of a senseless and tragic error.

Cartel's female victims

Narco terrorism is but a violent form of exerting power over others. In Juarez, it was unusual for drug dealers who killed women to be arrested, mainly because the killers were part of an organized crime network that purchased police protection. A drug dealer's motives for attacking a woman could range from personal jealousy to turf battles over the sale and distribution of illegal drugs.

In Juarez, the Carrillo Fuentes organization or its individual members disappeared men and women routinely. Their victims include Abigail Sanchez, who was last seen alive in 1994; Heidi Slaquet Armengol, who was kidnapped from a Juarez taxi in 1995; and Alma Diaz, a former intern at the Mexican consulate in El Paso, who was abducted in 2002 on her way to a kindergarten. Their bodies have not been found, but it may be presumed that they were killed.

Abigail Sanchez was married to Saul Sanchez Jr., a U.S. Navy veteran who invented several devices capable of intercepting airplane and ground communications. Mexican investigators used the devices with success to detect the activities of drug dealers. The couple was abducted while on their way to watch a performance at a Juarez theatre. They left behind two young children who never heard from or saw their parents again.

Because of his inventions, Mexican law enforcement, politicians and drug cartel operatives courted Saul Sanchez. A border resident familiar with the case said Sanchez also provided equipment for former Mexican presidential candidate Cuauhtemoc Cardenas, whose campaign staff reportedly used it to spy on the candidate's rivals. Sanchez's inventions were of concern to drug-traffickers and to U.S. and Mexican intelligence agencies.

A group of people that included federal police kidnapped the Sanchezes, according to a Mexican federal agent. The agent, however, lost track of the couple after they were transported to a garage across the street from a Juarez television station and does not know what became of them.

Jaime Hervella, a businessman in El Paso and Saul Sanchez's godfather, cries each time he talks about his frustrating quest.

He knows that Sanchez was working on a project to set up vast communications networks in several places in Mexico. He said many people visited Sanchez in El Paso to discuss his devices. And, later, Sanchez moved into a Mexican company's office in Juarez.

Another suspicious case that sent shockwaves throughout the community involved the strangulations of four engineers and technicians who were hired by the State of Chihuahua to install special communications equipment for the state police that could deflect interceptions. Three of the employees worked for Motorola in Mexico City. *Frontera Norte Sur* reported that the fourth victim was from Chihuahua City. The medical examiner's office said they were blindfolded with duct tape and strangled with cords. Their bodies were found August 7, 1998, during Governor Francisco Barrio's administration. The deaths are unsolved but bear the marks of organized crime. State officials put the unused equipment in storage.

Patricia Garibay said she has eight relatives who were killed or disappeared by the drug cartel or its operatives. Relatives of other cartel victims have shared in anguish the accounts given by police and other authorities to explain the fates of their loved ones.

The reports include that they died in extrajudicial executions or were thrown out of aircraft over wooded areas or the sea.

Another explanation is that, like some of Mexico's political dissidents, they are being held at secret military camps elsewhere in Mexico. People who are knowledgeable about the drug cartel say that fortunate captives are released back to their families after a few years of work in farm fields in Chiapas and other Mexican states. Chiapas is considered a major transit state for trafficking in arms, drugs, and people.

"I was told at one point that my brother Jorge's case was tied to "Operation Casablanca," but I could never find out how," Patricia Garibay said.

In 1998, the U.S. Customs Service announced the results of a secret investigation known as "Operation Casablanca." It led to indictments against numerous bankers, most of them from Mexico, on money laundering charges.

In a CBS-TV *60 Minutes* report in 2000, the U.S. Customs official in charge of the investigation complained that the U.S. government put a stop to it before it could look into Mexican President Ernesto Zedillo's secretary of defense. The Mexican government criticized the investigation because it was not informed of it until the results were made public in the press.

12.

AMADO'S CARTEL

Under Amado Carrillo Fuentes, the Juarez drug cartel became a relentless death machine that sometimes extended its reach north of the border. Amado Carrillo was a slight man who hardly appeared threatening at first glance. He liked to dress up for a night on the town and was known to throw lavish parties.

Many drug dealers are partial to expensive jewelry, and he was no exception. According to an account in a Mexican document, Carrillo and other drug dealers once spent five million dollars in a single night buying new jewelry. His brother, Vicente Carrillo, liked to drive a yellow Corvette and preferred Versace pants with a 34-waist size.

Vicente Carrillo liked bleached-blonde women. While Amado Carrillo preferred to socialize at home parties, his brother Vicente preferred hanging out in Mexican cantinas. He was seen around Juarez without bodyguards, and in public places that included a popular sports book on Juarez Avenue, only a couple of blocks from the international line and the reach of U.S. law enforcement.

A book by Amado Carrillo's former lawyer, Jose Alfredo Andrade Bojorges, said the drug lord viewed himself as a business executive who wanted to help the Mexican economy by working with several major industries. He wrote that as a part of his quest, the drug kingpin contacted (and later enlisted) a prominent business leader in Juarez.

Amado Carrillo would personally wait on friends who stopped by his house at late hours. "Ana," who knew him, said, "I got see him make the coffee and heat the tortillas for his guests – that's how he was." The drug cartel leader also liked to play the host.

Another Juarez resident said Amado Carrillo courted a young woman who worked in small office and once brought her flowers. Vicente Carrillo was more flamboyant, favoring ostrich leather boots and large gold belt buckles. Both brothers liked Mexican *corridos* and *norteña* music. Of course, they inspired some of the "narco corridos," popular folk songs about those in the drug trade.

It was widely reported that Amado Carrillo was fascinated with pop singer Gloria Trevi, who was arrested and jailed in Chihuahua City on charges that she and her manager Sergio Andrade corrupted minors they trained as backup singers. Other sources alleged the cartel was behind Trevi's imprisonment. According to a Mexican government document, Amado Carrillo had a crush on the singer and pursued her. Supposedly, she angered him by rejecting his advances. Trevi, who gave birth to a child while being held in a Brazilian jail, denied the Chihuahua State charges. After her extradition to Mexico, Chihuahua state authorities dropped the charges against Trevi in 2004 and she was released from jail.

Melina's untimely death

In 1993, relatives filed missing person's reports on both sides of the border for seventeen-year-old El Paso resident Melina Garcia Ledesma. Thanks to the persistence of the FBI, her body was found years later – not in Juarez as some had suspected, but in the backyard of her El Paso home. In Juarez, it is customary for drug dealers to dispose of bodies in this manner. The woman's husband, Alex Ledesma Jr., who was convicted of possessing cocaine in 1997, was convicted in an El Paso court of killing Melina and burying her body in their backyard.

The couple lived in an old middle-class neighborhood in Central El Paso. Prosecutors said the husband killed her in a fit of jealous rage. They said Alex Ledesma, who comes from a family of drug dealers, also had their pet dog killed after it dug up part of his wife's body. Alex Ledesma's father, Alejandro Ledesma Sr., fled to Juarez to avoid testifying against his son. At one point during the trial, the victim's parents, who had spent all their money paying private detectives to search for their daughter, became visibly upset when their former son-in-law gave his lawyer a high-five and made jokes after the judge made a ruling in the defense's favor.

At the time, the accused's mother, Enedina Mendoza-Ledesma, was serving a sentence at the Juarez Cereso prison for possessing opium gum. Authorities said she was a common-law wife of Gilberto "Greñas" Ontiveros, a border drug dealer who was jailed in Mexico in 1989.

Ontiveros was the only major Juarez drug lord arrested on either side of the Juarez-El Paso border in more than a decade. Police alleged Ontiveros had another common-law wife in El Paso who ran a topless club and bore him a daughter.

Authorities transferred Ontiveros to a different prison after learning that he was signing out of the Juarez prison on weekends to go dancing at local nightclubs. He also occasionally kept a pet lion at the prison, which terrified other inmates.

Neither U.S. nor Mexican authorities ever captured a major leader of the Juarez drug cartel during the 1990s and the first half of the following decade. Those years saw the Carrillo Fuentes cartel grow into the most powerful and brutal criminal organization on the border. Only the Arellano Felix cartel in Tijuana drew as much blood.

Mexican police documents and witnesses confirm that drug kingpins Amado and Vicente Carrillo regularly traveled to El Paso without problems. Their predecessor, Rafael Aguilar Guajardo, divided his time between living in El Paso and Juarez.

The Carrillo Fuentes brothers had their father hospitalized in El Paso, and, according to Charles Bowden, author of *Down by the River*, the cartel once owned a bank in El Paso. Several sources say they saw Amado Carrillo slap a high-level Chihuahua State law official during a dinner meeting at the Cafe Central in downtown El Paso. That official served in Governor Francisco Barrio's administration and later worked for President Vicente Fox. Eduardo Gonzalez Quirarte, a cartel lieutenant who worked closely with drug lord Jose Juan "Azul" Esparragoza, also frequented friends in El Paso. Gonzalez, who attended Jefferson High School on the U.S. side of the border, reportedly allowed a top aide of President Ernesto Zedillo to live in one of the kingpin's homes in Mexico City.

To cross the border unimpeded as often as they did, the drug lords had to have some form of consular or police cover. The FBI confirmed this suspicion when the agency disclosed that Amado's brother, Vicente

Carrillo, kept a Mexican federal police credential at his girlfriend's home in West El Paso. The card bore the alleged signature of a former Mexican federal attorney general. The card had Vicente's picture on it and an alias instead of his real name.

Ironically, an FBI special agent lived next door to the drug lord's girlfriend. The agent was shocked when his fellow agents arrived at the woman's house armed with a search warrant.

"El Brujo"

Two other murder cases linked to the drug trade were especially shocking for their brutality. In May of 2002, Deissy Salcido Rueda, of El Paso, and her cousin Eli Rueda Adame, of Juarez, were dismembered and buried in the backyard of Juarez resident Martin Guerrero Noriega. Guerrero was known as "el Brujo" (the witch) because he performed magic rituals and sold amulets.

On March 13, 2004, a Juarez judge sentenced him to fifty years in prison for the deaths. Members of Salcido's family were threatened when they tried to get authorities to investigate other potential suspects, including a relative of Salcido's and someone identified as "Beltran." A story in *Norte de Ciudad Juarez* newspaper said revenge over a cocaine deal gone sour may have been the true motive for the slayings.

Guerrero told the Mexican judge that two people had paid him to set up Salcido and her cousin. He said he lured them to his house by offering a special magic ritual to bring them prosperity. "El Brujo" said two men grabbed and killed the cousins after they arrived at his home. He said their bodies were cut into pieces so they could fit into his small backyard grave.

Police confined their investigation to "el Brujo." After the judge announced the sentence, Guerrero said he would rather spend fifty years in jail than tangle with the real killers. He refused to identify them.

A cocky drug dealer

The murders of three women whose bodies were discovered in 2003 in shallow graves east of Juarez sent shockwaves throughout the border city. The authorities classified their deaths as "crimes of passion," a common euphemism for family violence. Felipe Machado Reyes, 31, a cocky drug dealer who appeared in a picture wearing purple western boots and a lime-colored shirt, was accused of ordering the slayings.

One of the victims was his wife, Candelaria Ramos Gonzalez, 22. The other two were the wife's cousin, Mayra Alamillo Gonzalez, 20, and a friend, Miriam Garcia Solario, 22. Machado's wife and her cousin were shot in the head. Their friend, who also was shot, actually died of asphyxiation. The medical examiner found sand in her lungs and concluded she had been buried alive.

Police said the women were killed July 23 following a heated argument between Machado and his wife at the Autotel La Fuente on Avenida Tecnologico (Panamerican Highway). The Autotel is a popular Juarez gathering place for young people from the middle and upper classes. It is also a popular hangout for drug dealers.

The place, across the street from the powerful Fuentes family compound, features a drive-in service area where customers can order drinks from parked vehicles, a motel with cheap rates for one-night stands and a clubhouse with live music and a bar. Police said the couple's dispute escalated before they and their acquaintances left. A couple of days later, passers-by noticed the bodies in a patch of desert and notified police.

Machado, who was sought in connection with the murders, hid out in El Paso until U.S. law enforcement received a tip on his whereabouts and arrested him. Although he was wanted in Texas on drug violations, U.S. authorities promptly sent him back to Mexico to face the murder charges.

A year before the three women were slain, a hotheaded Machado had threatened the bouncers who threw him out of the Changada nightclub for being disorderly. Machado allegedly drove by later and shot up the front of the Changada as club patrons walked out. The gunfire killed a young woman who had nothing to do with the earlier scuffle. Despite eyewitness accounts, Juarez police did not arrest Machado.

But the three women's murders in 2003 was an act so flagrant the authorities could no longer afford to overlook him. This was not always the case.

Shooting at the Vertigo

On December 7, 1997, Rosa Arellanes Garcia, 24, was shot to death inside the Vertigo nightclub in Juarez. The Vertigo is a popular nightspot among teenagers from El Paso and Southern New Mexico. Initially, Mexican authorities ruled her death a homicide, and alleged that Victor "el Cubano" Lazcano was responsible. In September 2000, while the Mexican case was pending, U.S. authorities indicted Lazcano and three others on drug-trafficking charges. An El Paso police document had linked Lazcano and others who lived in El Paso to an El Paso police officer, who, through his lawyer, denied any wrongdoing. Lazcano was tried, convicted, and served a short sentence before being sent back to Mexico to face the Vertigo homicide charge. By that time, however, Chihuahua authorities had decided that the young woman's death was accidental. Lazcano went free.

Big Shadow and Little Shadow

"There are some death reports that the public never hears about because they are filed away in a locked cabinet," said a Chihuahua State official familiar with the Juarez homicide investigations. "We are forbidden to discuss them with anyone." One such case was leaked, however, and the disclosure nearly got Special Prosecutor Suly Ponce into lethal trouble. Agents in the state attorney general's office warned her that she could end up in the trunk of a car because of such leaks.

The official, who provided information from the case file, said the murder of Alejandra del Castillo Holguin in 2000 was part of a bigger case that actually involved several other homicides and disappearances in late 1999 and early 2000. The account was profoundly troubling, for it laid bare the abuse of power and authority on behalf of the killers. According to investigators, Alejandra Holguin had a sister named Perla Karina Holguin who was at the heart of the case. The sisters were known for their good looks. Their mother, Martha Holguin, was a magazine editor who moved to Juarez from Hermosillo, Sonora. Once in Juarez, Perla Holguin married or lived with an older man.

U.S. investigators said the man Perla Holguin was involved with was a major drug dealer who operated east of Juarez. His nickname was "Big Shadow." He had a young child by Perla Holguin and older children by a previous wife, including a son nicknamed "Little Shadow." "Big Shadow" lavished expensive gifts on Perla and gave her a daily allowance of more than $1,000 cash. At one point, he began to suspect that she was cheating on him and asked the family bodyguards to report to him if this was the case. Eventually, the bodyguards informed "Big Shadow" that she was having an affair not with a man but with a woman identified only as "Graciela."

The news angered "Big Shadow," who ordered "Graciela's"

death and had her body incinerated. Perla Holguin searched for "Graciela" until "Big Shadow" told her to stop looking because she was dead. Then Perla Holguin did the unthinkable. She avenged "Graciela's" death by hiring someone to kill the powerful drug dealer. She had him buried in their backyard.

"Big Shadow's" family began to miss the patriarch. When "Little Shadow" queried Perla Holguin about his father, she made the mistake of telling him that Mexican federal police had picked him up on drug charges. The son knew the federal police and quickly established that they were not involved. The son confronted Holguin, discovered the truth and allegedly had her killed. He also moved his father's body from the backyard grave to the family's cemetery plot.

"Little Shadow" learned Perla Holguin's young child was staying with Perla's sister, Alejandra Holguin. He reportedly had the sister, who was several months pregnant, killed and took Perla Holguin's child by "Big Shadow."

Mauricio Zuniga, a friend of the two slain sisters, confronted "Little Shadow" about the two women's deaths at the Changada club. Then, Zuniga turned up missing.

In the meantime, "Little Shadow" was trying to track down a large and missing sum of his father's money. He began to look for Perla and Alejandra Holguin's mother.

Martha Holguin, who feared she would be the next to die, abandoned any hope of recovering her grandchild and fled to the United States. Everyone was looking for her, the Mexican police, the FBI, the drug dealers.

"There were other deaths and disappearances linked to this case that will go unsolved forever," concludes a Chihuahua State official. A former DEA officer correctly described this case as a modern Shakespearean tragedy. Although Martha Holguin was well known in Juarez press circles, a few journalists who were familiar with unreported details of the case said their editors did not allow them to write the full story. Only Alejandra Holguin's death in March 2000 was made public.

A U.S. Consulate communiqué referenced a Mexican media account about the grisly crimes that mentioned Perla Holguin's 1999 disappearance. A Mexican official said that unless the community gets wind of certain deaths, some bodies are taken straight to the *fosa comun,* (common grave) the public common graveyard reserved for unidentified or unclaimed bodies. Vicky Caraveo, a former state official, said an unknown number of women's bodies are buried in the city's two common graves.

13.

Heidi and Isabel

The 1995 disappearance of Heidi Slaquet Armengol has haunted her friend Isabel Arvide for years. Arvide wrote about Slaquet in a book, *Muerte en Juarez* (Death in Juarez). DEA sources said the Juarez drug cartel bought copies of the book in bulk to limit its circulation. On both sides of the border, people who knew Slaquet, a European, said she was a charming and alluring woman who attracted men wherever she went. She operated an art gallery in El Paso, and Arvide said she dated such famous men as Spanish matador Manuel "El Cordobes" Benítez Pérez and opera singer Placido Domingo.

The day she disappeared, Slaquet was on her way to meet Arvide, her friend of twenty years, at the Juarez International Airport. She took a taxi, but never made it to the airport. The cab driver, Domingo Bernardino Delgado, was found dead inside the taxi, but there was no sign of Slaquet. Arvide now says that she ended her book before she realized that officials like the late Francisco Minjares, then in charge of the state's anti-kidnapping unit, intentionally misled her about the case.

An El Paso woman called "Ana" said she met Slaquet at parties hosted by drug capos in Juarez. Ana said Slaquet brought women from El Paso's beauty pageant crowd to the parties. Former DEA official Phil Jordan said one of his El Paso relatives who did volunteer work for the pageants was a friend of Slaquet's during this period. Important people attended these social gatherings, including mayors, police chiefs and business leaders. The late federal police commanders Guillermo Gonzalez Calderoni and Rafael Aguilar Guajardo socialized with Slaquet, too.

"When the El Paso women from the pageant arrived," "Ana" said, "the drug dealers would say, 'Here comes the good stuff.' These women were not forced in any way. They understood they were bought and paid for the minute they walked through the door. Heidi was the one who procured them."

Lino Herrera, a drug dealer who was later slain, was one of the circuit's popular party hosts. "Ana" cited differences in the women who were paid to help entertain the men. "The Mexican women wore less expensive clothes and tended to be more shy, but the beauty pageant women (from El Paso) were glamorous. They were dressed to the hilt. And they made pretty good money."

U.S. federal law enforcement sources said they knew something of Slaquet's disappearance. Their most compelling theories are that she was killed by the Arellano Felix drug cartel from Tijuana or the Carrillo Fuentes organization. Former DEA official Phil Jordan said Slaquet was a money courier for the Carrillo Fuentes cartel, and "she was probably killed because she was suspected of skimming money from the cartel, or because she was targeted by the Tijuana cartel that was trying to make inroads in Juarez at the time. The money couriers are the first ones they target whenever the drug dealers try to take over a territory."

If Slaquet was buried on a Carrillo Fuentes property, as some have asserted, then it is likely that Amado Carrillo's cartel was behind her disappearance. If the Tijuana cartel had her killed, then the killers probably would have sent a message to their rivals by exhibiting the body in a public place. The Carrillo Fuentes cartel was known to terminate people on the mere suspicion that they might be hurting the organization.

Arvide disputes any theories that cast aspersions on her friend's reputation. She believes Slaquet was killed because she found out that major drug kingpins had planned a summit in a designated place in Mexico. News accounts about that meeting later alleged that drug lords had paid a Mexican general $60 million dollars to protect the summit. "They felt she was going to tell me about it. And because I was a journalist, they feared that I was going to write about it," Arvide said.

One of the few clues Arvide has is a picture of a handsome man who was Slaquet's benefactor. People described him only as "el Compadre," a word that means a godfather or close friend or benefactor. People in Juarez who have looked at his picture said the mystery man was known by the surnames of Gallardo and Borunda.

In one photograph, the man is standing between two well-known matadors. The bullfighters told Arvide they could not recall "el Compadre's" name. No one knows where to find him, and some say he may have joined the long list of people whom the cartel disappeared during the 1990s. Other people in El Paso and Juarez who knew Slaquet are afraid to say anything about her or the mysterious man in the photograph. The cartel has that effect on people.

Threats against Arvide

Arvide frequently writes about corruption and the drug trade and because of a previous attempt on her life, the Mexican federal government assigned federal agents to guard her around the clock. I first met her in January of 2002, when she came to Juarez to resume her investigation into Slaquet's disappearance.

I accompanied her to the parcel where the bodies of eight women were found in November 2001 and to a couple of other sites that conceivably could yield Slaquet's body someday.

Jesus "Chito" Solis had just been named Chihuahua State's new attorney general. Arvide recently had accused him of having connections to drug traffickers, which the official vehemently denied. His appointment prompted federal officials to increase Arvide's security during her stay in Juarez. During the trip, Arvide's entourage included eleven federal agents and three bulletproof sport utility vehicles.

In the evening, two officials from the federal attorney general's office, Cuauhtemoc Perez and Rolando Alvarado, joined us for dinner at the Shangri-la restaurant. Perez pulled out a thick wad of cash and plunked down the *pesos* for the best tequila in the house and an especially pricey meal at the upscale eatery. "I bet they were living it up with my tax money," said Loren Magaña, an advocate for the missing who got into an argument later that week with Arvide.

The police death squad

Before her visit to Juarez was over, Arvide's armed federal guards escorted us to Hooligans nightclub. Three months earlier, the club had been the scene of a dispute that ended tragically for four young men.

Witnesses said a brawl ensued after one of the men asked a woman to dance. That offended the boyfriend who had escorted the woman to the club, and a fight broke out. One of the four young men knocked down the woman's boyfriend.

A bartender and club bouncers rushed to break up the fight, urging the young men to leave. Club employees told the five young men they had no idea who they had just tangled with.

The men left but were intercepted later by city police for no apparent reason. The police left after a few minutes, and four pickup trucks arrived with several men aboard. This was a death squad.

The armed group beat and abducted four of the five young men they encountered. They left behind a fifth man because they thought he was dead. The wounded man later identified one of his attackers as a state police officer.

The injured man's friends were found dead the next day, their bodies bearing signs of severe torture. One of them had his fingers pulled out of the sockets. Officials privately said the unfortunate men did not know that the disgruntled customer they fought that night at Hooligans was related to drug kingpin Amado Carrillo Fuentes. The woman he escorted that night was a dancer for a nightclub in El Paso.

The father of one of the slain men was a former police officer.

He tried to investigate but was threatened and had to drop his quest. He figured out in time that the police had no plans to solve the case.

Federal Attorney General Rafael Macedo de la Concha said in a news conference that the same drug kingpin's relative was involved in the 2001 attempt on the life of Chihuahua Governor Patricio Martinez. The authorities never arrested him in connection with the serious allegation. Instead, Macedo de la Concha received threats and was forced to quit his post. The government transferred him to another post outside of Mexico.

Arvide's warning

In 2002, Arvide, who had had a long romance with a general, was working on a new book about corruption in Mexico's military.

She abandoned the project after strangers tried to kidnap her son as a warning. "They sent back word to me that if I dropped the book about the military, they would leave my son alone," she said.

Arvide, who was unjustly jailed twice at the Chihuahua City prison on defamation charges, became worried when she learned from the federal police that Vicente Carrillo Fuentes reportedly paid a "brujo" or witch from another country $100,000 to conduct a sacrificial ritual as retribution for something she had written about the cartel.

Mexican federal agents told Arvide that the drug-related shooting of a Juarez man reportedly served as the proxy human sacrifice for the ritual aimed at the writer.

Human sacrifices

Many drug dealers, including members of the Colombian and Mexican cartels, are highly superstitious, pray to special patron saints or carry amulets and consult with mediums. Investigators for the Mexican Federal Attorney General's Office have documented cases of blood rituals carried out for drug traffickers, but the most notorious case on record was related to a criminal group that operated in Matamoros during the 1980s.

The group conducted human sacrifices, and one of their victims was Mark Kilroy, 21, a Texas pre-med student, who crossed the border into Mexico during spring break in 1989. Mexican police stumbled on the grisly activities at a ranch by accident. They found body parts and occult paraphernalia and made several arrests. Adolfo Constanzo, leader of the drug cult, asked members of his group to shoot him dead rather than allow police to take him into custody.

According to the Associated Press, one of the cult members testified that the late Mexican Interpol Commander Florentino Ventura Gutierrez was one of the cult's disciples. The commander committed suicide after shooting his wife and another person.

At least three other federal police officials, including a high-level drug investigator, also were linked to the group suspected of participating in more than twenty human sacrifices on the border and in Mexico City.

Arvide's jail sentence

Isabel Arvide narrowly escaped a third detention in Chihuahua City, when a state judge sentenced her on March 3, 2006, to a year in jail and a $20,000 fine. The sentence was for allegedly defaming former Chihuahua State Attorney General Jesus "Chito" Solis. The Committee for the Protection of Journalists in New York formally condemned the judge's action.

The committee also was busy responding to attacks against other journalists in Mexico, including the stabbing death of a Nuevo Laredo editor, reportedly the victim of competing drug barons, and grenade attacks against a newspaper in Quintana Roo.

Another high-profile complaint involved alleged attempts by officials to orchestrate the irregular detention of Lydia Cacho, a journalist and activist in Cancun.

During the previous year, the Mexican president's wife sued Argentine author Olga Wornat over her book about the first family, *Cronicas Malditas* (Damned Chronicles), and a businessman in Puebla sued Cacho for her book about pedophiles in powerful circles, *Los Demonios del Eden* (Demons of Eden). The lawsuits transformed the writers into martyrs, gained them public sympathy, and increased the demand for their books.

Under pressure from activists and journalism organizations, the Vicente Fox administration created a special federal prosecutor's office to investigate violence against journalists.

For Arvide, there was no point in turning to the new special prosecutor for journalists, because the man who oversaw that office was Mario Alvarez Ledesma, a federal deputy attorney general who was the subject of one of her scathing columns. Arvide laughed at the irony of expecting help from the official's staff. Friends warned Arvide to consider leaving Mexico for good.

Patricia ends her search

After five emotionally charged years, Patricia Garibay's search for her missing brother, Jorge, finally ended. She had sought help from many sources on both sides of the border. She met with human rights groups, with politicians, with Mexican and U.S. law enforcement, with anyone who might advance the investigation. During this long quest, which was not without its dangers, she had put any semblance of a normal life on hold.

Amnesty International had noted that the Juarez drug cartel was suspected of engineering the kidnappings of numerous people in Chihuahua state. Efforts to bring to justice those responsible behind her brother's abduction are likely to remain stalled. The same holds true for hundreds of families that continue to search for their missing relatives.

But, finally, Garibay is confident she knows what happened to her brother, and why it will do no good to try to recover his body for burial. Jorge Garibay's two El Paso companions probably met the same fate.

"We won't be able to bury him, or find something that was left of him," she said wistfully. "We were told, and we are satisfied that the information is correct, that Jorge was taken to a place where he was kicked and beaten severely, and that acid was poured over him to dissolve his body. Now that I know what happened to him, I feel the need to move on with my life."

The cartel's "bad girls"

Although men do most of the killing in Juarez, a few women have emerged as ruthless thugs in their own right. For example, a woman nicknamed "Madonna," considered the "queen of cocaine" in the city, was a suspect in several deaths and disappearances. Undercover officials said she is a foul-mouthed bleached blonde who works for the Carrillo Fuentes cartel. Her victims are cartel employees who crossed her somehow, or anyone who gets in her way.

The woman previously referred to as "Ana" said Madonna looks nothing like the famous singer. "She once walked into a club she owns and started snapping her fingers and asking her crew to round up a couple of men she suspected of cheating her. She had them killed– just like that. She's horrible." Like other cartel operatives, the Juarez press does not mention her, although everyone knows about "Madonna." She instills fear in people, and that is why the cartel leaders like her.

According to a U.S. court indictment, another woman associated with the cartel, Ana Pineda Monti, who used the aliases Ana Montti-Almaraz and Ana Montti, paid two people in the drug trade to kill a woman in El Paso. She suspected the woman was having an affair with her common-law husband. (This Ana is unrelated to the "Ana" quoted elsewhere in the book.)

The victim, Mercedes Caballero, was slain in her El Paso home in January of 2000. El Paso police said one of her children was inside the house at the time.

Before police arrested Ana Pineda Montti in Mexico on an extradition warrant, she was planning a traditional fifteenth birthday celebration for her daughter, which Mexicans refer to as a *quinceañera*, a rite of passage for girls. According to a person who received an exclusive invitation to the party, drug lord Vicente Carrillo Fuentes was to be the guest of honor because he was asked to be the girl's godfather.

The drug lord did not show up for the event at the Mision de los Lagos Club Campestre (Country Club), but drug investigators who conducted surveillance spotted Ana Pineda Montti. A short time later, Mexican police arrested her and the common-law husband, who was also using an alias. That man turned out to be Adrian Almaraz, nephew of the prominent lawyer, Sergio Dante Almaraz Mora. Dante was defending one of the bus drivers accused in the 2001 cotton field murders.

Her return, a bad omen

However, the Mexican government did not extradite the woman to confront the murder charge in El Paso. A Mexican official has said that cartel operatives who work for the government are able to stall extradition requests indefinitely – for the right people.

In 2005, Ana Pineda Montti returned to Juarez and called on her old boyfriend. Soon after that, a feuding faction of the drug cartel abducted

Adrian Almaraz and ten other men in the Valle de Juarez, west of the city. The missing man's father said his son Adrian Almaraz was last seen alive during a social meeting with Pineda Montti.

No one could account for the missing men. Adrian Almaraz's father and Sergio Dante Almaraz filed missing persons' reports with state and federal police.

"At first, none of the police officials wanted to process our complaint," the father said. "We were able to get one of the Juarez newspapers to report on the incident, but later the news media in Juarez said they could not follow up on my son's disappearance because the issue was too hot," he said. "They said the cartel had sent word to the media that it did not want to air its dirty laundry in public."

Frustrated, Sergio Dante Almaraz traveled to Mexico City to meet with Federal Attorney General Rafael Macedo de la Concha, shortly before the official resigned. Almaraz filed a report with De la Concha, and also with Jose Santiago Vasconcelos. During this trip, Almaraz discovered that Ana Pineda Montti, of El Salvador, had obtained Mexican citizenship. She was also exonerated by a Mexican judge on the U.S. extradition petition for lack of evidence.

Almaraz is murdered

The invisible force that guides Juarez selected January 25, 2006, as the date to sentence Sergio Dante Almaraz to death. He was driving a sport utility vehicle through downtown Juarez and had reached the intersection of Francisco Villa and Ignacio Mejia when two men pulled alongside his vehicle and fired ten rounds at him. He died instantly. The attack took place in the afternoon, shortly after 3 p.m. The lawyer was on his way to meet his wife for dinner and had just called her. He had a passenger in his car.

Ironically, or perhaps intentionally, his killers picked the same area to slay him where Juarez young women had vanished over the years. His brother Miguel Almaraz alleged that state officials had threatened him and Sergio Dante Almaraz during an intense argument over the lack of progress in Miguel Almaraz's missing son's case.

Miguel Almaraz, whose family fled Juarez after the very public murder, said he felt overwhelming impotence after losing his son and his brother in less than a year.

Shortly before the shooting, the outspoken lawyer had had a confrontation with officials at the state deputy attorney general's office. He may have felt threatened, because he made a point of telling a Juarez radio station that he would hold state officials responsible if anything happened to him. His slaying was a high-impact murder that sent shudders throughout the community.

The lawyer was fatally shot the same week a contingent of activists and artists from Spain had traveled to Juarez as part of a series of events to protest the women's murders. The advocates were supporters of a traveling forum against gender violence, led by Cristina Del Valle, an international singer and activist. More than thirty journalists from Europe accompanied the Platform of Women Artists against Gender Violence.

The group began their visit to Mexico with a high-profile concert featuring top artists like Juanes and Barry White in Mexico City's Zocalo. A smaller concert in Juarez brought together relatives of victims who held hands on stage with the artists after the performances. But the warm feelings went cold when gunfire killed the lawyer whom several Spanish journalists planned to interview that week.

Among other things, Sergio Dante Almaraz liked to dabble in politics. He had been named state director for the Convergence Party in the State of Chihuahua. Mexico's citizens were going to elect a new president on July 2. Previously, the lawyer had worked for presidential campaigns in support of candidates Porfirio Muñoz Ledo and Cuauhtemoc Cardenas. And, in 2006, he supported presidential candidate Manuel Lopez Obrador.

"Cerillo" grieves death

The fiery lawyer no doubt had a long list of enemies. But the most dangerous case he took on was the defense of Javier "Cerillo" Garcia Uribe, one of the accused in the 2001 cotton field murders. It was the same case that killed lawyer Mario Escobedo Anaya four years earlier.

The lawyers also treaded dangerous ground when they pursued the torture allegations against state police officers who allegedly mistreated their clients. One of them, the second bus driver accused in the eight murders, died in custody in 2004.

A state judge had finally set Garcia Uribe free for lack of evidence. But the accused, whose unjust imprisonment had destroyed his family, continued to press for an investigation into the torture police allegedly used to force a confession out of him.

Almaraz's murder also suggested police complicity. The journalists from Europe marveled at the sudden public airing of allegations that law enforcement officials might be involved. Names of possible suspects were tossed around freely in the press.

It also was demonstrated that the security cameras that should have caught the shooting on tape were manipulated. One of the cameras inexplicably malfunctioned, and the second one was frozen in one position, looking away from the intersection for forty-five minutes, before, during and after the attack on Almaraz.

The city police emergency command center operates the security cameras. Garcia Uribe went to the funeral of the lawyer who defended him through several excruciating years without charging him a cent. He could not afford a lawyer, much less one so skilled at working the system. Garcia Uribe wept openly when he bent over to look at the lawyer's body in the casket. Almaraz could have been killed for any number of reasons, but the hit was a clear sign about who ruled the border city. The lawyer had been scheduled to speak a few weeks later at a symposium on the women's murders at New Mexico State University.

The passionate and outspoken lawyer who suffered the same fate as Mario Escobedo Anaya did in 2003, also had recently agreed to defend Abdel Latif Sharif Sharif, at one time Chihuahua State's primary suspect in the Juarez femicides. For a lawyer with Almaraz's skills, dismantling the government's case against Sharif would be easy.

Supporters of Almaraz, a man who liked to laugh and speak loudly, thought his high visibility had afforded him some degree of safety. But Mary Lu Andrade, sister of 2001 victim Lilia Alejandra Garcia Andrade, said his death proved that no one was safe in Juarez anymore. No one.

14.

THE CARTEL WARS

The drug cartel's corruption of Juarez police at all levels – city, state and federal – explains how certain crimes can be sustained for years. These include the abductions of men and women, public shooting deaths to settle scores and *femicides*, the systematic murders of women. The onslaught could not continue without the influence of the Carrillo Fuentes drug cartel and its vast sums of bribe money.

U.S. drug enforcement officials said terror was the tool Amado Carrillo Fuentes wielded to eliminate rivals and maintain discipline within his organization. It was apparent the drug lord decided to employ the same tactics that had worked for the brutal Colombian cartels.

Former DEA official Phil Jordan said DEA and Mexican federal drug officials confirmed that the Juarez cartel had infiltrated the National Action Party in Chihuahua State since the early 1990s. Carrillo Fuentes actually began to court PAN politicians as far back as the late 1980s. Amado Carrillo exploited the fact that Chihuahua voters had grown weary of the Institutional Revolutionary Party (PRI) and were leaning toward the conservative opposition party.

In Mexico, the PAN is associated with big business and the Catholic Church. But in 1993, when PAN won the Chihuahua governor's office, the only change the people of Juarez experienced was the wave of violence that the Carrillo Fuentes forces unleashed on their community. The new drug lords disdained the old codes, which protected women and children.

In the new cartel, anything goes.

Intelligence sources said that the cartel negotiated its accords with the Chihuahua State government during Governor Francisco Barrio's administration. His election was seen as an important symbol of change and reform in Chihuahua. Before becoming governor, Barrio was the first opposition party member elected mayor of Juarez. While Barrio was governor, Juarez was ruled by a series of mayors from his political party, Francisco Villarreal, Ramon Galindo, and Gustavo Elizondo.

When Vicente Fox became Mexico's first non-PRI president in more than seventy years, he hired several former Chihuahua officials to help him run the country. Fox, a member of the PAN, made Barrio his anti-corruption czar. But along the way, something happened that upset the new administration. It began at the U.S. federal courthouse in El Paso with an extradition hearing for a Juarez lawyer. Lucio Cano, an attorney accused by Mexican officials of being part of the Carrillo Fuentes drug cartel, was spared extradition because Mexican officials did not testify or provide proof of their allegations. However, the most significant revelation to emerge from the proceeding had nothing to do with Cano.

An explosive document

The bombshell was found in a document the Mexican Federal Attorney General's Office had sent in support of the extradition request. In Mexico, that document is known as the *maxi proceso*, and it actually totals several volumes. The single tome that made its way to El Paso was a foot-high stack of legal-sized papers.

It traveled through U.S. and Mexican embassy channels, bore a red wax seal, and was held together with string. The U.S. State Department had instructed the U.S. District Clerk's office in El Paso not to take it apart.

The document is part of a Mexican federal indictment against the alleged heads of the Carrillo Fuentes cartel. *La Historia Secreta del Narcotrafico* (The Secret History of Drug-Trafficking), a book by Amado Carrillo's lawyer, Jose A. Andrade Bojorges, contains excerpts of the document.

Hoping to review Andrade's book for the *El Paso Times,* I called the publisher to get contact information for the author. A woman at the publishing company in Mexico City said, "Haven't you heard?" The author was disappeared, and the family had publicly requested that his body be returned for a proper burial. He is still missing. Jorge Fernandez Menendez, author of *Narcotrafico y poder* (*Drug-trafficking and power*), said the reason he faced no repercussions from his book, which was released the same year, is "because I was not Amado's lawyer."

At the El Paso extradition hearing, the U.S. federal judge agreed to enter the document into evidence. It was filled with the names of Mexican law enforcement officials and politicians who allegedly were involved with the cartel or protected it.

Carlos Huerta and Rafael Nuñez, two reporters from *Norte de Ciudad Juarez*, were the only other journalists who went to the district clerk's office to read the document. It took the three of us to lift it so we could make copies without damaging the seal and the string.

I returned to the *El Paso Times* newsroom with documents alleging that two Mexican federal agents had observed Vicente Carrillo Fuentes visit Juarez without arresting him, and that former Chihuahua Governor Francisco Barrio, the new federal anti-corruption czar, had received protection money from Amado Carrillo Fuentes.

Serious allegations

One of the documents said Vicente Carrillo Fuentes stopped at the Autotel La Fuente before heading to a meeting at a home in the Juarez Club Campestre (Country Club) neighborhood. A Mexican politician laughed loudly when asked why federal agents had failed to arrest the drug lord. "The federal agents were his security guards while he was in Juarez," the politician said, "and they were just reporting back to their bosses that Vicente had come and gone."

What the other Mexican document alleged about Barrio was devastating, considering that Fox was about to name him his anti-corruption czar. According to the document, a man named Tomas Colsa McGregor, who was Amado Carrillo's jeweler and accountant, told Mexican federal investigators that Barrio and other Mexican governors had received protection money from the drug kingpin.

The stories in the *El Paso Times* about Vicente Carrillo Fuentes' undisturbed visit to Juarez and the allegations that Barrio had solicited and received protection money from the drug cartel created a stir in Mexico. Vicente Fox was forced to defend Barrio, who later was a presidential hopeful. The episode provided a strong hint that despite the election of an opposition party member to the Mexican presidency, nothing fundamental was going to change, certainly not in Juarez, and not for a long time. It also meant that justice for the dead women would be delayed once more.

Barrio, who has a nephew who is an FBI special agent in El Paso, never responded to the newspaper's telephone calls for comment about the allegations. Instead, as is customary in Mexico, he took out full-page ads in Mexican newspapers to deny the allegations. The Mexican Federal Attorney General's Office, in turn, said then that the *maxi proceso* represented an open investigation.

Barrio's die-hard supporters said he was incorruptible. Nevertheless, whether Barrio knew it or not, someone in his administration received bribe money from the cartel and did so in his name. The Carrillo Fuentes cartel flourished during his administration, even as Barrio failed to stop the murders of women in the State of Chihuahua.

Jeffrey Davidow, a former U.S. ambassador to Mexico, disclosed in his book, *El Oso y el Puercoespin*, that drug allegations during Mexico's presidential campaign almost hurt Vicente Fox. U.S. Customs Service agents in Texas had detected drugs in a cargo of vegetables linked to Fox's export company in Texas. After being contacted by Fox's lawyer, who considered the timing suspicious, the U.S. government agreed to withhold publicity about the investigation.

According to Davidow, Fox was in the clear because customs investigators learned that the cargo had been repackaged in the United States. This meant the investigators could not prove a direct link between Fox's company and the drugs because a third party could have slipped the contraband in among the vegetables.

Fox: Cartel scores goal

Barrio's successor, Chihuahua Governor Patricio Martinez, survived an assassination attempt in January of 2001. Initial news reports said the bullet grazed his head. But a photograph distributed by the Associated Press told a different story. In the photo, Martinez, a member of the Institutional Revolutionary Party (PRI), was on the floor of the governor's palace with a thick stream of blood next to his head.

Victoria Loya, a state policewoman, was charged in the shooting and jailed immediately. Martinez never forgave President Vicente Fox's tasteless remark to the press about the attack. "The cartel scored a goal," Fox said. Many suspected Loya did not act alone, but she was the only one charged in the shooting. And she never offered a believable reason for the attack.

The governor complained to the Mexican press that the FBI had advance knowledge of the planned attack but did not warn him. A U.S. federal agent, however, said he personally notified Martinez of a possible plot against the governor, a scheme allegedly orchestrated by the Carrillo Fuentes cartel. The governor responded by beefing up his security. But he was caught off guard when he was shot on January 17 in Chihuahua City.

U.S. intelligence sources said the cartel tried to kill Martinez because someone in his staff wanted to negotiate with both the Arellano Felix cartel and the rival Carrillo Fuentes organization.

Later, Martinez threw a big community party in Juarez to celebrate the anniversary of his surviving the attempt on his life. Bands played live music and free food was served.

Outside the party, however, several people protested the murders of women in Juarez. Miriam Garcia, then wife of Victor "Cerillo" Garcia Uribe, was there, too, asking that her husband be released from his unjust detention. But like his predecessor, Governor Martinez could not stop the killing spree.

In 2004, toward the end of his six-year term, Martinez felt compelled to grant a lengthy interview to the *Heraldo de Chihuahua* newspaper in Chihuahua City. He used the interview to deny swirling allegations that he struck his wife, divorced her, and had an affair with a former backup singer for pop star Gloria Trevi. For the record, the governor said adamantly, none of the rumors was true.

Rumor: Amado is alive

The Carrillo Fuentes brothers are natives of Sinaloa, a state whose capital, Culiacan, is overrun by drug gangs. During the 1990s, the U.S. government was mostly concerned that the North American Free Trade Agreement was enforced with the least trouble possible, and that no one interfered with the U.S.-owned maquiladoras.

Collectively, the assembly plants operating in Juarez raked in billions of dollars for their shareholders, according to statistics of the Association of Maquiladoras. The drug cartel, meanwhile, had become a transnational corporation that also made billions of dollars. It hardly mattered to Mexico's political hierarchy that in the process Juarez had become a highly dangerous war zone.

Amado Carrillo Fuentes is said to be alive, and even some U.S. law enforcement officials are starting to consider the possibility. A knowledgeable source claims Amado Carrillo is in Malta, and that his brother, Vicente Carrillo, moved to Chile. Anti-drug officials say the cartel continues to extend its tentacles throughout Latin America.

Quoting unnamed U.S. intelligence sources, reporter Rafael Nuñez reported another version in 1998 alleging that Amado Carrillo became a CIA informant and used that leverage to help capture the Amezcua brothers (methamphetamine dealers) and Juan Garcia Abrego (Gulf cartel leader). The story in *Norte de Ciudad Juarez* further alleged that the CIA then killed (or pretended to kill) Amado Carrillo during his plastic surgery in Mexico City in 1997.

In June of 2005, authorities in Spain acting on a request from the FBI, detained two alleged members of the Juarez drug cartel on suspicion of drug-trafficking. The FBI arrested a third man, who lived in El Paso, Texas, in the same case.

The FBI office in El Paso was not exempt from the cartel's reach. In 2003, Mario Castillo, 36, a translator for the FBI, was sentenced to five years in federal prison for leaking and selling sensitive investigative information to a drug cartel member in Mexico.

Castillo, a Chihuahua City native and naturalized U.S. citizen, was hired by the FBI in 1998. "We don't know the full extent of the damage he did," said Hardrick Crawford Jr., the FBI's special agent in charge at the time.

Cartel troubles

On September 11, 2004, Rodolfo Carrillo Fuentes, brother of Amado and Vicente, was gunned down in a shopping center parking lot in his home state of Sinaloa.

The date gunmen picked to eliminate Rodolfo Carrillo Fuentes, the anniversary of the terrorist attack on the United States, was an obvious message. But for whom? His death was a significant event that ignited a war within the Juarez drug cartel.

Joaquin "Chapo" Guzman Loera was battling the Carrillo Fuentes brothers and Jose "Azul" Esparragoza for control of the Chihuahua smuggling corridor that included Juarez.

This and other incidents led to external battles with other Mexican drug organizations, as well as to widespread violence along the border and elsewhere in Mexico.

Drug traffickers recruited former elite soldiers to their ranks and were using such military-grade weapons as rocket launchers and heavy machine guns to wage war on rivals. They threw grenades at police stations in the state of Guerrero, where two lucrative corridors, Acapulco and Zihuatanejo, were at stake. Cartels also used beheadings and videotaped murders – tactics political terrorists used in other parts of the world – in the states of Baja California and Guerrero. Amado Carrillo Fuentes' real or feigned death in 1997 occurred in Mexico City on another date of importance to the United States, the Fourth of July.

Because of the enormous influence that drug traffickers wield in Mexico, it is as important to keep up with the power structure of the drug cartels as it is to follow the elections of mayors and governors. CISEN, Mexico's federal intelligence agency, has information that one of Mexico's top drug lords is a pedophile who is protected by officials in return for huge bribes. Residents of the border region must wonder whether the next kingpin of the Juarez corridor to emerge victorious will be the lesser of the evils.

15.

THE POLICE CARTEL

It was common knowledge in Juarez that the police were somehow involved in the women's murders. In fact, police officers who had killed women or were accused of rape rarely answered for their actions. People often asked whether the police in Mexico were incapable of investigating the murders or lacked the resources to do so.

The FBI and other law enforcement agencies in the United States offered assistance, but the Juarez police insisted they had everything under control. Although they lack the resources of their U.S. counterparts, police in Mexico are no less capable than officers anywhere else in the world.

The problem with the police in Juarez is that many of them worked for someone other than the public. They worked for organized crime. It is impossible to comprehend why the murders continued for so many years without understanding the role of law enforcement in a corrupt system.

The police enforced a strict code of silence that meant certain death for anyone who broke ranks. This system bore little resemblance to such almost-quaint traditions as soliciting bribes for minor traffic offenses. Police at all levels were involved in kidnappings and execution-style murders. U.S. federal law enforcement officials said the principal duties of Juarez police were to protect drug dealers and drug shipments.

Police kill Lardizabal

The death of Javier Felipe "El Negro" Lardizabal is a powerful symbol in the history of the Juarez women's murders. According to the criminal complaint filed by his sister, the former city police officer disappeared in May of 1993 while conducting an undercover investigation into corruption within the Chihuahua State police. He had gathered detailed evidence about police agents and commanders involved in the drug trade, auto thefts, and other rackets. One of those he was investigating was Sergio Rodriguez-Gavaldon, blamed by police for provoking the 2001 shooting deaths of the young daughter and common-law husband of Dr. Irma Rodriguez Galarza, the state forensic specialist.

Witnesses last saw Lardizabal alive when he was a guest at the Montecarlo Hotel in Juarez. Javier Benavides, deputy director of the Chihuahua State judicial police, used one of the hotel rooms as his office. Benavides later became Juarez city police chief. According to Lardizabal's relatives, Governor Francisco Barrio's staff had hired Lardizabal for the undercover investigation, something the governor's office denied after his death.

Lardizabal's mutilated body was found in November of 1993 in Lote Bravo, which two years later became a clandestine cemetery for young women who were raped and brutally murdered. It is a remarkable coincidence. A videotape of his autopsy shows that handcuffs were used to bind the tall, mustachioed Lardizabal. They were not his handcuffs, but the serial number (visible on the tape) indicates they were police issue.

In 1993, Lardizabal's sister, Rosa Lardizabal, formally accused Jesus Buil Issa, a Chihuahua State judicial police commander, of being involved in the disappearance of her brother. The dead policeman's sister served as a Juarez City Council member in 2003, during the administration of Mayor Jesus Alfredo Delgado. Buil Issa, whom U.S. law enforcement officials had linked to the Juarez drug cartel, denied the allegations.

After Lardizabal's murder, there would not be another local investigation of Juarez police corruption until 2004. His death was symbolic because it set the stage for what was to come for the next dozen years. His murder also heralded the emergence of the Juarez police cartel.

Prime suspect is murdered

Rosa Lardizabal began her term on the Juarez City Council with the Revolutionary Democratic Party (PRD), but later switched to the National Action Party (PAN). In the beginning, she was hopeful the Mexican Federal Attorney General's Office would investigate her brother's murder. Her term ended in 2004, and nothing happened. Since 1993, the case of the former police officer who dared to investigate the drug cartel's police connection remained unsolved.

But something monumental occurred a year after Rosa Lardizabal left office. Jesus Buil Issa was abducted in Juarez by one of the mysterious armed commandos that roam the region. Buil Issa, who tended to keep a low profile, rarely traveled to the border without heavily armed guards. Women described him as exceedingly handsome. Men feared him.

Before Buil Issa was killed, his captors had tortured him, reportedly to learn the whereabouts of Joaquin "Chapo" Guzman Loera. Buil Issa's death in 2005 was one of few visible signs of fissures within the Juarez drug cartel's hierarchy. "Chapo" was a drug baron who was trying to wrest control of the Juarez corridor from the Carrillo Fuentes brothers.

Rosa Lardizabal said she did not wish on anyone what happened to Buil Issa. But she nonetheless viewed his death as a form of justice for her brother's kidnapping, torture, and murder at the hands of police.

Another mother seeks justice

Identifying Lardizabal's body was one of the early cases assigned to Dr. Irma Rodriguez Galarza during her assignment in Juarez. Then, in July 2001, two hit men known as the "Garcias" who were chasing a former policeman killed her daughter, Paloma Villa, and her common-law husband, Sotero Alejandre Ledesma, and injured her son, Vladimir Villa. The shooters were chasing Sergio Rodriguez-Gavaldon when he sought refuge in Rodriguez Galarza's home on Del Trigal, a few blocks from the U.S. consul's home in Juarez.

Dr. Rodriguez Galarza was in Mexico City attending a work conference. The family members were gunned down as they stood on their front porch. Once inside the house, the man being pursued called someone on his cell phone and said, "Hurry and pick me up because this thing has heated up." A housekeeper said he left quickly through a back door, without bothering to check on the victims or call an ambulance.

Officials said Rodriguez-Gavaldon was the intended target of the attack. According to U.S. law enforcement, Rodriguez-Gavaldon, a former police officer and the son of a former Juarez police official, has a domestic violence charge pending against him in El Paso. He is unrelated to Dr. Rodriguez Galarza, the forensic specialist who at the time was reconstructing the remains of unidentified male and female homicide victims.

During Governor Patricio Martinez's administration, superiors forbade Dr. Rodriguez Galarza from reporting any statistics or names of Juarez victims in the textbooks she had authored. At the time, the state deputy attorney general's office in Juarez also prohibited officials from releasing statistics of rape victims to the news media.

Following the deaths of her husband and daughter, Rodriguez Galarza was removed from the state forensics staff, although she remained on call to help when needed. Officials allowed her to continue teaching at the state police academy, but they monitored her movements closely.

Rodriguez Galarza began her law enforcement career as a police officer for the State of Chihuahua. Then, she studied law. After finishing her legal studies, she decided to specialize in odonatological forensics. She said she turned in her official issue handgun soon after she transferred to Chihuahua City.

"If anything happens to me, no one will be able to claim that I committed suicide by shooting myself with that gun," she explained.

Her son, Vladimir Villa, who survived the attack provoked by Rodriguez-Gavaldon's detour into her home, is a grandson of Mexican revolutionary hero Francisco "Pancho" Villa.

To cope with her pain and loss, Rodriguez Galarza painted a large portrait of Paloma Villa, and displayed it in the middle of her living room. She and her daughter were close. With a great heaviness in her voice, she said "We did everything together.

We went shopping. We talked about life, and we joked a lot with each other."

"We were mother and daughter as well as friends. I feel a great emptiness without her. I warned them at the state attorney general's office that if they did not solve the case within a year, I was going to join the other mothers and plant my daughter's cross in front of the state office building."

16.

TERROR WITH A BADGE

In 2002, the Chihuahua State Attorney General, Jesus "Chito" Solis, flew from Chihuahua City to the border to personally intervene in a case involving the violent rape of an eleven-year-old boy in Praxedis, a village in Valle de Juarez, which is east of Juarez.

Angry Praxedis residents had marched into Juarez to demand justice. Authorities identified the boy's attacker as Edgar "Topo" Fernandez Jurado, an alleged regional drug dealer whom police seemed unwilling to arrest. With prodding from Solis, the state police finally arrested Fernandez.

Later, Alberto Quiñonez Alonso, a state police commander who oversaw Praxedis, was alleged in press accounts to have protected Fernandez. After "Topo's" arrest, the policeman was shot to death at a busy intersection.

I asked a detective who worked for Grupo Zeus, the state police task force charged with investigating organized crime-related shootings, why they never arrested anyone in these execution-style murder cases. "They know where our families live," was his candid response.

But who else protected "Topo"? Three years after his arrest, people in the judicial system warned that Fernandez ("Topo")

was about to be released. That produced such a public outcry that the possibility of his release was not mentioned again until 2006. The authorities in Juarez rushed to revive a weapons charge against him and said he would remain in jail, for now.

At first glance, it appeared that Fernandez was a common delinquent hardly worth all this trouble. But, as with so many others, it was suggested that family or political connections might hold the key.

Four years after Fernandez's arrest, federal authorities identified members of a group of drug dealers known as the "Escajeda band." Mexican police said the band operated in the Valle de Juarez and was suspected in confrontations with U.S. law enforcement officials at the border. It came to light then that seven of the alleged members were relatives of "Topo."

High-profile cop is killed

Francisco Minjares, former chief of the Chihuahua State Attorney General's anti-kidnapping unit, and Antonio Navarrete, a former state judicial police official in charge of Juarez homicide investigations, supervised the 1996 cases against Abdel Latif Sharif Sharif and the alleged "Rebeldes" gang.

They were among the police questioned by Mexican federal officials during the 1999 binational "Plaza Sweep" investigation. Enrique Cocina, one of the Mexican federal investigators, said Minjares showed up for his interview with armed state police agents who surrounded the building while Minjares was indoors answering questions.

Cocina said then that he had enough evidence to arrest Minjares for extortion, "but I'm waiting so I can gather enough evidence to charge him with homicide." During the "Plaza Sweep" investigation in Juarez, Cocina said he and his staff slept on the floor to avoid the range of gunfire in case someone fired at them through the windows.

Minjares, who wore wire-rimmed glasses and kept a low profile, resigned abruptly in January 2002. He quit after federal officials asked to see his files on dozens of forced abductions dating back to 1993.

His execution-style death on September 11, 2003, created a sensation in U.S. federal law enforcement circles, where Minjares was known as a corrupt official linked to numerous slayings and kidnappings. Law officials in another Mexican state had publicly accused him of orchestrating kidnappings that he later claimed to solve.

According to police sources, a top Chihuahua law enforcement official ordered Minjares' death because he knew too much and posed a risk to the organized-crime structure. Others suggested his death had more to do with large cocaine shipments that were intercepted by U.S. authorities at the border. The seizures represented multimillion-dollar losses. Yet a third theory contended that his private kidnapping unit had the temerity to extort drug dealers. In police circles, Minjares was a cop of all cops, much as Jesus Buil Issa had been.

Police under fire

Antonio Navarrete was a Juarez city traffic police official when I interviewed him about the 1996 murder investigations that he and Minjares had worked on. He described it proudly as "the most expensive and professional investigation we ever had in the State of Chihuahua."

Navarrete, who had a beer belly and wore a uniform, said he was in charge of the part that involved the "Rebeldes" gang but that "Minjares was the architect of the investigation against Sharif." Navarrete laughed off the allegations by one of his superiors, city police Lieutenant Martin Arce de Botello, that he protected drug dealers.

People who know Navarrete, who also investigated the Hester Van Nierop case, said he liked to dress up as a biker and ride motorcycles. They said he liked to fancy himself as the main character of the movie "Easy Rider." After leaving the city police force in 2001, *Norte de Ciudad Juarez* reported, Navarrete began to dabble in politics, and helped Mayor Jesus Alfredo Delgado with his election campaign.

Another detective who worked on the 1996 "Rebeldes" case said he and other investigators did not get credit for their extensive undercover work. He said the investigation was taken over by higher-ups like Navarrete, who took credit for the arrests of the alleged "Rebeldes" gang members.

Experts suspect police

Two criminologists from Mexico City, Oscar Desfassiaux and Eduardo Muriel, traveled to Juarez in late 1998 to help with the women's murder investigations. They had come at the invitation of the Francisco Barrio administration but did not arrive until shortly after Patricio Martinez became governor. The investigators said their efforts to assist were blocked at every turn, and they blamed that on alleged police involvement in the crimes.

Feeling unwelcome and frustrated, the two returned to Mexico City. During their short-lived investigation, they learned gruesome details about the 1998 death of Irene Salazar Crispin, a twenty-four-year-old maquiladora worker. "They penetrated her vagina with a knife and cut it into pieces. They did the same with her mouth. Her lips looked like flower petals scattered over her face, a mound of ripped flesh."

Desfassiaux said that Fabiola Zamudio Calderon, a 1995 victim, was found dead at the Ranchito Motel. The criminologist did not know it at the time, but it may be relevant that Zamudio was found in Room 21, reportedly a relevant number for the man who killed Van Nierop in 1998.

Two other cases exhibited interesting coincidences. Patricia Palafox Zavala, 14, was stabbed to death in 1996. Maria de los Angeles Hernandez Deras, 28, was killed in 1995. Their bodies were found in August, although a year apart, at different places on a street named Mercurio. Initially, it was reported that Hernandez was stabbed, but later, authorities said she died from gunfire.

In 2004, federal Special Prosecutor Maria Lopez Urbina accused Navarrete and other former and current Chihuahua State officers of mishandling the investigations. Navarrete, a former state homicide investigation chief, responded by obtaining an *amparo* (a document similar to a writ of habeas corpus) to protect himself against arrest.

Capo was a former cop

Long after he stopped traveling through El Paso, the FBI posted billboards and offered a reward of $5 million dollars for information that would lead to the arrest of Juan Jose "Azul" Esparragoza Moreno, one of the chiefs of the Carrillo Fuentes drug cartel. During 2003, Esparragoza was seen in El Paso escorted by a Mexican federal official, reportedly on his way to check on business matters in Texas and New Mexico. Why the billboards and reward for the drug lord *now*? Incredibly, FBI officials said they did not realize before how big "Azul" was in the organization.

Like Rafael Aguilar Guajardo, Esparragoza was a federal police officer before he became a major drug dealer. Author Jorge Fernandez Menendez considers him to be "one of the most violent (cartel) operators." In 1993, after joining the Carrillo Fuentes organization, Esparragoza worked out of the State of Morelos. During the administration of Morelos Governor Jorge Olea Carrillo, residents of Cuernavaca said cartel associates would hold lavish parties in that city that lasted for days.

Top bands were flown in for the festivities, and the revelers could count on state police for security. Sergio Estrada Cajigal, the governor of Morelos after Olea Carrillo, made headlines in 2004 when he was linked socially to Esparragoza's daughter Nadia in Cuernavaca. Estrada Cajigal belongs to the National Action Party, as does President Vicente Fox. The states of Morelos, Jalisco, Mexico, and Chihuahua functioned as a single territory for the Juarez drug cartel.

Letter from Guadalajara

Shortly after publication of the 2002 *El Paso Times* series on the murders, I received a letter from Guadalajara, the capital of the State of Jalisco. The writer said to look into the Mexican federal officers who were implicated in numerous rapes in Mexico City in the late 1980s.

The men accused in the crimes were part of federal Deputy Attorney General Javier Coello Trejo's security detail, and two of the accused officers were his relatives. Initially, U.S. authorities heaped praise upon Coello Trejo, whom they nicknamed the "man of iron," for his alleged tough stance against drug traffickers. The three-page letter from Guadalajara was signed.

Proceso, Mexico's respected investigative magazine, published several accounts about the multiple rape charges against Coello Trejo's officers. According to the issue of April 2, 1990, Mexico City special prosecutor Rene Gonzalez de la Vega said, "The leaders of the police rape gang are the nephew and another relative of Coello Trejo. (Both are) deputized federal agents." As many as eight federal police agents were suspected of participating in the Mexico City rapes. Half of the accused officers were convicted, and the rest set free.

Isabel Arvide, editor of another magazine at the time, was the first Mexican journalist to cover this issue extensively. Arvide said she got involved because the families of several rape victims asked for her help. They wanted to file charges, but everyone was afraid to go up against the powerful and dreaded Coello Trejo.

"Throughout this ordeal, everyone was threatened," said Arvide, who went to see Mexico City's federal prosecutor, Ignacio Morales Lechuga, on behalf of the victims and their families. Morales agreed to take on the case, a decision that ignited a fierce dispute between his office and Coello Trejo, who claimed that the charges were politically motivated.

Mexico City officials said the federal police assailants had a *modus operandi*. They staked out upscale nightclubs in the south end of the city and waited for couples to leave. The agents used at least two vehicles to follow a targeted couple, and then cut them off and pulled them over.

After taking the couple's vehicle to a remote site, the federal agents would take turns raping the woman in every way possible. Sometimes they forced the victim's boyfriend to watch. Other times, they stuffed the boyfriend inside the trunk of the car.

About fifty such attacks occurred before the federal agents were stopped, but only a fifth of the complaints were prosecuted. Arvide said some witnesses told authorities that a high-ranking law enforcement official personally observed (supervised?) several of these attacks. The investigating officials that knew his identity did not disclose it. Investigators said the federal agents who took part in the gang rapes used vehicles during the attacks that were assigned to Coello Trejo.

The former federal commander is mentioned in the 1999 book written by Amado Carrillo Fuentes' disappeared lawyer, *La historia secreta del narco* (*The secret history of drug trafficking*). Author Jose Alfredo Andrade Bojorges claimed that Coello Trejo acted as a middleman in negotiations to have Carrillo Fuentes released from jail "in exchange for several million dollars."

Coello Trejo had denied any involvement with the drug cartel.

There seems to be no logic in federal agents who guarded a powerful law enforcement official executing a series of planned sexual attacks that scandalized the Mexican capital. How could Coello Trejo be oblivious to his security team's criminal activities? The answer probably lies beyond the attacks. The systematic rapes in Mexico City may have served as training for the police mafias that proliferated in Mexico during the 1990s. Were they "trained" to infiltrate the cartels in undercover roles?

If the attacks occurred under official cover, then these criminal activities actually served a different purpose. These organized attacks helped to desensitize the participants and reinforce the code of silence. The fact that several officers committed the rapes in front of the others discouraged any one of them from denouncing the crimes. The gang nature of the attacks made them all accomplices.

Experts said gang rapes served as an initiation rite for police fraternities or brotherhoods that assisted organized crime in illicit activities, such as trafficking in drugs, weapons and women and children. Some street gangs also employ collective crimes to test new recruits.

A retired U.S. military intelligence officer, who analyzed reports of murders along the U.S.-Mexico border, said he had confirmed the existence of Mexican police networks that used rape and other forms of violence to initiate members. High-level law officials in Mexico City also have confirmed the existence of a powerful police brotherhood that supports organized crime.

Carlos Ramirez, editor of the left-of-center *La Crisis* magazine in Mexico, has reported in depth about Mexico's "police brotherhood." Arturo "El Negro" Durazo Moreno, the Mexico City police chief appointed by

President Jose Lopez Portillo, is associated with creating an elaborate and brutal law police structure that delved in extortion, drug-trafficking and prostitution. Victims of the "dirty war" also linked him to the political persecution of members of the September 23 Communist League.

The late Durazo headed the powerful police mafia between 1976 and 1982, which analysts believe dispersed after his departure and continues today in various forms. He also built a replica of the Parthenon in Zihuatanejo, Guerrero, a private mansion known for orgies and wild parties. Alfonso Durazo Montaño, a nephew of the notorious police chief, who is not linked to any wrongdoing, served as a personal secretary to President Vicente Fox and to the assassinated PRI presidential candidate Luis Donaldo Colosio.

Historically, human rights groups have criticized Mexico for allowing its police to force confessions from people by torturing them. In what could be another clue, several of the murdered women were tortured and mutilated.

An enigmatic commander

Javier Coello Trejo and his security team visited the Juarez-El Paso border several times while he was Mexico's anti-narcotics deputy attorney general. In 1990, the *El Paso Times* reported an incident involving Coello Trejo's wife, who was intercepted by the El Paso police during a shopping excursion. Police had questioned her need for an armed escort. Susie Azar, El Paso's mayor at the time, issued an apology for any mistreatment Coello Trejo's wife may have experienced in her encounter with the local police.

During the U.S. trial of Juan Garcia Abrego, the former kingpin of the Gulf cartel, a witness in a Texas court testified that Coello Trejo was paid about $1.5 million a month in bribes by that cartel. Coello Trejo, who did not testify, denied the allegations.

Maria Teresa Jardi, a former federal attorney general official who served in Chihuahua State, said startling things in a 2001 interview with *La Cronica de Hoy*, a Mexican national newspaper. "Powerful commanders led by Javier Coello Trejo passed through the state of Chihuahua," she said. "These commanders had at their disposal up to 300 people, who did not appear on any registry so they could not be traced, and who worked as unsalaried police with a badge and official vehicles and weapons."

In 2003, author Sergio Gonzalez Rodriguez had a book presentation at the annual book fair in Guadalajara, home city of the letter-writer who brought the police gang rapes to my attention. After the presentation, Gonzalez said he and a couple of friends went to a nearby cafe to relax.

Sitting next to their table was a man who obviously strained to hear their every word. Gonzalez and the others recognized him immediately. "It was Javier Coello Trejo," he said.

In 2004, a Mexican newspaper reported the execution-style murder in Juarez of a man who was suspected of being a hired killer. The account said the dead man was one of Coello Trejo's former federal agents.

And, what became of the Mexico City police rapists, and who were the mysterious commanders in charge of marauding police armies that Jardi said were given free rein in the State of Chihuahua?

17.

POLICE BLOTTER

A long procession of law enforcement officials oversaw the women's murder investigations. But, without exception, these powerful officers were unable or unwilling to exert the forces of law and justice to save lives.

One of them, former Chihuahua State Attorney General Francisco Molina Ruiz, was severely criticized for public comments he made about the forced abductions in Juarez during the 1990s. Jaime Hervella, co-founder of the International Association of Relatives and Friends of Disappeared Persons, was among his harshest critics.

"Molina said the people who were being disappeared met with their fate because they were either 'drug addicts' or 'homosexuals,'" Hervella said.

Molina belonged to the National Action Party and served under Governor Francisco Barrio. One source, an expert on U.S. national security issues, said he was appalled that the DEA's office in Mexico City had promoted Molina's bid to become Mexico's new federal attorney general under Vicente Fox.

"The DEA considered him a helpful asset, and they were actively backing his effort to become the next attorney general," said the expert, who requested anonymity.

Molina was the Chihuahua State attorney general when the women's murders began, and the crimes attributed to the Carrillo Fuentes drug cartel escalated. He later served as Mexico's anti-drug czar under President Ernesto Zedillo.

Antonio Lozano Gracia, the federal attorney general who also belonged to the PAN, was considered Molina's political benefactor. During their administrations, the Carrillo Fuentes cartel flourished, and the volume of cocaine smuggled into the United States grew exponentially. After Fox appointed Barrio as his federal anti-corruption czar, Barrio hired Molina as his security chief in Mexico City. His other employees included former Juarez police chiefs Javier Benavides and Jorge Ostos, two officials who ignored early warnings by state criminologist Oscar Maynez Grijalva that a serial killer was on the loose in Juarez.

Blotter: Juarez police

Over the years, several police officers in Juarez were accused of killing or sexually assaulting women. They were never prosecuted. In some cases, officials said, they lost track of the suspects after they fled the region.

One of the accused officers, Pedro Valles, was charged with fatally shooting his girlfriend in 1998. The body of Rocio Barraza was found inside Valles' police vehicle in the parking lot of the Chihuahua State Police Academy. Valles, who became a fugitive, was assigned to the unit that investigated the women's murders.

In 1998, a woman named Maria Talamantes accused four Juarez city police officers of sexually assaulting her inside the downtown city jail. One of the accused officers was a woman. Talamantes claimed the police showed her a photo album with pictures of dead women. All four officers denied the allegations. They were arrested in October of 1999, but a judge released them, citing a lack of evidence. Activist Judith Galarza said she followed this case closely.

Also, during the 1990s, Melchor Baca, a federal police officer, threatened his estranged wife and chased down and fatally shot one of her co-workers, Ruben Vasquez. This occurred in front of witnesses at the federal courthouse, where the man and Baca's wife worked. Baca, who belongs to a politically connected family, was never arrested.

Three years ago, two women accused Juarez city police officers of raping them inside their official camper vehicle after the officers offered to help them find a child caught in a custody dispute. Shortly after that, another city policeman was detained, though only temporarily, after a woman caught him placing a cloth soaked with a chemical over the face of a prostitute who had agreed to have sex with him. None of the three policemen in these cases was prosecuted. Other cases involving police arose during the decade, but most of them dead-ended.

Police allegedly rape U.S. woman

By 2005, the State of Chihuahua had a new governor, and Juarez had a new mayor. It made little difference to police bent on breaking the law. That year, a woman from El Paso accused Juarez city police of raping her inside their camper truck in the Pronaf business district. She and her husband were leaving a nightclub to drive back to El Paso, when police intercepted them in the parking lot. The officers said the husband violated Mexican law by carrying an open alcoholic beverage outside the club. The woman offered them fifty dollars to let him go, but they said that was not enough. Then the officers ordered the woman inside a police camper truck, where they raped her, while the husband was placed in another police vehicle. Then, they allowed her to rejoin her husband. The couple rushed back to El Paso but returned to Juarez after they decided to file a complaint with the Chihuahua State authorities. The U.S. consul's staff in Juarez found the woman's story credible and agreed to monitor the case. The Pronaf district features upscale nightclubs that are popular with Americans.

Concerns across the border

Over the years, people from El Paso who own or operate businesses in Juarez have voiced concerns about the murders. I once asked Susie Azar, a former El Paso mayor who had operated a maquiladora in Juarez, for her thoughts on the disappearances in broad daylight with no one seeing or hearing anything. Without hesitation, she replied, "The police are doing it. If nobody sees or hears anything, then the police have got to be doing it."

Lance Levine, a member of Amigos de Bush, who also works in the maquiladora industry, said former Juarez Police Chief Javier Benavides once told him that the women's murders was a case too big even for the FBI.

Benavides told him that labor organizations opposed to the North American Free Trade Agreement and eager to hurt the maquiladora industry were committing the murders. In fact, a Mexican federal investigator actually connected the murders to concerns over free trade, but not as Benavides described it.

This was not the first time a Juarez law official had suggested a political agenda for the femicides. Jose Refugio Rubalcaba Plascencia, a city police chief under Mayor Jesus Alfredo Delgado, served only a couple of months in 2003 before he resigned under fire. He alleged that rich and powerful men were behind the women's murders. Another source said a man who was implicated in the femicides, and who supported one of the mayoral candidates, nearly became city police chief. That possibility still exists.

Police fear killers

Activist Judith Galarza recalled an unusual encounter in the 1990s with Arturo Chavez Chavez, who succeeded Francisco Molina Ruiz as state attorney general under Governor Francisco Barrio. Chavez was present at a private gathering that included several people from the Juarez community. Galarza said Chavez told the group that organized crime was involved in the women's murders, "and that his men were afraid to go up against them (the criminals)."

During the encounter, which Galarza confessed made her nervous, a woman who is prominent in political circles asked her to tone down her protests against officials. "The woman told us we were not being fair to the PAN (National Action Party)," Galarza said, "and that we should give the party a chance to work. She also referred to the victims as 'whores.'"

After Fox became president, Chavez was recruited to work in his Cabinet over the protests of activists and relatives of the victims.

The Juarez killer cops

In January of 2004, an informant's tip led to the discovery of a clandestine grave in the backyard of a Juarez home. Acting on information from the U.S. Immigration and Customs Enforcement (ICE), agents from the

Mexican Federal Attorney General's Office under Jose Santiago Vasconcelos unearthed the bodies of twelve people whose deaths were linked to the Carrillo Fuentes drug cartel.

One was a man from El Paso County who had attended Socorro High School. Authorities said the victims had been tortured before they were killed.

The ICE case that generated the lead resulted in the arrests on drug charges of several people in El Paso and other parts of Texas. One suspect killed himself in a jail in the Texas Panhandle.

A break in the investigation came when an El Paso County Sheriff's deputy stopped a car for a routine traffic check. He called ICE agents after realizing that the U.S. Marshal's Service was looking for the man in the car. The suspect was Heriberto Santillan-Tabares, an alleged lieutenant in the Juarez drug cartel.

According to ICE officials, Santillan had ordered the deaths of the victims buried in the yard of the middle-class home in Juarez. That was only half the scandal. The drug smuggler had allegedly hired Chihuahua State police agents to abduct and kill the men.

The active participation of police in drug-cartel hits was out in the open now.

Mexican federal authorities transported a couple, their son and thirteen police officers to Mexico City for questioning in connection with the grisly discovery.

A Chihuahua State police commander, Miguel Loya Gallegos, became a hotly pursued fugitive. Three other state judicial police accused of being his accomplices also fled. Several Juarez activists said they recognized Loya as one of the policemen who had been involved in previous investigations of the women's murders.

Cops work for cartel

The U.S. Attorney's Office indicted Santillan in five of the twelve murders, while Mexican officials continued to dig away in several Juarez properties where other bodies might be buried. Although the murders took place in Mexico, U.S. officials said they were able to charge Santillan and the others because the deaths were part of an ongoing criminal enterprise that operated on both sides of the border.

The U.S. case, however, was not without its problems. An internal ICE memorandum revealed that a U.S. informant had supervised the murders ordered by Santillan, which created a dilemma for the U.S. investigators.

The informant Eduardo Ramirez, a former Mexican federal highway police officer, reportedly was wearing a wire when several of the men were killed. Inexplicably, the U.S. agents failed to react in time to prevent the murders. A former DEA official said ICE officials restrained Ramirez only after learning that his band nearly killed two undercover DEA agents in Juarez.

Sandalio "Sandy" Gonzalez, the ranking DEA official in El Paso at time, said his superiors ordered him to keep quiet concerning the case. Relatives of two of the twelve victims filed a wrongful death lawsuit against the U.S. federal officials involved in the case. By then, officials who represented ICE were fighting the informant's request for asylum. They wanted to surrender him to Mexican federal officials.

On October 15, 2006, *Proceso* magazine published a story with a provocative cover about Ramirez's allegations before a U.S. immigration court that people in the Fox administration had ties to the Juarez drug cartel. A spokesman for the Federal Attorney General's Office in Mexico City denied the allegations. Several months earlier, a daughter of Amado Carrillo Fuentes had celebrated a wedding in Ojinaga, Mexico, across the border from Presidio, Texas. Many people were invited, and among the distinguished guests who were reportedly seen at the celebration were an administrator in Fox's Interior Secretariat and a former high-level federal law enforcement official.

A $100,000 bribe

Embarrassed Chihuahua State officials ordered drug tests for many of its state police officers. Several came back positive for marijuana and cocaine use, and these officers were fired. A Chihuahua State official said that in one year alone, about 250 city police officers, nearly a fourth of the force, tested positive for drug use.

Previously, one of the special prosecutors investigating the women's murders tested positive for cocaine, but nothing came of it. According to U.S. federal law enforcement, that official had accepted a $100,000 "respect" bribe from the Juarez drug cartel. Another official assigned to the state special prosecutor's office was the cartel's designated money man. In that role, his job was to distribute bribes among employees of the Chihuahua State Attorney General's Office.

Suly Ponce, one of the special prosecutors for the women's murders, had a brother-in-law whose 1994 disappearance was attributed to the drug cartel. This conflict alone should have disqualified her from serving in the sensitive post.

The American movies "Traffic" and "Kingpin" portrayed how the drug trade envelopes families with law enforcement connections. But this reality surpasses anything Hollywood could invent.

On both sides of the border, relatives of politicians and law enforcement officials were arrested on charges of drug possession or smuggling.

Others were disappeared by the drug cartel.

It is impossible to investigate the Juarez women's murders without also considering the drug trade's effect on law enforcement.

Official's alleged sex ring

The Chihuahua State Attorney General's Office was barely getting over the scandal of its police acting as drug-cartel enforcers when it was hit with allegations that a high-ranking state law enforcement official was recruiting teenage girls for a sex ring.

The scheme unraveled after a teenager told her parents that a man and a young woman had offered her money to have sex with important businessmen. Hector Lastra Muñoz, head of the department that processes all state criminal complaints in Juarez, was accused of being the pimp for at least six teenagers. In his official position, he could accept, reject, or detour criminal complaints.

Authorities were obliged to arrest Lastra because he was caught in the act, attempting to recruit a teenager who worked at a fast-food restaurant. The other girls told authorities that two brothers who worked with Lastra had photographed them for an album from which clients selected girls. Lastra denied the allegations and claimed he was framed. He also threatened to expose corruption in the Chihuahua State Attorney General's Office.

According to initial reports, police officials and important businesspeople paid to have sex with the girls at a rented house in the upscale Club Campestre (Country Club) neighborhood. Through his lawyer, Lastra later said that no one else was involved. Then he was released after posting a $30,000 bond and promptly dropped out of sight. Authorities said the alleged sex ring was in its early stages, and a judge ruled that it was unnecessary for police to search the house where the sex encounters took place.

When news of the sex ring broke, Samira Itzaguirre and her fellow radio announcers contacted me. They speculated on the air that the case might lead to a broader investigation that could encompass the previous murders and disappearances of young women. I predicted that state officials would contain the investigation and shut it down quickly. The investigation would not get beyond Lastra. If prominent people were involved, then state officials would do everything possible to keep their names from coming out.

Others wondered whether Lastra would be silenced, or whether the sex ring was an elaborate scheme to blackmail wealthy clients.

In September of 2004, state officials under Governor Patricio Martinez turned over the hot Lastra case to the new governor's staff. As far as anyone could tell, nothing more was done with the case.

Cristo Negro yields another body

Chihuahua State Attorney General Jesus "Chito" Solis resigned on March 8, 2005, the International Day of the Woman. Governor Martinez was facing mounting pressure from even his own political party to remove Solis in the wake of the latest police scandals. The governor left the state on March 9 for an extended trade mission to China, just after 200 federal agents from Mexico City arrived in Juarez for an undisclosed operation.

On March 11, the body of Rebeca Contreras Mancha, 25, was discovered in the Cristo Negro vicinity, where the bodies of six other young women had been found between October 2002 and February 2003. Given the heated political climate, her death was viewed as yet another message from the mafia.

According to unofficial sources, her body was actually discovered on March 8, but that authorities withheld the information until Solis could resign and the governor had time to leave the country. Activists surmised that the killer or killers intentionally selected March 8 to plant the body, perhaps to frighten them or discourage the investigations.

A Colombian accent

Yet another scandal occurred in the summer of 2005. A teenager accused a foreigner's bodyguards of raping her. The girl had answered a newspaper ad for a company that was recruiting girls as models and aides. She was promised as much as $300 a day, a lot of money for a member of the city's working class. But first, she had to attend training sessions to learn such skills as etiquette and how to dress properly. She and other girls who responded to the ad were excited about the possibility of appearing in television commercials.

A man identified as "the engineer" showed up one day to hire one of the girls. He pointed to the girl in training but was told she was not ready. At first, the man got angry and left. Then, he returned, flung money at the counter, and insisted on the girl. She was instructed to accompany him. When she got into his vehicle, a cover was placed over her head so she could not see where they were going. When the cover was removed, she found herself in a large bedroom.

The girl's family said the man, who others said had a "Colombian accent," fondled the girl but did not have sex with her. Instead, he told his eleven bodyguards to have their way with her. Later, one of the guards, who did not participate, dropped her off near a roadway and threw cash at her. A Juarez reporter notified Federal Commissioner Guadalupe

Morfin Otero, who in turn asked the family to report the alleged attack. The case made for sensational headlines for a few days.

Before the investigation was shut down, state officials characterized the girl as a liar and a prostitute. She and her family were harassed and threatened. The girl's mother, who works at a maquiladora, said her daughter is severely depressed, and is afraid to leave their home for any reason. The authorities never explained why the "engineer" needed almost a dozen bodyguards.

The "narco" cops

Rafael Aguilar Guajardo, the city's first major drug kingpin, was a federal police official before he began smuggling drugs. For many border residents, he represented the old guard of organized crime. On orders from rival drug lord Amado Carrillo Fuentes, he was slain in April of 1993 while in Cancun with his family. As a point of demarcation, 1993 is the year that Carrillo seized control of the Juarez corridor. Pablo Escobar, the powerful Colombian drug lord who planned on retiring from the drug trade, also was killed that year. From that moment, all hell was unleashed on Juarez.

Over the course of a decade, nearly 2,000 men and women would be killed or disappeared. These are war conditions, and as in any war, women and children are the most vulnerable.

Phil Jordan, former director of the DEA's El Paso Intelligence Center, said the main job of Juarez police was to protect the drug trade. U.S federal investigators admit keeping active files on police in Juarez, because so many of them worked for the drug trade. Given the dizzying amounts of money involved, some police officers become drug dealers or their associates full time.

One of them, former Juarez city police commander Roberto Corral Barron, a cousin of Mexican federal Senator Javier Corral, was gunned down in 2002 to settle a drug-related debt.

Before he was killed, Corral allegedly protected a drug dealer who was accused of sexually assaulting an eleven-year-old girl. A city policeman who responded to the assault complaint at a ranch in south Juarez was about to arrest the drug dealer when orders came down from Corral's office to get away from the place. The commander explained that city police had no jurisdiction in such matters. City police, a preventive force, technically must defer to state police, which has primary jurisdiction over sexual assaults.

Although the Mexican press reported the incident, the drug dealer's identity was not revealed.

Silvia and Griselda

Hundreds of violent deaths went unpunished in Juarez because of the pervasive corruption of the police and the breakdown of the judicial system. It was a total meltdown. Police at the city, state and federal levels were implicated in homicides and sexual assaults, crimes the judicial system mostly ignored.

In 1998, two Mexican federal agents were accused of being involved in the disappearances of Silvia Arce, 29, and Griselda Mares, 24. Before they were reported missing, the two women worked at Pachangas, a nightclub at the corner of Gomez Morin and Del Trigal.

Police, at least initially, and the missing women's relatives, began asking questions. Then, literally overnight, the club changed names and owners. Police told Silvia Arce's mother, Eva Arce, that there was no longer any recoverable evidence because the place had a fresh coat of paint and the former staff was gone.

Eva Arce said her daughter and Mares sold jewelry and maintained the restrooms at the nightclub. Both were attractive women who had men hovering around them. The day her mother last heard from her, Silvia Arce said she was going to the club to collect her money. The mother never heard from her again.

Arce tried to interview former club employees, but they told her they were afraid to talk. She heard rumors that her daughter, whose husband had abused her, had been dating a federal agent.

Unknown to Arce at the time, a dancer at the club gave Chihuahua State authorities a statement describing what had happened. Apparently sensing she was in danger, the dancer then left town after telling police what she knew. Her courageous account, which was in the original missing women's case file, was kept under wraps.

According to the dancer, two federal agents named Carlos Cardenas Cruz and Jorge Garcia Paz stored weapons at the club as part of an arms-trafficking operation. The agents panicked when they went to the club and could not find the weapons.

They suspected club employees had stolen them and had several workers rounded up and taken to a ranch, where they were interrogated. Silvia Arce and Griselda Mares were among the first to be questioned. Arce, who said she knew nothing about the weapons, allegedly was tortured and killed. Mares also denied any knowledge of the weapons and suffered the same fate.

The federal agents eventually questioned the dancer, who told them that the weapons had not been stolen at all. She said a male employee nicknamed "el Jotito" had moved them to a safe place. That revelation came too late for Arce and Mares.

Although Chihuahua State authorities sought the two federal agents for questioning, the agency they worked for transferred them to Queretaro State in southern Mexico. The Mexican Federal Attorney General's Office in Juarez said it did not keep track of former agents, or of their superiors once they leave the district.

Later, one of the federal agents wanted for questioning denied any wrongdoing, and officials said the second man no longer worked for the agency. Authorities elsewhere in Mexico said one of the former federal agents allegedly worked for the "Zetas" (enforcers of the Gulf cartel) and was arrested in Texas, where he served time on a drug-related conviction.

The club formerly known as "Pachangas" went through a succession of new names and owners. At one stage, a federal police official in Juarez warned reporters to stay away from the place but would not say why. It was named the Caribbean Queen before it was razed in late 2003 to make way for a strip shopping center.

State police refused to disclose the location of the ranch where Arce and Mares were questioned, and their bodies have not been found. After

Arce spoke out against the authorities for failing to investigate her daughter's disappearance, she suffered several attacks and threats from strangers who warned her to stop making waves.

The intimidation increased markedly after the Inter-American Commission on Human Rights agreed to look into the case. In 2006, another tragedy befell the Arce household. Octavio Atayde Arce, 18, Silvia Arce's son, was killed by gunfire during a party of young people. The blow to Eva Arce's psyche was profound. The boy recently had received a scholarship to study abroad, but he died in a senseless shooting before he could escape the city's death trap.

Mexican federal police

Jose Santiago Vasconcelos, head of the Mexican Federal Attorney General's anti-organized crime unit in Mexico City, met with me in August of 2002, two months after the *El Paso Times* published the "Death Stalks the Border" series about the women's murders. The encounter took place at Landry's Restaurant in East El Paso. Mexican journalist Isabel Arvide accompanied him.

Because security was a concern, U.S. federal law enforcement officers discreetly posted several agents outside the restaurant. Vasconcelos had collaborated with U.S. authorities in the 1999 "Plaza Sweep" investigation that linked the Juarez drug cartel to the murders of several men. As a result, he was uneasy about traveling to the border and was unaware that U.S. officers were providing security.

I asked Vasconcelos about the allegation by Jorge Campos Murillo, a federal deputy attorney general, that "juniors" were involved in several of the Juarez women's murders. Campos first mentioned the "juniors" during a press conference in Mexico City in early 2002. Then he traveled to Juarez, where reporters asked him about this new line of investigation. At the time, Campos also said he was going to ask the FBI for assistance and would make the formal request through the Mexican consul's office in El Paso. A couple of weeks later, Campos was reassigned to another unit within the Federal Attorney General's Office in Mexico City.

In response to the question, Vasconcelos said, "That Campos doesn't know anything."

I also asked him about the two federal agents who were accused of torturing and killing Arce and Mares. Vasconcelos jotted down something and said he would look into it. At the end of the discussion, he reiterated that Federal Attorney General Rafael Macedo de la Concha was genuinely concerned about the women's murders.

In June of 2002, when the series was published, the El Paso newspaper had calculated that about 320 girls and women had been killed since 1993. In January of 2004, at the request of President Vicente Fox, De la Concha named Maria Lopez Urbina, a 15-year veteran of the agency, as the first special federal prosecutor assigned to look into the Juarez women's murders.

On the eve of International Day of the Woman, March 7, 2004, Amnesty International conducted a news conference in Mexico City to update the number of deaths. Amnesty said 417 girls and women, including the Chihuahua City victims, had been murdered. Since the meeting with Vasconcelos in 2002, nearly 150 additional girls and women were killed in Juarez before the federal government decided to act. By the end of this investigation, the number of victims was closer to 470.

Police: Jobs for sale

As time went on, the police corruption in Chihuahua State became more evident. In the year 2000, two federal attorney general administrators in Chihuahua State, Norberto J. Suarez Gomez and Jose M. Diaz Perez, were accused by federal officials of attempting to "sell" their positions for a large sum of money. Their posts were equivalent to the positions held by the El Paso FBI special agent in charge and assistant special agent in charge.

These two Mexican federal agents had attended meetings of the Border Liaison Mechanism, which brings together U.S. and Mexican law enforcement and consular officials from the El Paso-Juarez region to discuss security issues.

Mexican federal authorities said Suarez and Diaz were detained on December 30, 2000. Officials said they were caught in Mexico City, "behind the federal attorney general's office, where (Suarez) was to meet (Diaz) to give him 500,000 dollars so that (Diaz) could get a different position."

Officials said Diaz, who was convicted in Mexico City on corruption charges, was not given witness-protection status because he refused to identify the source of the money. Federal authorities later said the money had come from the Carrillo Fuentes drug cartel.

U.S. intelligence officials, including former DEA official Phil Jordan, said they have learned over the years that cartel leaders handpick key law enforcement officers for the key border corridors, including Tijuana, Juarez, and Matamoros. In Juarez, city police officials also were accused of selling "promotions" to the ranks of lieutenant or commander to the highest bidders.

Police captains, young woman disappear

Another high-profile case that hit a wall involved the disappearance of two Juarez city police captains, Marco A. Portillo and Oscar Arellano. They disappeared two weeks apart in the summer of 2001. Relatives said the officers became targets because they had information about corruption among higher-ups. Jorge Ostos, the police chief at the time, initially responded to their disappearances by dropping both men from the city payroll for failing to report for work.

Authorities looked to city police Commander Roberto Corral Barron for an explanation, but he chose to resign rather than answer questions about the missing captains. In March 2002, Corral Barron was riddled with bullets while driving near his Juarez home.

Raul Rodriguez Quiroz, another former police officer, was killed in the same manner on February 13, 2002. Like Corral Barron, he was accused of protecting drug dealers. David "Cristian" Sanchez Hernandez, a notorious drug dealer and former police officer who controlled narcotics sales in downtown Juarez, supposedly reported to Rodriguez Quiroz on drug matters.

Juarez newspapers, including *El Mexicano* and *Norte de Ciudad Juarez*, carried front-page stories about the slayings of the former cops.

Rodriguez also was linked romantically to a sister of Alma Diaz, 27, a woman who vanished on February 25, 2002, twelve days after his death. Diaz was a college graduate who had just completed an internship at the Mexican Consulate in El Paso. She and the two police captains are still missing, and the deaths of Corral Barron and Rodriguez Quiroz remain unsolved.

Police protect corrupt mayor

According to officials, Juarez police were called on during the deadly years to remove the body of a man who died inside the home of a Juarez mayor. Although the circumstances are unclear, officials said the death stemmed from a voluntary sexual act.

The death did not appear in any public police reports, but other sources in Juarez corroborated the account. The mayor involved in the incident was a cross-dresser whose nickname in transvestite circles was the "Doll." A video that U.S. officials were aware of showed him in compromising situations with young boys. That former mayor owed the police cartel a large favor for keeping it quiet.

18.

SHARIF THE EGYPTIAN

Irene Blanco was still in a state of shock when Judith Galarza and I spoke with her at the Medical Specialties Hospital in Juarez. Her son, Eduardo Rivas Blanco, had sustained three bullet wounds, and doctors were working to save his life. Blanco, not coincidentally, was representing Abdel Latif Sharif Sharif, the state's trophy suspect in the women's murders.

The shooting occurred on May 21, 1999. Rivas and a friend, Ivan Molina, were traveling along Avenida de la Raza in a Silverado pickup truck. Rivas was driving and each was holding an ice cream bar when a Ford pickup with tinted windows pulled alongside them. A stranger in the Ford rolled down his window and began firing 9-millimeter rounds at Rivas. Despite his injuries, Rivas had the wherewithal to floor the accelerator and drive like crazy to the hospital emergency entrance.

The smear campaign was instant. Two Juarez television stations reported that a drug dealer named "Eduardo Blancas" had been shot.

Although the drug dealer's name sounded similar to her son's name, Rivas believed that police intentionally gave the news media misleading information. The real Eduardo Blancas is a convicted drug dealer and a relative of a former Juarez police chief. Irene Blanco suspected rogue police were behind the attack but could not prove it.

Shortly after the shooting, a couple of police officers barged into the emergency room, against the doctor's pleas, to interrogate "Pali," as Blanco called her son. "They just wanted to see if Pali was still alive," she said. His survival was almost miraculous. He was shot in the leg, abdomen, and chest. For Blanco, the message meant to back off the Sharif defense.

The daring daytime assault was never investigated. Someone stripped "Pali's" Silverado in the city impound lot, and police never bothered to remove the bullets embedded in the chassis.

The usually stoic Blanco trembled as she spoke that day. A few weeks earlier, a message on her telephone answering machine warned that she would be hit where it would hurt the most. "It didn't matter what they did to me," Blanco said. "But I never dreamed that they would go after my family. For their sakes, I have to rethink whether I should continue with this case. I have a young daughter to worry about, too."

Blanco no longer felt safe, and she and her children eventually left Juarez. They stayed in the city only long enough to pay off her son's hospital bill and sell their pet dogs and furniture to raise money for the move.

Judith Galarza, an activist who had lost a sister in Mexico's "dirty war," also left Juarez. She became an officer for an international human rights organization based in South America.

Blanco was highly regarded by leaders of the National Action Party, and former Governor Francisco Barrio was among the VIPs who stopped by the hospital to pay their respects. Barrio urged caution. "There is a powerful mafia here that one should not interfere with," he told Blanco.

Mayor Gustavo Elizondo offered her a city police detail to guard her family. She declined when she learned that a police station associated with Commander Antonio Navarrete would be in charge of protecting her. Navarrete's investigation had helped to put Sharif in jail.

Questions elicit reprisals

Blanco said the threats began soon after she began asking why authorities were not investigating a man called "Alejandro Maynez" as a suspect in the murders. He was mentioned frequently by Juarez residents and even the police. Among them were two police officers who said they were drinking at the Club Safari with a man identified as "Maynez." They alleged that he bragged about killing several women.

Sonia Valle, a reporter for the *CIMAC* news agency in Mexico City, happened to be in Juarez one day when state police responded to a homicide. Another woman's body had been found, and Sonia went to report the story. "A police commander who was at the scene told me that the murder was the work of Maynez,"

she said later. "I didn't question him further because he made it sound as though it was widespread knowledge in Juarez." I told Sonia that I, too, was pursuing information about the man who called himself "Maynez." (He is not related to the criminologist Oscar Maynez Grijalva.)

The Egyptian

They called him "the Egyptian." Considering his criminal record in the United States, Sharif seemed at first to be a most promising suspect in the string of murders of young women in Juarez. He was arrested twice in Florida for sexual battery, once in North Palm Beach in 1981 and again in Gainesville in 1983. Convicted and sentenced to 12 years in prison, he served only two years and six months of the sentence.

He escaped from custody at one point but was quickly recaptured. His former wife told the *Fort Worth Star-Telegram* that she divorced him after he "beat her bloody." After that, a woman in Midland, Texas, accused him of sexually assaulting her. The charge allegedly was dropped on condition that he leaves the United States. Florida authorities said there were other women who had violent encounters with Sharif but were afraid to press charges.

Sharif's pattern of behavior seemed to fit neatly with Mexico's culture of *machismo*. In Mexico, men who physically abused their wives and other women have become mayors and governors.

On September 28, 1993, a U.S. immigration judge in El Paso, Texas, ordered that Sharif be deported to Egypt, but he appealed. In June of 1994, Sharif withdrew his appeal and volunteered to leave the United States. He chose to make his new home across the border in Juarez. Why Mexican authorities allowed someone with his record to enter the country is incomprehensible.

The foreigner, described as handsome, well dressed, and outgoing, soon became a fixture at nightclubs like the Noa Noa on Juarez Avenue and Joe's Place in the Mariscal red light district. Sharif quickly developed a reputation as a party animal, and once won a dance contest at the Noa Noa. But the good times ended on October 3, 1995, when Chihuahua State police arrested him on suspicion of raping a prostitute named Blanca Estela. He remained in jail until his death eleven years later.

Blanco to the fire

Francisco Villarreal, the Juarez mayor in 1996, told his assistant, Irene Blanco, that he suspected Sharif was a scapegoat. "I leave you in charge of him," he told her. Why the mayor asked her to take on the moral duty of watching out for Sharif is unclear, but, because she deeply respected the popular Villarreal, Blanco did not hesitate.

After Sharif ran out of money for lawyers, Blanco agreed to become his legal representative. In Mexico, an accused person can designate anyone to represent him or her in judicial proceedings. Blanco was an excellent analyst, and she consulted experienced lawyers for advice.

Before she came on board, Sharif had had a series of good lawyers, including Maximinio Salazar, Mario Chacon and Juan Fernandez Ordoñez. All of them risked their careers by defending such a controversial figure. Chacon said a judge cleared Sharif of the 1995 rape charge after a medical exam proved that no forcible sex had taken place between him and the woman. The alleged rape victim later recanted her statement. The authorities, however, had no plans to release the Egyptian.

In the 2002 *El Paso Times* series, "Death Stalks the Border," the newspaper outlined several flaws in the investigations against Sharif. The series also questioned why authorities were so intent on suspects of dubious guilt while ignoring others. Attorney Salazar felt he had the answer:

In Sharif, the authorities have found the perfect scapegoat. He was a stranger who did not speak Spanish, had no support network in Juarez and had the right kind of criminal record. Fernandez said Sharif was a victim of politics, of the pressure the authorities were under to solve the murders.

Evidence was lacking

In January of 2003, Manuel Esparza Navarrete, an official in the Chihuahua deputy attorney general's office, insisted the state "had a lot of evidence against Sharif," but that revealing it would jeopardize the investigation. The evidence did not materialize.

Higher-ups often called on Esparza, who speaks English fluently, to help with the perpetual public relations crisis. He translated for Robert Ressler when the famous former FBI profiler lectured at a psychology conference in Juarez. Esparza also dealt with most of the English-language media that sought interviews about the murders.

Two Juarez homicide cops grudgingly admitted that they were not sure what Esparza does, although he had been at the state deputy attorney general's office in Juarez for more than six years. His co-workers said Esparza liked to play with an online Ouija board, which also was a popular pastime of other state investigators. Together, they asked the electronic Ouija board to tell them who is killing women in Juarez. Esparza so impressed foreigners that at one point Canadian police wanted him to work for them.

Ressler, who interviewed Sharif at the Cereso prison, said the Egyptian fit the profile of someone who could be involved in the murders. I asked Ressler if Mexican officials had ever allowed him to review their evidence against Sharif. "We never got into evidence or anything like that," Ressler said. Mexican officials have accused Sharif on two separate occasions of masterminding the deaths of up to twenty-four young women. In 1996, he was accused of paying members of an alleged gang called the "Rebeldes" $1,200 a month to kill seventeen women in order to deflect suspicion from himself.

It is customary in Mexico for authorities to present suspects to the news media, and at the 1996 press conference, Sharif appeared bewildered as he sat down in a room filled with reporters, photographers, and TV cameras. A Juarez reporter who spoke English asked him if he knew why he was there: "Don't you know that you're accused of being a mass murderer?"

Juarez lawyer Gustavo de la Rosa Hickerson, director of the Cereso prison in 1995 and 1996, said he had Sharif and his alleged accomplices monitored closely at all times.

"I never saw any evidence that they had plotted together to kill anyone," he said.

The Rebeldes: 1996

Police initially netted more than 300 people in 1996 raids on downtown bars as part of an undercover investigation into the women's murders. During one of the raids, however, they managed to overlook one of their main suspects, a man nicknamed "El Diablo." They had to go back to arrest him.

Most of the alleged "Rebeldes" gang members were released, but several men and a woman were indicted on charges of kidnapping and killing women for Sharif. The "Rebeldes" suspects were Sergio Armendáriz Diaz, José Juárez Reyes Rosales, Luis Andrade, Juan Contreras Jurado, Héctor Olivares Olivares, Carlos Barrientos Vidales, Romel Ceniceros García, Fernando Gremes Aguirre, Carlos Hernandez Molina Mariscal, and Erika Fierro.

Shortly after his arrest, Reyes Rosales was released. But Chihuahua State authorities later claimed to have new evidence, and had him arrested in Dallas, Texas, where he was living at the time. Eventually, Hernandez, Olivares, Fierro (accused of luring women for the gang), Gremes and Ceniceros were freed. The five men who remained in custody denied the allegations and claimed police commanders "Navarrete, Tovar and Vidal" had tortured them.

Fierro said one of the policemen jammed her head into a toilet bowl filled with urine to convince her to sign statements prepared before she was even interviewed by police. State police denied that any torture took place and insisted the arrests stemmed from a serious investigation.

Francisco Barrio, the governor in 1996, called a news conference to announce the spectacular results of the "most expensive and professional investigation" in the state's history.

Flaws in case surface

The State of Chihuahua's 1996 case against Sharif began to unravel early on. At one stage, his lawyers were able to convince a judge that police Commander Antonio Navarrete had pointed a gun at a witness during videotaped testimony against Sharif. The judge tossed out the testimony after defense lawyers showed him where the videotape had been edited.

Luis Hernandez, a Chihuahua State human rights official, came to Juarez after relatives of alleged witnesses complained that police, including the late Commander Francisco Minjares, had coerced them into signing statements that incriminated Sharif. State police, without offering any proof, accused the state human rights official of accepting a bribe to help Sharif. Hernandez quit under duress.

The bodies of some of Sharif's alleged victims bore bite marks, and state officials ordered tests to determine whether his teeth matched the bites. Dr. Irma Rodriguez Galarza, the forensic specialist, said she was taken off the Sharif investigation "because I determined that Sharif's bite did not match the bite marks on some of the victims."

Bites marks also figured in a later case. On January 19, 2002, passersby found the body of Lourdes Lucero Campos, 26, in a ditch near El Millon (in Valle de Juarez), a drug-trafficking stronghold at the northeastern edge of the city. Her body showed bite marks. Police focused their investigation on her husband and an alleged boyfriend.

Before she was killed, Campos worked as a nutritionist at a maquiladora. After police closed the case, the victim's family took her body to Chihuahua City for burial. The family said authorities could not match the bite marks to either the husband or the alleged boyfriend. The family also said authorities instructed them not to discuss the bite marks with anyone.

Other irregularities marred the case against Sharif. He was charged at one time with the death of Elizabeth Ontiveros. The "victim" reported in person to the Chihuahua State police office to prove that she was very much alive. The body that been had identified as hers was then exhumed. It turned out to be the remains of seventeen-year-old Silvia Rivera Salas, a 1996 victim unrelated to Sharif's case.

As other "evidence," police Commander Minjares offered a statement alleging that Sharif had been seen with teenage victim Adriana Torres in the evening of May 7, 1995, the day before she disappeared. Her relatives said that was impossible because she was with them the entire evening. Torres was last seen alive Monday, May 8 in front of a Tres Hermanos shoe store near the Juarez downtown cathedral.

The Toltecas, 1999

Three years later, Chihuahua State authorities announced the arrests of five men, including four bus drivers, in connection with the murders of several young women who were killed at different times. They claimed that Sharif also paid these men to murder women for him.

The 1999 suspects were Jesús "Tolteca" Guardado Márquez (also nicknamed "Dracula"), José Ceballos Chávez, Agustín Toribio Castillo and Bernardo Hernandez Fernández. The fifth suspect was Victor Moreno Rivera, a former El Paso resident with a petty-crime record for burglary and drug possession. Moreno was living in Juarez at the time.

During a 1999 press conference at the Cereso prison, these men pulled off their shirts to show reporters bruises and burn marks. They claimed police tortured them until they confessed to the crimes. They had requested permission to meet with reporters and publicly recant their signed confessions. They said they did not know Sharif and had never killed anyone.

Guardado's background was similar to Sharif's, in that he had served time in prison for a sexual crime and had mistreated his wife, officials said. In fact, it was Guardado's wife who turned him in to police in Durango State after he allegedly beat her. He admitted to sexually attacking "Nancy," a fourteen-year-old girl he had left for dead in 1999. The girl identified him as the bus driver who attacked her.

Over the objections of state officials, Abelardo Gonzalez, the prison director, authorized the 1999 press conference requested by the five suspects. The prison director also said he was asked by a senior state official about the prison's visitor logs.

Gonzalez told him nothing in the logs connected Sharif to any of the five suspects. The official, Gonzales said, suggested that he "modify" the logs. He refused. Almost immediately, state officials launched a campaign to oust the prison director. Gonzalez had no choice but to resign under fire.

During a radio interview, Special Prosecutor Suly Ponce said Sharif was a psychopath who should be locked up for life. She also said his Egyptian background contributed to his aggression against women. However, a psychological exam ordered by officials showed that Sharif was in good mental health.

In 1999, a judge cleared Sharif of eighteen women's murders due to a lack of evidence. Still, he was not released. State authorities then charged him with the 1995 death of Elizabeth Castro, one of the earlier femicide victims who had a triangle carved on her back. Sharif was sentenced to thirty years in prison for Castro's death.

He appealed, and the sentence was revoked. Then, the state appealed the revocation, and Sharif was resentenced to twenty years in prison. To keep him jailed, he was charged later in the 1995 death of Silvia Rivera Morales.

Sharif's patents

Suly Ponce alleged that Sharif got the money to pay bus drivers to kill women through patents he had developed for companies in the United States. She claimed he kept the money in secret U.S. bank accounts, which made it difficult for Mexican authorities to investigate.

The FBI, which had helped with early inquiries at the request of Mexican officials, found no evidence of such bank accounts. Sharif had developed seventeen patents, but his former U.S. employers said the patents belonged to the companies and Sharif received no royalties or income from them.

David Harry, an executive with Benchmark Research and Technology, said, "None of the inventors are paid for (the patents). They, including Sharif, developed these patents for us as a part of their employment." Harry also said he lamented what had happened to Sharif in Mexico. "Sharif was a brilliant chemist. I considered him a friend."

In 1999, the *Fort Worth Star Telegram* published a lengthy series about Sharif, which suggested he might have had other victims in the United States.

The series contained an intriguing allegation that Sharif was a suspect in the 1977 death of New Jersey flight attendant Sandra Miller. Two connections caught the eye of the New Jersey detective investigating the murder. Sharif was working in the region at the time, and both he and Sandra Miller had been seen at the same club and hotel, although not together.

Chris Andreychak, the New Jersey detective quoted in the series, told me on two separate occasions that he did not consider Sharif a lead suspect in Sandra Miller's unsolved murder. "Unfortunately, the suspect we were leaning toward is deceased. For this region, it was an isolated case," Andreychak said.

"The only thing we knew about Sharif that made him a possible suspect was that he was in the area around the same time as Sandra Miller. I tried calling him once, but I was told that he wouldn't talk to me without his lawyer present. I don't consider him a strong suspect."

19.

INVESTIGATIONS ON TRIAL

A Chihuahua State official shared a disturbing account of how things worked at the state deputy attorney general's office in Juarez. He said Sharif's defense team had hired a specialist to evaluate whether Elizabeth Castro's body had been properly identified. Sharif's representatives contended that the body could not be hers because the height, facial features and other physical traits did not match. The specialist's findings supported those claims, at least initially.

According to the official, Chihuahua authorities later hired the same specialist as a fulltime state employee — on condition that he reverse his findings in Castro's case. His new report concluded that officials had correctly identified the body. For reasons that remain unclear, Castro's family has refused to exhume the body to settle the dispute over her identity.

The state transferred Sharif, the 1996 Rebeldes suspects and the other five murder suspects, to the Cereso prison in Chihuahua City. The move to the state capital was highly irregular, and the location 250 miles south of Juarez made it difficult for their lawyers or relatives to visit them.

Whenever Irene Blanco tried to visit Sharif, prison officials threw obstacles in her path. During his imprisonment, Sharif converted to Roman Catholicism. He kept an image of the Virgin of Guadalupe in his cell, and his only regular visitors were his lawyers, a priest and his religious godmother, Celia Simonetti, an elderly woman in El Paso, who said she was forced to curtail her visits because of poor health.

Following the September 11 terrorists attack on the United States, Sharif called me to ask for the FBI's telephone number. "I want to work for the FBI or the CIA. I want to volunteer. I know the Farsi language, and I can help them interpret over in Afghanistan, or wherever else they want to send me. I can help them find the terrorists."

Sharif was desperate to get out of the Mexican prison and said he would have accepted any dangerous assignment. The Egyptian Embassy in Mexico helped Sharif with his legal defense, but quit after he lost another round against Chihuahua State. After the last time a judge ruled against him, Sharif broke down in sobs.

Irene Blanco returns

Perhaps it was poetic justice or just fate. In 2003, as a result of Mexico's proportional representation system, Irene Blanco became a federal congresswoman for the National Action Party. She represented a district in the State of Quintana Roo. She was also appointed to a federal legislative commission, led by Marcela Lagarde, which was charged with overseeing the progress of the investigations into the Juarez women's murders. Blanco eventually left the commission because she felt the required teamwork was lacking.

She paid Sharif a visit in 2004, bringing a human rights official to meet with him. This time, the Chihuahua City prison staff that used to give her such a hard time, flung open the doors to welcome her. This time, Blanco had no trouble arranging to talk to Sharif. This was the woman who had endured death threats and a shooting attack against her son in 1999, and who was forced to abandon Juarez.

Sharif complained to her that he was being forced to take pills that seemed to make him sick. Blanco was able to confirm that prison officials were giving Sharif a medication for epilepsy, a condition that Sharif did not have.

During a later interview at the Mexico City airport, the modest and dignified Blanco said she never imagined herself becoming a congresswoman. She also never pictured herself investigating official corruption for the federal government or serving on the special legislative commission. The cloud of grief that hung over her was gone. She was determined to make her country a better place.

"Impunity is the main reason the cases in Juarez have not been solved," she said. "That is why the crimes are not solved and why they continue." After our interview, she grabbed her briefcase and headed off to catch another plane. The old Irene Blanco was back, and her fighting spirit was intact.

Sharif dies in custody

The "Egyptian" died on June 1, 2006, in Chihuahua City after he was transported from the prison to a medical facility for treatment. The authorities issued a five-paragraph statement that was part biographical. Ricardo Marquez Horta, the corrections director, said Sharif was taken to a clinic's emergency room because he had internal bleeding. The officials said he died a short time later from a heart attack.

The statement said Sharif was born on September 19, 1946, in Egypt, was divorced and had a doctoral degree in chemistry. His sentence for Elizabeth Castro's murder was under appeal. Officials said Sharif had heart problems and was in therapy because he was constantly depressed. His most recent lawyer told the press that Sharif taught other inmates how to speak English, "and probably died from sadness."

Jorge Orona, director of the Convergence Party in Chihuahua State, said the timing of Sharif's death was suspicious. A judge was going to rule on Sharif's federal *amparo* within a week or two of the day he died. His lawyer Jose Antonio Nieto said his release was imminent. Irene Blanco said the news of Sharif's death "chilled my soul." The Egyptian embassy in Mexico decided to have him buried quietly in Juarez. Nieto said the embassy owed him back pay for his defense of Sharif.

Cotton field suspects: 2001

Two bus drivers, Gustavo "Foca" Gonzalez Meza and Javier "Cerillo" Garcia Uribe, were charged in the next chapter of the city's multiple murders. They were accused of abducting, raping, and killing eight young women whose bodies were found in November of 2001. The bodies were discovered on a Tuesday and Wednesday, and police had detained the two men by Friday. According to a law enforcement source, the word came down from the governor's office in Chihuahua City to "get this solved by Monday or else."

On Sunday, a day before the arbitrary deadline, state Attorney General Arturo Gonzalez Rascon held a press conference in Juarez to announce the arrests. He also said it was possible that Sharif could be linked to the eight murders. Some reporters who were present audibly groaned in disbelief at what they heard. The official said the two bus drivers might have killed up to eleven women and read off the victims' names.

Later, the suspects' defense lawyers said police wearing Halloween masks grabbed the two men at their homes and took them to a safe house, where they tortured them until they confessed to the murders. To help with this mission, officials dispatched several law enforcement officers from the state capital to Juarez. The bus drivers were blindfolded and could not see where they were or who was applying the electric prods.

They said at one point a woman who identified herself as a state human rights representative asked them how they were being treated. They complained to her. Then the torture resumed. One of the suspects said he recognized her voice from television interviews as the voice of Suly Ponce. The former special prosecutor, who was now serving in a different state post, denied having anything to do with the detentions. Zulema Bolivar, the new Chihuahua State special prosecutor, washed her hands of the whole thing. She said officials from Chihuahua City took over the case completely.

The two Juarez bus drivers were taken to the prison in Chihuahua City, where officials had detained the other mass murder suspects. An official inside the police state offices leaked pictures of the two men taken soon after the torture sessions.

They had bruises and burn marks on various parts of their body, including their genitals. Their lawyers said they were nearly suffocated. The other bus driver suspects from 1999 also claimed that police had placed plastic bags over their heads to create a frightening sensation of suffocation.

Faced with the photographic evidence, authorities in 2001 contended that the two bus drivers had tortured themselves to gain public sympathy. Before they were taken to Chihuahua City, the two suspects made a stop at the Cereso prison in Juarez, where they were subjected to a medical examination to certify their physical condition at the time of their incarceration.

Sex, lies and videotapes

The Juarez Cereso prison director, Carlos Gutierrez Casas, released results of the medical exams to the suspects' defense lawyers. The documents indicated both men arrived at the prison with bodily injuries.

The new prison director, who had married an inmate, was forced to resign after providing those documents to the lawyers. Like Abelardo Gonzalez, the previous Cereso director, Gutierrez received threats and was driven to quit his post.

State authorities alleged that the two bus drivers had ingested cocaine and smoked marijuana before they went out to hunt for women to abduct rape and kill. Because they were commercial drivers, they were required to submit to periodic drug tests. The results of those tests, on file at state transportation offices in Juarez, were negative for drug use.

The state's own records contradicted the ever-fragile case that authorities had assembled. The van that police said the two bus drivers used to abduct the women had not worked in a long time. Officials had no physical evidence, no hairs, fibers, blood, or semen, linking the bus drivers to the victims.

With such damning disclosures, state authorities faced a credibility crisis. They responded with a videotape, which, they said, proved conclusively that the two men were not tortured.

State officials had TV stations throughout Mexico broadcast the tape and presented international human rights organizations with a copy.

But the accused men's wives and lawyers quickly pointed out that the torsos shown in the state's videotape with no burns or bruises were not the torsos of the two bus drivers. It was obvious that models were used for part of the tape.

Once people got wind of these Hollywood tricks, state authorities pulled the video out of circulation. The videotape became so rare that a Juarez television cameraman offered a copy to a California journalist for $500. In February, three months after the arrests, state police killed Mario Escobedo Anaya, the lawyer of one of the bus drivers. The police involved in the incident alleged self-defense. A year later, bus driver Gustavo "Foca" Gonzalez Meza, who was Escobedo Anaya's client, died at the Chihuahua City prison under suspicious circumstances following a simple hernia operation.

Defense lawyer Sergio Dante Almaraz Mora said their deaths were "crimes of state." Almaraz did not realize it then, but death was stalking him, too.

Federales: Organ-trafficking

Things seemed to be looking up when the Mexican Federal Attorney General's Office finally agreed to investigate the serial murders. Then the federal agents assigned to the investigation stunned the border community when they announced in 2003 that they were looking into the possibility that up to fourteen young women were killed to harvest their organs.

The cases they cited included the eight victims discovered in 2001 in the cotton field and six others found in the Cristo Negro vicinity in late 2002 and early 2003. Rolando Alvarado, a federal official who took part in the 1999 binational "Plaza Sweep" investigation, was in charge.

The surprising turn was taken when a T-shirt vendor named Juan Vazquez Villegas accused two Juarez men, Javier Garcia, and Hernando Valles, of abducting women for their organs. He offered the allegation when police asked him why he had a cell phone that had belonged to Mayra Najera Larragoiti, a young woman who was reported missing and was presumed dead.

U.S. law enforcement officials scoffed privately at the organ-trafficking probe but did their best to help the *federales* find a suspect on the U.S. side of the border, a man identified only as "William."

Vazquez alleged that Garcia and Valles killed their victims inside a two-story house and removed their organs in the bathroom. Later, he recanted the story, saying he made it up out of fear that he might be accused of killing Mayra Najera. Chihuahua officials were not sure then that Najera was dead since an earlier DNA test failed to confirm her identity.

Five months later, federal Deputy Attorney General Jose Santiago Vasconcelos conceded there was no evidence to support the organ-trafficking charges and set the suspects free. To his credit, he made it clear he would not use fabricated suspects to solve the murders.

In El Paso, a private investigator said he had stumbled on a group that was involved in the traffic of body parts, which does not require elaborate medical support. Body parts are sold to medical schools or research laboratories throughout the world. When pressed for details, the investigator refused to elaborate.

Enrique Juarez, another independent researcher in Mexico, said he developed an elaborate analysis that strongly suggests that women were being killed to harvest stem cells from their bodies. He based his findings on the ages of the victims and the approximate times selected for their abductions. Although no evidence exists to support these theories, in Juarez speculations persist that some of the crimes involve the trafficking of body parts or organs.

Death has a saint

Over the years, the murders have generated an assortment of theories about who was killing the women and why, including pornographic movies, snuff films and satanic rituals. FBI officials did not rule out the possibility that women were being killed to produce snuff films; however, in twenty years of investigating, the agency's national headquarters in Washington, D.C., said it had yet to see an authentic snuff video. But, in these modern times, perhaps things have changed. For example, in 2006, U.S. police accused a couple in the sex-murder of a woman in a Midwestern state. The authorities said the couple allegedly filmed the attack, including the victim's death. It is not beyond the realm of the possible that killers in Juarez filmed a rape or a slaying and kept the tape private to relive the event.

Of course, the risk of filming such acts is that the tape could serve as evidence against the killers. Andrew Luster, the Max Factor heir accused of drugging and raping women in California, taped sex acts with his victims. Luster fled to Mexico in 2003 but was caught and extradited to the United States, where he is now serving a prison sentence.

Several people in Juarez said they spent years compiling information on an alleged link to satanic rituals on both sides of the border. Perhaps two or three of the homicides were occult-related, but if so, they appeared to be isolated cases. Nevertheless, the Mexican team drew a sketch map of the sites where past serial murder victims had been found in Juarez and El Paso. They said that devil worshipers were using each new site to complete a pentagram shape over the El Paso-Juarez border region.

The "Santa Muerte" (Holy Death) movement represents one of the fastest growing cults in Mexico. Chapels and images used to venerate the patron saint of death have turned up in Juarez as well in recent years. Some gang members wear the image of this "saint" as a tattoo.

Another independent investigator, a teacher in El Paso, said he suspected that some of the Juarez women's murders were related to people associated with the El Paso serial murders of 1987. Wood was convicted in the murders of six young El Paso women whose bodies were found in shallow desert graves. Wood, who was 29 at the time of his arrest, is on death row in Texas for the six deaths. He denied killing anyone. El Paso police consider him a suspect in the disappearances of three young women, who went missing in 1987; Wood denied any link to them.

Mexican officials, including federal Commissioner Guadalupe Morfin Otero, raised questions about the possibility that registered sex offenders in El Paso County were responsible for killing women in Juarez. El Paso County Sheriff Leo Samaniego, among others, had complained that the State of Texas was dumping sex offenders in El Paso from other parts of the state. In 2001, a five-year-old Alexandra Flores was abducted from a Walmart store in El Paso and killed. The El Paso man convicted in her death, David Renteria, was a registered sex offender.

The concerns about sex offenders are valid because Mexican immigration authorities rarely ask for identification at the Juarez side of the international bridges. Sometimes, U.S. officials catch sex offenders at the border when they return to the United States, after checking their identification against police data bases. Sex offenders often are on parole or probation, and usually are sent back to prison if they are caught making trips to Mexico. However, Mexico did not consider it a sufficiently serious issue to institute checks on its side of the border.

Security forces suspected

In January of 2006, a Border Patrol agent from the El Paso region was charged with fondling an undocumented mother and daughter from Honduras. Alicia Gaspar de Alba, an American academic, suspects that someone connected to the Border Patrol is involved in the Juarez murders and gives credence to the idea that sex offenders living in El Paso have crossed the border to kill women. U.S. officials have deported Mexican citizens convicted of molesting children in the United States. Although the Mexican officials' concerns were duly noted, the main difference between El Paso and Juarez is that El Paso has a tracking system for sex offenders. Mexico does not keep track of sexual predators.

Another important difference is that serious crimes, including those committed by police or officials, are far more likely to be prosecuted in the United States than in Mexico. Other officials in Mexico said they noted with concern that Fort Bliss, a major Army installation in El Paso, houses soldiers who could cross the border and commit crimes in Mexico. They said they worried about the mental health of Iraq war veterans at the border.

But Juarez also has a military installation, and Mexico's army is highly secretive. Mexican soldiers who took part in kidnappings and torture during the "dirty war" (1968-1982) are as likely to need treatment as are any U.S. service members who experienced extraordinary trauma in combat. According to *Proceso*, a group of soldiers assigned to guard election ballots in a small town in Northern Mexico were accused of openly raping women and attacking several men following a bar fight in July 2006. Nothing happened to the service members who allegedly terrorized the community.

A retired Mexican general confided that he entered therapy because of the atrocities he was ordered to commit as a young officer. The same concerns could be said of soldiers and police who carried out torture, abductions, and murders for the drug cartels.

20.

Escaped killer

The border city's red light district is adjacent to Juarez Avenue and other downtown streets traversed by numerous victims. The Plaza Hotel, where Hester Van Nierop, a student and tourist from the Netherlands, was found dead in 1998, is in the district. The young woman's parents traveled to Juarez for the first time in the summer of 2004.

Roland and Arsene Van Nierop, her father and mother, said they wanted to see the place where Hester had spent the last hours of her life. They were upset at the lack of progress in their daughter's case. During this trip, the couple met with Mexican officials who finally contacted Interpol for help in locating a suspect mentioned in Hester's file.

The suspect was a man who had signed the hotel register as "Roberto Flores." While the Van Nierops were in town, Chihuahua State authorities distributed an artist's sketch of the suspect to the press. This occurred after the officials met with the parents, who also met with the FBI in El Paso.

The name "Flores" turned up in the register of the hotel on Segundo de Ugarte, where the young woman was strangled in 1998. A housekeeper found her nude body under a hotel bed. Hotel employees said the man who checked in with Hester spoke Spanish like a *norteamericano* (an American).

Whoever he is, he was also seen with Van Nierop at Norma's Club nearby before they checked into the hotel. Van Nierop's family learned that a witness had said that Hester appeared to accompany the man reluctantly. Unaware of the city's dangers, the Dutch visitor may have thought Juarez was like Amsterdam, where women can walk alone at night, even in its red light district, without being harassed, much less stalked for murder.

Suspect's sketch

According to Mexican documents on the case, Chihuahua State authorities had not done any work on the murder investigation in six years — until the parents came to the border. The suspect reportedly lived in the United States and had told another woman that U.S. authorities were looking for him in connection with the accidental death of a relative. According to Mexican police, the man preferred to stay in hotel rooms that ended with "21." The room where Van Nierop's body was found was No. 121.

After Van Nierop's murder, authorities reported the death of Perla Patricia Hernandez at the Motel Fronterizo, in Room 25.

Her body was found in the same position as Van Nierop's body. Fabiola Zamudio Calderon, a 1995 victim, was found dead at the Ranchito Motel in Room 21. Coincidentally, "21" is the symbol that "Aztecas" gang members use to identify themselves, according to U.S. drug investigators. The gang's affiliate, on the U.S. side of the border, called itself "Barrio Aztecas."

Many people wondered why Mexican authorities waited six years to release the suspect's sketch in Van Nierop's case. The description witnesses gave of the man did not seem to match the sketch police produced for the public. The Van Nierops also said that their daughter's backpack was missing, and that police told them that they never recovered it. However, Lorena Mendez-Quiroga, a California television reporter, recalled that several years earlier Chihuahua State officials allowed her to enter their evidence room to film Van Nierop's belongings, including the backpack.

Half a dozen women were found dead in Juarez hotels over the course of twelve years, but the authorities always said there is no connection. Former state Commander Antonio Navarrete, who helped develop the case against the "Rebeldes" gang in 1996

for the Lomas de Poleo murders, also supervised the initial investigation into Van Nierop's death.

Her parents made a return trip to Mexico in December of 2005, for a forum in Mexico City on the women's murders that Radio Netherlands sponsored. In light of the lack of investigation in Mexico, the Van Nierops said they were hoping the European Parliament would act on their petition to intervene.

Roland Van Nierop said, "We believe a serial killer murdered our daughter," a theory that Mexican authorities denied.

Juarez serial killer escaped

Felipe Pando, a former homicide investigations chief for Chihuahua State police, said he did not understand why Mexican authorities were not actively searching for a man named Pedro Padilla Flores. Pando said, "Padilla was a serial killer who killed and raped women in the same manner as some of the victims we've seen in recent years. He is one of the top people they should be looking for."

Pando said Padilla abused drugs and usually dumped his victims in the Rio Grande. "The U.S. authorities had helped us catch him," he said. According to stories in the *El Paso Times* archives, Padilla was arrested in 1986 in Juarez and indicted on charges of raping and murdering several women. Although he confessed to killing more women, he was convicted of the murders of only two women and a thirteen-year-old girl.

Before his arrest, Padilla had lived in an unkempt apartment in the Mariscal red light district of downtown Juarez. Pando said Padilla has been a fugitive since he escaped from a rehabilitation center in 1991. The Chihuahua State officials in charge of the women's murder investigations said they had never heard of Padilla, even though his case was widely reported by news media on both sides of the border. What is worse, they could not find his case file. Padilla Flores may be another untouchable, which could explain his escape and the missing file for his case.

An elusive suspect

"Alejandro Maynez" is a name that keeps coming up in relation to the women's homicides. He is an elusive man who fled the area and is said to have gone underground. His adoptive relatives named Maynez said his real name is Armando Martinez, and that "Maynez" is but one of several aliases he uses. The Maynez family is not related to the criminologist Oscar Maynez quoted elsewhere in this book.

Chihuahua State officials issued an arrest warrant for "Alejandro Maynez" in connection with the 1992 death of a young woman from Chihuahua City. Former state police Commander Refugio "Cuco" Rubalcava arrested him, but Pando, a state police official at the time, reportedly enabled his release.

Juarez lawyer Francisco Peña said "Alejandro Maynez" also came up in the case of Ana Benavides, who served a sentence at the Chihuahua City prison for killing and dismembering a Juarez couple and their child in 1998.

Peña said he represented Benavides, a petite woman who knew "Maynez" and several of his friends. "My client told the authorities that "Alejandro Maynez" was the intellectual author of these deaths. She became the scapegoat, while he and the others continue to go free."

Liliana Herrera, who served as one of the state special prosecutors for a short time, said her office had received a tip about "Alejandro Maynez," but she could find no information about him in the police files.

"Despite his earlier arrest, I couldn't find a single mention of him in our files. I couldn't even find a copy of the *amparo* (similar to a habeas corpus) that he allegedly had obtained."

Before his retirement in 2001, El Paso Police Sergeant Pete Ocegueda said he recalled that Juarez police had asked the El Paso Police Department for help in finding "Alejandro Maynez" in connection with the murder of a Norma's Club dancer named Lorenza Gonzales Alamillo, whose body was found off the Panamerican Highway in south Juarez. She had been strangled and mutilated.

"They thought (Maynez) might be a U.S. citizen because he came back and forth across the international bridges all the time, but we didn't have anything for him under that name," said Ocegueda, who had not been told the suspect's real name.

Missing or on the move

Mexican authorities said they believe the man known as "Alejandro Maynez" fled Mexico. His adoptive relatives said he married a U.S. citizen and lived near El Paso or in New Mexico under a different alias. One of his Juarez relatives, who asked not to be named, said, "I don't know why he started calling himself "Alejandro." He has always been Armando - that's his legal name."

Other journalists and I attempted to find this man so we could interview him. We went to virtually all the Juarez cantinas owned then by the adoptive family, including the Club Safari, El Papillon, Club 16, La Rueda and Club Monterrey. The family-owned bars feature attractive barmaids who wear low-cut tops.

At one of the clubs, an adoptive relative said, "There are some things we are not meant to talk about."

Guillermo Maynez Sr., the man's adoptive father, was at the Papillon when he said, "I don't ever want to see him or talk to him or know anything about him." The elder Maynez believed the man who grew up in his home was deeply troubled, and said he even took him to see a highly recommended therapist. However, the therapist grew fearful of the patient, and the therapy sessions ended.

In 1995, a gang from Sinaloa State abducted millionaire Valentin Fuentes and Guillermo Maynez Jr., the elusive man's adoptive brother. The two kidnapped men were freed after their families paid hefty ransoms. In their case, the Fuentes family reportedly paid the captors several million dollars. The late Commander Francisco Minjares, who was in charge of the state's anti-kidnapping unit, handled the two cases.

Minjares also supervised the investigation against Sharif. Minjares, an alleged business associate of "Alejandro Maynez," was accused of solving kidnappings that he himself orchestrated. A source in the federal attorney general's office, said people in El Paso and corrupt Mexican federal police were involved in the widely publicized kidnappings.

A troubling account

In 1997, Ramiro Romero, a federal police agent, and Victor Valenzuela, a state auxiliary policeman, told Chihuahua State authorities that the suspect "Alejandro Maynez" may have killed several women in Juarez. Valenzuela, who was an inmate at the Cereso jail at the time, claimed that Chihuahua State police framed him on a phony drug charge after he gave the information to Special Prosecutor Suly Ponce. Carlos Camacho and Alma Vucovich, members of the Mexican federal Congress, were present during the interview with Valenzuela at Cereso, along with *Reforma* journalist Sergio Gonzalez Rodriguez.

Valenzuela said, "We were at the Club Safari when "Alejandro" told us that he (and a cousin) raped and killed women. He once invited us to come along with him to rape women, but we turned him down. He said nothing would happen to him because his father was a very important man." Valenzuela said "Maynez" told him and Romero that he would walk across the border from El Paso and pick up one of the family vehicles in Juarez to scout for victims.

"(Maynez) said that sometimes he and a cousin would kill together, and at other times, they would have a contest to see who could kill more women," Valenzuela said.

A different source alleged that the "Maynez" cousin was actually one of the man's biological relatives who helped him dispose of bodies.

Valenzuela said he and Romero at first tried giving the information to Francisco Molina Ruiz, the former Chihuahua State attorney general. They were directed instead to Commander Francisco Minjares.

"When we saw that nothing happened, we went to see Sharif in case it might help him with his (defense) case," Valenzuela said.

Sharif used the information to file a complaint from prison against "Alejandro Maynez," but state authorities ignored it. It was then that the mysterious man filed for an *amparo* against arrest. Federal Agent Ramiro Romero was killed in the drug wars in 1998, and Victor Valenzuela left Chihuahua. Valenzuela said he returned to Juarez on the chance that things had changed under the new administration of Governor Patricio Martinez. After our interview at the prison that day,

Congressman Carlos Camacho said, "I was so disgusted by what I heard that I wanted to vomit."

El Paso's FBI office previously had received information that the man known as "Alejandro Maynez" had been killed in Mexico. Other sources said he was incarcerated in California. Numerous Juarez residents saw him in 2001 at the funeral of former Chihuahua Governor Teofilo Borunda, owner of the parcel where Lilia Alejandra Garcia Andrade's body was found earlier that year.

In an interview, "Maynez's" adoptive brother, Guillermo Maynez Jr., was asked if he thought the man he grew up with was capable of killing women. He paused momentarily before answering, "I don't know. It's for the authorities to investigate."

Valenzuela, who survived three Juarez prison riots, was released from the Cereso prison toward the end of 2003. He left a message at the *El Paso Times* newsroom to the effect that he was leaving the state of Chihuahua for good.

The elusive suspect's name came up again in 2004, this time in connection with a circle of people linked to the stabbing death of Ramon Navarrete Islas, a Catholic priest in Juarez. Another priest, who tried to investigate the clergyman's murder, told the news media he received death threats and warnings to leave the case alone. Police said the priest's vehicle was stolen and concluded that robbery was the motive.

A border resident who had moved to Colorado said the suspect, or at least someone believed to be him, turned up in that state. Others claim they saw him in Santa Fe, New Mexico.

The Mexican federal government's 2006 report on the Juarez women's murders excludes any reference to "Maynez," a name police files previously included. The federal report mentions others who were jailed in the death of the Norma's bar victim, but it leaves out the previous reference to the suspect that Chihuahua State Commander Refugio Rubalcava had arrested.

The "Railway Killer"

Angel Maturino Resendiz (alias Rafael Resendiz Ramirez) should not be overlooked as a suspect in the Juarez murders, said FBI profiler Robert Ressler and criminologist Candice Skrapec. Despite the fact that Maturino was known to cross the border often at Juarez-El Paso and Anapra-Sunland Park, N.M., the Chihuahua state authorities eliminated him as a suspect.

They offered flimsy explanations for not investigating him. Chihuahua officials said they had heard that the "Railway Killer" murdered only Anglos. Juan Manuel Carmona, spokesman for the Chihuahua Deputy Attorney General's Office in Juarez, said Maturino could not be a serial killer "because he did not target victims with similar profiles, women in this case, nor did he kill his victims in the same manner each time."

Ressler, a world expert on serial murderers, said serial killers do not always use the same methods to kill their victims. And, he said, they will keep on killing until someone stops them. He also said serial killers have killed both men and women, as was the case with Maturino. When Maturino was arrested, Ressler recommended that he be investigated in connection with the Juarez murders. Before Maturino surrendered at the El Paso border, the FBI was searching for him in the deaths of twelve people in the United States whose bodies were found near railroad tracks.

Maturino traveled across great distances – to Mexico, the United States and Canada - by hopping trains. He also crossed the U.S.-Mexico border frequently, albeit illegally. Skrapec had seen the autopsy reports for some of Maturino's U.S. victims. She is also familiar with at least 200 of the Juarez women's murder files.

"Based on what I saw, there are similarities, and that's why (Maturino) should be investigated. Some of the bodies found in Juarez were found near or along railroad tracks," she said.

For example, the strangled body of Mireya Hernandez Mendez, 20, was found in 1993 next to railroad tracks. At the time of his surrender, Maturino had a strong bond to Juarez. His mother lived there. He alternated between living in Villa Ahumada, a village south of Juarez, and in

Anapra, an extension of Juarez where some of the victims came from. Maturino denied killing anyone in Mexico or anywhere else before the U.S. murders.

Ressler said it is unlikely that Maturino began his killing spree that late in life. "Most serial killers do not start killing in their middle-age years. They usually begin in their adolescent years by fantasizing about killing, and they kill their first victim around their early adult years."

Maturino, who was 39 when he was taken into custody, had raped and killed a woman in Texas. He also had other victims that he never sexually assaulted. He was known to stab, shoot and even bludgeon victims with an ax. Chihuahua authorities probably had no interest in investigating Maturino, because it could affect the cases they had against the suspects they said were responsible for the Juarez femicides. Chihuahua officials also may have been reluctant to investigate Maturino due to his suspected his connections to drug-traffickers.

Luis Gutierrez, an inmate at the U.S. immigration detention center in El Paso, was able to shed light on these strong possibilities.

He said he knew Maturino and contacted the FBI in El Paso to provide U.S. agents with details about the suspect's life and habits. The FBI wanted to know only where to find Maturino and disregarded Gutierrez when he could not provide that detail. Gutierrez said Maturino was aggressive, smart, and consumed drugs. Police said he used as many as thirty aliases and was deported more than a dozen times. The U.S. Border Patrol, which later blamed computer glitches, released Maturino while he was the target of a national FBI manhunt. After his release, Maturino returned to the United States and killed more people.

Gutierrez said the "Railway Killer" belonged to the "Renteria gang" in the Mexican state of Durango that used trains and other vehicles to transport stolen construction materials, weapons, and drugs. "(Maturino) was related to some gang members that came from drug-trafficking families in Durango," Gutierrez said. "I met some of his cousins and they look like him. The territory they covered in Texas included Laredo and San Antonio."

The State of Texas executed Maturino on June 27, 2006, for the brutal rape-murder of Dr. Claudia Benton in the Houston area.

He was forty-six years old. He was charged with seven murders but was tried for only one of them. Several accounts published online allege that Maturino confessed to killing several people in Mexico. Before his death by lethal injection, he asked the families of his victims to forgive him. His body was taken to Durango for burial. One of his sisters was killed in a car accident in Juarez, and his mother moved away from the border city.

El Paso suspects

Former El Paso Assistant Police Chief J.R. Grijalva said that in 1998 El Paso police and Robert Ressler came up with the names of two men they considered potential suspects in the Juarez femicides. Both were Hispanic males with criminal records. Ressler said they were flagged because they fit a certain profile, based on past behavior, of someone who could commit such crimes.

Ressler had theorized that the likely killer or killers were male, Hispanic, and able to cross the border easily. The person or persons could blend in without arousing suspicion within the border's Hispanic culture. Grijalva said El Paso police monitored one of the two ex-convicts but found nothing incriminating. They lost track of the second man after he left the area.

It is not out of the question that someone from the U.S. side of the border was killing women in Juarez. Numerous citizens of Mexico live in El Paso and work in or own businesses in Juarez. Among them are Mexican police, as well as suspected drug dealers and their enforcers.

In modern times, El Paso has produced two serial killers: David Leonard Wood, a death-row inmate, and Richard Ramirez, the notorious "Night Stalker," who was in a California prison for the murders he committed there. The police did not link either man to murders in Mexico.

Guatemalan serial rape suspect

During Governor Patricio Martinez's administration, state authorities concealed from the public the existence of a serial rapist who was terrorizing women in Juarez and Chihuahua City. Officials admitted they were searching for such a suspect only after an official leaked the information to a newspaper.

The state police later arrested Ulises Ernesto Mijangos of Retalule, Guatemala, in August of 2005, in connection with several burglaries. After that, they charged him in the sexual assaults. He is suspected of committing as many as fifty rapes in the two cities over a span of two years.

Authorities described him as a man who shaved his body and occasionally wore women's clothing. During a search of his home, investigators found pieces of jewelry that he allegedly took from his victims. Officials have not explained how Mijangos was able to travel frequently and unhindered between Guatemala and the State of Chihuahua despite not having a steady job.

State Attorney General Patricia Gonzalez Rodriguez said DNA tests linked Mijangos, 34, to several cases in Juarez and Chihuahua City between 2003 and 2005. Officials said he belonged to a gang that operated in Mexico and the United States but acted alone in the sexual assaults attributed to him.

"Richy's" letter

A man known as "Richy" surfaced in El Paso in 2003.

Some thought he could be the person who, in the mid-1990s, wrote cryptic letters about killing and raping women in Juarez.

Someone had submitted to a Juarez newspaper a collection of letters that came to be known as "Richy's diary," giving birth to the legendary albeit mysterious character. Authorities searched quietly for the author of the letters, after a young woman identified only as "Sandra" allegedly committed suicide after receiving one of "Richy's" letters.

The man who later aroused interest in El Paso was an illegal immigrant who was arrested on drug charges. In checking his background, law enforcement officials learned he had sexually abused his young children. He had no formal education and had trouble writing a coherent sentence, making him a potential candidate for the author of the "Richy" letters, which were filled with grammatical errors.

One of "Richy's" letters, dated July 1997, is addressed to a girl named "Berenice." In the letter, "Richy" says he has an apartment in El Paso and asks Berenice to help him lure and drug two girls, ages thirteen to fourteen years old, whom he is planning to rape.

The letter also refers to a couple of acquaintances coming in from Sinaloa state who were said to like raping women. No one knows if "Richy" exists, or if the letters were a particularly cruel hoax.

Over the years, Mexican authorities have either lost or failed to collect evidence that could link individuals to certain crimes. So, having a potential suspect in custody in El Paso for different crimes did not mean much if he could not be tied to any of the attacks in Juarez.

Devastating U.N. document

The United Nations sent a group of international experts to the border in 2003 to conduct an analysis of the Mexican investigations. It was the first time such a group was invited to examine the police and judicial procedures used to accuse suspects in the Juarez femicides. At that time, Sharif, the "Rebeldes," the "Toltecas," and one of the bus drivers arrested in 2001 were in a state of judicial limbo. Except for Sharif, none had been convicted and sentenced.

Sharif had been convicted for only the death of Elizabeth Castro. He had been in jail since 1995, and the "Rebeldes" since 1996. The "Toltecas" had been in custody for four years. Because they had not been convicted, the inmates also could not appeal their cases. Under Mexican law, their detentions were irregular if not unconstitutional. In its 2003 report, Amnesty International criticized the State of Chihuahua for using confessions obtained through torture to solve the high-profile crimes.

The United Nations Office Against Drugs and Crime (UNODC) that sent the group issued a report of the experts' 2003 analysis of the state investigations. The special task force for the U.N. Juarez mission was composed of top-notch investigators:

Stanley Pimentel, a former FBI official assigned to Mexico; Carlos Castresana, a special anti-corruption prosecutor for Spain's National Court; Carlos Franco, a police official in Spain; Stefano Fumarulo, an organized crime consultant in Italy; Carlos Prieto, a consultant for the United Nations; and Edgardo Buscaglia, the U.N. mission chief.

The U.N. delegation met with Chihuahua State officials and with officials of the FBI's El Paso division. "I told our FBI liaison Sam Camargo to give them the unvarnished truth," said Hardrick Crawford Jr., the FBI special agent in charge.

The experts were given access to the Mexican files, and they were alarmed at what they found. The special task force wrote its conclusions and recommendations in an eighty-page report, which the Mexican government made public only after pressure by human rights organizations, families of victims, and participants of the 2003 "Maquiladora Murders" conference in UCLA.

Experts detect corruption

The UNODC report was devastating. It cast serious doubts on the state investigations that went all the way back to Sharif's detention. The task force also analyzed the case files for the "Rebeldes," the "Toltecas," and the 2001 "cotton field" murders. It was no longer journalists and activists who claimed that the investigations were flawed. This time, an objective group of international specialists with unquestioned credentials had arrived at the same conclusion.

Among other things, the special task force made note of the fact that torture was a crime under Chihuahua State law. Yet, none of the state judges or other officials ever investigated the torture allegations. They questioned the decision to transfer the cases from Juarez, where they belonged, to Chihuahua City.

They also criticized the lack of scientific evidence, such as DNA tests, to corroborate the alleged "confessions." The experts said judges did not act as impartial officers, and suspects should not have been accused in the deaths of several unidentified victims.

The report said few convictions and sentences existed despite the great number of previous investigations and judgments. The experts also said, "it is probable that the presence of organized crime (interferes with) adequate investigations and judicial processes in these cases." The analysis uncovered a pattern of corruption suggested by systematic errors and problems in the investigations.

Their analysis could not be more blunt. Several months after they issued their report, a couple of the experts, including Castresana, returned later to the border region. They were surprised to learn that Chihuahua State officials had not made any progress on their recommendations to rectify the problems.

In light of the report, I asked Vicky Caraveo, then the director of the Chihuahua State Women's Institute, what should be done now?

"Start over from scratch," she responded.

Judicial chaos

Facing mounting pressure from international human rights organizations, Chihuahua State officials decided to take definitive actions in the cases before them. On January 6, 2005, the Day of Epiphany, two state judges in Chihuahua City issued verdicts and sentences for the men accused in 1999 of killing several women in Juarez. Judge Victor Talamantes imposed forty years on Jesus "Tolteca" Guardado, Jose Gaspar Chavez, Agustin Toribio Castillo, and Victor Moreno Rivera, in the deaths of Brenda Patricia Mendez, Irma A. Rosales Lozano, Elena Garcia Alvarado and an unidentified victim.

Guardado also was convicted and sentenced in the brutal sexual assault of Nancy Villalva Gonzalez. Without explanation, the judge absolved Bernardo "Sanber" Hernandez, one of the five men accused in the murders. All of the men continued to insist on their innocence.

On the same day, Judge Javier Pineda Arzola sentenced members of the alleged "Rebeldes," believed by then to be a fictitious gang, for the murders of other women. Sergio Armendariz Diaz, Carlos Barrientos Vidales, Juan Contreras, Romel O. Garcia, and Gerardo F. Molina also were sentenced to forty years each.

The judge found the five "Rebeldes" guilty of the deaths of Guadalupe Veronica Castro and two other victims known only as "Tanya" and "Lucy." Jose L. Rosales, another alleged "Rebeldes" member, was sentenced to twenty-four years in connection with the death of Rosario Garcia Leal. Both groups of suspects – the bus drivers of 1999 and the "Rebeldes"– claimed they were tortured into confessing.

Shortly before the sentencing, Guardado ("Tolteca") spoke out for the first time since his 1999 arrest, saying he had testified falsely against Moreno and the four bus drivers. He also said he had not known Sharif. The 1999 suspects blamed former Special Prosecutor Suly Ponce for their plight. Later, Ponce was defending herself against allegations of having mishandled the investigations.

Chihuahua State authorities had prepared an order to detain her and other officials named by federal Special Prosecutor Maria Lopez Urbina. Ponce and the others who were singled out for punishment said they had merely followed orders. She also made a couple of stunning claims in a televised interview in Mexico: The killers are still free, and anonymous callers threatened to kill more women if her (Ponce's) staff dared to investigate further.

In another development, in the latter part of 2004, the Mexican federal authorities agreed to investigate Javier "Cerillo" Garcia Uribe's claims that he was tortured into confessing that he and Gustavo "Foca" Gonzalez Meza killed the eight women whose bodies were found in a cotton field in 2001. For this investigation, the authorities agreed to apply the United Nations Istanbul Protocol, an international guide designed to document cases of torture and human rights abuses.

After completing the protocol, the federal authorities determined that Garcia had been tortured, but returned the case without action to Chihuahua State officials. In turn, the state officials did not sanction anyone in connection with Garcia and Gonzalez's irregular detentions. Finally, a

Chihuahua State judge ordered Garcia released for lack of evidence in the 2001 "cotton field" murders.

The ruling came too late for the co-accused, Gonzalez, who died in custody in 2004. Two state police officers had visited Garcia at the prison before his release and asked him to drop the torture charges. He refused. Two years later, his lawyer Sergio Dante Almaraz Mora was murdered. The decisions to issue hasty rulings and bury the torture allegations appeared to be the result of backroom negotiations. Political interests, and not justice, were the order of the day.

PART III

*Injustice is a sixth sense,
and rouses all the others.*

Amelia Barr

21.

THE FBI: PLAZA SWEEP

The FBI office in El Paso, Texas, had assisted the Mexican government with investigations involving three different categories of mass murders and disappearances. The Bureau provided the basis for the only homicide charges pending against a top leader of the Juarez drug cartel, Vicente Carrillo Fuentes. The drug baron was suspected of ordering the deaths and abductions of men and women during the 1990s, and U.S. authorities indicted him for ordering several murders tied to the 1999 binational "Plaza Sweep" investigation.

The FBI also provided Mexico with a detailed investigative report about the Mexican military's role in that nation's political "dirty war." Although Mexican officials did not mention the FBI, the information they were given about Mexico's "dirty war" led to the eventual indictment of army officials for their roles in this dark era.

Over the years, the FBI also provided Mexico with compelling leads in the women's murders. Mexican federal and state authorities did not actively pursue those leads and resisted efforts to involve the FBI directly in the investigations.

Details about police and military involvement in systematic crimes, including the protection of drug-traffickers, demonstrated that the groundwork for the femicides began before the 1990s.

The social and judicial decomposition in Juarez that resulted in the women's murders did not occur overnight. The seeds for the widespread violence and impunity were sown decades earlier, beginning with the Mexican government's violent repression of dissident social and political movements.

Operation: Plaza Sweep

The U.S. public had its first glimpse into the drug cartel's inner workings through "Operation Plaza Sweep." The unprecedented binational investigation broke new ground in several ways. David Alba, FBI special agent in charge in El Paso at the time, reached out to Mexican federal officials after receiving credible information that the drug cartel had buried the bodies of men and women in several of its Juarez properties.

Most people remember this operation for the initial reports that up to a hundred or more bodies might be unearthed. The FBI was particularly interested in the fate of missing U.S. citizens who were last seen alive in Juarez. Because of the FBI's effort, the bodies of four El Paso men were recovered.

FBI sources said they had a key informant who provided specific details about where bodies were buried. At first, the informant went to the DEA office in El Paso, "but was laughed off," according to a U.S. official. But the informant, determined to tell his story, was not to be dissuaded. He then went to the next floor of the El Paso Federal Building, where the FBI had its offices. Although agents were skeptical at first, the informant refused to leave until someone listened.

Eventually, he spoke with an agent who was the Bureau's resident expert on the Juarez drug cartel. After interviewing him, FBI agent Hector Camarillo concluded that the informant and his information were credible. Only someone intimately acquainted with the cartel could know what he had described. The FBI agent immediately consulted with his superiors. As many as thirty U.S. citizens, including U.S. Navy veteran Saul Sanchez Jr., were among the people who were reported missing at the time.

Alba's staff met with resistance from the FBI liaison at the U.S. Embassy in Mexico City. Alba was seeking reassurance that the Mexican government was interested in jointly pursuing the sensitive case. The FBI staff in El Paso was divided on whether to proceed with such a risky investigation on the Mexican side of the border.

Alba became puzzled when Edmundo Guevara, an FBI official assigned to the U.S. Embassy in Mexico City, told him that Mexican officials were not interested. (Guevara later succeeded Alba as special agent in charge of the El Paso FBI office). Alba decided to quit wasting time on diplomatic red tape.

He reached out directly to Mexican federal Attorney General Jorge Madrazo. The case possessed undeniable complexities, including the possibility of U.S. federal agents having to work with Mexican law enforcement officials who were compromised. Alba met with Madrazo, who, after reviewing the FBI's intelligence, agreed to the investigation. Madrazo wanted to start the operation in September 1999, but the FBI said more time was needed to prepare the logistics.

The FBI office received approval from its headquarters in Washington and called on numerous agents and forensic experts for assistance. Alba assigned Frank Evans, his assistant special agent in charge, to oversee the operation. Evans was highly qualified due to his background in drug and violent crimes investigations. Before coming to El Paso, he had investigated activities of the Italian Mafia in the United States. His training for that investigation included learning to cook gourmet meals for mob associates.

"We could not work with the local Juarez police because of the *omerta* (code of silence) they observed," Evans said. "That's why we decided to work with Madrazo's trusted staff."

For the operation, the FBI set up a temporary morgue in El Paso and deployed a satellite communications system so that senior officials could observe the excavations from their offices in El Paso. (The U.S. military later adapted the same communications system for the war in Iraq.)

Mexico was to provide extraordinary security for the FBI staff working in Juarez. Madrazo dispatched hundreds of Mexican soldiers and federal agents from Mexico City to guard the U.S. investigators. It came to light later, that FBI officials received death threats from the Juarez drug cartel.

Media reports on the operation

After U.S. and Mexican officials launched the operation, my assignment for the *El Paso Times* was to report on the activities at the main ranch in south Juarez, where five bodies were unearthed. For the first day of our coverage, I filed five stories for the next day's paper and appeared by remote interview on Ted Koppel's ABC TV's *Nightline* program. As details emerged, Americans unacquainted with the border could not imagine how hundreds of people could vanish without a trace, right across the border from El Paso.

I explained to *Nightline* that the *modus operandi* was the same in most cases: Groups of armed commandos wearing police uniforms and wielding assault rifles would show up at a house or business and whisk away as many as a dozen men at a time. Some had suggested that these armed commandos were imposters rather than real police. Yet, numerous witnesses reported seeing Mexican police in the area during the abductions and did nothing to stop them. In fact, they apparently acted as lookouts. Sometimes, local police escorted the armed commandos with their captives. To the public, the alleged police raids appeared to be legitimate arrests.

The 1999 excavations in Juarez attracted reporters from around the world. Local Juarez police, who were kept out of the loop, took down notes and photographed the activities from a distance.

The painful truth would set in later once relatives checked in with the investigators about missing family members. The local Juarez police usually responded by saying they knew nothing about the victims or their whereabouts.

Jaime Hervella, co-founder of the International Association of Relatives and Friends of Disappeared Persons, said former Chihuahua State Attorney General Arturo Chavez Chavez gave him an intriguing reply when he asked about one of the missing men. Chavez served as the Chihuahua State attorney general under Governor Francisco Barrio. Hervella said, "Chavez told us then that, 'I must confess that this time (federal Attorney General Antonio Lozano Gracia) failed to notify me that they were picking up someone.'"

The people who were being disappeared in this manner included businessmen, lawyers, military officers, police commanders, and a few women.

Reportedly, some of the missing victims were thrown from aircraft while flying over the Chihuahua Sierra mountains.

Mexican authorities in Juarez generally disowned the matter and blamed the drug cartel and the victims for the mysterious abductions. Mexican federal and state officials tossed these cases back and forth. No one wanted to investigate them.

Chihuahua State officials said federal officials should investigate because the cases were related to the drug cartel. Federal officials argued that the cases fell within the jurisdiction of state police. Mexican authorities treated the cartel murders in the same manner. No one would touch them. The cartel enforcers were brutal.

They killed people in broad daylight, in front of witnesses, and with children looking on.

Loren Magaña, Hervella's co-director in Juarez, said their association had documented the disappearances of hundreds of people, mostly men, between 1993 and early 2004. Her brother-in-law, police Commander Alfonso Magaña, was among the many persons who vanished.

Not all of the missing had drug ties. Some were simply in the wrong place at the wrong time. Others were disappeared out of revenge for reasons wholly unrelated to drug-trafficking.

Claudia Margarita Rincon, 27, an El Paso resident, vanished on July 14, 2000, while on her way to meet Fernando Flores, the son of a Juarez city police official. Gustavo Elizondo was the Juarez mayor at the time. The FBI looked into Rincon's case, but was limited to the U.S. side of the border while the prime suspect remained in Mexico. The FBI said a person of interest failed the FBI's polygraph test, but the agency did not have anything more to work with. Rincon is still missing.

Juarez activist Judith Galarza criticized the FBI's operation because it did not focus on finding the city's missing and murdered women. She noted that several women's bodies were discovered near sites associated with drug-traffickers.

It was apparent that the femicides could not be isolated from the drug trade's influence. The cartel's corruption of officials was one of the main reasons the femicides continued unabated, and why investigations tended to fall apart. The cartel also provided the perfect cover for some of the killers who preyed on girls and young women. Because of the focus on the "Plaza Sweep" case, plans to publish a news series on the femicides were put on hold.

Officials silent

Prior to "Operation Plaza Sweep," a guarded silence was the only response the families of missing people had received from the Mexican government. Threats and harassment also discouraged many families from filing missing person's reports. Between 1993 and mid-1999, a Chihuahua State homicide detective had counted about 1,100 men's homicides in Juarez, an unprecedented number. Hundreds were killed later. When you add up all the Juarez slain, plus the missing men and women, you are confronted with a staggering human toll.

Considering the city's criminal environment, it is likely that most of the abducted men and women are dead. Historically, Juarez has been an important staging area for human-trafficking. Until the U.S. government made human smuggling an enforcement priority, Mexico generally did not investigate whether women were being trafficked within Mexico, to the United States or elsewhere in the world.

Shortly after the Zapatista uprising of 1994 in Chiapas, advocacy groups alleged that the Mexican army had recruited women to work as prostitutes for soldiers assigned to the conflict zone. There was no information available on where the women came from or what became of them later.

"Plaza Sweep" critics

The binational investigation attracted sharp criticism from Mexican politicians who regarded FBI involvement as an affront to Mexican sovereignty. Yet the FBI was in Mexico at the request of Mexican officials. One of the operation's vocal critics was federal Senator Francisco Molina Ruiz, Mexico's former federal anti-drug czar and a former Chihuahua State attorney general during the Francisco Barrio administration.

Investigators involved in "Plaza Sweep" encountered rebukes, mainly because all the bodies the public was led to believe might be found in Juarez failed to materialize. The FBI unearthed a total of nine men's bodies at four different sites. Investigators said the victims were tortured severely before they were shot to death and buried. U.S. officials said drug kingpin Vicente Carrillo Fuentes was present during some of the murders.

Officials said the cartel's top enforcer in most of these cases was a violent man nicknamed "Chaky" (Chucky). According to investigators, some of the victims were killed at homes in the city's exclusive Club Campestre (Country Club) neighborhood. The killers then took the bodies to various ranches for burial.

U.S. federal authorities indicted Carrillo Fuentes in seven of the nine deaths. Besides the five bodies found at the site nicknamed "Rancho de la Campana" (bell ranch) in south Juarez, two others were found at a cartel compound about three miles south of the ranch.

Investigators also unearthed two bodies at a remote ranch in Santa Rosalia, a property that officials said was associated with drug cartel leader Eduardo Gonzalez Quirarte. The sprawling ranch, thirty-six square miles of desert, is about a thirty-minute drive south of "Rancho de la Campana." Although FBI officials were told that other victims, perhaps dozens of them, were buried at the Santa Rosalia ranch, their sources had specific information about the burial sites of only two men.

During the FBI-led excavations, earth-moving machines dug twelve feet deep in some places in search of bodies. Former FBI official Frank Evans said that without more specific details, it was simply too much ground to cover.

Polygraphs for officials

For the "Plaza Sweep" investigation, the FBI administered polygraph tests to the top Mexican federal officials assigned to work with them. The Mexican officials volunteered and even insisted on the tests and background checks to assure the FBI that they were not compromised.

Trini Larieta and Dr. Miguel Aragon were two of the federal attorney general officials who requested and passed the tests.

The FBI agents who crossed the border on November 29, 1999, to find murder victims wrapped up the excavations and returned to El Paso in mid-December. On both sides of the border, the investigation petered out. Before it was completely shut down, the FBI promoted Alba and transferred him to Washington, D.C. He left Evans, the acting special agent in charge, to continue the investigation. But the operation ended soon after Guevara took over as the new FBI chief in El Paso. FBI staff members said Guevara insulted Dr. Aragon, who had a work area at the FBI offices during the operation. Sensing that he was no longer welcome, Aragon returned to Mexico.

FBI staffers said Guevara shut down the U.S. end of the investigation and had the agents who worked on it reassigned to other work. In Mexico, Madrazo and his staff paid dearly for their part in the groundbreaking investigation. Larieta, who was nearly dragged into a scandal, left the Mexican Federal Attorney General's Office along with Dr. Aragon.

After Vicente Fox took over as Mexico's president in 2000, Madrazo was sent to work at a Mexican consulate in the State of Washington. And the Mexican official who was the brains behind the *maxi proceso*, the voluminous Mexican indictment against Juarez drug cartel leaders, was banished to a consulate in Europe.

The *maxi proceso* contained the names of numerous politicians, law enforcement officials, businesspeople, and others who allegedly protected the Carrillo Fuentes cartel or profited from it. The cartel continued its reign of terror in Juarez, and more women were killed. Shortly after the "Plaza Sweep" investigation ended, two important regional drug dealers, Jesus and Daniel Sotelo, were killed in Juarez execution-style.

Jesus Sotelo's body was left next to the "Rancho de la Campana" in 2001, and Daniel Sotelo, a relative, was gunned down later in Chihuahua City, where the murders of young women were beginning to worry the state capital's residents. It seemed that things were back to business as usual.

"Chaky"

According to *El Universal* newspaper, a Mexican national daily, a hit man in Mexican custody named Arturo "Chaky" Hernandez Gonzalez handled the "Rancho de la Campana" murders for the cartel. The article quoted several academics who studied "Chaky's" career path as a cartel enforcer.

Their research into the phenomenon of hired killers found that such men operate without boundaries and are ideal employees for transnational crime syndicates.

Before going to work for the cartel, "Chaky" reportedly ran errands for a Mexican army general accused of protecting the cartel and of taking an active role in the violent repression of political dissidents during a part of Mexico's "dirty war."

One of the bodies found in Juarez during the 1999 FBI excavations was that of Castor Alberto Ochoa Soto, a top Colombian drug dealer. Cartel leaders ordered "Chaky" to "take care" of Ochoa as soon he crossed the border into Mexico from El Paso, where a U.S. federal court had just released Ochoa. The Colombian beat a proceeding against him on drug-smuggling charges but encountered death after the border crossing.

Plans to destabilize

"Chaky" is a prototype of the new enforcer for the drug trade. He reportedly received police training and was skilled in torture techniques. Law enforcement academies would benefit from learning about such men, their psychological profiles and how they are used to destabilize communities and entire regions. "Chaky's" preparation was similar to the training that military and police counterterrorism specialists received.

The Mexican academics *El Universal* interviewed, Luis Astorga, Javier Dondee and Gabriela Gutierrez, are breaking new ground by adding to our knowledge about the strategies of major crime organizations.

Before his assassination in 1998, Juarez drug lord Rafael Muñoz Talavera wrote a letter to Mexican President Ernesto Zedillo and other Mexican government officials in which he denied allegations that he was involved in the Juarez violence. He also denied being a drug-trafficker. He had the letter published in several newspapers.

Muñoz claimed he could tell government leaders who was behind the recent "destabilization" of the region. The letter suggested that he was aware of a strategy for wresting control of the Juarez smuggling corridor; his missive should have served as an early warning to the community. Chihuahua officials turned down the invitation to meet with Muñoz, who owned the popular Florida restaurant on Juarez Avenue, and who officials said was a former associate of Amado Carrillo Fuentes and Rafael Aguilar Guajardo.

"Destabilization" is a word which is more commonly associated with political disruption. In his letter, the El Paso-born Muñoz was alluding to the Carrillo Fuentes cartel. U.S. drug investigators said witnesses had linked Muñoz to the biggest cocaine seizure in history, a 21-ton cache found in 1989 in a warehouse in Sylmar, California. Before his death, drug investigators said, Muñoz broke with the Carrillo Fuentes organization, and was trying to work with the Tijuana-based Arellano Felix cartel. Tijuana was experiencing drug-related disappearances, too, which authorities attributed to internal drug wars. According to an investigator in Mexico, the underworld in Tijuana referred to a forbidden pastime in that border city known as *noches Juarenses*, or "Juarez nights," which allegedly involves killing women.

22.

MEXICO'S DIRTY WAR

The FBI's contribution to "Operation Plaza Sweep" did not end with the nine bodies investigators found or with the U.S. indictment against a brutal kingpin. The operation led FBI investigators into uncharted territory. They had not imagined at the beginning that their investigation would produce explosive findings about Mexico's politically motivated disappearances of the 1970s and 1980s.

Revealing what the FBI discovered during "Plaza Sweep" would have caused a political earthquake for Mexico, a U.S. official acquainted with the details said. Aspects of that part of the FBI's 1999 investigation are disclosed here for the first time. The era of Mexico's political repression helps to explain how the current organized crime network got started, and how soldiers and police were conditioned to eventually fill the ranks of the drug cartels and their support networks.

Rosario Ibarra de Piedra

Rosario Ibarra de Piedra visited Juarez in 2002 to express solidarity with the mothers of young women who were murdered or missing. The former Mexican legislator was at a home in Juarez where several of the mothers had gathered. Among those present were Marisela Ortiz, co-founder of Nuestras Hijas de Regreso a Casa (May Our Daughters Come Home), COLEF Professor Julia Monarrez and criminologist Oscar Maynez Grijalva.

Ibarra, a former legislator in her 70s, is a widely respected human rights activist. She has fought the Mexican government for decades in her quest to find out what happened to her missing son, Jesus Piedra Ibarra, a medical student. Officials had alleged that her son was a leader in the country's communist movement and belonged to the Liga Comunista 23 de Septiembre (September 23 Communist League), which also had members in the state of Chihuahua.

After nearly three decades, Mexican prosecutors sought an order to detain Miguel Nazar Haro in connection with Piedra's 1975 disappearance in Monterrey, Mexico. Nazar was a former director of the Federal Security Directorate. Witnesses and police told the mother that law enforcement officers had picked up the college student and, that after a struggle, took him to the infamous Military Camp No. 1 in Mexico City. Witnesses reported last seeing him alive there in 1976.

Witnesses also said Nazar Haro tortured some of the people detained during the "dirty war," but he has denied torturing or killing anyone. Nazar Haro admitted that he was a founder of the "White Brigade," a secretive government paramilitary group that tracked and detained political dissidents in several states, including Chihuahua.

The notorious organization consisted of more than 200 police and soldiers who worked on-call as needed at Nazar Haro's direction. For more than thirty years, the Mexican government denied the brigade's existence.

Mexico's systematic crackdown on political dissidents occurred during the administrations of Presidents Gustavo Diaz Ordaz, Luis Echeverria, Jose Lopez Portillo, and Miguel De la Madrid. Survivors alleged they were tortured by soldiers and police and held illegally at clandestine jails and military installations. Given the years of official denials, the biggest obstacle these people and their families faced was just getting anyone to believe them.

Activist encourages mothers

Ibarra sat that day among the mothers in Juarez, encouraging them to persist in their search for the truth. It had taken her a lifetime to get at least some answers, and along the way she had helped many victims of the government's political war. Among other things, she obtained the release of people being held illegally at a military camp in Mexico City, even after officials denied holding anyone there.

But the justice she so desperately sought for her own family continued to elude her. Vicente Fox, who in 2000 became the first opposition-party candidate elected president in seventy years, was simply the latest president to hear her demands. That day in Juarez, Ibarra and the others had no idea that the FBI in El Paso held the key to their government's carefully guarded secrets about the fate of hundreds of Mexico's missing sons and daughters.

Mexico receives the file

The U.S. government kept the "dirty war" investigation under wraps, as the FBI discretely turned over a voluminous file to Mexico's federal authorities. Jorge Madrazo, the Mexican attorney general during the "Plaza Sweep" investigation, never uttered a word about the explosive FBI file. My first clue about it came when I received a message to "ask about the Mexican generals." The information emerged much later.

In August of 2001, the *El Paso Times* published a story about the arrests of Mexican Generals Mario Acosta Chaparro and Francisco Quiroz Hermosillo. Madrazo's office announced that they were charged with protecting the Carrillo Fuentes drug organization. At the time, neither Madrazo nor his assistant attorney general, Trini Larieta, said anything about other politically sensitive allegations the generals might face related to the "dirty war."

FBI documents 600 deaths

In its extensive investigation, the FBI had several vital tools at its disposal, from informants to an impressive array of intelligence files. "No investigator in Mexico knows what the FBI has. The capabilities of the FBI go beyond anything the PGR (Federal Attorney General's Office) can begin to imagine," an FBI source said. For this aspect of its investigation, the FBI was authorized to tap into key U.S. intelligence banks to develop a detailed file on the Mexican military's role during the 1970s and 1980s.

"As a result, we were able to document the deaths of 600 people in Mexico that involved the military," the FBI source said. The Bureau gathered eyewitness accounts and corroborating information.

The FBI gave the Mexican Federal Attorney General's Office the names of the military principals involved and of witnesses who were present during military-led abductions of civilians, their imprisonments, and their extrajudicial executions. The rest was up to Mexico.

"We gave the Mexican officials enough information for them to use as a basis for their own investigation," the FBI source said. It was then just a matter of locating the people who participated in or had direct knowledge of what had taken place. Knowing what information, the FBI possessed, Mexico could no longer postpone the inevitable, the prosecution of military elites who up to then were considered untouchables.

The FBI report said Generals Acosta and Quiroz were junior officers when they and other members of the Mexican army participated in the violent and irregular raids. Other members had retired, quit the military, or had died.

But the Mexican government did not act promptly on the FBI's information. A U.S. official said one explanation involved internal FBI politics: "Ed Guevara's closing of Plaza Sweep severely delayed an aspect of the case that would have had a deep impact on the core of the Mexican government."

Mexico appoints special prosecutor

Eventually, the Mexican government appointed a civilian prosecutor to investigate the military's role in the political disappearances. According to a U.S. State Department report on human rights in Mexico, Generals Quiroz and Acosta were "implicated in the deaths or disappearances of 143 persons during the 1970s." A military tribunal decided, however, that they could be tried for only twenty-two deaths. The military proceedings were closed to the public.

In November of 2003, a man by the name of Horacio Zacarias Barrientos Peralta, 55, was found shot to death in Guerrero state. Barrientos, who was mentioned in the FBI file, had been scheduled to testify against some of those accused in the "dirty war." Ignacio Carrillo Prieto, the civilian special prosecutor, said his murder would not hurt the government's case because officials had other evidence.

Human rights activists noted that General Acosta was an alumnus of the U.S. School of the Americas, where he reportedly learned the torture techniques the military used in Mexico. Amnesty International and other non-governmental organizations had questioned whether Mexican Attorney General Rafael Macedo de la Concha, also an army general, was genuinely interested in pushing the investigation to its limits. Mexico's military wielded great power and many politicians feared the institution.

The witness

In August of 2002, Mexican officials disclosed that a key informant in the case against the generals was former army Captain Gustavo Tarin. Because he was in U.S. custody, Mexican authorities interviewed him at length in El Paso, Texas. Among other things, Tarin alleged that Quiroz had authorized the use of military planes during the 1970s to transport political prisoners, as well as illegal drugs. Publicly disclosing Tarin's identity also put him in danger.

Tarin, one of the FBI informants for "Plaza Sweep," claimed that during some of those trips, political dissidents were thrown out of military aircraft. In the 1990s, the drug cartel reportedly also eliminated people by throwing them from government aircraft while in mid-flight. It seems the military officers and their associates were putting to new use what they had learned in the "dirty war."

Political repression

Nazar Haro managed to evade arrest for "dirty war" crimes until 2004, shortly after the death of former President Jose Lopez Portillo, who reportedly had protected him. U.S. law enforcement officials previously had arrested Nazr Haro in the United States in connection with an auto theft ring. However, a U.S.

intelligence agency intervened on his behalf, arguing that he had provided the U.S. government with valuable information. Nazar Haro fled the United States after posting bail.

Mexican authorities had long denied there was ever a "dirty war" against political dissidents and insisted the "White Brigade" was a myth. Today, they have referred to the Juarez femicides as a myth. Activists and U.S. government sources said federal and local police officials in Chihuahua State served or took orders from the "White Brigade." They further alleged that some of the Mexican police, who learned torture and other terrorist techniques from the "White Brigade," later put those skills to use for the Mexican drug cartels.

Police in Mexico's "dirty war"

Juarez activist Judith Galarza said she and others knew that police in the state of Chihuahua worked for the secret government organization or were ordered to help with its operations. She said former federal Commander Salvador Siller was among them. In the 1990s, activists familiar with Siller's background managed to derail his nomination for a top city post after they disclosed his role in Mexico's "dirty war."

Activists said former state Judicial Police Commander Refugio "Cuco" Rubalcava, as well as an unnamed former Chihuahua State attorney general, assisted federal officials in identifying or detaining political dissidents in the state of Chihuahua. In the 1990s, Rubalcava and his two sons were found dead inside the trunk of a car left in the middle of the international Bridge of the Americas. U.S. authorities charged drug lord Vicente Carrillo Fuentes with their murders. Rubalcava is the former police official who had "Alejandro Maynez," (Armando Martinez) arrested in connection with one of the Juarez femicides. The connections for apparently disparate crimes in Juarez seemed endless.

Secret U.S. foreign policies

Most Americans do not know that the U.S. government played an indirect role in the Mexican reign of terror that lasted from the late 1960s to the 1980s. It began after the U.S. government pressured Mexico to keep communist movements in check. This secret U.S. foreign policy extended to other countries in Central and South America, where a series of dictators ordered the abductions and deaths of hundreds (perhaps thousands) of people viewed as potential or suspected guerillas.

The Mexican government responded to the U.S. request with the elite "White Brigade," which spied on civilians, and abducted and tortured hundreds of suspected dissidents. Many of them were held in clandestine prisons, but others were victims of extrajudicial executions.

Juarez activist Judith Galarza said "gringos" were present during a "White Brigade" raid of her Juarez family's home in the 1970s. "They acted as if they were the ones in charge. They spoke only English, and they instructed the Mexican officers to make sure they looked in the closets and other places," she said.

Kate Doyle, a senior analyst for the National Security Archive (NSA), a private research institute in Washington, D.C., told the *Washington Post* that recently declassified documents proved U.S. officials were aware of how the Mexican government had worked to "eliminate its opponents" during the dirty war. But the U.S. government decided to stick to issues that "mattered most to Washington," such as trade and oil. Today, time and circumstances suggest that things may not be much different when it comes to the femicides.

In December of 2005, I ran into Rosario Ibarra de Piedra again, this time at a forum on the Juarez murders in Mexico City. I urged her to ask the Mexican Federal Attorney General's Office about the FBI's investigation into the military's role in the "dirty war." The Mexican prosecutor's cases against the military had stalled, and nothing was happening.

The unsanitized report

Then, in March of 2006, the NSA and several Mexican and U.S. media published extracts from an unsanitized document that exposed in gruesome detail how political leaders had ordered the military to carry out a systematic campaign of repression that included abductions, rapes, illegal detentions, and murders. Federal Special Prosecutor Ignacio Carrillo Prieto served on the task force that was to produce a final version of the document for the federal government.

The damning account was out in the open. It named people, including former President Luis Echeverria. The military's campaign bore striking similarities to what took place in Juarez in the 1990s. It was evident the drug cartel had adapted "dirty war" techniques to serve its needs in important drug corridors and other places on the map of drug-trafficking. In 2004, Jose Santiago Vasconcelos, Rafael Macedo de la Concha's right hand, hinted strongly in comments to the press that the Mexican government would not prosecute any prominent citizens linked to the "dirty war" or the Juarez femicides.

"What a disappointment," confided a U.S. official. "We used to count on Vasconcelos. The truth is, there is no one else left to work with."

In 2006, Javier Coello Trejo, Mexico's former anti-drug czar, made headlines again when he presented himself as Miguel Nazar Haro's lawyer in a complaint against Ignacio Carrillo Prieto, the special prosecutor who charged Nazar Haro in connection with atrocities during the "dirty war." Nazar Haro accused the prosecutor of fabricating evidence, defamation, and conflict of interest.

Shortly before the presidential election of July 2, 2006, Mexican authorities placed former President Echeverria under house arrest on suspicion of genocide. A couple of days later, a judge ruled that the statute of limitations for the charge against him had expired in November 2005. Former military Captain Miguel De la Barreda, accused in the disappearance of a member of the September 23 Communist League, also was exonerated.

Mystery "Rambos"

During President Miguel De la Madrid's administration, according to authors Laurie Freeman and Jose Luis Sierra, the CIA trained an elite group of Mexican soldiers to form part of a special intelligence unit. The team was instructed to hunt down drug lords and develop strategies to dismantle the drug cartels.

De la Madrid was president from 1982 to 1988.

Then, in 1996, the U.S. military created a program to train a new breed of Mexican anti-drug troops known as GAFEs (Special Air Mobile Forces

Group). These elite commandos were commissioned to operate throughout Mexico to find and detain drug dealers, particularly in the state of Jalisco and along the U.S.-Mexico border, Freeman and Sierra said.

As had happened with other similar programs, several of the GAFE troops deserted the military to join the drug cartels. U.S. officials have confirmed that former Mexican soldiers, referred to as "Zetas," work as enforcers for the Gulf cartel. Advocates for the Juarez femicide victims said one of the men implicated in the 1998 disappearance of two Juarez women was a "Zeta." Some of these soldiers had received U.S. training.

To most rational people, it seems unlikely that after years of gathering intelligence on the cartels, none of these special units ever managed to capture drug lords like the Carrillo Fuentes brothers, Jose "Azul" Esparragoza, Eduardo Gonzalez Quirarte, Osiel Cardenas, Joaquin "Chapo" Guzman Loera or the Arellano Felix cartel leaders. That seems possible only if official complicity impeded their work. None of the big names in the Juarez drug cartel had been touched.

Mexican and U.S. intelligence sources point to corruption. They alleged, for example, that Mexican federal officers had captured "Chapo" in September 2005, but a high-level government official ordered his immediate release. This kind of ethical failure allowed the cartel wars to continue throughout Mexico. It suggests that the government's unwritten policy is one of letting drug dealers fight each other, instead of confronting them, in an endless war of attrition.

Operation: "Dropkick"

In places where the Pentagon was practically dispatching special anti-drug teams to Mexico, something new was going on. This was a "Rambo"-style war against drug-traffickers. And the cartels responded in kind. The disputed territories were the fabulously profitable smuggling corridors, and the future sites for the femicides.

To complicate matters, in the year 2004, a privately financed band of armed commandos introduced its own tactics in the war against drug-trafficking organizations. These "commandos" could be described as members of an ad-hoc paramilitary group. "Terry Sheron," moniker of the band's U.S. leader, said the mission of "Operation: Dropkick" was to infiltrate and bring down the Arellano Felix cartel of Tijuana.

He said the Tijuana cartel had already spent millions in unsuccessful efforts to find the group's members. Although the cartel killed several of these men, the self-styled "Rambos" claimed to have so infiltrated the Tijuana cartel that they cannot be identified. "Terry Sheron" said some of the evidence his team gathered includes details about off-shore accounts the cartel uses to pay corrupt Mexican and U.S. officials.

"Sheron," a former U.S. Special Forces soldier, said, "We cannot be corrupted because we do not work for any government. My men are the real heroes." The band's leader also said some of the men he recruited had friends or relatives who were victims of the cartel's brutal violence. One had a daughter who was raped and killed by cartel operatives.

One of these privately hired soldiers claimed to have stumbled onto a suspect in the Juarez femicides. The band allegedly had secured evidence against the suspect, but for a different crime. Through their intelligence network, one of the band's members said they also learned that low-level drug dealers had murdered women in Juarez "because they knew they could get away with it."

In August 2006, the DEA announced the detention of Francisco Javier "Tigrillo" Arellano Felix, a leader of the Tijuana drug cartel, in international waters. U.S. officials said the kingpin was in a boat fishing off the coast of California. "Sheron" claimed his team provided the lead that led to the drug baron's capture. Time will tell whether "Operation Dropkick" succeeds where so many others have failed. One of the operation's leaders also said not to expect any help from the Mexican government related to the femicides because of the Juarez drug cartel's grip on the city.

Military implicated

Mexican soldiers or the anti-drug officers who worked with the army were suspected in the deaths of Digna Ochoa and Norma Corona, both lawyers and noted human rights advocates.

Because of its intelligence resources in Mexico, the CIA may very well know who killed them.

The agency likely also is familiar with the evolution of the Juarez femicides, although it seems to treat this knowledge as a state secret. The same thing happened during the dirty war. U.S. intelligence sources knew what was going on, but political agendas imposed other priorities.

Here, we must ask, who benefits from the silence?

According to *La Crisis* magazine, U.S. intelligence agencies once used a ranch belonging to Mexican drug baron Rafael Caro Quintero to train Contras from Nicaragua, allegedly with the knowledge of former Mexican Interior Secretary Manuel Bartlett. Mexican journalist Dolia Estevez wrote about this in a column for *El Financiero*, in which she quoted alleged CIA deserter Ralph McGehee.

It was not for nothing that a top drug cartel leader once told "Ana" (she is mentioned elsewhere in this book) "that there was nothing anyone could do about the femicides."

General signed paychecks

Mexican General Jesus Gutierrez Rebollo told Mexican author Rafael Loret de Mola that during his short term as the nation's anti-drug czar he became aware of an elite group of law enforcement officers who collaborated with U.S. intelligence agents in undercover missions.

The general, jailed in Mexico on charges that he protected Amado Carrillo Fuentes, told the writer that Mexico had its own "Rambos." He said the group included about thirty men who were trained by the CIA, FBI, and DEA, and set loose in the country in 1997, ostensibly to infiltrate the drug cartels.

Gutierrez said that neither former federal Attorney General Antonio Lozano Gracia nor then anti-drug czar Francisco Molina Ruiz bothered to brief him about the group's mission. The general said he found out about these super cops with carte blanche because "I signed their (payroll) checks but I never saw their faces." Gutierrez said a Chihuahua engineer identified only as "Meste," whose resume showed extensive experience in guerilla and terrorist tactics, was the coordinator of this secret force.

The existence of such a group raises several obvious questions. What did the U.S. government learn along the way about the women's murders, and why did it keep silent?

A U.S. official confided that a U.S. Embassy officer in Mexico City was adamantly opposed to the FBI becoming directly involved in investigating both Mexico's drug-related abductions and the women's murders "because it was nasty business."

Did some of the U.S.-trained "Rambos" go awry and become involved? Or perhaps the government felt it was more important to protect its covert operations than to save lives.

Training Argentine style

Mexican intelligence sources alleged that the U.S. government trained Argentina's military in torture techniques, and Argentina taught Mexican soldiers the same skills. Argentina is a Latin American country that is slowly recovering from the massive repression of a former police state.

In 2004, Argentines learned that some of the nation's soldiers had "practiced" torture and other degrading acts so they could understand the limits of physical abuse in the interrogation of suspects. Newspapers published graphic pictures of these training sessions that shocked Argentines. This kind of training, which employs physical abuse and psychological terror, certainly ruins anyone for civilian law enforcement. This contrasts with the goal of normal police work, which is to protect communities.

But crime cartels and some governments may rely on this kind of preparation to condition certain trainees for a lifetime of crime and terror. This could explain the Mexico City police rapes that seem to lack a clear motive. Crime organizations, including drug cartels, would be interested in recruiting police and soldiers with this kind of training.

The U.S. State Department, the United Nations and international human rights organizations have criticized Mexico for continuing to rely on confessions obtained through torture to solve homicides and other serious crimes. Except for Sharif, all the suspects in the high-profile femicide cases claimed they signed confessions because they were tortured. Police had to learn their torture techniques somewhere.

"Dirty war" victims

Leticia Galarza, sister of activist Judith Galarza, was a victim of Mexico's "White Brigade." Judith Galarza said the government suspected that her sister was a member of the September 23 Communist League. She was abducted in 1978 by government security forces in Mexico City and has not been seen or heard from since then. According to her family, after her sister left Juarez, she became active in the conservative National Action Party (PAN) in Mexico City. From the PAN, she reportedly made the leap to the leftist group. While searching for her, the family discovered she may have given birth while she was imprisoned. Her Juarez relatives were able to locate and recover the child but hit dead-ends when it came to Leticia Galarza.

Julian Mata, an activist with the Latin American Federation of Associations of Families of Detained or Disappeared Persons (AFADEM), traveled to Juarez in 2001 to meet with members of the International Association of Relatives and Friends of Disappeared Persons.

His visit was to discuss possible international avenues to pressure Mexican authorities into finding out what happened to those reported missing during the 1990s, and whose disappearances U.S. and Mexican officials attributed to the Juarez drug cartel.

In an interview, Mata said some of the women incarcerated during Mexico's "dirty war" were raped as a form of torture. When they became pregnant, their captors extended the torture by threatening to take away their children.

He said some women suspected of being rebels were jailed on fabricated charges, such as prostitution, and some of the children born to them in jail were stolen. These incidents are reminiscent of the issues dramatized in "The Official Story," a 1985 Hollywood movie about the Argentine military dictatorship. Except to those close to the issue, the accounts sounded surreal.

Trained to rape and kill?

The "White Brigade" also carried out raids in Juarez, in operations so well concealed, that Americans across the border in El Paso did not have the slightest idea of what was happening. Until the Mexican government's draft report was leaked in 2006, no one except the families of victims believed the atrocities were real.

On February 28, 2006, the Associated Press said the report "alleges that (Mexico's) presidency orchestrated an anti-insurgency campaign in which soldiers carried out summary executions, raped women and set entire villages on fire."

Mexican high-level officials were unable to contain the report because it was leaked to U.S. and Mexican media, and the National Security Archive posted it on its website. Mexico's shame was exposed for the world to see. Kate Doyle, the NSA's Mexico Project director, called the government's actions "a savage counterinsurgency campaign."

Part of the NSA report alleges that officials recruited young men for elite groups such as the "Halcones" (falcon or hawk) to carry out counterinsurgency missions. They looked for athletic men who were skilled in martial arts and could be counted on to carry out orders without question.

The young men infiltrated dissident organizations, acted as provocateurs, and killed on orders. They were trained to kidnap, rape, and torture in the name of the government. They were implicated in student massacres and other atrocities. Their leaders had received military training in the United States and other countries.

Mexico may not have seen the end of groups like the "Halcones." In a 2006 article, *La Jornada* published a story alleging that the government had trained a new generation of security forces to infiltrate, discourage and disband "subversive" activities. Unlike those before them, members of the new secret group receive more formal education and better salaries. The article said they will be directed to target leaders of civil resistance movements and conduct discreet detentions.

According to the newspaper, "Halcones" are assigned to the Federal Preventive Police (PFP) and the Federal Investigative Agency (AFI), and that former "Halcones" are among the people who trained them. The article by Gustavo Castillo Garcia also revealed that a former leader of the Mexican "Halcones" was sent to Chile shortly before the 1973 coup that toppled President Salvador Allende and installed Augusto Pinochet as a military dictator.

The following day, the newspaper published a letter by Brigadier General Francisco Aguilar Hernandez, which denied the Mexican National Defense Secretariat (SEDENA) had anything to do with the training or use of its facilities for such purposes. Other Mexican federal security agencies did not comment regarding the article.

Chihuahua's victims

Mexican officials have yet to account for about a dozen people who were abducted from the state of Chihuahua during the "dirty war" era, activist Judith Galarza said. One of the notorious cases involves Alicia de los Rios Merino, who was detained on January 5, 1978, by Mexican soldiers and members of the Federal Security Directorate. According to the Centro de Derechos Humanos Miguel Agustin Pro Juarez, Merino was last seen alive with other detainees at Military Camp No. 1 in Mexico City. Officials accused her of being a member of the September 23 Communist League. She is still missing.

The "White Brigade" also conducted raids in Chihuahua State, where other residents vanished. Some, like Minerva Armendariz Ponce, were fortunate and obtained their liberty later. According to *Reforma's* news wire service, Armendariz was sixteen years old when she was abducted in 1973 and taken to the Fifth Military Zone of Chihuahua before federal officers took her to a clandestine jail in Mexico City to be tortured. Her brother, Carlos Armendariz Ponce, a member of the Movimiento Armado Revolucionario (Armed Revolutionary Movement), was assassinated in the Tarahumara Sierra, along with other students.

In a 2004 interview, Minerva Armendariz told reporters: "The fallen, the disappeared, all those families that were destroyed, deserve justice .... These were crimes against humanity."

Two other survivors, Aleida and Lucio Gallangos Vargas, brother and sister, were reunited after the "dirty war" had separated them for thirty years. Aleida was living in Juarez when she found out that her brother was in the United States. Their parents, who belonged to the September 23 Communist League, disappeared in 1975.

Assuming the Mexican government exhausts the leads the FBI has provided, Galarza may live long enough to see a resolution to her missing sister's case. Officials said the FBI's investigation of Mexico's "dirty war" focused mainly on activities in the state of Guerrero, which today represents one of the fiercest drug smuggling battlegrounds.

The Lomas de Poleo artifact

These cases demonstrate that Mexico's war on political dissidents was not a myth, as the government once claimed. The complicity of high-level officials with the drug trade decades ago, combined with their approval of tactics involving human abuses, set the stage for the unprecedented government corruption that saw its climax with the Juarez women's murders. The networks of complicity were woven before the 1990s, and they planted their terror and instability in much of Mexico.

The states of Chihuahua, Mexico and Morelos simultaneously experienced the rise of a new industry of kidnapping for money, the explosive spread of retail drug markets and extreme violence. The "Colombianization" of Mexico's drug trade, an apparent strategy of the Carrillo Fuentes cartel, has created "narco democracies" in some regions.

The wooden board that Juarez residents found in Lomas de Poleo several years ago, with its crude drawings of soldiers, marijuana plants and nude women, turned out to be a precise portrayal of conditions in the border city.

23.

THE FBI AND FEMICIDES

The FBI's David Alba always believed that binational police cooperation was the key to solving the border's most baffling crimes of the 1990s. These included forced abductions in Juarez, which involved increasing numbers of U.S. citizens, and the countless missing and murdered women.

Before he came to El Paso as special agent in charge, Alba had worked on other investigations along the U.S.-Mexico border. He viewed the unprecedented "Operation Plaza Sweep" of 1999 as the beginning of a new era of collaboration between U.S. and Mexican law enforcement.

"The stars were aligned just right at the right time for this," Alba said. The El Paso-Juarez region is known for the kinds of crime that an international border facilitates – drug-trafficking, human-trafficking, vehicle thefts, arms-trafficking, and homicides. Theoretically, people on the U.S. side could plan murders on the Mexican side, and this would be enough in some cases for U.S. authorities to charge suspects with conspiracy to commit crimes in Mexico, officials explained.

After the success of "Plaza Sweep," Alba had intended to continue with a similar investigation into the Juarez women's homicides. Some of the women who were killed in Juarez were U.S. citizens or U.S. legal residents. Without U.S. intervention, their cases seemed destined to remain unsolved.

Because of "Operation Plaza Sweep," the Carrillo Fuentes cartel put a $250,000 bounty on the heads of FBI officials who played lead roles, including Alba and Frank Evans, at the time the No. 2 man at the FBI office in El Paso.

At first, the FBI tried working with the Chihuahua State authorities. "That's why we came up with the idea of asking the FBI profilers to help out," Alba said. FBI headquarters approved the request and sent several profilers from the FBI academy in Quantico, Virginia, to meet with officials the Mexican border city. FBI Special Agent Al Cruz said the profilers were reluctant to come, mainly because they feared they would lose control of their work. In fact, those fears were realized, and it set back U.S. involvement in the women's murder investigations for years.

The FBI profilers

In 1999, Arturo Gonzalez Rascon was the Chihuahua state attorney general and Suly Ponce was the special prosecutor assigned to oversee the women's murders investigations. Frank Evans said the FBI had developed a long list of recommendations to assist the Chihuahua investigators, including "strategies for capturing the killers." Retired FBI official Robert Ressler, who pioneered criminal profiling at the FBI, was the first notable expert to advise the Chihuahua state police about the cases.

During his 1998 visit, Ressler also met with officers at the El Paso Police Department. He made subsequent trips at the request of the Chihuahua authorities, usually when public pressure mounted.

Back then, Ressler surmised that one or more serial killers were at work, and that the person or persons were most likely Hispanic or Mexican-American. He said it was "someone who could blend in easily and not call attention to himself ... perhaps someone who took advantage of crossing the border to commit the crimes."

The FBI profilers traveled to Juarez in March and April of 1999. Their trips coincided with the arrests of several bus drivers who Chihuahua State officials accused of killing women for Abdel Latif Sharif Sharif in exchange for money. The press nicknamed the suspects "the Toltecas."

I was at the *El Paso Times* newsroom when we received a faxed press release from Chihuahua State officials about their conference with the FBI profilers. The Chihuahua officials sent the same statement to news media throughout Mexico. The news release claimed that the FBI experts concurred with Chihuahua authorities that Sharif was responsible for the murders. I was reluctant to write a story based solely on the Mexican press release without first checking with the Bureau.

FBI Special Agent Al Cruz asked me to send him a copy of the press release. A couple of hours later, Cruz called back and asked that we not publish the statements attributed to the FBI in the Chihuahua press release. He said the FBI did not want to create an international incident and stated for the record only that the FBI experts had not made the statements attributed to them in the press release.

During the profilers' visit to Juarez, the Chihuahua authorities selected case files for the FBI experts to review. Of those, the experts kept copies of several that they wanted to analyze further. On their second trip to Juarez in April 1999, the profilers met with state officials, including Special Prosecutor Suly Ponce, and gave an oral report of their preliminary findings. Al Cruz, who accompanied the FBI profilers, said the Chihuahua State officials thanked the FBI experts for their help, but said they already had suspects in custody.

Cruz said the Chihuahua officials asked the FBI profilers what they thought about their case against Sharif. "The only thing the profilers said was that it was a 'novel theory,'" Cruz said.

Most Mexican reporters did not check with the FBI and filed stories across Mexico based on the Chihuahua government's press release. I told Juan Manuel Carmona, press secretary for the Chihuahua State Attorney General's Office, that the FBI had denied making the statements attributed to them in the press release. Carmona chalked it up to "possibly an error in the translation."

Chihuahua State officials were not interested in anything the FBI profilers had to offer. "I was disappointed," said Alba. After that experience, FBI officials in El Paso decided they would work only with officials from the Mexican Federal Attorney General's Office in Mexico City.

FBI: serial killer at work

FBI officials later explained that the profilers from Quantico had reviewed the Mexican files for seventy-eight homicides and chose twenty-five to thirty for an in-depth analysis. One of their preliminary findings was that a serial killer was involved in about thirty of the murders. The profilers had hoped to return to the border to develop a more comprehensive conclusion.

The FBI also wanted to explore the possibility that a group or gang may have committed several kidnappings and murders. FBI experts said a group psychology would be different from that of a lone serial killer or of a serial killer acting in concert with someone else.

Robert Ressler said he would be surprised if the profilers came up with anything different from what he had found in 1998. "They (the profilers) probably had been students of mine at the FBI Academy," Ressler said.

The FBI suggested various recommendations to help advance the Chihuahua investigations, such as applying established protocols and standards, and designating a single forensic team to respond to each crime scene to ensure uniformity.

"Many of the cases were tainted by multiple forensic investigators, (and) each had to show they were *el supremo*," said Frank Evans, former acting special agent in charge of the El Paso FBI office. "The strategy must include plans to inveigle the subjects, utilizing established profiling techniques and recommendations.

"Forensic team members must be part of the investigative effort. (And) all investigative records must be centralized, computerized and accessible (to) the investigative team," said Evans.

The FBI's efforts to assist Mexico slipped to a back burner after Evans left the agency and until a new chief arrived with an interest in pursuing cross-border collaborations.

New FBI chief on board

Hardrick Crawford Jr., special agent in charge after Edmundo Guevara left, was in El Paso only a few months when he peered outside the FBI's offices one day and saw several people with protest signs in front of the federal building. They were members of the International Association of Relatives and Friends of Disappeared Persons. They wanted to know why the FBI had dropped its "Plaza Sweep" investigation.

It was November 2001, the second anniversary of the initial excavations, and they were desperate to learn what had become of their missing relatives. Crawford, who had heard about the "Plaza Sweep" investigation before coming to El Paso, met with them later. The members said they found Crawford to be open, friendly, and sympathetic.

Before coming to El Paso in the summer of 2001, Crawford had worked on several high-profile cases, including the terrorist attacks on the U.S. Embassy in Kenya in 1998 and the arrest in 2001 of James C. Kopp, a top federal fugitive. Richard Schwein, a retired FBI official in El Paso, called Crawford, "an outstanding investigator."

Crawford appeared genuinely interested in what was going on across the border. He could see Juarez from his office window.

"There is probably nothing we can do about the women's murders that have already occurred, but we can at least try to do something to prevent any more deaths from happening," said Crawford. "We need to find out what is happening with all those missing ladies." Then he pointed to a picture of his college-age daughter and said, "If anything were to happen to her, you know I would be out there looking for the killer."

Crawford: Crimes against humanity

Shortly after the bodies of eight young women were discovered in a Juarez cotton field in November of 2001, the FBI began receiving calls and visits from writers, journalists, and advocacy organizations, all wanting to know what the FBI was doing about the murders in Mexico. The FBI explained repeatedly that it could not operate across the border without an official request from the Mexican government.

Crawford surprised many people, especially Mexican authorities, when he appeared on an ABC *20/20 Downtown* television segment about the murders. The program aired on January 31, 2002. At the time, Crawford told ABC journalist John Quiñones that he was interested in helping.

In July 2002, the FBI office received a faxed letter inviting Crawford, or a designated representative, to attend a special meeting in Juarez to discuss solutions to the women's homicides. Mexican congressman David Torres Rodriguez, who served on a legislative commission looking into the murders, spearheaded the meeting at the Lucerna Hotel.

"We got very short notice. The invitation came over by fax the night before the day of the meeting, and when I arrived, I could tell that they really weren't expecting me to show up. They were very surprised when I walked through the door,"

Crawford recalled.

The two-hour meeting heated up, particularly when Lorenzo Aquino, the highest-ranking federal law enforcement official in Juarez, began offering excuses for why the Mexican federal government could not get involved in the state investigations.

Someone at the table asked Crawford for his opinion. He recommended a binational task force to investigate the murders, just what FBI official David Alba had in mind when he had served at the border.

Crawford told the group that law enforcement agencies in El Paso had set aside jurisdictional differences when five-year-old Alexandra Flores was kidnapped from an El Paso store in 2001. He described how police shared their resources to work together on the case. He told the Mexican officials that when the FBI worked on the "Green River" serial murders in the Northwestern United States, "it made no difference to the agency that the victims in that case were prostitutes."

Crawford also told the astonished group that "what was happening in Juarez was a crime against humanity." His words made front-page headlines in the Mexican press.

Soon after that, Mexican President Vicente Fox began to make noises in the press about asking the FBI for help. Crawford got wind of it and called Quantico to find out if the Bureau's profilers would be willing to come back to the border. He designated a senior official at the El Paso office to oversee a task force, in the event Mexican officials formally requested the FBI's assistance. Despite the fiasco of 1999, the FBI profilers said they would return to lend their expertise.

The same week after he met with the Mexican legislators, Crawford went to the El Paso Club for dinner with his wife. Several of the Mexican waiters approached the FBI official, asking to be photographed with him. They showed him the *Norte de Ciudad Juarez* newspaper that used his "crimes against humanity" quote for a front-page headline.

The waiters had rushed out to purchase a disposable camera.

After the picture-taking was over, they thanked Crawford for caring about the women of Juarez. The encounter moved him.

A couple of FBI employees with relatives in Mexico also told Crawford how much they appreciated his interest and willingness to help solve the crimes.

El Paso Crime Stoppers

On both sides of the border, advocacy groups were searching for the key that might open the way to a breakthrough. One group invited me to a brainstorming session. I suggested asking whether Crime Stoppers might be interested in taking calls about the murders and offering a reward for information.

A couple of former El Paso police officials agreed that this was a plausible idea. "An international case would be a feather in the cap of El Paso's Crime Stoppers," said J.R. Grijalva, a former assistant El Paso city police chief.

People on both sides of the border might be willing to provide leads on a confidential basis. Witnesses in Juarez were afraid of the police, who readily gave suspects the home addresses of their accusers. The fears were real.

Carlos Martinez, father of Carly Martinez, a college student who was savagely murdered in southern New Mexico in 1998, told El Paso human rights activist Victor Muñoz that he would support the proposal. Martinez served on the El Paso Crime Stoppers advisory board, and his recommendation would carry weight.

The proposal was defeated, however, by the implacable opposition of one board member. Muñoz was upset at the outcome. He said, "The board member felt that it would offend the police in Juarez."

A toll-free hotline

The setback did not end things there. In 2003, the FBI and the El Paso Police Department, in agreement with Chihuahua State authorities, set up a toll-free hotline to receive tips about the Juarez women's murders. The number set for this was 800-237-0797. Under the arrangement, the FBI and El Paso police would receive the calls, analyze the information, and pass on to Mexican authorities anything they considered useful.

Rafael Navarro, editor of *El Mexicano* newspaper in Juarez, published the toll-free number almost daily, but other Juarez news media did not. As a public service, *El Mexicano* also participated in a website called "Pesquisas en Linea" (Online Searches), which is devoted to disseminating information to the public about missing men, women, and children. The site includes photographs of missing Juarez persons. In 2006, the Juarez newspaper moved to a different website.

FBI report leaked

Lilia Alejandra Garcia Andrade was seventeen when she was murdered in February 2001. Nine months later, someone in the Mexican Federal Attorney General's Office in Juarez leaked a report from the FBI about the teenager's murder. According to the intelligence in the report, several hit men working for drug dealers abducted the young maquiladora worker and held her captive for several days. The leak exposed confidential informants who had given sensitive information to the FBI and Mexican authorities.

The witnesses said they tried giving the information to Special Prosecutor Suly Ponce, but that she brushed them off. After that, they decided to visit the FBI. At the time, Ponce was trying to pin Andrade's murder on circus workers at a shopping mall across the street from where Andrade's body was found. Ponce backed off after two circus workers accused her of trying to bribe them to implicate a fellow worker. Ponce denied the allegations.

After the FBI report was leaked to the Mexican press, people who claimed to be FBI agents knocked on the doors of Juarez homes where some of the witnesses lived. Two Juarez residents who provided information about the Andrade case said they received threats and were forced to leave the city twice. The FBI imposters were never identified. The episode illustrates the dangers ordinary citizens wanting to help face in the border city.

Report: Drug gang involved

The FBI report, based on raw intelligence, said one of the men who attacked the girl was named "Raul." It said "Raul" was "a well-known drug dealer" who associated with someone at a Dominguez television repair shop, where witnesses said the suspects had parked a white Mercury or Thunderbird.

The FBI report said: "There is a woman who has a friend who is married to a man who works for Raul packaging drugs and constructing (hidden) compartments for vehicles. On one occasion, when the first woman visited her friend, Raul was present and offered her a job in drug-trafficking. They told her that in order to work for them, she would have to kill a member of her family. The people killed by Raul's group supposedly are mutilated, (which) includes ripping their testicles and breasts."

Several witnesses walked past the white sedan parked on Rancho Becerra on February 19, 2001 and saw a young woman in the car who was identified later as Andrade. The witnesses said the teenager was struggling with one or two men inside the car.

They said that a man who appeared to serve as a lookout went inside the TV repair shop.

Taxi drivers about twenty feet from the white sedan looked on but did nothing. Their cabs were distinguished by the Tres Hermanos shoe store ads on top of the vehicles. It was ironic that several previous victims were seen at a Tres Hermanos store or had worked in one before they disappeared. Mexican state investigators said they never found a connection.

One of the witnesses that evening was an American woman who was returning from the Walmart on Ejercito Nacional, which is perpendicular to Rancho Becerra. She knocked on a door of a nearby house and asked the residents to call police "because something terrible is happening to a young woman in that car." A second witness, who was a Juarez judge, and a third unnamed person had to call police before a patrol car finally showed up. Another witness said in an interview she suffers a deep sense of guilt "because I felt I could have done more to save that girl. I'm seeing a therapist now."

Jorge Dominguez, owner of the TV repair shop and a former Philips maquiladora technician, emphatically denied any association with the men involved in the attack. "They did a DNA test on me and I came out clean," he said. Norma Andrade, Lilia Alejandra's mother, said that while Dominguez is correct about the DNA test, Chihuahua State police did not run a DNA profile for "Raul," who was mentioned in the FBI report. He worked at a business a few blocks from the TV repair shop, but later moved from the area.

Ponce said she looked into the FBI report allegations but dismissed them as groundless.

Zulema Bolivar, who succeeded Ponce as special prosecutor for the women's murders investigations, said she knew that people in Juarez had gone to the FBI with information. "As you know, we don't have a witness protection program like they do in the United States," Bolivar said.

When the police car finally arrived at Rancho Becerra that night, the white sedan with the teenager inside had already left. Juarez city police dispatchers said they did not send a unit after the first call because they thought it was a prank.

Personal altar

Lilia Alejandra Garcia Andrade's violent death took on a personal importance for me. She symbolized the persistence of these murders, and the apparent unwillingness of the authorities to end them.

I went out one day to look for the place where her body had been found. There, I stumbled upon a tall wooden cross dedicated to her memory with her name on it. The cross had been erected in her memory in the middle of a triangular-shaped parcel across the street from the Juarez Plaza Mall. The parcel also sits across the street from the maquiladora that employed her. The same grassy lot is located adjacent to a narrow street of a middle-class neighborhood.

Co-workers said they last saw her when she left the assembly plant at the end of her shift. Former Chihuahua Governor Teofilo Borunda owned the property where the killers dumped her body. The prominent politician died later that year of natural causes.

Garcia had married when she was fifteen and had two young children. At the time of her death, she was separated from her husband and lived with her parents. It is not unusual for Mexican women to marry at such a young age. Norma Andrade, her mother, was an elementary school teacher.

I was staring at Garcia's cross when I heard a baby's cries from a nearby home. It was at that moment that everything hit me at once. I saw the daughters, mothers and sisters who did not make it home one day because someone decided to make them the next victim. Then I began to cry. There at Garcia's cross, I cried.

Until then, I had been unaware of the emotions that had built up inside of me since I began investigating the murders. It was as if a dam somewhere inside me had burst. I was oblivious to the strangers who walked by, wondering what was wrong with me. They must have imagined that I was a friend or a relative of the victim.

From that day on, Garcia's cross became my personal altar. I believed that her case held the key to solving some of the brutal murders of young Juarez women.

Cases with common traits

Oscar Maynez Grijalva, the former Chihuahua State forensic chief, was familiar with Garcia's autopsy. He said her "death and the deaths of three of the eight women whose bodies were discovered in 2001 showed some of the same characteristics of the serial murders we saw in the early 1990s." The autopsy indicated that Garcia had been dead only a few hours before her body was discovered on February 20, 2001; she was abducted only a few days earlier, on February 14.

The autopsy indicated that Garcia had been tied up, raped by several men, and strangled. Maynez said the autopsy also revealed that she ate a meal on the day she was killed. "This meant she was held captive for several days, and her captors fed her to keep her alive," said Maynez.

Garcia's mother scolded the former governor, who owned the vacant parcel, for ordering a bulldozer to raze the land. She said the bulldozing destroyed any evidence the killers might have left behind.

The teenager's captors took her on Valentine's Day. She was seen in the white car several days later, on the night before she was killed. The car in which she was seen was parked next to the Saint Valentine shopping center. Adding to the odd set of coincidences, the killers tossed her body in the parcel which is bounded by Saint Valentine Street.

The Garcia family received a tip later that a police official had selected the victim as a Valentine's Day "gift" for an influential man. The family was unable to confirm the allegation.

To a casual observer, it appeared that the allusions to Saint Valentine were intentional. Perhaps it was a message. But for whom? Nine months later, a cotton field about two miles east of where Garcia had been abducted, became the latest graveyard for eight young women.

Fear and loathing

Heliodoro Juarez was a lawyer, professor, and former president of the Chihuahua State Human Rights Commission. In January of 2002, he said he wanted to investigate the femicides, out of his own sense of frustration as a citizen who lived in the city. He planned to recruit a team of law students to assist with the investigation. We agreed to meet again in a few months to report on our investigations and compare notes. When I saw him later that summer, Juarez was a changed man. He said he wanted nothing to do with the murders, and called off the investigation. He started to draw me a map of the place where Alejandra Garcia Andrade's body was found and of other relevant sites nearby. Then, he abruptly stopped drawing and crumpled up the paper.

"I know a lot about her case. Stay away from it," Juarez warned. "It is dangerous. It involves hit men who cut off the breasts of women, and who work for the Dominguez drug dealers." He never specified which Dominguezes he feared, and Dominguez is a common name in the border region.

U.S. and Mexican investigators confirmed that several people with that surname are in fact notorious drug-traffickers. Heliodoro Juarez was offered a job elsewhere and left the border for several years. Later, others would describe something more ominous than what the Juarez lawyer had discovered.

24.

BOTCHED OPERATION

During Hardrick Crawford Jr.'s administration, the FBI in El Paso attempted another joint border operation that required the collaboration of Mexican federal and city officials in Juarez. Given the pervasive corruption of Mexican police, people in the border community marveled that the FBI even considered it.

Crawford wanted to trust his Mexican counterparts and believed that Juarez Mayor Jesus Alfredo Delgado genuinely wanted to help U.S. law enforcement officials put an end to another crime: burglaries of Union Pacific trains that traveled east and west along the border.

For several years, a gang entrenched in Anapra, an extension of Juarez, regularly stole cargo from U.S. trains that were forced to slow to a crawl when they reached a sharp curve along the border. Whenever a train reduced its speed to maneuver the curve, thieves from Mexico would rush over to the U.S. side, jump aboard the freight cars, and make off with televisions, VCRs, and other items.

The gang became adept at crossing the border through openings in the chain-link fence between Anapra and Sunland Park, New Mexico. The thievery had cost Union Pacific millions of dollars in losses. The thieves who operated from the impoverished community of Anapra were not ordinary gang members. U.S. officials viewed the young thugs as hardened criminals who smuggled people and drugs and committed murders for organized crime. Juarez police looked the other way, reportedly because gang members paid officers for protection. A Juarez city council member referred to the gang's territory as "no man's land."

The binational operation against the gang received the green light. About sixty FBI and Border Patrol officers took part on the U.S. side of the border on the night of September 12, 2002. On the Mexican side, another sixty federal customs and city police officers stood by in case they were needed.

But something went terribly wrong. After the operation began, the Anapra gang that had crossed border brutally attacked two FBI special agents, Samantha Mikeska and Sergio Barrio. It happened when Mikeska tried to catch a gang member at the fence line. Other members jumped in to help their fellow thug. They dragged Mikeska through a hole in the fence. When Agent Barrio came to her aid, he, too, was attacked. The gang kicked and beat the two agents with sticks, stones, and a baseball bat.

The brutal attack ended only after another FBI agent fired his weapon in the air. After the attack, Mexican police rounded up about a dozen gang members from Anapra homes and turned them over to the FBI at the border. The severely injured agents were rushed to the El Paso county hospital, where their treatment included drug-induced comas.

The agents recovered after extensive therapy. FBI Special Agent Sergio Barrio, highly respected by his peers, is former Chihuahua Governor Francisco Barrio's nephew. Another FBI agent in El Paso also is related to another former Chihuahua State governor. The border can be a small world.

The FBI was pressed with questions from the news media about the disastrous turn of events. U.S. officials criticized Crawford for not being at the scene to personally lead the mission.

Mexican officials faced harsh criticism from their politicians, who accused them of allowing the FBI to invade Mexico's sovereignty. Not long after that, several persons who represented the gang members that the FBI had detained, filed complaints against the Mexican officers who assisted the FBI with the operation.

There were suspicions on both sides of the border that organized crime elements had financed the legal proceedings for the Anapra gang. The complaints charged that Mexican police had committed treason. The complaints expressed no concern for the courageous U.S. agents who suffered severe injuries while in the line of duty. No thanks either were offered for the U.S. effort to crack down on a gang that had terrorized Juarez residents for years.

According to the FBI's review of the operation, a breakdown in the agency's chain of command was responsible for the disaster that nearly killed two of its agents. As a result, a mid-level FBI official was disciplined.

Crawford leaves the FBI

In 2003, the FBI's Crawford was caught in a Mexican political crossfire that cut short his career. Before that, a very promising development in the women's homicides appeared on the horizon. Top Mexican federal officials flew to Juarez to discuss the murders with Crawford and Chihuahua State officials. "It was a huge development," said Crawford. "The Mexican officials asked for our collaboration in investigating the women's murders and the drug cartel."

The officials at the meeting included Jose Santiago Vasconcelos, head of Mexico's federal organized crime investigative unit, and federal Assistant Attorneys General Jose Campos Murillo and Carlos Vega Memije. Campos was the first high-level official to mention openly that "juniors," the sons of wealthy families, could be involved in the Juarez women's murders.

A storm ensued soon after that. Jorge Carpizo, a former Mexican federal attorney general, alleged that Jose Maria Guardia, owner of the Juarez racetrack concession, and Juan Sandoval Iñiguez, a Roman Catholic cardinal in Guadalajara and former Juarez bishop, were laundering money for drug-traffickers. Crawford was caught in the line of fire because of his association with Guardia and the cardinal.

Mexican writer Isabel Arvide criticized the FBI official's new friendships, referring to them as "dangerous liaisons." She also said Carpizo was a highly regarded law expert. According to the Mexican press, Carpizo readily conceded that the allegations were based on an "anonymous" letter he received about Guardia and Sandoval. However, the information was sufficient for federal Attorney General Rafael Macedo de la Concha to launch an investigation.

Guardia claimed that Carpizo's allegations were retaliation because Guardia and the cardinal previously had accused Carpizo of conducting a shoddy investigation into the 1993 assassination of Guadalajara Cardinal Juan Posadas Ocampo.

Mexico's national media published stories about Crawford and his controversial friends.

Before the attacks against Crawford, the FBI office in El Paso had disclosed that it was in possession of a Mexican federal police credential that bore a picture of drug lord Vicente Carrillo Fuentes. The card had the alleged signature of Diego Valades, a former Mexican federal attorney general and a close friend of Carpizo's. Telemundo network reported on the drug lord's police I.D. for a documentary titled *Ciudad sin Ley* (Lawless City).

FBI officials said privately that Vasconcelos was convinced that U.S. officials intentionally embarrassed the Mexican Federal Attorney General's Office by disclosing the card to the media.

Before the controversy, Sandoval was viewed by some leaders in the Catholic Church as a contender to succeed John Paul II as pope.

Crawford, who felt compelled to help his new friends, stated his support for Guardia and Sandoval during a news conference in May of 2003 at the Juarez racetrack. It was to be his undoing.

Minutes before the news conference, Valentin Fuentes, a prominent Juarez businessman, urged the cardinal to stay away from Guardia or risk being dragged down with him. Guardia, who was on the telephone with the clergyman, got wind of this and swore at the cardinal in anger. Guardia read Crawford's hastily prepared remarks, and the cardinal headed for the racetrack after discarding the businessman's advice. Crawford, Guardia, and the cardinal appeared together at the news conference.

Crawford under fire

To play it safe, Crawford said, he had asked the FBI staff in El Paso to investigate Guardia, but not the cardinal. Crawford said he believed the cardinal was innocent. FBI agents said they had warned Crawford about the rumors regarding Guardia. During U.S. court testimony, FBI employees testified that Guardia did not pass the entire polygraph test that Crawford had requested for him.

Then, after Crawford resigned from the FBI, it came to light that his wife had worked for the Juarez racetrack as a marketing consultant. The U.S. Justice Department began an inquiry to determine whether Crawford had benefited from his wife's membership in El Paso's Coronado Country Club, one of her employment perks. Crawford insisted he did nothing wrong and that he had disclosed his wife's source of income as required by the FBI.

Crawford said he befriended Guardia only after others at the FBI office suggested that he become acquainted with the racetrack operator. He said Special Agent Art Werge suggested that the FBI could benefit from having a contact like Guardia, who moved in high political and business circles.

Guardia considers himself a friend of Cuba's Fidel Castro, and appears in personal photographs with the dictator. He also was close to the late Fernando Gutierrez Barrios, a powerful Mexican politician who liked to play tennis during his visits to El Paso. Among other things, Gutierrez Barrios was an informant for the U.S. government. Guardia apparently also had friends in Washington. One of his "proofs" was his invitation to an exclusive ball at President George W. Bush's inauguration ceremony.

At the height of the controversy, a confidential intelligence source in Mexico City claimed Guardia was a U.S. intelligence asset, Crawford's wife was clean, and the "mafia" wanted to get rid of the FBI official. Unknown to Crawford initially, his trouble with the U.S. Justice Department resulted from sworn statements that Guardia gave U.S. officials about his relationship with Crawford. The former FBI official said he was unaware of this betrayal until shortly before his trial in 2006.

Mexican official complains

Jose Maria y Campos, a Mexico Foreign Ministry official and a friend of Carpizo and Valades, complained in writing to the U.S. Embassy in Mexico that Crawford was interfering in Mexico's internal affairs. The letter prompted U.S. Ambassador Tony Garza to pull Crawford's country clearance, a move that prohibited Crawford from entering Mexico in his role as an FBI official. He could cross the border only for social purposes or as a tourist.

Cardinal Sandoval met with President Vicente Fox to discuss the money-laundering investigation that put him and the others under a cloud.

A couple of months later, federal Deputy Attorney General Jose Santiago Vasconcelos announced that the Mexican investigation found no wrongdoing on the part of Guardia or the cardinal. The federal government had pulled Guardia's gaming license but returned it after the investigation cleared him.

Crawford, however, opted to retire. "This is not how I wanted to end my law enforcement career," he confided.

According to the Associated Press, a federal jury convicted Crawford on August 16, 2006, on two charges–that he concealed certain facts about his relationship with Guardia and that he made false statements about gifts from Guardia on his financial disclosure statements. He was acquitted of three other counts alleging that he lied to investigators. He repeatedly denied any wrongdoing.

Guardia, who stayed away from the trial, was not required to testify. Cardinal Sandoval testified for Crawford's defense.

Advocates see a setback

The turn of events stunned advocacy leaders on both sides of the border. They believed that with Crawford's departure they had lost an important ally.

In an interview, I asked Sandoval what he thought about the unusual women's murders, which began the same year that Cardinal Juan Posadas Ocampo was gunned down in Guadalajara. Sandoval said powerful people had to be involved for the deaths to continue as long as they had.

Guardia, who has important friends in Mexico, also has powerful rivals. He said one reason "they were after my [gaming] license is because [backers] of Jorge Hank Rhon wanted him to take over the Juarez gaming concession. In order to do that, they first have to get me out of the way. A couple of years ago, Jorge Hank Rhon quietly opened two Caliente betting counters in Chihuahua, so he's already in the state."

Hank comes from a powerful family with businesses in Mexico and Costa Rica. He owns the racetrack concession in Tijuana, and his family has strong ties to politicians in Chihuahua State. Former Chihuahua Governor Fernando Baeza Melendez, who preceded Governor Francisco Barrio, worked for several Hank family members in Costa Rica. According to a U.S. Customs Service investigative report, Jorge Hank Rhon previously lived next door to Juarez magnate Pedro Zaragoza in San Diego, California.

Hank ran for mayor of Tijuana in 2004 and won as a candidate for under the Institutional Revolutionary Party (PRI). During his mayoral campaign, the controversial Hank, who has a private collection of exotic animals, was pressured by Mexican women politicians to apologize for telling reporters that "la mujer" ("the woman") is his favorite animal.

Hank opened a Caliente branch in the Juarez Pronaf district. By 2006, his new sports betting counter was doing business on Avenida Juarez, only a few feet from the Paso del Norte International Bridge and a block from Guardia's sports betting counter. The Caliente consortium also moved into the building on Juarez Avenue that used to house Rafael Muñoz Talavera's Florida Café.

At the end of 2005, Guardia was having problems with his racetrack, and employees complained they were not getting paid. He placed his house in West El Paso on the market and continued to avoid Crawford.

Juarez police chief quits

Across the border, Juarez Police Chief Refugio Rubalcaba Plascencia quit under fire the same year that Crawford resigned. He is not related to the late Chihuahua State police official of the same last name. Mayor Jesus Delgado recruited him. However, the flamboyant official who liked to wear military-styled uniforms, served only for forty-five days before resigning in March of 2003.

The gregarious police chief nicknamed the "General," was popular with the general public. In response to the city's gang violence, he had recommended a curfew for teenagers, but that idea was shot down. During his brief administration, he was given the distasteful task of leading the forced removal of hundreds of squatters from Lote Bravo, a disputed development where the bodies of several women had been found in 1995.

Juarez reporters regularly pestered him about such things as his new sport utility vehicle, his growing number of bodyguards and his Rolex watch. Weary of such questions, he lashed out at reporters and asked them, "Would you prefer to have a fucked-up police chief, instead of one who has something to show for all his hard work over the years?"

Ex-chief makes startling allegations

The day after he left the police force, Rubalcaba told a Juarez newspaper that he had received death threats. He also made startling allegations about the women's murders.

"There is someone in Juarez who does not want the women's murders solved or for the city police to investigate," said Rubalcaba. "There is someone here with a lot of economic power who has a lot of hatred for Juarez, a small group that enjoys the pain of women (and) that enjoys watching the murders of girls on videotapes."

"When one gets in the way, when one disturbs this powerful group, then this happens," said Rubalcaba, alluding to his sudden departure from the Juarez police department.

City police are considered a crime-prevention force in Mexico. They are not authorized to investigate homicides. However, after the bodies of six women were found in the Cristo Negro area in 2002 and 2003, Rubalcaba let it be known that city police would, in fact, investigate.

No government official in Juarez at any level bothered to interview Rubalcaba about his explosive assertions. During a news conference in El Paso to announce the new FBI hotline for the murders, I asked Juarez Mayor Jesus Delgado if Rubalcaba's allegations were being investigated. In response, Delgado, said "We are following every possible line of investigation." After a few more questions from reporters, the officials quickly ended the news conference.

Chihuahua State Attorney General Jesus "Chito" Solis, Chihuahua State Special Prosecutor Angela Talavera, El Paso Police Chief Carlos Leon, El Paso Mayor Raymond Caballero and FBI Special Agent in Charge Hardrick Crawford Jr. attended the news conference.

Before she left, I asked Talavera about Rubalcaba's allegations. She said he should file a formal complaint if he had information about the murders. She conceded that she had made no effort to contact him. I pressed upon her that Rubalcaba was "not just any guy off the street, he was the police chief."

The killers are protected

Several years ago, I met with reporter Sonia del Valle at a cafe in Mexico City. She was a correspondent for CIMAC, a prestigious women's news service in Mexico, and was chasing a promising lead that several other reporters also were pursuing.

Del Valle said she contacted her sources about the Juarez women's murders, and that an official at the Federal Attorney General's Office warned her to stay away from the issue. The source told Del Valle that the murders involved "protected people," and that no one in Mexico could protect her if she persisted in her investigation.

I did not hear from Del Valle again for a long time, but her source with the friendly warning proved to be right.

Journalist suffers reprisal

Mexican journalist Sergio Gonzalez Rodriguez was pistol-whipped so badly in Mexico City in 1999 that he had to be hospitalized. One of his attackers showed him a police badge and told him the attack was at the request of a police commander. The assailant told Rodriguez that it was related to the "Juarez matter." Gonzalez was working on a book about the murders titled *Huesos en el desierto* (*Bones in the Desert*).

Later, an official who flashed a badge for the Mexican federal Interior Secretariat approached Gonzalez at a cafe in the port city of Veracruz. The government operative told Rodriguez that he had been warned.

Around this time, a Chihuahua State official sent word to his staff that the state police were to pick up Gonzalez "the moment he steps on Chihuahua soil, so we can find out who's been filling his head with this pack of lies."

The *El Paso Times* published a series in 2002 about the Juarez women's murders and abductions titled "Death Stalks the Border." It helped to break the silence about who was killing the women and why. People began to come forward with more crucial information.

Several women shared personal testimonies about gang rapes at sex parties where influential men were present. One of them, a university student, said she was fortunate to be alive after being raped by influential men at such a party. She was too frightened to file a complaint.

On another occasion, several people told a U.S. immigration official that the Egyptian Abdel Latif Sharif Sharif did not kill the women. They told the immigration official that the men responsible were "the juniors," the sons of wealthy families. Asked why they did not report this to the Mexican police, they responded, "because the juniors will kill us."

Mexico: A sensitive file

During a religious event at the border, a church minister felt compelled to share a dream he had about the Juarez murders. "I saw the killers in my dream. They are from well-known and important families," the minister said. It seemed that the issue of the Juarez women's murders had permeated the community's collective consciousness.

A health professional who said he possessed knowledge about the crimes said, "The murderers are known. But they are so highly placed that the police and government are afraid to crack down on them."

Fear gripped even top government officials, particularly in the state of Chihuahua. A Foreign Ministry official once alleged that the governor at the time was given a file that revealed the likely killers. "Governor Patricio Martinez knows," the official said. "He had the file on his desk. He said to me once, 'There it is. Where would you like for me to begin?'"

Apparently, former Governor Francisco "Pancho" Barrio also had an idea about who was involved. According to a Barrio relative, "Pancho wanted to do something. He wanted to bring the best investigators, but he became aware that rich and powerful men were involved, and (that) nothing could be done."

Barrio tried to do something to end the crimes while he was governor. His staff brought former FBI profiler Robert Ressler to the border in 1998. His staff also invited Spanish expert Antonio Parra, who consulted with Chihuahua officials. His staff also had invited the two criminologists from Mexico City, although they did not arrive in Juarez until shortly after Barrio had ended his term in office.

Mexico's "Intolerable Killings"

Vicente Fox's rise to the Mexican presidency and Barrio's election as governor of Chihuahua followed parallel paths.

Both men belonged to the opposition National Action Party, and each was elected with great expectations for change and reform. And, in both cases, the post-election results were the same: a disastrous rise in insecurity in Chihuahua State and the nation.

During Barrio's administration, young women were brutally murdered in the state. After Fox became president, new similar slayings of women were reported in other parts of Mexico.

It will be up to the people of Mexico to judge whether Barrio truly was unable to stop the women's murders while he was governor.

25.

MODUS OPERANDI

In March of 2003, a Mexican official leaked another report about information the FBI had received regarding the femicides in Juarez. The official said the Mexican Federal Attorney General's Office also had a copy of the report. The raw intelligence described how victims might have been lured to their deaths without arousing suspicion. It alleged that the killers used a music store, several bars, and an old cafe in downtown Juarez to target potential victims.

The report was alarming because it said there were plans to kill four more girls within two weeks. Only a few weeks earlier, the bodies of four young women had been found in the Cristo Negro area. If the report were accurate, what could be done?

I felt as though I were swirling in a sea of impotence. It was as if the fate of young women in Juarez depended on those of us who possessed the information. Lives were at stake.

From the recent news accounts, it appeared that the FBI and the Chihuahua state authorities were entering into a new era of collaboration. And Mexico's federal officials were getting involved in the femicide investigations. At this stage, it seemed the only option left was to give the authorities a chance to pursue the leads.

Mexico's top investigators

The Mexican Federal Attorney General's Office assigned Rolando Alvarado to supervise the initial investigations. I had met Alvarado before, through Mexican writer Isabel Arvide. For security reasons, Alvarado's

Mexico City team wanted to keep a low profile. Nonetheless, he agreed to meet us at the Shangri-La in Juarez, where we had met a year earlier. Kent Paterson, a journalist based in New Mexico, and others from the U.S. side of the border, joined us. We wanted to be sure Alvarado had the latest FBI leads. U.S. officials had said that sensitive information they sent to Mexico sometimes failed to reach the right people. Alvarado said he was in Juarez for an indefinite period to investigate the women's murders. He said he was not aware of the uncorroborated intelligence the FBI recently had sent Mexico.

During the meeting, Alvarado introduced us to a couple of his trusted agents. One of them said he had worked on the investigation of Luis Donaldo Colosio's assassination. Colosio, a Mexican presidential candidate, was assassinated on March 23, 1994 in Tijuana. A persistent theory about his death is that he refused to meet with a drug cartel leader during the presidential campaign. Mexican legal experts compared his death to the assassination of John F. Kennedy, in that it will never be solved to the public's complete satisfaction.

Alvarado's assignment was a difficult one. The Mexican press was reporting that all levels of law enforcement were cooperating on the femicide investigations, but the reality was another story. His agents said they knew that several Juarez police worked for the Carrillo Fuentes drug cartel, and this added a layer of danger to their work. They also were aware that local police were monitoring his team's every move, including our meeting.

The report

The report that the FBI sent Mexico, which the Bureau characterized as raw intelligence, contained the first account of a possible *modus operandi* for the femicides: two men, assisted by police and others, were involved in enticing young women. Part of the account, which was translated from Spanish to English, is reproduced here:

"There is a club in Juarez called the Club [redacted] on Avenida Juarez … [Name redacted] knows who is responsible for the homicides of young women that are abandoned in areas of Juarez. [Name redacted], together with his assistant, a young man with a mustache who is skinny and arrogant, act as lookouts to recruit new girls. They first come into contact with the girls who visit the ... [Name redacted] store on [Avenida] 16 de Septiembre, across from the cathedral. Once the girls go inside the store, they find themselves alone. Then, they are followed, but without realizing it, by other young people who will approach them and ask them for personal information for a school called ECCO along the same street."

Other parts of the report contained more frightening allegations: "Somehow, the girls are contacted and directed to the [Name redacted] restaurant ... Once inside the restaurant, they are tied up, tape is put over their little mouths, and they are taken out through an alley proliferated by prostitutes. The one who is in charge of transporting them is nicknamed "Guero" ("Blondie") who belongs to the Juarez drug cartel. [He] also operates in other clubs, such as Safari and Nereidas. Together with "Ritchie," if that is even his real name, they are in charge of paying off police to get rid of the bodies. I am warning you that Police Chief [Name redacted] is Ritchie's first cousin. [There] are plans to kill 4 more (girls) within the next two weeks."

The report alleged that the attic of the one of the clubs was used to store souvenirs of the victims, such as hair, and that one of the suspects "showed them off as trophies" to his customers.

One of the clubs, an old watering hole in the tourist district, is near the Glamour Institute, where Juanita Sandoval, 17, worked and attended cosmetology classes. She was one of three victims whose bodies were found February 17, 2003, in the Cristo Negro area. The others were Esmeralda Juarez, 16, and Violeta Alvidrez, 18.

All the places mentioned in the report were within short walking distances of each other in downtown Juarez, where in the past other teenaged girls had vanished or were last seen alive.

Evidence lost

Time passed and nothing seemed to happen. Were Mexican officials truly working with U.S. counterparts to prevent new femicides? An FBI source said people at the Bureau were skeptical. Part of that skepticism was related to the Cristo Negro cases.

"Chihuahua officials told us that they had recovered a semen sample from Violeta Alvidrez's body," said an FBI source, "and we told them to bring it in so we could run a DNA analysis and come up with a DNA profile of her attacker. Whenever they came up with a suspect, they could check the DNA profile against the evidence to see if it matched."

The FBI source said Manuel Esparza Navarrete, an official with the Chihuahua State special prosecutor's office, responded with some bad news. "(Esparza) told us that the evidence was used up or got misplaced, and that heads were going to roll for this," the FBI source said. "We knew then that they weren't serious."

Over the years, Chihuahua state authorities lost or destroyed a great deal of evidence, including victims' clothing. Cadavers were misplaced. Case files were missing or burned accidentally. The clothing of victims ended up on the bodies of other victims. Families of victims in Juarez and Chihuahua City constantly questioned the identities of the bodies they had buried.

Under Mexico's system, the Chihuahua State Attorney General's Office has the primary jurisdiction for homicide investigations and is legally responsible for safeguarding files and evidence.

Another common complaint was that police often failed to exhaust all lines of investigation. Mexico's National Commission of Human Rights, under Jose Luis Soberanes, was the latest institution to question this issue in relation to several of the cases. In this regard, the commission specifically criticized the case of Esmeralda Alarcon, one of the six Cristo Negro victims.

Commission provides leads

According to a witness quoted in the commission's 2004 report, "A man who worked at the [downtown] Tres Hermanos shoe store said he wanted to marry [Esmeralda Alarcon]. [He] was 40 years old ... and he was always asking me to help him so Esmeralda would listen, but she didn't like him."

The witness alleged that [Alarcon] had dated a doctor "who had the bad habit of consuming cocaine."

In the case of Juanita Sandoval, another Cristo Negro victim, a witness said a suspicious doctor "would ask me and my friends if we wanted to watch pornographic videos on the computer .... [On] one occasion, before watching the video, the doctor asked us if we had had sex relations, how we did it and if we were virgins," the government report said.

In the case of Violeta Alvidrez, the report said a relative of the girl alleged that, "despite the fact that [an unnamed relative] had provided information of her whereabouts, [the authorities] never did anything, and even threatened [the relative] so she wouldn't tell the news media."

The Chihuahua State authorities did not follow up on any of the leads that the federal commission provided.

Computer schools mentioned

More time passed, and there were still no signs that the authorities were pursuing leads in the FBI report. The report's reference to an ECCO computer school did not appear to faze the Chihuahua officials, despite the fact that more than a dozen dead or missing girls in Juarez and Chihuahua City had enrolled in or had some other connection or contact with ECCO schools.

The *El Paso Times* had reported on the concerns over ECCO schools in April of 2002. Special Prosecutor Liliana Herrera acknowledged then that at least eight missing or dead girls were ECCO students or had some connection to the schools. Despite her short tenure as the special prosecutor for the femicides, Herrera came across as someone who genuinely wanted to investigate the murders. She was hampered by a lack of experience and the lack of support from her staff and superiors.

She was, in fact, blocked at every turn. In 2002, Herrera tried to find out what information the FBI had about the murders, but for some reason the FBI never fully explained, her attempt turned into an unpleasant encounter that discouraged her from seeking any further assistance from the Bureau. At the FBI, she said, "They insulted me and treated me as less than a professional."

FBI officials said she was turned away because she failed to follow the proper protocol for contacting the Bureau.

ECCO had two schools in downtown Juarez, and another one in downtown Chihuahua City. Teenagers with profiles similar to the Juarez victims, and with connections to an ECCO school, also had disappeared in Chihuahua City, the state capital. In Juárez, Liliana Holguín de Santiago, 15, Maria Acosta Ramírez, 19, and Lilia Alejandra García, 17, had links to ECCO schools. One of the six Cristo Negro victims (2002-2003) also was enrolled in an ECCO school.

Octavio de la Torre Jimenez, an ECCO manager in Juarez, and Aaron Anibal Castañeda, an ECCO manager in Chihuahua City, denied any wrongdoing. "We had nothing to do with what happened to those girls," De la Torre said.

According to the company's publicity, the ECCO corporation operated thirty-six computer schools in several Mexican states. *Reforma* newspaper reported that a businessman who is influential in sports circles was a principal in the corporation. No one ever suggested that he was involved in any wrongdoing. Yet, the ECCO managers in Juarez and Chihuahua City refused to identify or provide contact information for the owners of ECCO and or its local branches. Several journalists elsewhere in Mexico tried without success to obtain the information about ECCO's ownership.

The ECCO managers in Juarez and Chihuahua City said that it was not necessary to interview the owners. In an email, Juan Gabriel Capuchin, an instructor who said he had worked for the computer company for twelve years, responded with this message: "You can be assured that if I had seen my workplace involved in something so vile, I would have stopped working for the company."

Later in 2003, the ECCO schools in Juarez and Chihuahua City reportedly changed owners and names. The former ECCO on Avenida 16 de Septiembre in Juarez became Incomex.

A mother's testimony

Several years before ECCO found itself in the spotlight, a mother and her daughter saw an employment ad for ECCO recruiters in Juarez and decided to apply. As the hiring process progressed, the mother said she grew increasingly uneasy about the job and left with her daughter. She shared an intriguing account of her experience.

"They had two kinds of people at the ECCO school. They had the students who enrolled in the classes, and the *promotores* (promoters) who recruited students and (other) potential recruiters. We did not tell them that we were mother and daughter because they told us they did not permit people who were related to each other to work for the company," the mother said.

"I noticed that they focused intensely on my daughter, who was starting to believe whatever they told her. They promised everything, including a lot of money and the potential for travel. It was too good to be true, and I started to get suspicious," she said.

ECCO managers then scheduled a talk for the prospective recruiters at a Juarez hotel. And they treated the prospects to a meal and conducted several interviews.

"In those days, they were sending men and women recruiters to some of the most remote neighborhoods of Juarez," the mother said. "They knocked on doors and invited people to join ECCO.

I don't know why but they kept took our original [identification] documents at another office on the second floor. I was afraid they would not give them back to us."

"After the meeting with everyone at the hotel, we went to the school on Avenida 16 de Septiembre. Through a glass partition, I could observe the man who was interviewing my daughter," the mother said. "I believe the manager was Guatemalan. I never saw him again. I could tell they were about to persuade my daughter to go work for them, but after everything I saw, I got us both out of there as fast as possible."

Several Juarez families, including Esmeralda Herrera Monreal's mother, had mentioned that ECCO promoters visited outlying neighborhoods like hers to recruit students. The promoters wanted Monreal's daughter to enroll and left her a brochure. Norma Andrade said her daughter, Lilia Alejandra Garcia Andrade, had stopped at an ECCO school to inquire about enrollment before she was abducted and killed in 2001. Another source said there were similar schools in Guatemala, with connections to Mexico, which also recruited young people.

Internet suspicions

In his research, New Mexico journalist Kent Paterson learned that several young women who were killed or disappeared in other parts of Mexico also had a connection to a computer school or internet cafe. Paterson, an editor for the Frontera Norte Sur news service at New Mexico State University, said, "Since 1995, at least 16 young women or girls who had some sort of contact with ECCO and other private computer schools in Ciudad Juarez, Chihuahua City and Nuevo Laredo have been murdered or disappeared. Many had been raped."

Considering Mexico's explosive growth in internet use in recent years, computers can become lethal tools for those who target young women for abduction, rape, and murder. Criminals now communicate over the internet to avoid using telephones that are easier for investigators to monitor. Without thorough investigation, it is difficult to determine whether computer schools or cyber cafes had a role in any of the cases of missing and dead women.

It is possible that killers used phony ECCO recruiters to approach potential victims, or that they were able to access computer records at the schools or internet cafes to harvest young women. A source in Chihuahua City said state police agents used ECCO cyber cafes as a hangout. He said corrupt police involved in stolen auto networks used the internet cafes to communicate with their associates.

Rolando Alvarado's federal team launched an undercover investigation of a Juarez computer school in March of 2004. The investigation, carried out long after it might have done any good, proved fruitless. The cross-country movement of young women – who seek work in maquiladoras, nightclubs, computer schools and retail stores–provides a perfect hunting ground for killers or sex-traffickers. Several young women who died or disappeared in Juarez were last seen alive on their way to apply for a job or to keep a job interview appointment.

In 2005, one of the Juarez television stations interviewed a woman who was identified as Maria del Rosario Gomez Solis, 26, who was reported missing in 1993. She said she managed to return to Juarez after having been kidnapped when she was fourteen years-old by a truck driver and forced into prostitution for several years in various Mexican cities. Her name was on a list of disappeared Juarez women that Amnesty International had compiled from police reports. Although many people watched her TV interview, the authorities in Mexico did not bother to investigate her harrowing account. Officials simply added her to the list of missing women that federal officials found alive in 2005. The document left out any reference to her odyssey, which her family said included giving birth to a baby that was taken away from her during her captivity.

26.

Operation Sagrario

Federal official Rolando Alvarado said in June of 2003, "I can't figure them out," and asked to be removed from the Juarez women's murder investigations. He also told the International Association of Relatives and Friends of Disappeared Persons that he had asked his superiors to put him back on investigations of drug-related disappearances, even though in five years he had not solved a single case.

Shortly after that, a federal agent who was working with Alvarado in Juarez confirmed that neither he nor the other agents had interviewed any of the witnesses mentioned in the raw intelligence report the FBI sent Mexican officials in March of 2003. Instead, one of the federal agents asked for help in arranging a meeting with flamboyant private investigator Jay J. Armes of El Paso, a request the famous private eye promptly turned down. Mexican federal authorities also had not approached the FBI to exchange information about the women's murders. One of the Mexican federal agents wanted to meet with the FBI, but discreetly and on an informal basis. "I do not want the Chihuahua State police to find out," the agent stressed. The FBI was considering his request – until controversy erupted over Crawford's friendships with Cardinal Sandoval and Jose Maria Guardia. Any plans for such a meeting were canceled.

In light of the official inaction, and the imminent threat that more girls might be sacrificed, several reporters from both sides of the border developed a plan for an operation to be led by journalists. It was called "Operation Sagrario," after one of the Juarez victims. Its purpose was to acquaint the press with the people and businesses mentioned in the report. We would seek answers about the allegations from the owners or managers of those places.

If the report were accurate, then "Operation Sagrario" would alert the community about specific dangers. If not, we could put to rest the fears raised by the report. We decided to do it on August 10, 2003, a Sunday. Amnesty International was scheduled to release its "Intolerable Killings" report the next day.

Aloof official

In the morning before the media blitz, Sergio Gonzalez Rodriguez, Kent Paterson, and I went to see Alejandro Gertz Manero at the Radisson Hotel in El Paso. Gertz was the Mexican president's national security secretary, a post equivalent to the one held by Condoleezza Rice before she became Secretary of State. Two officials with the Mexican Federal Preventive Police accompanied Gertz. He introduced one of them as his intelligence coordinator.

Gertz gave us his trademark high-brow discourse on crime and corruption, then proceeded to make excuses for why Mexican federal police could not usurp Chihuahua State jurisdiction in the murder investigations.

In Mexico, Gertz is viewed as an intellectual, and he regularly wrote columns for newspapers on various topics. We gave him a copy of the same FBI report that Alvarado had, which he promptly passed on to his intelligence officer without first reading it. After our discussion ended, the only thing Gertz wanted to know was how we found out what hotel he was staying at. In response, I rose from the table and thanked the Mexican national security secretary for his time and bother.

On a human level, Gertz did not seem at all interested in the fate of poor young women in Juarez. His indifference was disillusioning. It seemed that the doors for possible options to help prevent more femicides were closing on all sides.

The following year, Mexico's *Milenio* weekly magazine published an interview with Juarez business executive Angelica Fuentes titled "Queen of Gas" that mentioned her imminent marriage to Gertz. Chihuahua Governor Jose Reyes Baeza Terrazas had appointed Fuentes, one of Mexico's richest women who resided in Juarez and El Paso, to be the state government's representative in Mexico City. Later, Gertz's relatives said he and Fuentes called off the wedding, and in mid-2004, Gertz abruptly resigned his post.

Miguel Fernandez, the Coca-Cola magnate, and the brains behind the *Strategic Plan for Juarez* (a blueprint for the border city's future), also jumped on the bandwagon to clean up the city's image by asking other community leaders to help put the murders in their "correct" perspective.

Later on, Roberto Madrazo Pintado, the 2006 presidential candidate of the Institutional Revolutionary Party, invited Fuentes to join his national campaign staff. She quit after a disagreement over the campaign's leadership style. Madrazo lost the election in a three-way bid that Felipe Calderon of the National Action Party won.

The media blitz

Shortly before the August 10 media blitz, someone urged us to ensure that our actions were not going to hurt a possible joint investigation by the FBI and Mexican authorities. It was a fair request, and with that in mind, we contacted an FBI source to discuss those concerns. The answer was surprising.

"Go for it. You are not going to jeopardize any investigation," the FBI source said. "You in the media don't have your hands tied like we do." Indeed, the news media is not limited by matters such as national sovereignty nor does it require government permission to investigate.

Several print, radio and television journalists wanted to collaborate, while advocacy organizations volunteered to serve as witnesses in case anything went wrong. Later, we learned that someone was nearby taking pictures for the FBI in case something got out of hand. Given the allegations of possible ties to the drug cartel, we harbored genuine fears for our safety. Some of the journalists came because they thought they could help.

The media blitz included reporters from California's *Orange County Register*, *La Jornada's* National Correspondent Jenaro Villamil, *Reforma* Editor Sergio Gonzalez Rodriguez (despite the threats against him), Radio KUNM journalist Kent Paterson, former *Norte* editor Graciela Atencio, a KINT TV camera crew, a reporter for *Norte de Monterrey*, a TV crew from Channel 4 of London and others. We gathered that day in the hot afternoon sun, took a deep breath and went inside our first stop, a restaurant.

Once inside, we identified ourselves as journalists to a man who said his name was Francisco Lopez and was in charge. His name was not in the report, but he proceeded to deny all of its allegations concerning the eatery. "People who are envious and malicious must have made up these things," he said. To prove he was telling the truth, he allowed us to check inside the restaurant to see for ourselves that no victims were being held there against their will. Lopez said nothing of the sort could happen at the restaurant because it was usually closed by 5 p.m.

Then a British reporter reminded Lopez that he had told her TV crew that various clients sometimes rented the place at night for private parties, and that important families were among his customers. The restaurant, in its current state appeared an unlikely place for significant social gatherings.

We also checked with the hotel next door. Rates for stays of less than an hour were posted in the lobby. A young girl at the desk became visibly nervous and fled, while a camera at the hotel entrance watched our every move.

Next, we went to a club around the corner and were told that the owner was not available. A bartender named "Chuy" gave us permission to go inside and climb a ladder into the attic, which the report had mentioned. The walls of the club were plastered with pictures of nude women in various poses. The bartender explained that the picture display was a "Juarez tradition." We then walked into a music store on Avenida 16 de Septiembre, also mentioned in the report. At the store, an employee told us she had not seen anything suspicious and had no idea when the owner or manager might return.

At a second club, around the corner from the restaurant, we were told that "Guero" (Blondie) was the owner but that he was not the "Ritchie" refenced in the report. The young woman who ran the bar at the club laughed and called the owner on the telephone for us. The purported owner said that neither he nor anyone else associated with the club was involved in anything illegal. He also said he did not know anyone at the other places mentioned in the report. He offered to meet with us at the club but called back a few minutes later to say he could not make it after all.

At that time, the ECCO on Avenida 16 de Septiembre was closed because it was a Sunday, but by then the public was familiar with the school's practice of using sidewalk recruiters to enroll new students.

No response from Mexico

FBI officials later confirmed that they had provided the Chihuahua State authorities with the report, but that Mexican officials never got back to them. FBI Special Agent Art Werge said, "We treated it as raw (unprocessed) intelligence. It involved El Paso suspects. We sent the information to the Chihuahua state attorney general's special prosecutor in March (2003), and they never mentioned it again or asked us to help or got back to us in any way."

Werge would not elaborate on the FBI's information concerning the "El Paso suspects." The part of the report we saw did not mention that anyone had a specific El Paso connection, so that background likely came from police files.

The day after "Operation Sagrario," Oscar Valadez, the Chihuahua State deputy attorney general, acknowledged having received the FBI intelligence. However, his only response then was, "We are still investigating. We have not ruled out anything." Valadez said he heard about our visits to the places mentioned in the report but made no further comments about the news media operation.

Several places mentioned in the FBI report had changed owners several times, and due to a legal practice of using *presta nombres* (third-party representatives or straw buyers), it was difficult to ascertain the real owners. Between November and December of 2003, one of the restaurant's and hotel signs disappeared. In their place were new signs for a business called the Hotel Condesa.

In its edition of April 24, 2004, *Norte de Ciudad Juarez* reported that public works inspectors temporarily shut down the place because it was operating as an alleged brothel without a hotel permit. The article said the closure stemmed from citizen complaints. According to *El Mexicano*, the man who had identified himself as the restaurant manager in August, was now in charge of the hotel.

On most nights, up to a dozen or so relatively young women would stand outside the hotel in the late hours attempting to flag down customers. It was a dangerous time for women to work in the city's sex industry.

Two journalists who were also present during the interview with Valadez quipped about his Rolex watch, while I kept an eye on the Uzi-like firearm behind his desk. Valadez, a distinguished-looking man, appeared surprised when I congratulated him on the state's capture of "Topo" Fernandez. The man was indicted in the violent sexual assault of a young boy in Valle de Juarez.

Valadez, who was polite and professional, said "we haven't had any more bodies turn up since February–when we found the Cristo Negro victims." He said that was proof that the femicides had ceased. But an FBI source said otherwise. The femicides had not stopped. The difference was that now the killers were disposing of young women in a more shocking manner. And that was why bodies were not being discovered.

Officials ignore leads

Other leads reportedly came to the attention of the FBI in El Paso. A Juarez man said he had hoped that the FBI would act on a tip provided by concerned citizens about a massage parlor in the Pronaf area. He said the business, allegedly linked to a notorious drug dealer, operated as a brothel that hired young women to service male clients in Juarez and El Paso. He also said two female employees who were sent to clients in El Paso were among the women authorities had reported missing. The book *Los Chacales de Ciudad Juarez* also mentions that Juarez-based prostitution services, disguised as massage therapy, "have extended to El Paso."

The tips kept coming but police failed to follow up. In December of 2003, *El Mexicano* reported that Chihuahua state police in Juarez had arrested four members of a violent gang, including its leader, Fernando Solis Delgado, alias "Piranha." The authorities accused them of attempting to rape a young woman and of marking her back with their gang symbol. Police did not divulge the symbol details. The newspaper article also alleged that the FBI gave Chihuahua State authorities information about "Piranha" more than a year before his 2003 arrest, linking him to the

Cristo Negro victims. The FBI's Art Werge said he could not corroborate whether the Bureau had forwarded intelligence to Mexico about the alleged gang members or had received information about the massage parlor.

The other men arrested with "Piranha" included Cesar Alvarez, alias "Poison," and two others identified only by their nicknames "Patotas" (Big Feet) and "el Pink."

Juarez city law enforcement officials estimated that as many as 500 gangs operated in the city. The acknowledged top two groups were the Aztecas and the Mexicles. At the Cereso prison, members of these rival gangs battled each other for control of the drug trade inside and outside the prison. The violence led to riots and the resignations of prison directors.

Patricia Gonzalez, the Chihuahua State attorney general, announced in 2006 that a new gang "more powerful" than these two had emerged; however, she would not disclose any details.

Dangerous drug dealers

According to a U.S. drug investigator, drug dealers who work for the Juarez drug cartel are responsible for some of the murders of women in that city. The source said these killers travel periodically to the border from the state of Durango to smuggle drugs into the United States.

"They stay at a ranch in Anapra and wait there for the right moment to take the drugs across the border," the investigator said. "To amuse themselves it got into them to hunt and kill women. They would come and go regularly. The police knew what they were doing, but they did nothing to stop them." Anapra is just south of the boundary that separates the Mexican community from Sunland Park, New Mexico. And it is adjacent to Lomas de Poleo.

In 2006, the *San Bernardino Sun* interviewed Hardrick Crawford Jr., the former FBI official, about Mexico's drug violence. Crawford told the newspaper that "Many of the women in Juarez were killed by people connected to the Juarez cartel. It's a reminder. It's the (cartel's) way of letting people know who's in charge."

Norte de Ciudad Juarez reported that Javier Galindo Vera, a Chihuahua state police officer who revealed the involvement of police and drug dealers in the abductions and deaths of men and women, had been murdered in 1994 to silence him.

Later, the *Dallas Morning News* quoted a Mexican document that alleged drug dealers had killed women in Juarez to celebrate successful drug runs. The Mexican document cited in the Dallas paper raises an important question. If Mexican officials possessed this information, why did they not arrest the suspects?

From these accounts, it is undeniable that drug dealers in the Mexican border region enjoy immunity from prosecution, and those with the right connections can get away with virtually anything. But while that fact might help explain some of the murders, it alone does not account for the broad range of motives involved in the femicides.

27.

MEXICO'S SECRET FILES

An FBI source finally shed some light on the crimes that had baffled the Juarez-El Paso border community for years. "Who's behind the murders? From the Bureau's view, it included one or more serial killers, a couple of drug dealers, two violent and sadistic gangs and a group of powerful men," the FBI source said.

Eventually, I learned that several Mexican federal investigators had in fact looked into the women's murders, and their findings were conclusive. I also found out that two Chihuahua State officials had tried without success to investigate a "junior," the scion of a wealthy Mexican family, in connection with the Juarez crimes.

During the Mexican secret federal investigations, which took place between 1995 and 2003, numerous people at the border came under surveillance. One of the investigators, who for his safety must remain unnamed, asserted that high-level officials were protecting the killers. "They know who the killers are, and their involvement has been proven beyond any doubt," the investigator said.

Another federal investigator said he wrote a letter to President Vicente Fox detailing what his investigation had uncovered.

After that, the investigator began receiving death threats.

A different Mexican official who worked in intelligence also alleged that powerful people involved in crimes bribed officials, who then ordered a purge of people (potential witnesses) who had assisted with the murders. They were considered a threat because they could point to the prominent authors of these crimes.

During an eight-month period, from August 2004 through March 2005, fifteen men whom intelligence officials had linked to the Juarez femicides, all low-level operators, were killed by organized crime elements. DEA experts say the drug cartels eliminate operatives who become liabilities to the hierarchy because they know too much. Other clues point to a high-level cover-up.

A double file

An FBI source alleged that Chihuahua State officials maintain two files on the women's murders, "the one they show to everyone and the one they keep to themselves, and we know what is in the one they keep to themselves."

When Patricio Martinez was governor of Chihuahua, he endorsed the arrests of suspects in connection with the deaths of young women in Juarez and Chihuahua City. One of the suspects was Cynthia Kiecker, an American who was charged in one of the Chihuahua City femicides. She and her husband, Ulises Perzabal, also charged in the death, vehemently denied the allegations, and claimed police had tortured them until they confessed.

Agents of three different federal security agencies, who took part in the previous undercover investigations, named others as the prime suspects. They claimed the people responsible for the systematic murders of women in Juarez and Chihuahua City are not the ones that are in custody. The law enforcement agencies these investigators represented are the Federal Attorney General's Office, the Federal Preventive Police and the Center for National Security Investigations (Mexico's equivalent of the CIA).

The Mexican federal government has never admitted that the previous investigations took place, much less their explosive findings. In fact, a CISEN source has asserted that several government operatives – instead of investigating - were assigned to search for and destroy the records of any of these early investigations. Anticipating exactly that response, several investigators said they decided to conceal surreptitious copies of their files.

Officials supplied women

The earliest federal attorney general investigation into the women's murders took place in Juarez during the mid-1990s. Jose "Pelon" Sanchez Naves, a federal judicial police official linked to the drug trade, was familiar with the earlier investigation. Sanchez was gunned down in 1998 in Mexico City before he could publicly reveal the details. Ernesto Zedillo was president of Mexico and Antonio Lozano Gracia was the new federal attorney general.

One of the Mexican federal investigators said they discovered that several high-level Chihuahua State law officials were helping to facilitate "orgies in which young girls who were reported missing later turned up dead." These investigators also said that state officials were suspected only of enabling the sex parties, not the deaths. No action was ever taken against the politically connected law officials.

Jorge Lopez Molinar, former Chihuahua State deputy attorney general in Juarez under Governor Francisco Barrio, was mentioned in a 1996 investigative report which asserted that he knew about the investigation. He died of natural causes in December 2005. Another Chihuahua state official who was mentioned in the investigative report was transferred from Juarez and promoted to a higher position in Mexico City.

A third former official, an alleged enabler, turned up on a list of officials who, according to Federal Special Prosecutor Maria Lopez Urbina, allegedly mishandled the women's murder investigations through negligence or abuse of authority. She submitted the list to Chihuahua State authorities, but nothing came of it. President Vicente Fox referred to Lopez Urbina's work in identifying allegedly negligent Chihuahua State officers during his fourth State of the Union address. Lopez Urbina, who received death threats during her Juarez assignment, was transferred to another Mexican state in 2005.

Deaths to protest NAFTA

According to a second Mexican federal investigation in 1999, authorities in Mexico City concluded that prominent men, known as "juniors," were involved in the Juarez women's murders. The principal investigator said the women were being killed to protest the North American Free Trade Agreement. The deaths were intended to send the government a message because these men suspected that free trade threatened their businesses. The investigators said the businessmen wanted more favorable trade conditions for themselves.

Over the years, the *El Paso Times* reported extensively on the free trade agreement. Initially, many Mexicans did not welcome the free trade accord, and the opposition went well beyond the insurgents known as the Zapatistas. The massive trade agreement between Canada, Mexico and the United States went into effect on January 1, 1994, the day the Zapatistas under rebel commander "Marcos" chose for their uprising in the southern State of Chiapas.

In the first few years of the trade pact, U.S. telephone companies reported widespread vandalism to their telephone lines in Mexico. In the El Paso-Juarez region, several U.S. dairies (Farmers Dairies and Price's Creameries among them) ran into considerable trouble getting their products to Mexican markets.

At that time, a Mexican company held a monopoly on the dairy business in Juarez, where U.S. companies reported the most severe attacks. Incidents included torching a milk delivery truck and destroying a U.S. company's entire milk inventory in a warehouse. The U.S. dairies decided to pull out of Chihuahua State until conditions improved. The leader of a union that represented dairy employees denied that Mexican union workers had anything to do with the attacks. Chihuahua State authorities never arrested anyone in connection with this economic terrorism.

Another free trade controversy arose over the movement of Mexican trucks. Under NAFTA, Mexican trucks are supposed to be able to drive beyond the 25- mile border zone and throughout the rest of the United States and Canada. Unions for organized U.S. truck drivers applied enough pressure to postpone the inevitable, but only for a few years. In Mexico, several trucking companies were implicated in drug-trafficking. The Mexican investigator in the probe that focused on free trade as a motive for the murders during the 1990s described his findings in a letter to President Vicente Fox. He does not know if the president ever got the letter, but the investigator was threatened and now fears for his life.

Investigators implicate "juniors"

A third, more extensive undercover federal investigation that lasted nearly a year and ended in 2001 uncovered startling information about the Juarez women's murders. It also found that powerful men were involved in the femicides. Adolfo Aguilar Zinser, Fox's national security advisor, had direct knowledge of this investigation and confirmed its existence. He died in a vehicle wreck on June 5, 2005.

Some of the names that surfaced during the 1999 investigation turned up again in this second investigation. Mexican federal agents used wiretaps and other techniques to identify the suspects. The effort began with a different goal, but after the agents stumbled on the women's murders and abductions, their probe became an investigation within an investigation.

This time, the federal agents said, women were being collected for orgies and killed for sport. The agents said some of the influential suspects involved in the orgies also participated in the slayings.

What motive did the Mexican federal investigators have for disclosing the sensitive information they had gathered? Their response was chilling:

"We turned over the results of our investigation to our superiors and nothing happened," one said. "We no longer know if we are working for the government or for organized crime." The investigators insisted that they had enough evidence to put the suspects in jail. They hope that one day their investigations will result in the arrests of these killers.

Other confidential sources provided additional information about the suspects. Some of their victims are buried on private property, which makes it difficult to investigate the murders. "Moreno" was the surname of one of their victims. One of the "juniors" reportedly has more than one wife. Another one of these suspects tried to commit suicide more than once with a firearm. These men are investors in the drug trade and allegedly paid law officials large sums of money to protect them. Several served as public officials.

One of them faces potential legal trouble but for a crime that is unrelated to the women's murders. Most of these men are highly superstitious and belong to a secret society that borders on devil worship. Their family political connections extend to U.S. and Mexican presidents. Several "juniors" were in therapy, where they mostly boasted about their misdeeds. On separate occasions, two different Chihuahua State officials were blocked from investigating one of the "juniors" mentioned by the federal investigators.

An FBI source said Bureau informants also said that prominent people are connected to the crimes. This may be why the FBI was blocked from investigating the crimes.

A U.S. intelligence source in 2002 was the first one to mentioned that prominent men were suspects in drug-trafficking or money laundering and in the femicides. In an interview in Texas, the U.S. source said, "We believe some of the same people are involved in the (women's) murders, and boy you should see some of the names."

A hellish flight

One of the "juniors" sexually assaulted a woman during a flight to Las Vegas, according to a member of Mexico's federal Congress. The legislator said a "junior" who had access to a $40 million jet in El Paso, Texas, had invited a couple of young women to accompany him and other friends to Nevada.

At first, the idea seemed exciting and appealed to the women. After boarding the plane, however, they became frightened because the man indicated that he and the others wanted to have an orgy during the flight. "They resisted the best they could, and finally got away from them in Las Vegas," the congressman said. Although the young women were from upper-middle-class families, they were nonetheless afraid to file a police report because of the power the "juniors" possessed, even though the assault took place while in flight over U.S. territory.

Another FBI source offered his reflection on the allegations against the "juniors." He said the crime spree against women "has to have an organized connection to some type of sanctioned or ritualistic behavior."

The suspects that frustrated Mexican agents believed were behind several of the grisly slayings represent enormous wealth and power. Their collective net worth is in the billions of dollars. They have been associated with leaders of Mexico's two major political parties. They have ties to other transnational businesses and wield power that reaches beyond the U.S.-Mexico border. Several of them contributed to Vicente Fox's 2000 election campaign, as well as to presidential candidates before and after him.

Two of the "juniors" have appeared in photographs with the Mexican president. Federal sources said they were uncertain that Fox knows about the "juniors," but that several of his subordinates were informed. One of the "juniors" controlled Mexican federal Customs in Juarez for years. A Mexican federal Customs official said this particular "junior" brandished a gun and threatened to kill him if he failed to play by the rules.

What was the official's offense? He seized contraband that was being brought into Mexico through the Juarez-El Paso border crossing. The local and powerful mafia made it clear that anyone who paid the proper authorities was free to smuggle anything in their trucks or train cars. The Customs official said he decided to avoid further problems by transferring out of Juarez.

Killers are untouchables

There are people who believe these men will never be brought to justice, that they are untouchables. A national leader of Mexico's Institutional Revolutionary Party said privately that powerful people associated with country's "ultra-right wing" were involved in the Juarez femicides. He said that because of what government officials know they are afraid to come near the issue.

U.S. journalist Maury Terry describes a strikingly similar scenario in *The Ultimate Evil*, a book about Americans who conspired to commit murders in the United States and eluded justice because of their powerful connections. Terry's remarkable investigation also linked the Son of Sam murders in New York to the cult killings in California orchestrated by Charles Manson. We can only speculate to what end the explosive Mexican femicide investigations were used. It may be that they were used to extort the killers or to blackmail people for political gain.

28.

PACTS OF POWER

Rita Laura Segato, a Brazilian expert on violent sexual crimes, analyzed the Juarez women's murders from her perspective as a social anthropologist. In 2004, she and Mexican activist Isabel Vericat cut short their visit to the border city during a special forum on the femicides. Vericat helped to organize the forum, and the anthropologist was a featured panelist. Segato and Vericat said they felt threatened by a series of events during their visit, including the death of a young Juarez woman just as the forum was beginning.

The community of activists had come to expect a woman's murder coinciding with such events. Segato said, "Juarez is as insecure as Argentina was during the repressive military dictatorship. I felt that kind of dread again in Juarez." Segato, a native of Argentina, was not familiar with the Mexican investigators' suspicions that powerful men were involved in the crimes. Yet, her theoretical analysis agrees with the facts that federal security agents had uncovered. Mexican author Sergio Gonzalez Rodriguez also asserts in his book *Huesos en el desierto* that powerful people are among the suspects.

Segato said the systematic murders are organized and serve as a signature for the crime organizations. She believes the murders evolved over the years and occurred at different times for different reasons. "The killers used the women's bodies to mark their territory and demonstrate their power. In some cases, it seems the deaths make no sense. They do not appear to be connected, but they are," she said. "The fact that the deaths continue serves to reinforce the pact of silence that exists within this co-fraternity or brotherhood."

The academic said she believes the same criminal network operates as a clandestine power structure parallel to that of the legitimate one. In the state of Chihuahua, it appears that organized crime actually has supplanted the legitimate power structure. In an interview for Channel 4 of London, Mexican criminologist Oscar Maynez Grijalva said "everyone knows that organized crime runs Juarez."

Experts: It is a power trip

In Segato's view, the networks of complicity have extensive security in place. "The violence serves as a system of communication among those who share in this code of power, which continues to unfold and becomes more complex each time. But its motive is to produce and exhibit impunity as a mark of territorial control and of the vitality of the groups. You cannot have these kinds of crimes go on for such a long time and with this degree of impunity unless there is a second state, with a power that is parallel to or of greater force than the power of the state."

"As long as drug dealers are viewed as marginalized elements to be discarded by the society, and as long as gender and sexual crimes are treated as a generalized evil of the region, no one else in Mexico or the rest of the world will feel threatened," Segato warned. "These murders are about something else. The killers are not marginal, and even though the form in which they torture, mark and eliminate their victims appears to be sexual, issues of gender alone do not explain their motivations."

Segato said the murders are not about sex, nor are they casual. The criminal brotherhoods commit these crimes when they open their doors to a new member, when a new member must prove he is worthy and capable, when they successfully close a new business deal, or when another group challenges their territory. "This implies that they must newly seal their complicity, in actions such as drug-trafficking and money laundering, to reinforce the group's loyalty," she said.

The murders could not continue without the authorization or complicity of corrupt police and government officials. It is the ultimate power trip. Mexican federal investigator Rolando Alvarado was right to complain "I can't figure them out," when the murders seemed to make no sense to him.

Krippner: They resent women

Dr. Stanley Krippner, a psychologist and author based in San Francisco, California, travels to Juarez regularly to lead training seminars for psychologists in the region. He attended the Sixteenth World Congress of Sexology in Havana, Cuba, in the summer of 2003, where experts from Juarez presented academic papers on the Juarez women's murders. After the conference, participants signed a petition urging government action to find the killers.

Based on what he knew about the murders, Dr. Krippner said, "It is likely that someone who resents women who work is involved, even if it is someone who is from a higher economic circle than the victims." He and other experts said they believe that someone with a sexual disorder began killing in 1993. Some of the deaths appear to be highly ritualized, with the bodies left in particular positions.

Dr. Krippner and other experts said the killing rituals included cutting off the victim's hair, tying them with their shoelaces, and stabbing, torturing, raping, and mutilating the young women. Many of the victims bore physical similarities, as well.

Sergio Rueda, a Juarez psychologist who collaborates with Krippner, said, "We probably have two or three people who practice the sexual sacrifice of their victims. The modus operandi might vary, but the goal is always the same–to sacrifice the victim. This can vary from verbal insults to torture or death."

Krippner said a lone serial killer or several of them working together could be involved. "You could have someone who is respected in the community, someone with authority, someone who has the resources to pay others to dispose of bodies for him. This makes it easier for him (or them) to avoid detection."

The American psychologist agrees with Robert Ressler and other experts that serial killers experience a form of relief or ecstasy during their crimes and are driven by a compulsion to kill. The experts said such killers are sociopaths, devoid of an internal sense of right and wrong. "Some of them acquire great power and status. If a community is alert, they can detect their behavior," Krippner said.

Segato's analysis supports the federal and state police investigations that uncovered the role of powerful people in the femicides. Krippner's assessment reinforces the theories of Robert Ressler, Dr. Candice Skrapec and Maynez Grijalva that serial killers are responsible for several of the murders. In 1999, FBI profilers theorized that one or more serial killers were involved in approximately thirty of the earlier murders. In all of these cases, it appears that the objective of the killers is to kill or "sacrifice" their victim. One set of killers does it to assert power, and the other does it out of compulsion. Under these scenarios, the community of accomplices is small enough that it is possible for the crimes and the criminals to overlap.

Mexico appoints new officials

During the latter half of Vicente Fox's administration, two women were appointed to lead new federal posts charged with looking into the murders. They were federal Special Prosecutor Maria Lopez Urbina, a veteran law enforcement official, and Commissioner Guadalupe Morfin Otero, a former Jalisco State human rights official.

It was evident from the limitations placed on them that the government did not intend to put anyone in jail for the femicides, at least not those described by Segato, the FBI profilers and the psychologists. If officials were serious about solving the murders, then they would the investigators who possessed useful information.

U.S. and Mexican intelligence files mention people with knowledge that could provide police with relevant leads. Among the surnames in their files of people that could be helpful are Molinar, Sotelo, Hank, Tafoya, Alvarez, Tellez, Solis, Sanchez, Rivera, Fernandez, Zaragoza, Cabada, Sanchez, Loya, Hernandez, Molina, Fuentes, Lopez, Urbina, Cardenas, Cano, Martinez, and Dominguez. None of the people who were contacted about what they might know volunteered any information.

Any of them that possesses knowledge that could prove useful to authorities ought to share it with the authorities. They could be holding back out of fear or from a reluctance to offend friends or relatives of powerful rivals. The drug cartels also have extensive intelligence networks, and it is likely that the cartel leaders also know the identities of the killers.

A possible strategy would be to offer potential informants a confidential polygraph test, to establish credibility. A neutral international body, such as the United Nations special task force that reported on the Juarez murders in 2003, could administer the test. Any information they provide will help prevent more women from being abducted or killed.

FBI's startling revelation

"Our informants tell us that they are still killing women in Juarez," an FBI official said, "except that now they are disposing of them in different ways. They are dismembering their bodies and are feeding the body parts to hogs at a ranch. Why hogs? Because hogs will eat anything."

During a previous interview with Oscar Valadez, the former Chihuahua state deputy attorney general, I asked him about the FBI's shocking revelation. But Valadez's only response was, "Oh–I hadn't heard that."

Sadly, the possibility is not far-fetched. In Canada, authorities there reported that an affluent farmer accused of being a serial killer was suspected of using his hog farm to eliminate the remains of his alleged victims.

29.

CHIHUAHUA CITY

Cynthia Kiecker's nightmare began when she and her husband, Ulises Perzabal, a Mexican citizen, joined the growing list of dubious suspects arrested in connection with the femicides in Chihuahua State. The couple with the "hippie look" stood out, and that, apparently, was enough for the state judicial police to accuse them of killing Viviana Rayas Arellanes.

The body of the sixteen-year-old Chihuahua City girl was found outside the state capital on May 28, 2003. Like other victims before her, she had been raped and tortured. The next day, police took Kiecker and Perzabal into custody.

Jose Rayas, Viviana's father, demanded swift justice for his daughter. Because he was a labor union leader of some influence, the authorities wasted no time in producing a couple of suspects. The problem is that they were scapegoats.

Kiecker and Perzabal said police used electric prods, near-asphyxiation, and psychological abuse to force them to confess to a murder they did not commit. Kiecker told her family police threatened to penetrate her with a wooden stake if she did not sign a statement that was prepared in advance of the torture sessions. She did not even know what was in the statement. "I could hear them torture Ulises. I could hear the screams," she said.

The story Chihuahua authorities came up with was filled with inconsistencies. They were under pressure because it seemed that Chihuahua City was turning into another killing field for young women.

At first, the authorities said that Kiecker and Perzabal operated a store that sold occult items and used drugs to lure young girls for satanic rituals. Police said Viviana Rayas was killed during a sex party at the couple's home. Later, the authorities said Kiecker bludgeoned the girl to death with a pipe because she was jealous that her husband was paying too much attention to the teenager. However, the state's autopsy report found that Rayas was strangled. It said nothing about blows to her head.

Victim's family skeptical

Jose Rayas said his family believed the authorities at first. But they later dismissed the official account and decided to conduct their own, investigation. Rayas told British journalist Sandra Jordan that private investigators he had hired to help him solve his daughter's case received death threats and were forced to leave the city.

Maurice Parker, the U.S. consul in Juarez at the time, sent a representative to interview Kiecker at the jail in Chihuahua City, which is about 250 miles south of the U.S. border. The consul's office followed up with a strong letter of protest to the Chihuahua state government, complaining about the conditions of her detention. U.S. officials also were concerned about the refusal of Mexican officials to investigate the torture allegations.

Kiecker, 44, a native of Bloomington, Minnesota, had lived and worked in Chihuahua for five years. She and her husband operated a small shop where they sold the jewelry that they made and designed. Kiecker and Perzabal, a musician, had even participated in marches to protest the violence against women in Chihuahua City and Juarez.

Protests against detentions

In their desperation to get Kiecker out of jail, her family sought help from American politicians. U.S. Senator Norm Coleman of Minnesota conveyed his concerns to Mexico's ambassador to the United States, Juan Jose Bremer. The senator also raised the issue in a letter to Mexican President Vicente Fox. In a written statement, Coleman said the U.S. consular officials who visited Kiecker in jail had "confirmed physical marks of possible torture."

Shortly after Mexican officials announced the murder charges against the couple, two witnesses told reporters in Chihuahua City that they were coerced into incriminating Kiecker and Perzabal. They called a news conference to retract the statements they gave police against the couple. The witnesses claimed that state police had tortured them, too. A third witness who gave police a statement incriminating the couple fled the area out of fear for his safety. Mexican federal Commissioner Guadalupe Morfin Otero pressed for an investigation into the torture allegations.

During Governor Patricio Martinez's administration, neither U.S. Consul Maurice Parker nor Morfin nor anyone else was able to get the Chihuahua authorities to release the couple. People were beginning to wonder who really ran the state of Chihuahua.

Other U.S. advocates sought help for Kiecker and her husband, including New Mexico Governor Bill Richardson, who has family ties in Chihuahua. Richardson traveled regularly to Chihuahua City and met often with Governor Martinez to discuss trade and economic issues.

Richardson, who was considered a potential presidential contender for the 2008 election, had served as the U.S. ambassador to the United Nations. In that post, he represented the U.S. government in internationally sensitive matters involving human rights.

After pressure from U.S. groups like Amigos de las Mujeres de Juarez, Richardson asked his staff to check into the complaints.

For the most part, though, the American governor appeared to activists to be more interested in brokering trade deals with Martinez than in trying to get a falsely accused American citizen out of the Mexican governor's state jail.

In April of 2004, Chihuahua trade and tourism official Leopoldo Mares Delgado announced that, thanks to agreements negotiated by Richardson and Martinez, a manufacturer in Chihuahua City was going to sell its underground fuel tanks worth $50,000 each to the City of Albuquerque, New Mexico. Publicly, Richardson remained silent about Kiecker's case and the femicides in general.

New Mexico State Senator Mary Jane Garcia, on the other hand, had denounced the femicides for years. She raised the issue with her Mexican counterparts at governmental binational meetings. "We're trying to get some help for the women of Juarez," Garcia said in an interview.

Kiecker: No interest in justice

Carol Kiecker, Cynthia's mother, attended the historic international V-Day rally and march in El Paso and Juarez on February 14, 2004. CNN's Anderson Cooper interviewed me remotely the day before for a program about the event. Hollywood celebrities Jane Fonda and Sally Field traveled to Juarez to take part in the protest.

Kiecker said her family had incurred crushing debts to help with her daughter and son-in-law's legal defense. "There seems to be no interest in giving my daughter and her husband any sort of justice," she said wistfully. The pained look on her face was unforgettable as she talked about Cynthia Kiecker's plight that day at the plaza in downtown El Paso.

Judges in Chihuahua state postponed any definitive action on the case while Governor Martinez was still in office. A new governor, Jose Reyes Baeza Terrazas, took office in October 2004, and the Kiecker family hoped things might change.

Femicides in Chihuahua City

After the death of sixteen-year-old Norma Luna Holguin in 1999, Chihuahua City began to experience a series of young women's murders similar to the slayings that had shaken Juarez for more than a decade. The victims were similar, and so, apparently, was the *modus operandi*.

Paloma Escobar Ledezma's parents traveled from Chihuahua City to Juarez in 2002 to discuss their daughter's case with border reporters. Lucha Castro, a courageous lawyer and activist from the state capital, accompanied the couple to the meeting at Sanborn's on Avenida Triunfo de la Republica.

Many people used the restaurant for meetings and press conferences. Carlos Slim, Latin America's wealthiest businessman, owns the popular chain of Sanborn's eateries and upscale retail stores.

Paloma's father, Dolores Alberto Escobar, could barely contain his tears as he and his wife, Norma Ledezma Ortega, described their futile efforts to convince the authorities to investigate Paloma's disappearance. The father, a former municipal police officer, turned away and rubbed his eyes, trying not to break down during the interview.

The teenage girl worked at the Aerotec maquiladora in Chihuahua City. She disappeared on March 2, 2002. Her mother, Norma Ledezma, said the family last saw Paloma when she left home in the afternoon. According to witnesses, others saw the teenager about fifteen minutes after she left home to head over to the downtown ECCO computer school she attended. She was seen with a man named Francisco Ramirez, an ECCO recruiter from the Mexican state of Chiapas.

Escobar's body was found on March 29, 2002, dumped in the outskirts of the city. Even as her body rotted amid the desert shrubs, state police urged the family not to worry. The police claimed they had seen the teenager at nightclubs with friends having a good time.

The police account was especially cruel considering the timing of the Escobar's death. According to her autopsy report, Escobar was killed within two days of her disappearance. "She was already dead when (the police) old us they saw her having a good time," Norma Ledezma said. "How is this possible?"

Planting evidence

A Chihuahua State police commander was accused of allegedly planting a picture of Paloma Escobar's boyfriend where her body was discovered. Witnesses told the authorities they had given the boyfriend's picture to the official, which meant police may have been trying to incriminate the boy in their rush to solve the case.

Escobar's relatives received death threats to discourage them from investigating the murder on their own. Many Juarez families and human rights groups said they had experienced exactly the same things. Norma Ledezma said things got so bad that her husband had to go into hiding for a time.

In its 2003 "Intolerable Killings" report, Amnesty International said state police in Chihuahua City failed to follow leads for several suspects in Escobar's case. "The man (ECCO promoter Francisco Ramirez who was a suspect) left the city, and the authorities claim that they lost trace of him," the report said.

The international human rights organization also said there were "clues and testimonies [that] seem to establish a link" between the cases of four other Chihuahua City girls reported missing:

Yesenia Vega Marquez, 16; Minerva Torres Albeldaño, 18; Julieta Gonzalez Valenzuela, 17; and Rosalba Pizarro Ortega, 16. But, for unknown reasons, police never investigated the possible links.

Later, authorities confirmed that Torres and Pizarro had been killed.

Just like Juarez

Chihuahua City was turning into another graveyard for young women. It was also beginning to resemble Juarez in another significant way. Terrifying execution-style murders linked to the drug cartels had now spread to the state capital. A knowledgeable source said that following the U.S.-Mexico "Plaza Sweep" investigation, high-ranking cartel leaders left Juarez and moved to Chihuahua City during the Patricio Martinez administration, to put more distance between themselves and U.S. authorities at the border. They wanted to avoid capture and extradition to the United States.

Manuel Esparza Navarrete, a former state official and a government spokesman for the women's murder cases in Juarez, told the *Arizona Republic* in July 2003 that he knew of only three or four cases of murdered women in Chihuahua City. By May of 2003, however, the capital city had recorded six such deaths.

He also insisted there was no connection between the murders in the two cities, and that sex was not the motive in the Chihuahua City murders.

Yet, Chihuahua City victims Miriam Gallegos and Erika Carrillo were found partially nude. Authorities in Chihuahua City had said that Paloma Escobar was found clutching pubic hair in one hand. Her family discovered later that state investigators never ordered a DNA test for the pubic hair evidence.

Neyra Azucena Cervantes

Another Chihuahua City case, the brutal death of Neyra Azucena Cervantes, also took a strange twist. She was murdered in May of 2003. While she was still considered missing, the girl's family sent word of her disappearance to relatives in the state of Chiapas. The news led her cousin, David Meza, to make the long journey from Chiapas to Chihuahua to help search for her.

Once Meza arrived, however, Chihuahua State police ordered him detained, and then allegedly tortured him into confessing to his cousin's death. Patricia Cervantes, the victim's mother, said none of her relatives believed David Meza had anything to do with the death of Cervantes. Police suggested that he was in love with his cousin and killed her because she had rejected him.

The young man was trapped by the same judicial system that held many other suspects who proclaimed their innocence: Sharif, Cynthia Kiecker, Ulises Perzabal, the "Rebeldes," the "Toltecas," and the two bus drivers arrested in 2001. One of the ways Patricia Cervantes helped to support her family was to cook meals for employees of the TOMZA gas company, which also employed one of her relatives.

David Meza's family in California asked U.S. lawmakers, including U.S. Representative Hilda Solis, to intervene in the case. A Chihuahua State judge finally issued a ruling that set Meza free for lack of evidence. His relatives attributed his release in the summer of 2006 to pressure from the international community.

One question remained, however: Who killed Neyra Cervantes?

California deputies get involved

In May of 2004, a group of mothers of victims from Chihuahua City and Juarez provided DNA samples to investigators from the Alameda County Sheriff's Office in Northern California. The deputies, investigating a "Jane Doe" murder in their jurisdiction, had noticed the unidentified victim bore an uncanny resemblance to Minerva Torres Albeldaño, one of the missing women from Chihuahua State. The deputies decided to travel to the border to find out whether the Chihuahua girl's family was willing to provide a DNA sample. To their surprise, several families offered to do this.

The deputies explained the situation during a meeting at the Casa Mayapan cafe in El Paso, Texas. Victims' families, federal Commissioner Guadalupe Morfin Otero, and U.S. Consulate officials were present. The deputies told the families that they would run the DNA tests "as a humanitarian favor."

After the tests were done, the Alameda County Sheriff's deputies reported that the skeleton Chihuahua State officials said belonged to Neyra Azucena Cervantes matched the DNA of her relatives. But, they said, the skull could not be hers because it was a man's skull.

According to a news release by Amigos de las Mujeres de Juarez, which the Alameda County Sheriff's office confirmed, "The skull in the [Chihuahua] photographs is that of a man, not of a woman. The teeth that appear in the photographs are not the same teeth that are in the pictures of Neyra when she was alive."

Investigations lacking

The advocacy group Justicia para Nuestras Hijas (Justice for Our Daughters) said fourteen young women were reported missing in Chihuahua City between 1999 and September of 2003. Several of them eventually were found dead. Others are still missing.

In another case, Justicia para Nuestras Hijas also looked into the disappearance of Karen Avila Herrera, 14, who vanished from Chihuahua City on February 4, 2003.

The adolescent turned up alive in Juarez, saying she escaped from a woman who had abducted her.

Avila alleged that after escaping, she sought refuge with a Juarez family, who then contacted her family in Chihuahua City. Avila's mother, Martha Herrera, traveled to Juarez immediately to bring her daughter home.

The girl told her family that she had been coerced into going to Juarez with a woman named "Yaritza," who wanted her to work as a prostitute.

Chihuahua lawyer Lucha Castro and activist Alma Gomez criticized the authorities for failing to investigate Avila's alleged abductor or any of the other information the victim provided. Instead, Gomez said, state officials tried to intimidate and discredit their advocacy organization. The activists said they suffered threats and violence because of their work.

With so many young women still missing, it is possible that some of them were victims of human-trafficking rings. But no Mexican officials, at the state or federal level, investigated that possibility.

A film crew from Channel 4 of London said they got a keen sense of Chihuahua-style justice during a 2003 visit to investigate the women's murders in Juarez and Chihuahua City. London reporter Sandra Jordan and her cameraman said they had covered many hot spots around the world but had never encountered the levels of corruption they found in the State of Chihuahua. The journalists said that while they were filming in Juarez, state police officers who also worked as security guards for prominent residents accosted them. The team's investigation was featured in a documentary titled *City of Lost Girls*.

30.

THE FEMICIDES SPREAD

Cynthia Kiecker, 45, and Ulises Perzabal, 46, were released after spending eighteen months in a Mexican jail for a crime they did not commit. They walked out of the prison on December 17, 2004, just in time for the Christmas holidays. The Chihuahua State judge who ruled in their favor said he could find no evidence linking the couple to the death of Viviana Rayas. The judge, however, refrained from commenting on the couple's allegations of torture.

Their release came just after the new Chihuahua governor, Jose Reyes Baeza Terrazas, took over the state government. Two weeks before Kiecker and Perzabal were set free, Cynthia called from the Chihuahua City jail to say she was optimistic that things would go well for her and her husband. Fortunately, she was right.

During Kiecker's imprisonment, she got to know Mexican singer Gloria Trevi before the famous performer was released from the same jail. Kiecker said prison officials allowed her to continue making her jewelry, and she sold several pieces to Trevi and to the wife and daughter of a Chihuahua State official.

"I told the official's wife when she came to the jail to please tell her husband that Ulises and I were innocent," Kiecker said.

After they walked out of the Mexican jail, U.S. consular officials and Mexican federal agents escorted the couple and watched as they crossed over to El Paso, Texas. Both governments wanted to avoid any incidents.

"What worries me most is how we are going to clean up the horrendous image of us that the Chihuahua authorities had fabricated," Cynthia

Kiecker said. "We never drugged anyone, and we were not devil worshipers. And we certainly were not killers. It was evil the way they presented us to the public."

Kiecker also said she was going to miss Mexico, where she had lived and worked, and where she had met her husband of twenty years.

Following their release, Perzabal mentioned an intriguing episode from his past. He and Kiecker were invited to speak at the University of Texas at El Paso, where they shared the harrowing details of their torture and unjust detention. During a dinner after the forum, Perzabal said he had also been a victim of Mexico's "Dirty War." He said Mexican security forces had linked him to the September 23 Communist League, an insurgent group that operated during the 1970s in Chihuahua and other Mexican states. "I was tortured during that era when they detained me," he said.

Perhaps that was the real reason, and not his hippie look, that Chihuahua State authorities decided to focus on Perzabal when Viviana Rayas was killed. The Mexican government likely already had a file on him from the "Dirty War" years. The couple moved to Minnesota, where they started a new jewelry business that features their original designs. They said they did not forget the others they left behind and advocated for the release of David Meza and Abdel Latif Sharif Sharif.

Crimes across Mexico

Five years after young women began turning up dead in Chihuahua City, Marcela Lagarde, a Mexican congresswoman, asked her government to look into the femicides that activists were reporting in various parts of Mexico. Brutal murders and disappearances of women were taking place in Chihuahua City, Tijuana, Mexicali, Ixtapa-Zihuatenejo, Mexico City, Reynosa, and Matamoros. A similar pattern of murders also appeared in the Mexican states of Nuevo Leon, Mexico State, Tamaulipas, Chiapas, Oaxaca, Quintana Roo, Veracruz, and Guanajuato.

Lagarde was chairperson of a special legislative commission tasked with investigating the increasing number of gender murders. Federal Congresswoman Irene Blanco, Sharif's former legal representative, served on the commission for a short time. Concerned Mexican legislators said the brutal violence against women was not normal. It was as if the country had suddenly awakened to the long-running terror.

Lagarde's commission conducted an analysis of the women's murders throughout the nation. The study, though well-intentioned, had its shortcomings. Police experts agreed that what is really needed is an investigation that leads to the arrests of the killers.

Other femicides

In 2003, *Cambio* magazine published an article about the murders of sixteen women that shocked the community of Leon, Guanajuato, in President Vicente Fox's home state. Writers Alejandro Suverza and Catalina Gaya said the deaths occurred at a rate of one each month between January 2002 and May 2003. The crimes were especially alarming in a state most Mexicans considered a relatively safe place. The deaths in Mexico were catching the attention of other Latin American countries, such as Argentina and Chile, which also published news accounts of the crimes.

In the northern Mexican border state of Nuevo Leon, an interdisciplinary group counted twenty-nine women's murders between January 2002 and August 2003. The Nuevo Leon Women's State Institute reported that ninety-four women were murdered in the state over a five-year period. According to human rights advocate Omeheira Lopez, the city of Reynosa recorded 136 women's homicides between 1999 and February 2004.

Amigos de Las Mujeres de Juarez, a U.S. advocacy group based in Las Cruces, New Mexico, took note of the alarming trend.

The organization sent letters in November 2003 to Mexican President Vicente Fox and Chihuahua Governor Patricio Martinez. "Evidence is also mounting that the killings have spread," the letters said. The new fear was that what had happened in Juarez could happen anywhere.

Police knew of abductions

A Mexican government official, who provided crucial information about the situation in Chihuahua State, recalled a disturbing account that suggests human traffickers may have been targeting young women.

During the 1990s, a Juarez family sought his help in finding a missing teenage girl. He then called on a police official and told him about the family's plight. The official asked him to wait while he checked with his contacts in Mexico City. The result was instant, and the girl was quickly located. The official who managed to find her said she would be sent back to her family provided that no one asked any questions or filed a police report. She made it back home safely, and that was the end of the story.

In another case, police abducted a teenage girl in Juarez and took her to a house that was still under construction. The police used the building as a safe house to stash drugs and hold meetings about drug deals with officers from other law enforcement agencies. In the meantime, the girl was passed around from police officer to police officer.

Eventually, one of the officers took pity on her and took her back to her home. He told her mother to be thankful that her daughter was not killed. He also warned the mother not to report the matter to the authorities. Fearing for her safety, the family removed the girl from Juarez and hid her elsewhere in Mexico.

Human-trafficking

Several cases involving human-trafficking in the United States have prompted the U.S. federal government to make human slavery an investigative priority. Armed with new legislation, such as the PROTECT Act, and a mandate from President George W. Bush to crack down on this global travesty, U.S. Immigration and Customs Enforcement (ICE) officials were able to rescue dozens of victims from foreign countries.

In one such case, ICE agents uncovered a ring in New Jersey in which teenage girls were smuggled from Mexico and forced into prostitution after arriving in the United States. Authorities identified six suspects.

Four were convicted and sentenced and two became fugitives. Investigators did not disclose the girls' Mexican hometowns.

A 2004 article in the *New York Times Magazine* about human-trafficking in Mexico quoted officials who claimed that extensive networks are involved. Peter Landesman's in-depth and controversial story also alleged that corrupt police and government officials protected the human-smuggling gangs.

Before that, in the year 2000, the United Nations Children's Fund (UNICEF) and Mexico's Integral Family Development Office (DIF) released a joint report about child sex exploitation, including sex tourism and child prostitution, in Juarez and five other Mexican cities. The report elicited hardly a yawn from Juarez officials.

A couple of U.S. and Mexican federal investigators offered a plausible explanation for the lack of response from the Mexican government. They said authorities are aware of videotapes that implicate a Juarez politician and a highly placed Mexican federal official in sexual situations with young boys. A Mexican official further alleged that people within his government protected a ring of pedophiles who served in high-level positions. The deeper one dug; the filthier things seemed.

In 1997, Mexican authorities detained three men on suspicion of child sex and pornography. One of them was a doctor and former government health official, and a second man was a construction supervisor in El Paso. Police in Juarez found videotapes of young children engaging in sex with adults, including the doctor. But the case was dropped after the accused successfully argued that children as young as nine and eleven years old were paid to have sex with the adults. That made the children prostitutes and the sex consensual, according to them. The doctor, who drove a Grand Marquis, was set free after paying a bond.

Tijuana déjà vu

Tijuana, another border city, is similar to Juarez in many respects. It has a thriving maquiladora industry, a growing population and a pronounced drug trade controlled by the violent Arellano Felix organization. It also has an opera company and active environmentalist groups. In May of 2003, I traveled to Tijuana to attend a border journalists' conference. During a break, I walked into a shopping center directly across the street from the conference hotel.

Inside the shopping center, I came across a kiosk with fliers that bore pictures of missing teenage girls and pleas for information. There was an ECCO computer school just a few feet from the kiosk. The faces of the missing girls on the fliers were not much different from the young women who had vanished in Juarez and Chihuahua City.

Over the course of the conference, *Zeta*, a Tijuana newspaper edited by the legendary Jesus Blancornelas, published an interview with former Chihuahua Governor Francisco Barrio, who was in Tijuana that week. Barrio was on the National Action Party's list of presidential hopefuls for the 2006 election. Asked about the Juarez women's murders, Barrio told the newspaper that the murders that occurred during his administration had been solved.

The feisty *Zeta* published a running challenge to Baja California's authorities with an article that asks, "Jorge Hank Rhon: Why did your bodyguards assassinate me?" The ad refers to the 1988 assassination of *Zeta* co-founder Hector Felix Miranda. Blancornelas said Felix frequently criticized Tijuana mayor Hank and his associates in his columns. Two men who worked for a Hank family member were jailed in connection with the journalist's death.

Hank has denied any connection to the writer's death. He has gambling operations in Juarez and Chihuahua City, and enjoys close ties to Chihuahua state government officials.

In 2004, another *Zeta* staff member was shot to death. Government investigators blamed drug traffickers, while the beleaguered Blancornelas continued to produce his newspaper.

Jane Fonda and Salma Hayek

The trail of brutally slain women actually stretches from the border city of Juarez to Central America. Actress Jane Fonda's trip to support the V-Day rally in Juarez in 2004 was inspired in part by the numbing murders of women in Guatemala. During her visit there, Fonda said she would return with "an army to stand beside Guatemalan women to say to the world what is going on here. ... You have even more women killed than in Ciudad Juarez."

Two years later, Fonda teamed up with actress Salma Hayek to perform Eve Ensler's "Vagina Monologues" in Mexico City in support of the women in Juarez. Hayek reiterated her commitment to help end gender violence during a star-studded event on June 22, 2006. According to EFE, Spain's news wire service, high-end fashion line Dolce & Gabbana sponsored the program at the Hollywood Roosevelt Hotel that honored Hayek and the Salma Hayek Foundation.

Various celebrities attended the function and watched an excerpt of Lorena Mendez-Quiroga's documentary about the Juarez femicides called "Border Echoes." At the event, Hayek said, "We are demanding justice for these women. This cannot be happening. We are not going to look the other way."

In 2004, Helen Mack, of the Myrna Mack Foundation in Guatemala, was a keynote speaker for a human rights forum in Juarez intended to foster the exchange of ideas between activists in Central America and in the Juarez and El Paso region.

Mack said she has spent more than a dozen years trying to get her sister's killers put away.

A military death squad assassinated her sister, anthropologist Myrna Mack Chang, in 1990. Helen Mack has resorted to international tribunals to prosecute the intellectual authors of Myrna's murder, who reportedly were high-ranking military officials.

Femicides in Guatemala

Helen Mack said 700 hundred girls and women were murdered in Guatemala between 2000 and 2004. Although gangs called "Maras Salva Truchas" were blamed for most of the murders, the truth is that the authorities have not produced any credible suspects or lines of investigation to explain the killings.

Juarez academic Julia Monarrez Fragoso refers to this violent trend as the "extermination of women." She said femicides are characterized by brutal acts of violence against a woman's body, such as rape, torture, strangulation, stabbing, and mutilation. Feminists like Jane Caputi and Diana Russell use "femicide" to refer to women's murders, regardless of who commits them (spouse, boyfriend, relatives, or strangers). They contend that femicides differ from most murders of men because they are motivated by a desire to assert power.

Femicides are similar to hate crimes but are based on gender instead of race or ethnicity, academics assert.

Rolando Alvarado, the Mexican federal official who supervised the federal investigation of several femicides in Juarez, said he "would not rule out hate" as a motive for the women's slayings. In that sense he is right; the manner in which the deaths are committed suggests a burning hatred of women.

According to a *New York Times* article dated October 21, 2005, "Guatemala has suffered an epidemic of gruesome killings of women that are as mysterious as they are brutal." The article said that when a young woman disappears in Guatemala, "her body turns up a few days later in a garbage bag or in an open field." The deaths appear very much like the murders in Juarez and Chihuahua City.

"Many of the women's faces and bodies have been mutilated, and many have been tortured sexually or otherwise. Some of the bodies have messages, like 'death to bitches,' scrawled on them," according to the article. Sources interviewed for the story said the killers might include people who took part in that country's civil war, either as insurgents or as police and soldiers.

In other words, a vast number of unemployed killers with access to firearms seem to still be doing what they were trained to do. This, too, sounds like what has happened in parts of Mexico. Advocacy groups began documenting the Guatemala women's murders in the year 2000.

There is another factor that links the Guatemala murders to the ones in Chihuahua State – the active presence of the Carrillo Fuentes drug cartel. In his 1999 book about Amado Carrillo Fuentes, author Jose Alfredo

Andrade Bojorges said the cartel had operations in Guatemala and El Salvador. From that, it is logical to assume that the cartel recruited many of its workers from the ranks of former insurgents and government security officers, and these began a terror campaign for the cartel.

In June 1993, Mexican drug lord Joaquin "Chapo" Guzman Loera was arrested in Guatemala and turned over to Mexican officials. "Chapo," who escaped from a high-security prison in Guadalajara, continues to operate out of Guatemala. Andrade's book outlines the cartel's relations and activities in some of the same Mexican states that experienced an increase in brutal women's murders.

Perhaps it is no coincidence that a man from Guatemala was arrested in Mexico in 2004, accused of numerous rapes in Chihuahua City and Juarez. The authorities said he traveled frequently, and unhindered, between the U.S.-Mexico border and Guatemala.

Authorities said Carrillo Fuentes cartel operatives purchased homes in Chile, while operatives of the Arellano Felix cartel bought a ranch in Brazil. Both groups sought to extend their reach into South America.

Femicides in the Americas

Alarmed by what is going on in Guatemala, the United Nations sent a representative to gather facts about violence against women there.

El Salvador, too, is experiencing a growing number of violent murders of women. In 2002 alone, El Salvador reported 238 women's murders that its government blamed on domestic abuse.

The geography of these femicides is vast, and extensive investigations are required to understand their nature, the motives, and the people and structures responsible for them. As a starting point, investigators must determine which of the crimes were committed by strangers, relatives, gangs, organized criminals, or serial killers. In many of the Mexican cases, the authorities have yet to identify the victims (the Jane Does), a basic and essential factor to arrive at the truth.

More research is needed to confirm exactly how many women are missing in those countries and whether organized crime is involved. Human-trafficking, sex slavery and organized crime may explain in part the transnational violence. U.S. Representatives Hilda Solis and Barbara Lee, both in California, are leading efforts to bring these atrocities to the attention of the U.S. Congress. The Juarez women's murders have served to raise the public's awareness of gender murders and abductions in North and Central American countries.

The cocaine trail

In April of 2005, Manuel Zelaya, the new president of Honduras, made a provocative statement. He well may be the only head of state in that region to speak the truth. In a news interview, he said the hard line employed by his predecessor against gangs like the Mara Salva Truchas served only to divert attention from the real source of generalized violence in his country – "the traffic through Honduras of Colombian cocaine bound for U.S.

streets." He also told the *Miami Herald*, "There was a ... political campaign to blame the crime on the youth."

Over time, scholars have documented "wars" for control of petroleum, trade routes, and even opium fields. The latest war appears to be over the lucrative cocaine market.

Canada's missing women

Organized crimes that cross boundaries and jurisdictions may prove overwhelming for conventional police forces that limit themselves to narrow locales. The new wave of global crime requires a police force with transnational authority and expertise in international investigations.

In Canada, Ruth Mustus, an activist, is trying desperately to inform the world about the approximately 500 mostly indigenous women who disappeared in her country over the past twenty years. Mustus says the women matter little to authorities because they are viewed as invisible victims who are marginalized by Canadian society. This, too, sounds a lot like Juarez, where the bodies of victims are treated like trash, tossed in dumps, sewage ditches and cement-filled containers.

Countries experiencing the systematic deaths of women must recognize what is happening, and their governments must pursue a collaborative course to alleviate the human destruction.

These crimes transcend the definitions of the U.S. federal Uniformed Crime Code for reporting crime statistics. In these times, police require the kind of training that enables them to analyze femicides from a broader sociological perspective than most law enforcement academies provide in their training.

The conventional paradigms no longer apply to this spreading cancer of gender murders. Unpunished crime fuels more crime.

If Mexico's government fails in Juarez, then the long-term results for its civil society will be social chaos, increased crime, and anarchy.

PART IV

"I said in my heart, God will judge the righteous and the wicked, for there is a time for every matter and for every work."

Ecclesiastes 3:17

31.

THE POLITICIANS

There is a saying that in Mexico, everything happens, yet nothing happens. This is especially true of Juarez. It is true of the drug corruption, it is true of the "dirty war" era, and it is true of the countless murders of men and women perpetrated by various mafias and tolerated by the government. The events that shaped Mexican politics over the past thirty years affected the nation as a whole, the U.S.-Mexico border, and conditions in Juarez.

For many years, Mexico operated as an apparent democracy. Since the Mexican Revolution of 1910, which killed a million people and displaced countless others, a single party known as the Institutional Revolutionary Party ruled Mexico.

The country had a vertical system of power, and the president was at the top of the hierarchy. State governors wielded absolute power over their territories. Elected officials benefited from prosecutorial immunity known as *fuero*.

During the 1980s, Mexico suffered two major convulsions. One was the 1985 earthquake in Mexico City that killed thousands more people than the government publicly admitted. The temblor forced many people to move to outlying areas, and some made their way to the border to find jobs in the maquiladoras.

Three years earlier, in 1982, the country experienced one of its worst currency devaluations ever.

Mexicans have come to expect peso devaluations at the end of every six-year presidential term. Political insiders said it was a way of looting the treasury before the next president was installed.

The next worst devaluation occurred after President Carlos Salinas de Gortari left office in 1994, when Ernesto Zedillo came on board as the new president. The 1994 peso crisis virtually destroyed Mexico's new rising middle class. It was the same year NAFTA went into effect.

The end of Zedillo's term did not produce a devaluation. Instead, it left the country holding the bag for the FOBAPROA banking scandal that cost taxpayers millions upon millions of dollars, nearly the price of another currency crisis.

Vicente Fox was the first president in more than seventy years to be elected from an opposition party, the National Action Party. During his administration, the power of the executive branch was decentralized, and the federal congress received more power. The judiciary was still trying to operate as an independent branch of the national government.

Official offenses ignored

Carlos Ramirez, a left-leaning Mexican political analyst and publisher of *La Crisis* magazine, has noted the unwillingness of Mexican presidents to punish their predecessors for serious national offenses, such as the recent banking-loan scandal. Human rights activists, including Rosario Ibarra de Piedra, have criticized presidents for failing to investigate the "dirty war" atrocities and for failing to deliver justice in several high-profile assassinations.

Officials have not cleared these murders, which include the 1984 death of Mexico City journalist Manuel Buendia during the administration of President Miguel De la Madrid. Buendia's death is pivotal because he was investigating the alleged roles of the Mexican government and the military in the drug trade.

His sacrificial death represents a demarcation in Mexico's modern history.

Although a government operative was arrested in the journalist's murder, many Mexicans suspected the order to kill him came from much higher in the government ranks, perhaps as high as Los Pinos (Mexico's presidential house). *La Crisis* publisher Carlos Ramirez has asked that the government reopen the investigation. "[Over] time, it was proven that Buendia's assassination was a political crime, which initiated [a] long cycle of instability and destabilization, and the first that drew the line of narco-violence," Ramirez wrote. Since then, many more journalists have died violently, in Chihuahua state and other parts of Mexico.

Ramirez said the arrest of a federal security officer in Buendia's murder ended an investigation that should have included the late General Juan Arevalo Gardoqui, former Interior Secretary Manuel Bartlett, and former President Miguel De la Madrid. All three denied any involvement in either the journalist's murder or a cover-up.

Among other things, Buendia was investigating connections between the government and drug dealers like Rafael Caro Quintero, Miguel Felix Gallardo and Miguel Fonseca, the drug barons of the 1980s.

Witnesses in the murder trial of slain DEA agent Enrique "Kiki" Camarena implicated General Arevalo Gardoqui, along with the three drug lords. The murder of Camarena, a U.S. federal agent assigned to Guadalajara, was traced back to the drug barons and police officials.

U.S. officials had notified the Mexican government about a giant marijuana plantation at Bufalo, Chihuahua, during the administration of Governor Fernando Melendez Baeza. In 2006, the former governor sought and obtained a federal senator's post in the July 2, 2006, election. Another big marijuana plantation was discovered in Chihuahua State shortly after Patricio Martinez ended his term in 2004. It was bigger than the one discovered at Bufalo in the 1980s. U.S. drug investigators said the notorious Herrera drug clan owned the new marijuana fields near Jimenez, Chihuahua.

A shocking video

The U.S. Customs Service disclosed a video showing how Mexican soldiers killed several Mexican federal agents who were trying to intercept an airplane carrying cocaine from Colombia. Writer Andrew Reding said the Mexican government under Salinas de Gortari chalked up the massacre in the state of Veracruz to a case of mistaken identity, but that the "autopsies revealed that some of the [federal agents] had been tortured, then executed." Under General Rafael Macedo de la Concha, the former federal attorney general, the soldiers involved in the 1991 attack were exonerated.

Other murders during the 1990s that shook Mexico and were never solved to the satisfaction of its citizens were the slayings of Roman Catholic Cardinal Juan Jesus Posadas Ocampo in 1993, PRI presidential candidate Luis Donaldo Colosio in 1994, federal Congressman Francisco Ruiz Massieu (Salinas' former brother-in-law) in 1994, and human rights lawyer Digna Ochoa in 2001. Ochoa had defended environmental activists in the state of Guerrero who allegedly were tortured by soldiers.

The deaths of Ruiz Massieu and Posadas Ocampo occurred during the administration of Salinas de Gortari, the president who brokered NAFTA. The president's brother, Raul Salinas, was jailed for several years during the Zedillo administration in connection with Ruiz Massieu's murder. Ochoa's murder, which the government labeled a suicide, occurred just before Zedillo's presidency ended.

Political pacts

The Juarez femicides overlapped the terms of three presidents: Salinas de Gortari, Zedillo, and Fox. The governors of Chihuahua state during that period were Fernando Melendez Baeza of the Institutional Revolutionary Party, Francisco Barrio of the National Action Party, Patricio Martinez of the Institutional Revolutionary Party and Jose Reyes Baeza Terrazas (Melendez Baeza's nephew) of the Institutional Revolutionary Party. The governors who were in office during the "dirty war" go back further, as do the mayors of Juarez and Chihuahua City.

Mexican political analyst Carlos Ramirez contends that Mexican presidents enter into pacts or agreements with predecessors that exempt them from prosecution. It was not until Zedillo's presidency that the federal government dared to arrest generals for complicity in the drug trade. And it was not until Fox became president that a former president, Luis Echeverria, was publicly accused of playing an active role in the country's political "dirty war" saga.

On June 30, 2006, authorities detained Echeverria under house arrest on charges of genocide. But his age, 84, and his political influence made it unlikely that he would be sentenced to prison. In fact, a judge ruled that the statute of limitations for the charges against him had expired in November 2005.

Within the same week, another judge ruled in favor of Luis De la Barreda Moreno, a former military captain accused in the death of a September 23 Communist League member and other crimes associated with Mexico's political repression.

President Lopez Portillo died in 2004, without having to answer for his role in the "dirty war" era.

When Salinas de Gortari was president, he was eager to build a legacy that credited him with bringing economic reforms to Mexico, including free trade with Canada and the United States. He also wanted to appease U.S. State Department demands for broader democratic reforms, which allowed several members of the National Action Party, including Francisco Barrio and Ruffo Appel, to become governors of strategic northern border states.

He also made it possible for Vicente Fox to become president by effecting a change in the Mexican constitution, which, for the first time, allowed Mexican citizens who were not born of Mexican parents to run for president. Fox's father is an Irish immigrant, and his mother is from Spain. However, the change could not take effect for six years - at the end of Zedillo's administration. After the peso crisis of 1994, Salinas de Gortari left Mexico and remained in self-imposed exile during most of Zedillo's presidency.

Salinas de Gortari's' return to Mexico after Fox's election showed that he had not lost his political power. He wasted no time trying to influence Mexico's political scene. He also helped his brother, Raul Salinas, get out of jail. After spending several years in a Mexican prison, Raul Salinas managed to fend off allegations in France and Switzerland that he made millions in protection money from drug cartels or other illicit sources. Their brother, Enrique Salinas, was murdered in 2004 outside of Mexico City. There were no arrests after more than two years of investigation.

More allegations

Allegations that high-level officials and prominent business leaders were involved in the drug trade also surfaced during Zedillo's presidency. The *Washington Post* reported in 1999 that Jose Liebano Saenz Ortiz of Chihuahua state, Zedillo's trusted personal secretary, was under investigation by Mexican officials for allegedly protecting drug dealers.

The *New York Times* carried a separate story the same year about the National Drug Intelligence Center's report alleging that Carlos Hank Gonzalez and his sons, Carlos and Jorge, had ties to drug cartels and "pose a significant criminal threat to the United States." Carlos Hank Gonzalez, a German-Mexican, was considered a powerful and corrupt politician who also came under the scrutiny of French investigators and the Costa Rican government.

The response from Mexico was swift and effective. It compelled U.S. Attorney General Janet Reno to announce that the Hank family was not formally under U.S. investigation, and a Mexican investigation requested by Saenz Ortiz cleared him of any wrongdoing. Family patriarch Carlos Hank Gonzalez died in 2001 from an illness.

Jorge Madrazo, the Mexican federal attorney general under Zedillo who showed courage for his role in the 1999 "Plaza Sweep" investigation, conducted an anti-crime summit in Juarez after maquiladora managers complained to the president about the city's rampant crime and violence.

Madrazo's staff promised to bring a federal team to investigate the drug-related disappearances, the women's murders, and well, everything. Madrazo's summit was good for a few news headlines, but he never returned to the border.

And he never followed through on those promises. The Juarez drug cartel kept gaining strength throughout Mexico, as did the Tijuana cartel under the Arellano Felix brothers. The women's murders in Juarez also continued.

Mexico's next president

Mexico's 2006 presidential candidates included four men and a woman. Roberto Madrazo Pintado, former Tabasco state governor, represented the Institutional Revolutionary Party and was in third place in most polls. Felipe Calderon, the National Action Party candidate, was Fox's energy secretary before launching his campaign.

Santiago Creel, former interior secretary, was unable to obtain the conservative party's nomination. Manuel Lopez Obrador, a member of the Democratic Revolutionary Party and former Mexico City mayor, was at the top of the polls in the early stages of the campaign. Polls showed that he and Calderon were tied just before the July 2 election.

The Mexican federal election commission said Calderon won by a very narrow margin. Lopez Obrador, however, refused to accept the preliminary results, and also proclaimed victory. He alleged that the election was stolen from him. Two weeks after the election, a million of his supporters joined him in Mexico City's main square to protest the election process.

Lopez Obrador hoped to do what Cuauhtemoc Cardenas was unable to achieve in two presidential bids – win in a transparent election. Cardenas, who questioned neoliberal economic models and free trade, reportedly won the election against Salinas de Gortari in 1988. However, according to some pundits, Mexico's power structure handed the victory to Salinas. Enrique Krauze, a prominent Mexican historian, said he considers fraud in the 1988 election to be a foregone conclusion.

The U.S. government maintained silence about the allegations that the Institutional Revolutionary Party had stolen the election from the left-of-center candidate. The U.S. government apparently did not suffer from a lack of awareness. *Proceso* magazine published an interview in 2006 with a former Central Intelligence Agency officer who alleged that the U.S. government knew the 1988 election was stolen from Cardenas. Two of the candidate's close campaign aides were murdered two days before the election, according to news accounts.

Author Jorge Fernandez Menendez alleged in an article for *Diario Milenio* that former federal Commander Guillermo Gonzalez Calderoni, who was murdered in 2003 in McAllen, Texas, was implicated in the deaths of Cardenas' aides. The deaths allegedly involving a scheme to acquire secret computer codes to break into Mexico's electoral systems. Before his murder, Gonzalez Calderoni threatened to divulge the Mexican government's dirty secrets; he also allegedly protected and later betrayed powerful drug barons, the article said.

A continuous thread ran through the years of various presidents: the strong suspicion that they tolerated the drug trade. Their passive negligence permitted the drug cartels to corrupt police and government officials. The Juarez women's murders are but an extension of this thread.

Presidential female candidate

Patricia Mercado Castro, the 2006 presidential candidate of the Social Democratic Party, was regarded by most political analysts as uncorrupted. She began and ended her presidential campaign at the Juarez cotton field where eight women's bodies were discovered in 2001. Mercado, a social activist from Sonora State, is a friend of Guadalupe Morfin Otero, the federal commissioner that Fox appointed to eradicate violence against women in the border city.

Mercado made it difficult for the majority-party candidates to ignore the femicides, a subject that Mario Alvarez Ledesma, a deputy federal attorney general for human rights under Fox, and other officials were supposed to put to rest for good before the election.

Roberto Campa Cifrian, the fifth presidential candidate, is a lawyer in Mexico City and a member of the Nueva Alianza (New Alliance) Party.

Zapatistas campaign

Toward the end of 2005, the leaders of the Zapatista rebellion announced "The Other Campaign," an alternative to the 2006 presidential election. In a communiqué dated November 20, 2005, the anniversary of the Mexican Revolution, the leaders said Subcommander Marcos, also known as "Delegate Zero," would be part of a national campaign to promote the three pillars of the movement: democracy, liberty, and justice. Unlike their armed rebellion of 1994, the Zapatistas said they had agreed that this movement would be a peaceful one.

Marcos, wearing his trademark ski mask, began his campaign tour to join the Zapatistas with other dissident groups in Mexico and to acquaint himself with their needs. *La Jornada* agreed to cover Marcos at his rallies and meetings throughout his campaign, just as it did the five presidential candidates.

The international community had saved the Zapatistas from extinction after a widely circulated memo by Chase Manhattan Bank in 1995 had urged the Mexican government to "eliminate" the insurgent group to ensure fiscal stability.

During the Zapatistas' campaign, Marcos emphasized that the group was not seeking power. He used the media attention to speak out against all the major-party candidates, including Lopez Obrador, whom he did not consider an authentic leftist leader. Marcos urged citizens to use peaceful means to recover what they had lost to neoliberal economic policies that benefited the elites of Mexico.

The revolutionary leader traveled to Juarez and Chihuahua City in 2006. He led a rally at the Stanton Street international bridge and criticized the U.S. government for building a fence at the border. A helicopter and dozens of police and federal agents manned the U.S. side of the border. In Juarez, city police vehicles followed the Zapatista entourage at a distance. Several amused photographers took pictures of a police unit with the number 666 on it.

Marcos met with several human rights groups and denounced the political disappearances of the "dirty war" and the unsolved women's murders. The van he used during his historic trip to the border was painted with small crosses and the words "no more femicides." During his talk in Chihuahua City, he attacked what he referred to as the "caceria de mujeres" (the hunting of women) in the state of Chihuahua.

U.S. politicians seek to help

U.S. politicians in border states were the first to get involved in the issue of the Juarez femicides. In Texas, state Senator Eliot Shapleigh and state Representative Norma Chavez, both Democrats from El Paso, spoke out against the women's murders and joined binational protest marches.

U.S. Representative Hilda Solis, a Democrat from Los Angeles, was the first member of Congress to take up the issue. She introduced a resolution in the Congress that, among other things, condemns the crimes. U.S. Senator Jeff Bingaman of New Mexico introduced a similar resolution in the U.S. Senate. The House and Senate unanimously approved the joint resolution in 2006, overcoming efforts by Mexican government lobbyists to defeat it.

U.S. Senator John Cornyn, who promoted U.S. laws against human-trafficking, asked the FBI in El Paso to brief him on the femicides before one of his official visits to Mexico.

In November 2003, Solis led a U.S. congressional delegation on a fact-finding mission to the El Paso-Juarez border. The group, accompanied by U.S. activist Dolores Huerta, members of the Washington Office on Latin America and Amnesty International-USA, received briefings from various sources, including the FBI, Mexican officials, advocacy organizations and families of victims. The delegation also included U.S. Representatives Ciro Rodriguez, Silvestre Reyes and Luis Gutierrez. After their meeting with the families of victims, a couple of the U.S. delegates emerged teary eyed for the news conference that followed.

Because of Solis' untiring efforts, the U.S. State Department and the U.S. Embassy in Mexico under Ambassador Tony Garza took a more active role in the matter. Garza announced a $5 million grant from funds earmarked for foreign countries to assist legal reform efforts in the State of Chihuahua and pledged any technical assistance requested by Mexican authorities.

City Councils in El Paso, Los Angeles and New York passed resolutions advocating justice for the victims.

In December 2005, the National Organization for Women conducted its national board meeting in El Paso, Texas, to bring attention to the women's murders. Europeans also tackled the problem. In its annual report on human rights around the globe, the European Parliament condemned the Juarez femicides.

After a visit to the border city, a European Parliament official recommended that Mexican authorities incorporate the term "femicide" in its legal code to set gender violence apart from other crimes. Several lawmakers from Spain also traveled to Mexico to find out what is being done to solve the murders.

Economic interests prevail

On a different front, the U.S. government had tried for several years to encourage the Vicente Fox administration to promote development of northern Mexico's natural gas resources. Massive blackouts in California and other U.S. states exposed serious stresses on the U.S. energy supply. It is likely that the U.S. government is reluctant to anger powerful Mexicans who are in a position to advance the U.S. energy development agenda, as well as to benefit from it. Before energy became a major bilateral topic, the development of NAFTA and the protection of the maquiladora industry were the overriding concerns.

In Mexico, presidential politicians routinely sought the favor and financial support of powerful Chihuahua state families with connections to energy industries and the government.

Business interests linking Mexico and the United States date back many years. Halliburton is a prime example. According to a news release in 2004, a Halliburton unit signed a five-year technology agreement that will benefit Petroleos Mexicanos (PEMEX), Mexico's national oil company. The announcement said PEMEX had enjoyed a fifty-year relationship with Halliburton, a conglomerate that counts U.S. Vice President Dick Cheney among its former CEOs. In the face of such political and business ambitions and of U.S. and Mexican economic interests, it is easy to see why the lives of poor, young women in Mexico rate low on the two governments' agendas.

Linda Jewell, a seasoned U.S. diplomat, met with Chihuahua State Attorney General Patricia Gonzalez in October 2004 in Washington, D.C. The former U.S. deputy assistant secretary of state with the Bureau of Western Hemisphere Affairs was attuned to the economic interests of Mexico and the United States.

According to a U.S. government cable, Jewell said at the meeting that "the murders in Ciudad Juarez had captured the attention of many in the U.S., including Congress and human rights organizations. It was damaging Chihuahua's image and would inevitably be an impediment to efforts to promote economic development. She stressed that the (U.S. government) wanted to help Chihuahua solve these terrible crimes and noted that the repeated question from the U.S. Congress and public was what [was] the (U.S. government) doing to help Mexico on this."

Later, Jewell visited the border to learn more about the situation. She asked U.S. Consul Donna Blair to arrange a meeting with key Mexican officials and human rights advocates at the consul's home in Juarez. Dr. Cynthia Bejarano of New Mexico State University was among those who were invited to attend. Juarez city police outside Blair's home wrote down the license plate of every vehicle that arrived for the meeting.

32.

THE PACT

My long journey in search of the truth ended seven years after it began. It ended over a cup of coffee in a city in the United States. It was on February 2, 2006, Mexico's *Dia de la Candelaria*, the Catholic holy day known as Candlemas. A couple of confidential sources had agreed to meet me. I went inside the café we had chosen for the rendezvous and sat down at a table to wait.

The aroma of espresso permeated the air. I stared at a poster of Antigua, Guatemala, that hung on a wall in front of me. It reminded me of two books about Guatemala I had just read.

The first was *Disappeared: A Journalist Silenced,* about Irma Flaquer's disappearance during her country's civil war. The other was *The Blindfold's Eyes*, a harrowing account of an American nun's ordeal by torture. Their stories are vivid testaments to the kind of injustices that power struggles can foment.

My mind skipped to the brutal murders of women in Guatemala in recent years and to the obvious comparisons with Juarez. The swooshing sound of the cappuccino machines interrupted my thoughts. It was all I could hear above the conversations at the adjoining tables. This was another world. Here, people talked about employers who gave them a hard time, their children's sports activities and getting over the flu. This world was alien to the one that brutal drug lords and their hired guns occupied.

One of my sources walked in the door and looked around until our eyes met. He wore a navy blue suit and looked like a banker. He said he had read the Spanish edition of this book, and that was what convinced him to provide additional information for this investigation. It was information that up to this moment had eluded me. It also gave me what I had been missing – an ending.

What he shared on this day was crucial and shattering. It broke down the final wall of secrecy that had protected those most responsible for the violence that ravaged the state of Chihuahua for a dozen years. Intuitively, I had sensed the existence of an inner sanctum that hid the real power behind the death and destruction. But I could not reach it. And now, like a banker with the key to a safe-deposit box, this man would unlock the final secret.

An unusual summit

The source, a lawyer, ordered a cup of coffee as we waited for the other person to join us. The three of us then decided to move to an isolated corner of the café, beyond the hearing range of others.

I knew I was about to hear about an event that had affected many lives. After exchanging a few pleasantries, the source began his account:

Some years ago, a meeting was called at the home of a politician in the state of Chihuahua. Important people were instructed to show up at the designated time. It was near the Christmas holiday season, when Mexicans traditionally take vacations for two or three weeks at a time. This is when maquiladora employees collect their annual bonuses and go on a spending spree for their families. Government officials customarily take time off and leave behind skeleton crews to handle the most basic needs of their offices.

The lawyer said he was expecting a holiday affair, one of the many soirées that take place in late December and early January. He expected the usual Mexican eggnog spiked with liquor known as *rompope*, colorful salads, corn tamales and traditional pastries. Around this time, homes are decorated with a nativity scene or small Christmas tree. People banter about work, boast of holiday trips in the works, toss in some politics and, as Mexicans are prone to do, give everyone a hug and wish each other well. This is what the source was expecting that day.

When he arrived at the house, the source was amazed to see a former president of Mexico at the center of the gathering. He had seen nothing in the press about his visit to the community, yet there he was. He could hardly believe he was at a party where the guest of honor had been Mexico's highest authority.

In fact, other guests told him that *Señor Presidente* had convened the meeting. Among those at the house that day were a general, a high-ranking police official, several federal judges, and a bishop. "During the meeting, several Colombian men were introduced," and they were the only ones the source did not recognize.

"The food was catered, and it was the best of anything you could have ordered. Drinks were served as well," the source said. After a short time, it became evident that the meeting was not purely social. Everyone was instructed to begin gathering around the dining room table to listen to the former president speak. There was not enough room for everyone to sit, and several people had to stand around the table. It was a most unlikely place for the kind of meeting that unfolded.

President: A new deal

"The president said the purpose of the meeting was to announce the 'new deal' and its terms," the source said. Several of the people present already had the benefit of some background and quickly explained a few details to the source. They told him Chihuahua state had been "sold" to one of the Colombian drug cartels and, like the spoils of war, the state had been divided up into several territories.

The president said "unimaginable sums of money" were to be made as a result of this pact. Soon after that, someone took out a piece of paper with a list of names on it and asked that it be passed around for everyone to look at before leaving. "The president said the new pact with the Colombians had certain conditions and come what may, one of them was (for law enforcement) not to interfere with any of the people on the list. They were 'untouchables." The names on the list included drug traffickers, powerful families, and even prominent men that Mexican federal investigators had implicated in the Juarez femicides.

The source, who suddenly felt out of place, was astounded that everyone else in the room seemed to take it all in stride.

"This was not done with any kind of subtlety," the source said. "They passed around that paper with the names on it in a very clumsy manner, and the group was told in no uncertain terms: 'Don't let it occur to you to do anything to any of these people.'" No one at the party acted surprised, and no one spoke out or asked any questions about the instructions.

Ramifications

The source was shaken to his core by what he had just witnessed. He understood at once that disclosing to the wrong people what had taken place that day would mean certain death. He said a range of emotions set in: fear, disgust, anger, grief. He knew instinctively that the pact the former president described would set in motion a horrible future for the state of Chihuahua. The source said he cried when he went home that day.

"We were afraid of the Colombian drug dealers because we knew they were bloodthirsty. Some of them were known to practice human-sacrifice rituals," the source said. "At least Rafael Aguilar [the drug lord who preceded Amado Carrillo Fuentes] was from Chihuahua state. He had family roots in Mexico, and he cared to an extent about what happened in his home. Now we were going to be at the mercy of the Colombians."

The new crime lords

For the pact to work, the old capos of the region had to be eliminated. Rafael Aguilar Guajardo, who was from Juarez and had family ties in Chihuahua state, was the original kingpin of the Juarez drug cartel. According to media accounts, he was assassinated on orders of Amado Carrillo Fuentes, who took over the Juarez corridor. Pablo Acosta, the capo based in Ojinaga, Chihuahua, across the border from Presidio, Texas, was also eliminated to make room for Carrillo Fuentes. Pablo Escobar, the powerful Colombian drug lord, died in a shootout in 1993, and others rushed in to fill the void. Leaders of the Carrillo-Fuentes organization came from Sinaloa, a state whose capital city, Culiacan, is notoriously overrun by violent drug gangs.

The pact had profound implications for the state's border region. It sealed the fate of hundreds of men and women for years to come. It condemned Juarez to a dark era marked by terror, abductions, torture, mutilations, rapes, and murders. It included the kidnappings and violent murders of young women because it guaranteed impunity for the perpetrators. People who were involved in laundering money or other support services for the new cartel were exempt from arrest and prosecution. The cartel sacrificed those who got out of line.

Police officers were transformed into bodyguards and enforcers for the drug-traffickers.

This truly was a pact with the devil, and it was sealed in blood. From the guests who were present at the politician's house that day, it appeared that the cartel had succeeded in corrupting all of the community's important institutions.

Because of what he witnessed that day, the source left Mexico.

He gave this information to U.S. officials, but he complained that they responded with indifference. Others like him who did not want to be a part of this diabolical scheme eventually also found ways to leave the region. Although he has hidden his identity, the source considers himself a dead man if he ever steps foot in his country again.

Other pacts

Other sources in Mexico and the United States confirmed that such a meeting took place in the state of Chihuahua. A U.S. intelligence source said it was true that Mexican officials had entered into a pact with the Colombians. The intelligence source said several people in the border community knew about it but mentioned it only in hushed whispers.

Although U.S. law enforcement officials knew about the Christmas holiday meeting attended by a former Mexican president, they were unable to provide details about what was discussed.

The state of Chihuahua is a strategic corridor for the Mexican drug cartels and their subsidiaries which transport Colombian cocaine to different destinations in the United States.

During the 1990s, the U.S. government was mostly concerned with getting the North American Free Trade Agreement established and preventing any interference with U.S.-owned assembly plants, or other U.S. economic interests. Collectively, the maquiladoras in border cities like Tijuana, Juarez and Matamoros raked in billions of dollars for their shareholders, according to the Association of Maquiladoras.

The drug cartel became a transnational corporation that also made billions for its investors. Former DEA official Phil Jordan said NAFTA contributed to the ability of drug cartels to expand their businesses. It hardly mattered to Mexico's political hierarchy if drug lords had turned these cities into perpetual war zones. Mexican author Carlos Loret de Mola alleges in his book *El Negocio* that the Mexican economy would collapse if the drug trade were removed.

Similar pacts were repeated elsewhere in Mexico, in places that sheltered the Carrillo Fuentes cartel and its Colombian associates. These included the states of Oaxaca, Mexico, Nuevo Leon, Queretaro, Morelos, Jalisco, Quintana Roo, Chiapas, Michoacán, Sonora, Guerrero, and others. Amado Carrillo Fuentes' disappeared lawyer, Jose Alfredo Andrade Bojorges, mentioned some of these states in the book that cost him his life.

Andrade also said Carrillo Fuentes family members were living in Santiago de Chile, while other members of the syndicate guarded important corridors in Guatemala. A few years ago, police in Chile reported a string of women's murders similar to the Juarez femicides near one of the coastal cities that Juarez drug cartel operatives used to transport drugs. And officials in neighboring Argentina revealed the existence of illicit funds in that country belonging to the Carrillo Fuentes cartel. Recent far-flung arrests illustrate the cartel's explosive growth.

At the request of the FBI in El Paso, two men associated with the Juarez drug cartel were arrested in 2005 at the Ritz Carlton hotel in Madrid, Spain, next door to the famous Prado Museum. The Queen Sofia Museum, which houses Pablo Picasso's famous "Guernika" painting, is not far from the Prado. When I first saw Picasso's work in Spain, I wondered whether the Guernica Hospital in Juarez was named for the painting. Andrade Bojorges discusses this in his book and said someone in Juarez indeed had suggested naming the hospital after Picasso's anti-war masterpiece. He did not identify who that someone was.

Shortly after the two arrests in Madrid, the FBI arrested a third man living in El Paso, Texas, who reportedly belonged to the same drug cell. Just as disturbing is the fact that intelligence sources had detected a couple of men in Spain that Mexican investigators had linked to the Juarez women's murders.

Religion and drugs

The reference to a church official at the sinister meeting does not suggest that all clergy of the Catholic Church in Mexico winked at drug dealers or accepted their dirty money. Far from it. Many priests and Christian evangelical ministers in Mexico have denounced the drug trade and the violence against women.

Some have said privately that corruption is at the root of the impunity in the Juarez cases. Last year, a bishop in Aguascalientes, Ramon Godinez Flores, came under fire for reportedly telling *La Jornada* that donations from drug dealers were "purified" when they proceeded from good intentions. Later, he claimed that his words had been twisted. Nevertheless, the article reflected the casual attitude toward drug-trafficking that exists in some Mexican communities.

In response to the comments attributed to his colleague, Isidro Guerrero, the bishop of Mexicali, Mexico, told *El Universal* that it is disastrous to have contact with drug dealers because they collect double for any favors. "They ask you for special Masses, and then ask you to store their vehicles in your garage," Guerrero said. The acclaimed 2002 movie "El Crimen del Padre Amaro" (The Crime of Father Amaro) portrays the involvement of Catholic clergymen with drug dealers in Mexico.

Pope Benedict XVI has denounced drug-trafficking, and he and his predecessor, Pope John Paul II, also condemned the Juarez women's murders.

Pacts across the border

The continuous thread of drug corruption does not stop at the border. During the 1980s, several Texas residents were witnesses to another frightening pact. This one involved a "multimillion-dollar cocaine transaction" at a private home in Horizon City, Texas, where a party was raging one night. The witnesses instantly recognized two of the prominent men who walked into the house, avoided the partiers, and headed downstairs to a closed-door meeting. They were a former El Paso politician and a former Juarez elected official. After they left, the party-goers were invited to help themselves to cocaine residue left on the meeting-room table downstairs. Several people who witnessed the events became fearful and moved away from the area.

It was during that era, that prominent Mexican families were invited to enter the drug trade to help fund the Nicaraguan war against the Sandinista communist rebels. It was in everyone's interest to keep the Marxist menace out of the continent, while making money to help the cause. During the 1990s, a Juarez government official confided that the late Juarez Mayor Francisco Villarreal once told him matter-of-factly, "We have no choice.

We have to pact with the *narcos*."

A Colombian drug dealer

A former U.S. law enforcement official said it was not unusual for Chihuahua State "to be sold and resold" for drug smuggling purposes.

An intelligence source added that the 1993 death of Cardinal Juan Jesus Posadas Ocampo in Guadalajara was related to the Colombian cartel's dealings with Mexico. The source alleged that the clergyman was supposed to deliver a Colombian politician's complaint to a Mexican politician that Mexico was not honoring its agreements with the Colombian drug lords.

Juarez residents said businesses owned by Colombians sprouted overnight in Chihuahua state. The new businesses included florists that sold drugs directly from the flower shops.

Castor Alberto Ochoa-Soto, a Colombian drug dealer, was among the nine men whose bodies were unearthed in Juarez during the 1999 "Plaza Sweep" investigation. He was tried on drug charges in a U.S. federal court in El Paso, Texas, but was set free after prosecutors were unable to persuade the court of his guilt.

Despite his importance in drug-trafficking circles, Ochoa-Soto's trial received hardly any coverage from the U.S. media. On February 11, 1995, two U.S. federal agents walked him and his lawyer to the Paso del Norte International Bridge. When they reached the Juarez side of the border, Mexican federal police acting on orders from the Carrillo Fuentes cartel picked up the two men. They were tortured and killed.

According to an article by U.S. journalist Rafael Nuñez, Ochoa-Soto lost six tons of cocaine during a deal with undercover agents, and Amado Carrillo Fuentes was hoping to keep another twenty-two tons of the white powder that Ochoa-Soto had stashed away in Mexico. The coke was worth more than $3 billion.

Ochoa-Soto was a high-ranking member of Colombia's notorious Medellin cartel and a relative of the Fabio Ochoa clan. His family has yet to claim his body from the Juarez morgue.

Dust in the desert

No one who lived in this border region between 1993 and 2005 can deny that Juarez was in a state of siege throughout the golden years of the Carrillo Fuentes cartel. More than a decade of cocaine smuggling from Colombia lined the pockets of police, military, and government officials, and perhaps even some church officials.

Mothers who lost their daughters during this era could not conceive how completely this corruption frustrated their quest for justice. The advice of a Mexican journalist in Mexico City several years ago is as accurate today as it was then: There is no one in Mexico who can protect anyone who seeks to investigate this.

The pacts that sealed the deaths of countless people in Juarez went beyond anything that Dr. Rita Laura Segato imagined in her pointed analysis. The pacts between crime lords and people at the highest levels of the Mexican government overwhelm the desires of well-meaning politicians, government servants, advocates, and honest police to end this nightmare.

My meeting at the coffee shop summed up the years of tragedy.

It had been a long odyssey. Along the way, mothers cried over the caskets of their young daughters. Juarez lawyers Mario Escobedo Anaya and Sergio Dante Almaraz Mora were assassinated. Fabricated suspects were unjustly imprisoned.

The drug cartel corrupted police who were sworn to protect the community. Mexico's "dirty war" was treated as a necessary secret. Along this road, hundreds of men and women who vanished are feared dead. What guided this journey was an inner voice that would not stop crying out for justice.

Today, a fine white dust still blows across the desert of Lomas de Poleo, one of the poor neighborhoods that became a hunting ground, and later a graveyard, for young, terrified women. No doubt they screamed, but there was no one to hear or help them.

The last people they saw were the malevolent men who killed them. The last image conjured in their minds before they died, I like to think, was a comforting one of a mother, a young son or daughter, a brother or sister, or a tiny pet canary.

That white fine dust that blows about in the wind touches everything in sight.

EPILOGUE

For the oppression of the poor,
For the sighing of the needy,
Now will I arise, saith the Lord.

Psalm 12:5.

Epilogue

The Mexican Federal Attorney General's Office issued a lengthy report on the Juarez women's murders in January of 2006. It undercounted the victims and left out information about suspects that may have pointed to serial killers. In statements to the press, the federal authorities flatly denied that serial killers were involved in any of the slayings. This contradicted previous finding of the FBI and of experts like Robert Ressler and Candice Skrapec.

Mario Alvarez Ledesma, the federal deputy attorney general for human rights, claimed activists exaggerated the problem and that more women are being killed in other places in Mexico. The PGR report, condemned as a whitewash by advocates, outraged families of victims. It failed to convince anyone that the federal government intended to solve the crimes. And it was not based on investigation. It was an analysis of information provided by Chihuahua State authorities about the murders and reports of missing women. The report received the Vicente Fox administration's views on the issue.

Amnesty International joined in the criticism of the report. While the Mexican federal document increased the count of Chihuahua State officers who allegedly mishandled the investigations from 81 to 177, it concluded that expired statutes of limitations protected them against prosecution or other penalties. "As a result," Amnesty International said, "the [federal Attorney General's] review appears to have failed to overcome some of the deficiencies of the original investigations."

United States: It's a problem

On March 8, 2006, International Day of the Woman, U.S. State Secretary Condoleezza Rice presented to Congress the State Department's annual Country Reports on Human Rights Practices, 2005. In the section on Mexico, the report states: "Violence against women continued to be a problem nationwide, particularly in Ciudad Juarez and the surrounding area. Government efforts to improve respect for human rights were offset by a deeply entrenched culture of impunity and corruption."

Some of the human rights violations noted in the report included kidnappings by police, torture and forced confessions, corruption in the judicial system, criminal intimidation of journalists, human-trafficking with official complicity, social and economic discrimination against indigenous people, child labor, and corruption at all levels of government. The U.S. report refers to the Juarez police rape reported in 2005 by an El Paso woman and her husband.

Human-trafficking concerns

The U.S. State Department highlighted additional areas of concern, including human-trafficking and generalized violence against women. "Trafficking in children for the purpose of sexual exploitation [also] was a problem, "according to the report. Contradicting what Alvarez Ledesma said only a few weeks earlier, the U.S. State Department reported, "The problem of violence against women was particularly grave in Ciudad Juarez and the State of Chihuahua."

It noted that Commissioner Guadalupe Morfin Otero's second report in 2005 attributed the slow progress "to a culture of impunity, dubious investigative techniques, including torture, and police corruption and ineptitude." The report also said human-trafficking victims alleged that criminal gangs had forced them to work in table-dance bars or as prostitutes under threat to them or their families.

Adriana Carmona of Justicia para Nuestras Hijas raised another worrisome issue in an interview with *La Jornada*. She alleged that several mothers seeking access to a federal assistance fund for families of victims were told they first had to sign a document waiving their right to petition for investigation.

Federal officials agreed to apply the Istanbul Protocol to determine whether Javier "Cerillo" Garcia Uribe was tortured, but at some point, they decided that the Federal Attorney General's Office should not release its findings. Publicly, federal officials said they had no jurisdiction. Instead of examining the torture allegations, a state judge released Garcia for lack of evidence. Chihuahua State officials also released one of the 1999 "Toltecas" suspects and one of the 1996 "Rebeldes" members.

In 2005, Chihuahua State Attorney General Patricia Gonzalez hired forensic anthropologists from Argentina to help identify victims' remains. They exhumed the bodies of several victims whose identities were questioned, but the alleged body of Elizabeth Castro, whose death was attributed to Abdel Latif Sharif Sharif, was not among them. Correctly identifying the body that authorities claimed was Castro's would have cleared Sharif, his defense lawyers argued.

Five individual complaints are pending before the Inter-American Commission on Human Rights: The 1998 disappearance of Silvia Arce in Juarez, in which two federal agents were implicated; the 2001 murders of Esmeralda Herrera Monreal, Berenice Ramos Monarrez and Claudia Ivette Gonzalez; and the 2002 sex-murder of Paloma Escobar in Chihuahua City. After intense international pressure, David Meza, unjustly accused of killing his cousin in Chihuahua City, was set free in June 2006.

Tony Garza alleges suspects

U.S. Ambassador to Mexico Tony Garza alleged on August 17, 2006 that Edgar Alvarez Cruz, who was in U.S. custody in Denver, Colorado, "is believed to be part of a gang of men who raped and murdered no less than ten women in Ciudad Juarez between 1993 and 2003." Garza said the detention presented "a major break" in the investigations into hundreds of women's murders in the state of Chihuahua. Alvarez was to be surrendered to Mexico. Mexican officials hinted that Alvarez and two other men could be suspects in the eight "cotton field" murders of 2001 and the six "Cristo Negro" slayings of 2002-2003. The other suspects were Jose Francisco Granados de la Paz, who also was in U.S. custody for an unrelated crime, and Alejandro "Cala" Delgado Valles, who was detained by authorities in Juarez.

De la Paz had a criminal history similar to that of the "Railway Killer," Angel Maturino. He crossed the border frequently, committed petty crimes in both countries, and, like Maturino, had served a short sentence in a New Mexico jail. Alvarez was to be processed for deportation by a U.S. immigration court for entering the United States illegally. Chihuahua authorities scrambled to investigate whether they had any evidence against the three men. Relatives of Alvarez and Granados de la Paz said the two men are in-laws and grew up together in Juarez. *Norte de Ciudad Juarez* reported that Granados de la Paz may have written one or more letters to his family implicating the other two men in the femicides. Their families told the newspaper that the men were incapable of committing such heinous crimes. Authorities did not confirm whether Edgar Alvarez was related to Cesar "Poison" Alvarez, an alleged gang member that *El Mexicano* previously linked to the "Cristo Negro" murders.

Mexican media accounts about the new suspects ranged from the guarded to the highly speculative. One news story alleged that Delgado Valles took police to several sites where bodies were allegedly dumped, and one of those places was near the "Caballito" (Little Horse) mountain in the outskirts of Juarez.

The Juarez community associates this area with drug cartel activities. Families of the suspects said they feared that the Mexican authorities, who were under pressure from the U.S. Embassy, might be tempted to make one or more of the latest suspects fit the crimes.

Bodies were misidentified

Chihuahua State authorities announced, also in August of 2006, that three of the eight "cotton field" victims were not dead but missing: Guadalupe "Lupita" Luna de la Rosa, Barbara Aracely Martinez Ramos, and Veronica Martinez Hernandez. The correction came five years after officials blamed two innocent bus drivers for the deaths of the eight young women that authorities named in a 2001 news conference. Two of the eight bodies from the 2001 case were now correctly identified as Maria Rocina Galicia Meraz and Merlin Elizabeth Rodriguez Saenz. According to a list of missing persons compiled by Amnesty International, Galicia, 17, who worked across the downtown cathedral, was reported missing in August 2001, and Rodriguez, 16, was last seen in April 2000. Barbara Aracely Martinez Ramos' mother, Maria de Jesus Ramos Villanueva, died of illness in March 2006. Her crusade for justice ended before she was able to determine with certainty if her daughter was dead or alive.

The other 2001 "cotton field" victims that the Argentine experts positively identified were Claudia Ivette Gonzalez, Mayra Juliana Reyes Solis, Esmeralda Herrera Monreal and Maria de los Angeles Acosta Ramirez. The eighth victim's identity is pending. The identity of Ramos was confirmed through DNA analysis by the Serological Research Institute of Richmond, California. Justice for the Women of Juarez paid for the test as a favor to the victim's family.

The Hester Van Nierop case, thanks to the persistence of her parents Roeland and Arsene Van Nierop, concluded with the arrest of her killer. It was a rare exception to the many other unsolved femicides. Roberto Flores (also known as Ramiro Adame) was extradited from a U.S. prison to Chihuahua after serving time for drug-trafficking. He was sentenced in 2017

to more than 30 years in prison. Witness reports and other evidence satisfied the Van Nierop family that Flores was the man who killed Hester in 1998.

In 2012, cousins Richard and Ruben Lopez of El Paso were sentenced to 20 years each by a Chihuahua state court in connection with the 1996 shooting deaths of sisters Victoria and Rita Parker, according to the *El Paso Times*. The FBI helped provide evidence that led to their convictions.

A new wave of drug cartel wars starting in 2006 swept across Mexico. In Juarez, the Guzman-Loera cartel continued to battle the Carrillo-Fuentes organization for control of the border trafficking corridor. Thousands of men and women died and disappeared in this war of attrition. The mostly foreign-onwed assembly plants known as maquiladoras continued operating without any major problems. According to published accounts, the total number of women's murders reported in Juarez between 1993 and 2020 had reached 2,198.

PHOTOGRAPHS

Lilia Alejandra Garcia Andrade's daughter visits her slain mother's grave in Juarez, Mexico. The young woman was abducted and killed in February 2001. [Victor Calzada/Courtesy of the *El Paso Times*.]

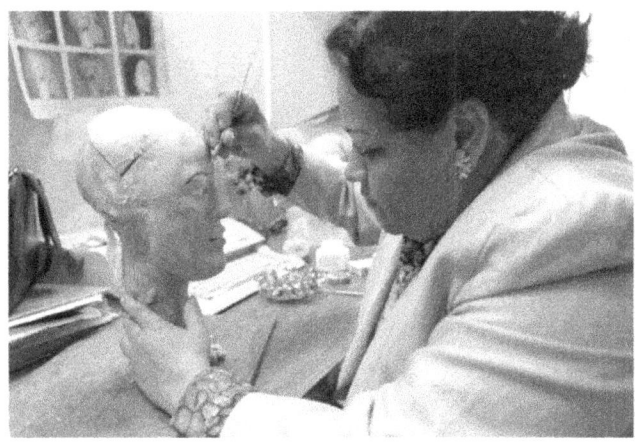

Dr. Irma Rodriguez Galarza works to reconstruct the remains of unidentified victims in Juarez, Mexico. [Leonel Monroy]

Frank Bender, a forensic expert based in Philadelphia, works to reconstruct the remains of Juarez femicide victims in May 2003. [DWV]

The cross at the Paso del Norte International Bridge between Juarez, Mexico and El Paso, Texas was installed in honor of the victims. [Leonel Monroy]

Abdel Latif Sharif Sharif learns at a news conference in 1996 that he is Chihuahua State's prime suspect in a string of murders of women. [Victor Calzada /Courtesy of *El Paso Times*]

Alleged gang "Rebeldes" members are detained in 1996 and accused of killing women for Sharif. [Norte de Ciudad Juarez]

Norte de Ciudad de Juarez front-page pictures show how bullets were planted in a police vehicle that pursued lawyer Mario Escobedo Anaya in 2002. [*Norte de Ciudad Juarez*]

U.S. Congressional delegation led by U.S. Representative Hilda Solis of Los Angeles addresses reporters in Juarez, Mexico, after meeting with families of victims in 2003. [Leonel Monroy]

U.S. and Mexican officials announce a new FBI tip hotline for the Juarez women's murders in El Paso, Texas, in 2003. [DWV]

Edith Aranda
Longoria

Laura Berenice
Ramos Monarrez

Rosalba Pizzaro

Mayra Yesenia
Najera

Maria de Los
Angeles Acosta
Ramírez

Yesenia Vega
Márquez

Guadalupe Luna
De la Rosa

Maria Isabel Mejía
Sapien

Alma M. Lopez
Garza

Julieta González
Valenzuela

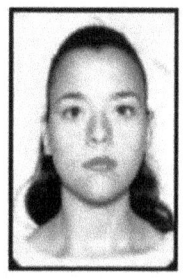

Minerva Torres
Albeldaño

Dead or missing in Juarez and Chihuahua City.

Paula Flores, mother of Sagrario Gonzalez, a 1998 victim, takes part in a *rastreo* (sweep) to search for bodies outside Juarez. [Leonel Monroy]

Guillermina Gonzalez, Sagrario's sister, attends a vigil for victims in Juarez. [Leonel Monroy]

Patricia Mercado, a candidate for president of Mexico in 2006, opened and closed her presidential campaign in Juarez in the place where eight young women's bodies were discovered in 2001. [Barbara Vazquez]

Unidentified woman was found 2005 in a sewage ditch in Juarez. [Raymundo Ruiz]

Residents of the Mexican border city look at a banner in the lobby of the Chihuahua State Attorney General's Office protesting the women's disappearances and murders. [Leonel Monroy]

Esmeralda Juarez Alarcon, a 2003 "Cristo Negro" victim, wears a traditional quinceañera dress. [Family photo]

Claudia Ivette Gonzalez wore overalls when she vanished in 2001. [Family photo]

Paloma Escobar, a Chihuahua City victim. [DWV]

Sally Field and Jane Fonda were among the celebrities at the V-Day March in February 2003 in Juarez. They called for an end to the gender violence. [Leonel Monroy]

Federal Commissioner Guadalupe Morfin Otero in her Juarez office. [Leonel Monroy]

Activists Jaime Hervella and Vicky Caraveo discuss the U.S. Congressional delegation's visit to the border in 2003. [Leonel Monroy]

Judith Galarza, a Juarez activist, lost a sister during Mexico's "dirty war" era. [DZN]

Irene Blanco, federal congresswoman, left Juarez after her son was shot. [DZN]

Arsene and Roland Van Nierop traveled to Juarez from the Netherlands in 2004 to check on the status of their daughter's case. Hester Susanne Van Nierop was strangled in a downtown hotel.
[Photo Barbara Vazquez]

Javier Felipe "Cerillo" Garcia was cleared as a suspect in eight murders.

Jesús Manuel "Tolteca" Guardado, a 1999 suspect.

Gustavo "Foca" Gonzalez, a suspect, died in custody in 2004. Photos by Norte de Ciudad Juárez

The "Toltecas" suspects were not part of a real gang as officials asserted.

Presentation of Spanish-language edition of book, *Cosecha de Mujeres (Harvest of Women)*, in Madrid, Spain. From left, Argentine journalist Graciela Atencio, Amnesty International representative Giulia Tamayo, Congresswoman Carmen Alborch, author Diana Washington Valdez, singer-activist Cristina del Valle and editor Rosa Galindo.

Candy vendor stands next to one of the crosses in Juarez that mark each woman's death. [Leonel Monroy]

U.S. Representative Hilda Solis (middle) joined a vigil in El Paso, Texas to commemorate Juarez victims. Dolores Huerta, United Farm Workers co-founder, at right, and New Mexico State Senator Mary Jane Garcia joined the ceremony. [Leonel Monroy]

Cinthia Irasema Ramos Quezada, 24, was left dead on a sidewalk in Juarez in 2004. She was added to the list of unsolved murders. [Raymundo Ruiz]

Cynthia Kiecker and husband Ulises Perzabal spent 18 months in a Chihuahua City prison for a crime they did not commit. They were accused in one of the femicides in the Chihuahua State capital and alleged they were tortured into confessing. Pressure from the U.S. government and international community helped set them free in 2004. They since moved to the United States. [Family photo.]

Zapatista leader Subcommander Marcos denounced the women's murders during his visit to Juarez in 2006. [Leonel Monroy]

Lawyer Sergio Dante Almaraz Mora was killed in broad daylight in downtown Juarez in 2006. [Hector Conde]

Glossary

Chihuahua State Attorney General's Office: Has primary jurisdiction in murder cases.

Femicide: The author's accepted term for the murder of a woman.

Institutional Revolutionary Party (PRI): A political party with a highly vertical system that controlled Mexican government for 70 years.

Los Pinos: The Mexican presidential house (Mexico's White House). Maquiladoras: In-bond assembly plants that were known also as "twin plants."

Mexican Federal Attorney General's Office: Investigates organized crime and drug-trafficking.

Mexican state police: Report to state attorney general's office and investigate murders and other serious violent crimes.

Mexican municipal police: Report to the city government and are a preventive force only.

Mexican state governors: Serve a one six-year term. Mexican presidents: Serve a one six-year term.

Names: It is the practice in Mexico and most other Spanish-language cultures to use the surnames of both parents (for example, Juanita Perez Gonzalez). It is not unusual to have the same paternal and maternal surnames, as in Juanita Perez Perez. Middle names frequently are used to further identify people (i.e., Juan Carlos Perez Gonzalez).

National Action Party (PAN): A right-of-center political party. Revolutionary Democratic Party (PRD): A left-of-center political party.

Notes

Sources: The use of endnotes and footnotes within the text was dropped in this edition to reduce the harassment and threats to people who provided confidential information.

Prologue

1. Project "Por Sagrario," by Hector Carreon, 1998-1999.

2. "Families, Officials, Claim Cover-Ups Keep Killings from Being Solved," *El Paso Times*, June 23, 2002.

3. Secret Societies. Arkl Daraul, 1989, pp. 80, 199 and 227; and www.united.non-profit.nl/pages/info02n9.htm and www.unitedagainstracism.com.

4. Interviews with Mexican agents and officials who investigated the crimes. They and U.S. officials who provided similar information will remain anonymous.

5. Recorded telephone calls in 2003 and 2004. Reported calls to police in El Paso, Texas, January 2004.

1. Border Safari

1. Interview with Irma Perez.

2. Interview with Dr. Julia Monarrez Fragoso.

3. Interview with intelligence sources.

4. *Drugs and Democracy in Latin America*, pp. 290-291.

2. Near Cartel Ranch

1. Interviews with Ramona Morales and Andrade family members.

2. Interviews with State of Chihuahua medical examiner.

3. Interviews with Dr. Irma Rodriguez Galarza.

3. Lomas de Poleo

1. Interviews with Victoria "Vicky" Caraveo, founder of Mujeres por Juarez, and director of the Chihuahua Women's Institute.

2. Ad signed by Fernando Martínez Cortes, "Tomza y la nueva fiscalía del Caso Juárez," *Norte de Ciudad Juárez*, 2004; "Trabajadores sindicalizados bajo amenazas de muerte," *La Hora* (*Guatemala de la Asuncion*), September 9, 2003, and testimony of Dr. Roy Godson for the United States Congress, "Threats to U.S.-Mexican Border Security," April 23, 1997.

3. Ad by business organizations defending Juarez business executive, *Norte de Ciudad Juarez*, 2004.

4. Confidential CISEN sources.

5. Interview with State of Chihuahua law enforcement official.

4. Atrocities

1. "Juarenses Demand Action in Slayings," *El Paso Times*, November 8, 2001 and the 1998 Mexican National Commission on Human Rights report on the Juarez women's murders.

2. Interview with Mark Leoni.

3. Panamerican Health Organization/World Health Organization report on mortality and morbidity in the border region, El Paso, Texas, 2000.

4. Mexican National Human Rights Commission report on the Juarez women's murders, 1998.

5. Interview with Dr. Cheryl Howard, University of Texas at El Paso.

6. "Intolerable Killings," Amnesty International report, August 2003.

7. Asma Jahangir, United Nations special rapporteur, news conference in Mexico, 1999.

8. Report on Juarez murders, Inter-American Commission for Human Rights, April 2003.

9. Teofilo Alvarado, "Ofreceran hoy conferencia sobre Juárez," *Norte de Ciudad Juárez*, April 29, 2004.

5. Sagrario's Death

1. Letter of Paula Flores, June 2004.

2. "Only Blaming Smelter Unfair, Ex residents Say," *El Paso Times*, August 5, 2002.

3. Isabel Velásquez, "Sagrario, un recuerdo," *El silencio que la voz de todas quiebra*, pp. 94-95.

4. Mario Héctor Silva, "Relatora de la onu para las mujeres asesinadas en Juarez," *El Financiero*, June 26, 1999.

5. Informe de la Subprocuraduría del Estado de Chihuahua, 1998.

6. El Paso County Medical Examiner autopsy report, El Paso, Texas, 1996.

7. Interview with Dr. Julia Monarrez, Colegio de la Frontera. She documented 363 women's murders in Juarez between 1993 and 2003, including 133 sex murders.

6. Gringo

1. Interviews with Adair Margo and Vanessa Johnson.

2. Interviews with Antonio Medina.

3. *El Mexicano* news editor Felix Gonzalez allowed me to inspect the photo albums and correspondence of the elderly American man referred to as "el gringo."

7. Cristo Negro

1. Case file for Elizabeth Castro.

2. Interviews with witnesses who saw the nine bodies at the Juarez morgue in the summer of 2001.

3. The author was present during the police removal of Lote Bravo alleged squatters in 2003.

4. Mexican National Commission on Human Rights report on the Juarez women's murders, 1998.

5. Investigative report, United States Customs Service, Code TECS. 3, Number SD02BR97SD0022, "Operation White Tiger," August 14, 1997.

6. Jamie Dettmer, "U.S. Drug Warriors Knock on Heaven's Door," *Insight Magazine, The Washington Times*, April 21,1997.

7. Interview with truck driver in El Paso, Texas.

8. City of Juarez public property registry document.

9. Sonia Aguilar, "Devuelve PGR a Estado caso Campo Algodonero," *Norte de Ciudad Juarez*, June 29, 2006.

8. Death of a Lawyer

1. "Lawyer for Suspect in Killings in Juarez Slain," *El Paso Times*, February 7, 2002; "Border is no Match for Some Family Ties", *El Paso Times*, November 11, 2002; Laura Cruz, "Drug Ties Suspected in 7 of 9 Fatally Shot Last Week in Mexico," *El Paso Times*, October 3, 2002 and intelligence sources.

2. Interviews with Mario Escobedo Salazar and Sergio Dante Almaraz, and article by Olga Aragón, "Un padre en busca de justicia," *Diario de Ciudad Juarez*, February 20, 2002.

3. Carlos Huerta, "Siembra bala pje," *Norte de Ciudad Juarez*, February 8, 2002.

4. FBI sources.

5. "Crimenes sin Respuesta," Televisio de Catalunya, TV3-Barcelona, February 28, 2006.

9. Cotton Field Murders

1. Interviews and collaborations with U.S. journalist Kent Paterson.

2. "Tears, rage in Guatemala," Associated Press, August 30, 2004, distributed by www.cbsnews.com/stories/ 2004/08/30/world/main 639545.shtml

3. "Intolerable Killings," Amnesty International report.

4. Interview with Candice Skrapec.

5. Government receipt for ad critical of Juarez radio journalist Samira Izaguirre, 2002.

6. Interviews with members of Justicia para Nuestras Hijas.

10. Crime Scene

1. Interviews at the site with Victor Muñoz, Dr. Cynthia Bejarano, Josefina Gonzalez. Photographer Linda Stetler was present during the sweep.

2. Interviews with Azul Luna, Lorena Mendez, Benita Monarrez and a medical technician in El Paso.

3. Mexican Congressman David Torres Rodriguez provided the Mexican federal government's DNA test results for the cotton field victims.

4. Justicia para Nuestras Hijas explained background about the cross installed at the Paso del Norte International Bridge.

5. The Associated Press reported that actress Jane Fonda voiced concerns over femicides in Guatemala during a news conference in December 2002.

6. Pablo Hernandez and Carlos Huerta, "Regresan las invasiones," *Norte de Ciudad Juarez*, Sept. 29, 1999.

11. The Drug Cartel

1. Interviews with Patricia Garibay.

2. Interviews with El Paso Police Department detectives in El Paso, Texas.

3. Interview with FBI sources, and testimony of FBI agent at a court martial in Fort Bliss, Texas in 2000, for a U.S. soldier accused of drug-trafficking, and "Drug Dealer Linked to Unsolved Deaths, *El Paso Times*, October 31, 2000.

4. The Mexican Federal Attorney General's affidavit, called the "maxi-proceso," against the alleged leaders of the Carrillo Fuentes drug cartel.

5. Luis Astorga, "Drug Trafficking in Mexico: A First General Assessment," MOST Discussion Paper No. 36; http://www.unesco.org/most/astorga.htm. Contains reference to Operation Casablanca.

6. Interviews with "Ana" in El Paso, Texas. She is referred to only by first name for safety reasons.

7. Paul Gootenberg, "The Birth of the Narcs: The First Illicit Cocaine Flows in the Americas, 1947-1964."

12. Amado's Cartel

1. Louie Gilot, "Police Still Seek Murder Suspects," *El Paso Times*, December 12, 2000.

2. "Murder Suspect's Cousin Caught in Mexico," *El Paso Times*, May 20, 2002.

3. Charles Bowden, *Down by the River*, p. 271.

4. Interviews with DEA officers, a Mexican intelligence officer, and former DEA official Phil Jordan.

5. Copy of the alleged Mexican Federal Attorney General credential issued to the drug lord (No. 000866); distributed to news media by the FBI in El Paso, Texas.

6. Interviews with FBI sources.

7. Luz del Carmen Sosa, "Sospechan que ex conyuge de la mujer está implicado en el caso," *Diario de Ciudad Juarez*, June 2, 2002, and *Norte de Ciudad Juarez*, March 14, 2004.

8. Louie Gilot, "Arrests Made in Juarez Deaths," *El Paso Times*, July 28, 2003.

9. El Paso Police Department document, and "Drug Dealer Linked to Unsolved Deaths," *El Paso Times*, October 31, 2000.

10. Interviews with State of Chihuahua officials.

11. Interviews with the International Association of Relatives and Friends of Disappeared Persons and Juarez reporters.

13. Isabel and Heidi

1. Interviews with Isabel Arvide, Phil Jordan, FBI sources

2. and "Ana."

3. Isabel Arvide discussed a controversial article that *Milenio* published in June 3, 2001.

4. Alberto Ponce de León y Armando Emanuel Vélez, "El patio de la muerte," *Milenio*, February 2, 2004, pp. 36-39.

4. Information provided by Mexican intelligence sources.

5. Jennifer Shubinksi, "Indicted woman has long record," *El Paso Times*, December 9, 2000.

6. Mexican intelligence sources.

7. Interview with Jorge Fernandez Menendez, and the "maxiproceso" document.

14. Cartel Wars

1. "Maxiproceso" documents and the Mexican Federal Attorney General UEDO-PGR memorandum related to the cartel.

2. Interview with a Mexican politician.

3. Jeffrey Davidow, *El Oso y el Puercoespin*, pp. 218-219.

4. "FBI Letter Alleges Cartel had Role in Attack on Chihuahua Governor," *El Paso Times*, April 20, 2001; "Alleged Plot Stirs Mexico," April 23, 2001; "FBI Warned of Attack on Chihuahua Governor," *El Paso Times*, July 28, 2001, and "Woman Gets 27 Years for Shooting Governor," *El Paso Times*, October 26, 2003.

5. FBI sources.

6. Interview with FBI official Hardrick Crawford Jr. regarding the Mario Castillo case.

7. "Matan a hermano del narco mexicano Amado Carrillo Fuentes," September 13, 2004, www.terra.com; www.terra.com/actualidad/articulo/html/act183107.htm.

8. "Gloria Trevi prepara su regreso a escena," September 23, 2004, Terra.com; www.terra.com/actualidad/articulo/html/act183814.htm.

9. Mexican intelligence sources; Jorge Fernandez Menendez, *Narcotrafico y poder*, p. 71; and Rafael Loret de Mola, *Confidencias peligrosas*, pp. 85-104.

15. The Police Cartel

1. Interview with Dr. Irma Rodriguez Galarza.

2. Interview with Juarez city Councilwoman Rosa Lardizabal, her brother Javier Felipe Lardizabal's case file, and a videotape of the deceased's autopsy.

3. Jorge Fernandez Menendez, *Narcotrafico y poder*, p. 60.

4. "Candidato perdedor de la gubernatura de Chihuahua," *Bajo Palabra*, July-August 2004, pp. 40-43.

5. "Families, Some Officials Suspect Police are Involved," *El Paso Times*, June 24, 2002.

6. Carlos Huerta, "Libran contra violador serial orden de arresto en Juarez," *Norte de Ciudad Juarez*, March 9, 2006.

7. "Families, Officials, Claim Cover-Ups Keep Killings from Being Solved," *El Paso Times*, June 23, 2002.

16. Terror With a Badge

1. Mary Jordan, "Former Spy Chief Arrested in Mexican 'Dirty War' Case," *The Washington Post*, February 20, 2004.

2. Interview with State of Chihuahua homicide detective.

3. Enrique Cocina's report to the International Association of Relatives and Friends of Disappeared Persons.

4. State of Sonora official.

5. Jeremy Schwartz, "Rebirth of the Gulf Cartel," *Corpus Christi Caller-Times*, November 19, 2001.

6. Interview with national and border security expert in New Mexico.

7. "Temo que Navarrete me mande matar: Botello," *El Mexicano*, November 8, 2002.

8. Memorandum of the United States Bureau of Immigration and Customs Enforcement, El Paso, Texas, expediente ENF-1:01:EP:LG, August 25, 2003.

9. Jacinto Segura, *"Lastra*, un Adrade, reclutaba niñas de 14 y 15 años," *El Mexicano*, March 3, 2004.

10. *Proceso*, Numbers 689 and 700; 2002 letter from Guadalajara and Maria Teresa Jardi, *La Cronica de Hoy*, January 22, 2001.

11. Andrade Bojorges, Jose Alfredo. *La historia secreta del narco*.

17. Police Blotter

1. Interview with Jaime Hervella.

2. "Death Stalks the Border" series, *El Paso Times*, June 22-23, 2002.

3. Interview with Judith Galarza, whose non-governmental organization assisted Maria Talamantes in filing the complaint.

4. The U.S. consul's staff in Juarez looked into the alleged police rape of the woman from El Paso.

5. "Detienen a policía por violación en Ciudad Juarez," www.elpueblo.com.mx, November 10, 2003.

6. Interviews with Lance Levine and Susie Azar, two Americans who operated maquiladoras in Juarez.

7. The ICE case received widespread publicity by media in El Paso, Dallas and Mexico. Narco News maintains an internet archive of the story.

8. Retired DEA official Sandalio "Sandy" Gonzalez and U.S. court documents.

9. FBI sources provided lead on $100,000 bribe.

10. Jacinto Segura, *"Lastra*, un Adrade, reclutaba niñas de 14 y 15 años," *El Mexicano*, March 3, 2004; and Moisés Villeda, "Pervertía Menores, Cae Jefe de Previas," *El Mexicano*, February 26, 2004.

11. Sources close to the case provided details about the man with a Colombian accent. A state judge dismissed the charges against three suspects of the alleged sex ring in 2006.

18. Suspects

1. Ramiro Romero, Mexican federal agent, and Victor Valenzuela, former state auxiliary policeman.

2. Interviews with Irene Blanco, Judith Galarza and Sonia del Valle.

3. Interviews with Sharif Abdel Latif Sharif and his former defense lawyers.

4. Interview with Robert Ressler.

5. Police documents on the "Rebeldes" case.

6. Interview with Dr. Irma Rodriguez Galarza.

7. "Death Stalks the Border," *El Paso Times*.

8. Interview with police Captain Sadie Darnell, Gainesville Police Department in Florida.

9. Interview with Manuel Esparza.

10. Interview with an investigator close to the Lucero Campos case.

11. Press conference in 1999 at Cereso in Juarez by the "Toltecas."

12. Tim Madigan, "A Monster Exposed," *Fort Worth Star Telegram*, August 8, 1999.

13. Interviews with Suly Ponce.

14. Interview with David Harry and other former employers of Sharif.

19. Investigations on Trial

1. Interviews with Gustavo de la Rosa Hickerson.

2. Interviews with Sharif.

3. *Fort Worth Star Telegram* series on Sharif, 1999.

4. Interviews with detective Chris Andreychak.

5. Interview with Irene Blanco.

6. "Temo que Navarrete me mande matar: Botello," *El Mexicano*, November 8, 2002.

7. Interview with Antonio Navarrete.

8. Guadalupe de la Mora, Adriana, *El silencio que la voz de todas quiebra*, pp. 121- 131.

9. Interviews with New Jersey Detective Chris Andreychack.

10. Documents on state of health for Gustavo Gonzalez Meza y Javier Garcia Uribe, 2002.

11. Drug urinalysis reports for Gustavo Gonzalez Meza and Javier Garcia Uribe, 2002.

12. Ryan Pearson, "Fugitive Max Factor Heir Caught in Mexico," Associated Press, June 18, 2003.

13. Interview with Mexican military intelligence agent.

14. "Intolerable Killings," Amnesty International report, 2003.

15. Report of the United Nations Task Force Against Drugs and Crime, Juarez mission, November 2003.

16. Testimonies of families of victims at UCLA, Los Angeles, California, 2003; compact disk of event produce by Professor Coco Fusco and testimonies of families of victims at New Mexico State University, Las Cruces, N.M., 2006.

17. Interview with INS inmate Luis Gutierrez.

20. Escaped Serial Killer

1. Interviews with Felipe Pando and Francisco Peña.

2. Interviews with adoptive relatives of Armando Martinez, alias "Alejandro Maynez."

3. "Who's guilty? A look at suspects," *El Paso Times*, June 24, 2002.

4. Interviews El Paso city police officers and Robert Ressler.

5. Interviews with U.S. federal sources.

6. Copy of a "Richy" letter.

7. Angel Subía García. "Dan 113 años de prisión a los Toltecas," "Dictan 40 años de prisión a los integrantes de la banda acusada de crímenes contra mujeres," *Norte de Ciudad Juarez*, January 7, 2005.

21. The FBI: Operation Plaza Sweep

1. Interviews with FBI sources.

2. Interview with Judith Galarza.

3. Interview with Frank Evans.

4. Interviews with relatives of disappeared people and with the International Association of Friends and Relatives of Disappeared Persons

5. ABC TV's "Ted Koppel" program on Juarez "mass graves" investigation, November 1999.

6. Mexican military intelligence sources.

7. CISEN sources.

8. Leaders of "Top Drug Trafficking Ring Indicted," https://www.peace-officers.com/articles/ar070803a.shtml; September 6, 2004.

9. *El Universal* story on "El Chaky," 2006, and story by Rafael Nuñez about Colombian drug lord and "El Chaky."

10. "Ligan a Estrada Cajigal al narcotráfico," Agencia de Noticias-Radio Fórmula, April 12, 2004, and Iván González, "Sigue bajo investigacion Estrada Cajigal: PGR," Noticieros Televisa, April 4, 2004.

11. "2 Mexican Generals Suspected in Mass Graves Arrested," *El Paso Times*, February 9, 2000 y "7 Generals Now Accused in Mexico's War on Drugs," *El Paso Times*, April 9, 2000.

12. Rafael Muñoz Talavera letter.

22. FBI: Mexico's "Dirty War"

1. Various FBI sources.

2. "Mexico: Don't Use Military Justice '"for Dirty War,'" Human Rights News, *Human Rights Watch*, September 30, 2002.

1. "Investigan asesinato de testigo de guerra sucia," NOTIMEX, November 28, 2003.

2. "Background Information for the New International Team for the Accompaniment of Human Rights Defenders in Mexico," Peace Brigade International Newsletter (Europe), Fourth Quarter, 2000; "El general Mario Arturo Acosta Chaparro encabezo una unidad de la Brigada Blanca."

3. Jesús Aranda, "Sabia el alto mando de los ilicitos de Quiros," *La Jornada*, August 12, 2002.

4. Mary Jordan, "Former Chief Spy Arrested in Mexican Dirty War Case," *The Washington Post*, February 20, 2004.

5. FBI sources.

6. Laurie Freeman and Jose Luis Sierra, *Drugs and Democracy in Latin America*, p. 277.

7. Rafael Loret de Mola, *Confidencias peligrosas*, pp. 63-64.

8. Jose Martínez M., *La Crisis online*, June 3, 2003.

9. Interviews with Judith Galarza.

10. Center of Human Rights/Miguel Agustin Pro Juarez.

11. *La Crisis* reported on Rafael Caro Quintero's ranch.

12. Communications with "Operation Dropkick" leader.

13. U.S. State Department report.

14. Kate Doyle, National Security Archive, Mexico project.

15. Agencia Reforma, "Exguerrillera chihuahuense exige a Fox no ser cómplice," *Norte de Ciudad Juarez*, July 26, 2004.

23. FBI: The Femicides

1. Interviews with David Alba, Frank Evans, Oscar Maynez Grijalva, Al Cruz, Robert Ressler, Hardrick Crawford Jr. and J.R. Grijalva

2. Interview with witnesses and Norma Andrade.

3. "Families, Officials, Claim Cover-Ups Keep Killings from Being Solved," *El Paso Times*, June 23, 2003.

4. Jose Maria y Campos letter, 2003.

5. ABC TV "Downtown 20/20," segment of January 30, 2003.

6. Edward Barrera and Sara A. Carter, "Slayings tied to cartels," *San Bernardino Sun*, February 28, 2006

7. FBI intelligence concerning kidnapped girl.

24. FBI: Botched Operation

1. U.S. Customs Service report.

2. Kevin Sullivan, "Eccentric Candidate Faces Test in Tijuana: Late Billionaire's Son Laughs Off Dark Rumors," *The Washington Post*, July 11, 2004.

3. Luz del Carmen Sosa, "Recibi amenazas: Ruvalcaba," *El Diario de Juarez*, March 21, 2003.

4. ICE and FBI sources.

5. Interviews with Jose Maria Guardia, Hardrick Crawford Jr., Cardinal Juan Sandoval Iñiguez, Sonia del Valle, Dr. Stanley Krippner, Sergio Gonzalez and U.S. and Mexican intelligence sources.

6. Jose Maria y Campos letter, 2003.

7. Telemundo "Ciudad sin Ley" special on Juarez, 2003.

8. El Paso news conference to announce FBI hotline.

9. PGR announcement.

25. Modus operandi

1. Intelligence report transmitted by FBI to Mexican authorities, 2003.

2. Interview with Rolando Alvarado.

3. FBI sources.

4. Mexican National Commission for Human Rights, 2004.

5. Interview with State of Chihuahua Special Prosecutor Liliana Herrera.

6. Email letter of Juan Gabriel Capuchino of INCOMEX and Octavio de la Torre defending ECCO schools.

7. Interview with a Mexican federal agent and Jay J.Armes.

8. El Paso mother's testimony about her experience with an ECCO school.

9. Meeting with Alejandro Gertz Manero.

10. Interview with Loren Magaña.

11. Interviews with Art Werge, Oscar Valadez.

12. Citizens who denounced massage parlor.

13. *San Bernardino Sun* interview with former FBI official.

14. Interview with Kent Paterson.

26. Operation Sagrario

1. "No action on Juarez killings," *El Paso Times*, August 15, 2003 and interview with FBI Special Agent Art Werge; Jenaro Villamil, "En el documento se mencionan personajes y lugares relacionados con los crímenes," *La Jornada*, August 16, 2003 and Graciela Atencio, "El circuito de la muerte," *Triple Jornada*, September 1, 2003.

2. El Paso Police Department detective.

3. "Clausuran restaurante," *Norte de Ciudad Juarez*, April 22, 2004.

4. Jesús Aguirre and Jacinto Segura, "Pandillero investigado por el FBI por crímenes contra mujeres," *El Mexicano*, December 12, 2003.

5. Alfredo Corchado and Ricardo Sandoval, "Suspicion of Police Ties in Juarez Killings Mounts; Report Says Women Killed as Celebration," *Dallas Morning News*, Knight Ridder News Service, March 3, 2004.

6. Jacinto Segura, *"Lastra*, un Adrade, reclutaba niñas de 14 y 15 años," *El Mexicano*, March 3, 2004.

7. "NAFTA Gets Mixed Reviews After 1st Decade," *El Paso Times*, June 22, 2003.

8. Rosa Isela Pérez, "Desaparecidos: el drama de nuestras familias," *Norte de Ciudad Juarez*, special series, May 11-17, 2003.

27. Mexico's Secret Files

1. Interviews with confidential Mexican federal security sources and U.S. intelligence sources.

2. Media account of Jose Sanchez Nava's murder; he was an official who was close to the 1996 confidential federal investigation.

3. FBI sources.

4. Interview with Mexican federal congressman.

5. Maury Terry, *The Ultimate Evil*.

6. Sergio González Rodríguez, *Huesos en el desierto*.

7. National leader of the PRI in Mexico.

8. U.S. State Department cable.

28. Pacts of Power

1. Information provided by a Mexican customs official.

2. Interviews with Dr. Stanley Krippner and Sergio Rueda.

3. Interviews with Dr. Rita Laura Segato; and Guadalupe Salcido, "El móvil de crímenes es perpetuar el poder de las mafias o cofradías," *Norte de Ciudad Juarez*, July 29, 2004.

4. Laurie Freeman and Jose Luis Sierra, *Drugs and Democracy in Latin America*, pp. 263-296.

5. Interview with Mexican federal Special Prosecutor Maria Lopez Urbina and Chihuahua State Deputy Attorney General Oscar Valadez.

6. U.N. special task force report, 2003.

7. Derived from the files of Mexican and U.S. officials.

8. FBI sources.

9. "Alert Issued over Meat from Pickton Farm," CBC News British Columbia, Canada, March 10, 2004.

29. Chihuahua City

1. Interviews with Cynthia Kiecker and her family and story by Edgar Prado Calahorra, "Se caen testigos, denuncian tortura," *Norte de Ciudad Juarez*, July 2, 2003.

2. Film documentary by Channel 4 of London, *City of Lost Girls*, 2003.

3. Rosa Isela Pérez, "Exige comisionada castigo a funcionarios," *Norte de Ciudad Juarez*, June 9, 2004.

4. Leopoldo Mares Delgado announced contract between the City of Albuquerque, New Mexico, and the State of Chihuahua, April 2003.

5. Alejandro Suverza y Catalina Gaya, "Las muertas de León," *Cambio*, September 21, 2003, pp. 10-16.

6. Report about women's deaths in Nuevo Leon, Instituto de las Mujeres de Nuevo Leon, www.rima.web.com/ar/violencia, December 29, 2003.

7. www.enlineadirecta.info y "Feminicidios en Mexico: ¿Se expande la epidemia?" *Mujeres Hoy*, www.desarme.org, August 13, 2004, and Edgar Prado Calahorra, "Young Woman's Body Identified near Chihuahua City, Others Missing," *Norte de Ciudad Juarez*, and www.frontera.nmsu.edu, June 27, 2003, plus interview with Kent Paterson.

8. "Intolerable Killings," Amnesty International report, 2003.

9. Tessie Borden, "Chihuahua City May Have Juarez-Type Murder String," *Arizona Republic*, July 20, 2003.

10. New release: County of Alameda, California, and Amigos de las Mujeres de Juarez in New Mexico, 2004.

11. Ruth Mustus, "500 Missing Indigenous Canadian Women: They Don't Seem to Matter," www.iaia.chronicle.org/archives, March 2005; and "Stolen Sisters," Amnesty International, October 4, 2004.

30. The Femicides Spread

1. Francisco Barrio interview published by Zeta in May 2003.

2. Jane Fonda news conference in Guatemala, Associated Press, December 2, 2003, and "Alarma por muertas en Guatemala: onu," *El Universal*, February 11, 2004.

3. "Detienen a 36 sospechosos de 397 feminicidios en Guatemala," AFP/*La Jornada*, December 12, 2004.

4. Laurie Freeman and Jorge Luis Sierra, *Drugs and Democracy in Latin America*, p. 277, and Kent Paterson regarding the Zihuantanejo femicides.

5. Diana Washington Valdez, "Couple Found Innocent of Teen's Slaying," *El Paso Times*, December 18, 2004.

6. Kent Paterson, "Femicides On the Rise in Latin America," IRC Americas Program Report, March 8, 2006.

31. The Politicians

This chapter relies heavily on the works of several Mexican political analysts who hold different views of the country's political history.

1. Carlos Ramirez, publisher of *La Crisis* in Mexico City.

2. Enrique Krauze, author of *Mexico: Biography of Power*.

3. Jorge Castañeda, author of *The Mexican Shock*.

4. U.S. Customs Service videotape of the soldiers who killed federal agents who intercepted an airplane with drugs and Andrew Reding's account of the event.

5. *The Washington Post* on Liebano Saenz.

6. *New York Times* on Hank family.

7. *Proceso* article on ex-CIA agent, 2006.

8. Jorge Fernandez Menendez, *Diario Milenio,* regarding Guillermo González Calderoni.

9. Zapatistas 2005 communiqué regarding Sub-Commander Marcos and his alternative campaign. *La Jornada* covered his campaign travels extensively.

10. Resolutions condemning Juarez femicides passed by the U.S. Senate and the Congress in 2006. Cities including El Paso, Los Angeles, Albuquerque and New York also passed resolutions related to the crimes.

11. Author was asked to brief the U.S. delegation that visited the border in 2003.

12. "Halliburton Awarded 175 Million Contract by pemex," Halliburton newsletter, May 6, 2004.

13. U.S. State Department unclassified cable dated October 2004.

14. See also Alvaro Delgado's book *El Yunque: La Ultraderecha en el poder*.

32. The Pact

This chapter relies heavily on the testimony of a former Mexican official who was at the meeting described in this chapter. U.S. and Mexican intelligence sources confirmed that such a meeting took place.

1. Carlos Loret de Mola Alvarez, *El Negocio*, describes the drug trade's enormous impact on the U.S. and Mexican economies.

2. Enrique Krauze, *Mexico: Biography of Power*, for additional background about Mexican politics.

3. Andrade Bojorges, *La Historia Secreta del Narco*, for reference to the hospital in Juarez and the Picasso painting.

4. Accounts in *La Jornada* and *El Universal* regarding clergy's statements about the drug trade.

5. Testimonies of people who were present at the Horizon City party.

6. Testimony of a Juarez politician. (Tamaulipas politician Humberto Martinez de la Cruz came under fire in 2006 for his candid statement on how government officials in Matamoros negotiated with drug dealers.)

7. Rafael Nuñez. "Colombian Drug Lord Unclaimed in Juarez Morgue," www.newspapertree.com, June 12, 2006.

Epilogue: The Fallout

1. Psalm 12:5, *Holy Bible*, Old Testament, King James Version.

2. Amnesty International's response to the 2006 Mexican federal government's report on the Juarez murders.

3. *Norte de Ciudad Juarez* article about Arturo Chávez Chávez.

4. Daniel Cabeza de Vaca 2006 news conference in Mexico City.

5. Condoleezza Rice presented U.S. State Department Report on Human Rights to Congress, 2006.

6. Interviews with Oscar Maynez Grijalva.

7. Juan Manuel Venegas, "Fox sobre el caso Juarez: a veces escasea la justicia en nuestro país," *La Jornada*, November 26, 2003, and interviews with victims' relatives who met with Vicente Fox.

8. President Vicente Fox Quesada's fourth state of the nation report, www.presidencia.gob.mx/actividades/index, September 1, 2004.

9. Interviews with Guadalupe Morfin and her first report for the Commission to Prevent and Eradicate Violence Against Women in Ciudad Juarez at Los Pinos in Mexico City, June 3, 2004: "Falta investigar y sancionar a los responsables de la violencia contra las mujeres y denuncias por tortura y sancionar a servidores omisos o cómplices."

10. *Reforma*, "Presenta libro en Nueva York, González Rodríguez," Oct. 17, 2003, and "Una década de feminicidio en Mexico," *Reforma*, March 5, 2004.

11. Forensic anthropologists from Argentina, part of an acclaimed team led by Mercedes Doretti, were invited by the Chihuahua authorities to assist. Frank Bender, a forensic sculptor in the United States, also assisted the Chihuahua state authorities.

12. Mexican Federal Attorney General's report on the Juarez murders, 2006.

13. U.S. Embassy in Mexico press announcement, 2006.

14. Drug Enforcement Administration statement about the Tijuana cartel arrest.

15. "Terry Sheron" of Operation Dropkick.

16. El Heraldo de Chihuahua, August 2006.

Bibliography

Interviews

Aguilar, Soledad. Mother of Cecilia Covarrubias.

Alba, David. Special Agent in Charge of FBI in El Paso, Texas.

Alvarado, Rolando. Regional director for the Mexican Federal Investigative Agency, Federal Attorney General's Office.

Amigos de Las Mujeres de Juarez, New Mexico; non-governmental organization. Andrade, Norma. Mother of Lilia Alejandra Garcia Andrade.

Andreychack, Chris. Detective for the New Jersey State Police. Armes, Jay J. Private investigator in El Paso, Texas.

Arvide, Isabel. Mexican author and journalist.

International Association of Relatives and Friends of Disappeared Persons; non-governmental organization in Juarez and El Paso.

Azar, Susie. Former mayor of El Paso, Texas; former owner of a maquiladora in Juarez, Mexico.

Barrios, Emilia. Mother of Violeta Alvidrez Barrios.

Bautista, Yanette. Principal investigator for Amnesty International in the Juarez case. Bejarano, Cynthia. Criminal justice professor for New Mexico State University in Las Cruces, New Mexico.

Benavides, Javier. Former Chihuahua state and city police official.

Bencomo, Elfego. Deputy attorney general for the State of Chihuahua Juarez. Blanco, Irene. Mexican federal congresswoman for the National Action Party. Bloom, Gregory. Author, online editor and radio journalist, New Mexico.

Bolivar, Zulema. State of Chihuahua special prosecutor for the women's homicide investigations in Juarez.

Camacho, Carlos. Mexican federal congressman for the National Action Party.

Caraveo, Victoria. Director of the Chihuahua Women's Institute; founder of Mujeres por Juarez.

Castillo, Bobby. Resident Agent in Charge of the Drug Enforcement Administration in El Paso, Texas.

Castro, Lucha. Lawyer and activist with Justicia para Nuestras Hijas in Chihuahua City.

Cervantes, Patricia. Mother of Neyra Azucena. Chacon, Mario. Lawyer in Juarez.

Chavez, Norma. Texas state representative.

Coalition Against Violence on the Border in El Paso, Texas.

Covarrubias, Oscar. Special agent for the Mexican Federal Attorney General's Office.

Crawford Jr., Hardrick. Agent in Charge of the Federal Bureau of Investigation in El Paso, Texas.

Cruz, Al. FBI special agent in charge, El Paso, Texas.

DeAngelis, George. Assistant chief of the El Paso Police Department in El Paso, Texas.

De la Concha, Rafael Macedo. Mexican Federal Attorney General.

De la Rosa Hickerson, Gustavo. Former director of the CERESO prison in Juarez. Escobedo Salazar, Mario and Escobedo Anaya, Mario. Father and son, lawyers in Juarez.

Evans, Frank. Acting special agent in charge, FBI El Paso division in El Paso, Texas. Galarza, Judith. Activist; officer of the Asociación de Familiares de Desaparecidos y Víctimas de Violaciones a Los Derechos Humanos; sister of Leticia Galarza.

Garcia, Mary Jane. New Mexico state senator.

Gertz Manero, Alejandro. Mexican federal secretary of national security. Garibay, Patricia. Sister of Jorge Garibay.

Gonzalez, Josefina. Mother of Claudia Ivette Gonzalez. González, Paula. Mother of Sagrario González Flores.

González Rodríguez, Sergio. Author of *Huesos en el desierto* and editor for *Reforma*. Grijalva, J.R., Assistant chief of the El Paso Police Department in El Paso, Texas.

Guardia, Jose Maria. Owner of the Juarez racetrack concession.

Gutierrez, Luis. Inmate at the U.S. Immigration and Naturalization Detention Camp, El Paso, Texas.

Harry, David. Executive with Benchmark Research & Technology, former employer of Abdel Latif Sharif.

Herrera, Liliana. Chihuahua state special prosecutor for the women's homicides in Juarez.

Howard, Cheryl. Sociologist and professor at the University of Texas at El Paso. Izaguirre, Samira. Show host and news reporter for Radio AM 1300, Juarez.

Integración de las Madres de Ciudad Juarez.

Johnson, Vanessa. FEMAP foundation representative in El Paso, Texas.

Jordan, Phil. Former director of the Drug Enforcement Administration El Paso Intelligence Center, El Paso, Texas.

Juarez, Heliodoro. Lawyer; former president of the Chihuahua State Commission for Human Rights.

Justicia para Nuestras Hijas in Chihuahua City. Kiecker, Carroll. Mother of Cynthia Kiecker. Kiecker, Claire. Sister of Cynthia Kiecker.

Krippner, Stanley. Psychology professor for the Saybrook Graduate School, San Francisco, California.

Kuykendall, Travis. Director of the West Texas High-Intensity Drug Trafficking Area and former DEA agent.

Lardizabal, Rosa. City councilwoman for Juarez and sister of former policeman Javier Felipe Lardizabal.

Ledesma, Norma. Mother of Paloma Escobar, Chihuahua City. Leoni, Mark. Former U.S. Consul official in Juarez.

Levine, Lance. Owner of a maquiladora in Juarez.

Lopez Urbina, Maria. The first Mexican special federal prosecutor assigned to investigate the women's murders in Juarez.

Luna de la Rosa, Celia. Mother of Guadalupe Luna de la Rosa.

Magaña, Loren. Co-director of the International Association of Relatives and Friends of Disappeared Persons.

Margo, Adair. Founder of the FEMAP foundation in El Paso, Texas.

Maria y Campos, Jose. Letter from the Mexican Foreign Ministry addressed to the U.S. Embassy in Mexico, 2003.

Maynez Grijalva, Oscar. Former Chihuahua state forensic chief and state criminologist; professor for the Autonomous University of Juarez.

Medina, Antonio. President of the Association of Clubs and Restaurants in Ciudad Juarez, a trade organization.

Mendez-Quiroga, Lorena. Independent filmmaker and journalist for FOX TV News en Los Angeles, California.

Morfin Otero, Guadalupe. Commissioner for the Commission to Prevent and Eradicate Violence Against Women in Juarez.

Molinar, Jorge. Former Chihuahua state deputy attorney general in Juarez. Monarrez, Benita. Mother of Laura Berenice Monarrez.

Monarrez Fragoso, Julia. Professor at the Colegio de la Frontera in Juarez. Monreal, Irma. Mother of Esmeralda Herrera Monreal.

Morales, Ramona. Mother of Silvia Elena Rivera.

Muñoz, Victor. Co-founder of the Coalition Against Violence on the Border, El Paso, Texas.

Najera Castro, Nahum. Former Chihuahua state deputy attorney general in Juarez.

Navarrete, Antonio. Former Chihuahua state chief of homicide investigations and city traffic police chief in Juarez.

Nuestras Hijas de Regreso a Casa in Juarez.

Ocegueda, Pete. Sergeant and detective with the El Paso Police Department. Ocho de Marzo.

Ortega, Jose. Chihuahua state deputy attorney general in Juarez. Ortega, Marisela. Journalist with *Norte de Monterrey*.

Pando, Felipe. Former Chihuahua state police official and uncle of Guadalupe Veronica Castro Pando and Airis Pando.

Pérez, Irma. Mother of Olga Alicia Carrillo Pérez.

Ponce, Suly. Former Chihuahua state special prosecutor for the women's homicides in Juarez.

Quijano, Alfredo. Editor of *Norte de Ciudad Juarez*.

Ramirez, Carlos. Editor of *La Crisis*, columnist and Mexican political analyst. Ressler, Robert. Former FBI profiler and author; he coined the term "serial killer."

Rodriguez Galarza, Irma. Forensic officer, author and a former Chihuahua state police commander. Mother of Paloma Villa.

Sadie, Darnell. Police captain for the Gainesville Police Department in Gainesville, Florida.

Salazar, Maximino. Lawyer in Juarez.

Sandoval Iñiguez, Juan. Cardinal of the Roman Catholic Church in Guadalajara, Mexico.

Schwein, Richard. Former FBI official in El Paso, Texas. Shapleigh, Eliot. Texas state senator.

Sharif, Abdel Latif Sharif Sharif.

Skrapec, Candice. Criminologist and professor in California. She had access to more than 200 of the homicide case files.

Solis, Hilda. United States Representative to Congress.

Talavera, Angela. Chihuahua state special prosecutor for the women's homicides in Juarez.

Rodriguez Torres, David. Mexican federal congressman; provided copies of the federal government's DNA results for the 2001 cotton field murders; National Action Party.

Valadez, Oscar. Chihuahua state deputy attorney general in Juarez.

Valenzuela, Victor. Former Chihuahua state police auxiliary agent; inmate at the CERESO prison in Juarez.

Varela, Héctor. "Benavides y el gran robo de joyas," www.todoseditores.com/semanario, October 24, 2000.

Vasconcelos, Jose Santiago. Mexican federal deputy attorney general.

Villagrana, Luis. "El Chandocan ordeno despedir a Botello," www.todoseditores.com/semanario, October 24, 2000.

Voces sin Eco.

Vucovich, Alma. Mexican federal congresswoman and president of the legislative Gender and Equality Commission, member of the Revolutionary Democratic Party.

Werge, Art. FBI special agent.

Books

Aguayo, Sergio. *La Charola*. Mexico City: Grijalbo, 2001.

Andrade Bojorges, Jose A. *La Historia Secreta Del Narco: Desde Navolato Vengo.*

Mexico City: Océano de Mexico, S.A., 1999.

Arvide, Isabel. *Muerte en Juarez*. Mexico City: Grupo Editorial Siete, 1996.

Benítez, Rohry; Candia, Adriana; Cabrera, Patricia; De la Mora, Guadalupe; Martínez, Josefina; Velásquez, Isabel; Ortiz, Ramona. *El silencio que la voz de todas quiebra*. Chihuahua City: Ediciones del Azar, 1999.

Bowden, Charles. *Down by the River*. New York: Simon & Schuster, 2002. Castañeda, Jorge G. *The Mexican Shock: Its Meaning for the United States*. New York: New Press, 1995.

Coronado, Irasema and Staudt, Kathleen. *Fronteras No Mas: Toward Social Justice U.S.-Mexico Border*. New York: Palgrave MacMillan, 2002.

Davidow, Jeffrey. *El Oso y El Puercoespín*. Mexico City: Grijalbo, 2003. Desfassiaux, Oscar. *Los Chacales de Ciudad Juarez*. Mexico City: Libros para Todos, 2004.

Fernandez Menendez, Jorge. *Narcotrafico y poder*. Mexico City: Rayuela Editores, S.A., 1999.

Freeman, Laurie and Sierra, Jose Luis. "Mexico: The Militarization Trap." *Drugs and Democracy in Latin America: The Impact of U.S. Policy*, editors Youngers, Coletta and Rosin, Eileen, Boulder, Lynne Rienner, 2005.

Gonzalez Rodriguez, Sergio. *Huesos en el desierto*. Barcelona: Anagrama, S.A., 2002.

Krauze, Enrique. *Mexico: Biography of Power*: HarperCollins. New York, 1997. Loret de Mola, Carlos. *El Negocio*. Mexico City: Grijalbo, 2001.

Loret de Mola Alvarez, Rafael. *Confidencias Peligrosas*. Mexico City: Océano de Mexico, S.A., 2002.

Poppa, Terrence. *Drug Lord*. New York: Pharos Books, 1990.

Psalm 12:5, Old Testament. *Holy Bible*, King James Version, Nashville: Thomas Nelson, 1972.

Rodriguez Galarza, Irma. *Identificación Forense Estomatológica*. Ciudad Juarez: Lazer, 2001.

Terry, Maury. *The Ultimate Evil*. New York: Barnes & Noble Books, 1999.

Vericat, Isabel. *Ciudad Juarez: De este lado del puente*. Mexico City: Instituto Nacional de las mujeres and Epikeia, A.C., 2004.

Documents

Amnesty International. *Muertes Intolerables: Diez años de desapariciones y asesinatos de mujeres en Ciudad Juarez y Chihuahua*, August 11, 2003; AMR 41/027/2003.

Amnesty International. Mexico. *Muertes Intolerables*. Statistical abstract, August 11, 2003.

Amnesty International. "Stolen Sisters," October 4, 2004.

Berdon, Eduardo. Memorandum of the Mexican Federal Attorney General's Office regarding activities of Vicente Carrillo Fuentes in Juarez, March 20, 1998.

City of Juarez. Municipal Public Registry. Property record of owner of the cotton field tract at Ejercito Nacional and Paseo de la Victoria (also called A.J. Bermudez Street).

Comunicado del Ejercito Zapatista de Liberación Nacional; carta del FZLN al EZLN. Comunicado del Comité Clandestino Revolucionario Indígena, Comandancia General del Ejercito Zapatista de Liberacion Nacional, Mexico, November 20, 2005.

El Paso County Medical Examiner's Office. Autopsy report for Sandra Vasquez Juarez, 1996.

Eskridge, Chris. "Mexican Cartels And Their Integration Into Mexican Socio-Political Culture," report for the International Conference on Organized Crime, Lausanne, Switzerland, October 1999.

Human Rights Watch. "Mexico: Don't Use Military Justice for Dirty War" *Human Rights Watch News*, September 30, 2002.

Instituto Chihuahuense de la Mujer. *Homicidios de Mujeres: Auditoria Periodistica* (January 1993-July 2003), Juarez, 2003.

Inter-American Commission for Human Rights (OAS). Report on the homicides of women in Juarez, 2003.

Juzgado Segundo de lo Penal/Estado de Chihuahua. Case file No. 11323/93-403: Felipe Javier Lardizabal.

Juzgado Tercero de lo Penal/Estado de Chihuahua. Case file No. 426/01/Homicide: Gustavo Gonzalez Meza and Víctor García Uribe.

Monarrez Fragaso, Julia. Feminicidio sexual serial en Ciudad Juarez: 1993-2001;

Debate Feminista, 13th Year, Volume 25, April 2002.

Mexican National Commission for Human Rights. Report on the homicides of women in Juarez, 1998.

Mexican National Commission for Human Rights. Report on the homicides of women in Juarez, 2004.

Mexican Federal Commission to Prevent and Eradicate Violence Against Women in Juarez. *Report*: November *2003 April 2004. Ciudad Juarez: Secretaría de Gobernacion,* 2004.

National Security Archive. Doyle, Kate. "Human Rights and the Dirty War in Mexico," May 2003.

National Security Archive. Doyle, Kate. "Report Documents 18 Years of 'Dirty War' in Mexico," February 26, 2006.

Oficina de Las Naciones Unidas Contra la Droga y el Delito. "Informe de la Comision de Expertos Internacionales de la Organizacion de las Naciones Unidas/sobre la Misión en Ciudad Juarez," Mexico, November 2003.

Pan-American Health Organization/World Health Organization in El Paso, Texas. Report and statistics on health in the border region Mexico-United States, 1995- 1997.

Plan Estratégico para Ciudad Juarez. Email letter that refers to the negative effect of publicity on Juarez about the women's murders, 2004.

Policía Judicial del Estado de Chihuahua. "Homicidios en Serie Efectuados en el Sector de Lomas de Poleo durante el mes de marzo al mes de abril de 1996," 1996.

Procuraduría General de Justicia del Estado de Chihuahua. *Informe* de *Homicidios cometidos en perjuicio de mujeres en Ciudad Juarez (1993-1998),* February 1998.

Procuraduría General de La Republica de Mexico. *Informe sobre los homicidios de mujeres en Ciudad Juarez,* 2006.

Procuraduría General de la Republica de Mexico. Arrest warrant against the alleged leaders of the Juarez drug cartel, UEDO "maxiproceso" documents, January 16, 1998.

United States Customs Service. *Operation White Tiger*, investigative report, Case No. SD02BR97SD0022; November 25, 1997.

United States Department of Homeland Security. ICE press release. "Four indicted in ICE probe of Brothel Where Mexican Women as Young as 14 Worked as Prostitutes," April 9, 2004.

United States State Department. *Report on Human Rights Practices, Mexico*; Bureau of Democracy, Human Rights, and Labor, 11-12, 2004.

United States State Department. *Report on Human Rights Practices, Mexico*; Bureau of Democracy, Human Rights, and Labor, 2006.

United States State Department, various agency documents obtained through the Freedom of Information Act at the request of Dr. Keith Yearman, College of Dupage., 1995-2005.

Multimedia reports

ABC Television "Downtown 20/20," Juarez murders, January 2003.

ABC Television "Ted Koppel," Juarez "mass graves" report, November 30, 1999. Aranda, Jesús. "Sabía el alto mando de los ilicitos de Quiros," *La Jornada*, August 12, 2002.

Aguilar, Sonia. "Devuelve PGR a Estado case Campo Algodonero," *Norte de Ciudad Juarez*, June 29, 2006.

Aguirre, Jesús and Segura, Jacinto. "Pandillero Investigado por FBI por Crimenes Contra Mujeres," *El Mexicano*, December 12, 2003.

Alvarez, Jorge. "Las muertas de Juarez. Bioética, poder, genero e injusticia," XVI Congreso Mundial de Sexología.

Atencio, Graciela. "El circuito de la muerte," *Triple Jornada (La Jornada)*, September 1, 2003.

Bañuelos, Claudio. "Bendice el Obispo Ramon Godínez las limosnas dadas por narcotraficantes," *La Jornada online*, September 20, 2005.

Barrio, Francisco. Letter from Francisco Barrio to *El Diario de Ciudad Juarez* responding to allegations in story by the *El Paso Times*, and the "maxiproceso" documents, October 16, 2000.

Borden, Tessie. "Chihuahua City May Have Juarez-Type Murder String," *The Arizona Republic*, July 20, 2003.

Borunda, Daniel. "Cartel suspects caught in Spain, El Paso," *El Paso Times*, August 5, 2005.

Cabildo, Miguel. "Consignados cuatro federales violadores, pero son cinco identificados y aún faltan," *Proceso*, January 22, 1990.

Capuchino, Juan. Electronic letter regarding computer schools, August 28, 2003. Carreón, Héctor. Para Sagrario Online Project, 1999.

Castañon, Aracely and Hernandez, Pablo. "Protestan miles por muertas," *El Diario de Juarez*, February 15, 2004.

Castro, Salvador. "Investigan ligas de exjudicial con narcos," *Norte de Ciudad Juarez*, November 2002.

Castro, Salvador. "Hallan osamenta en Km 30," *Norte de Ciudad Juarez*, April 15, 2004.

Castro, Salvador and Chaparro, Ana. "Ejecutan sicarios a Dante Almaraz," *Norte de Ciudad Juarez*, January 26, 2006.

Dettmer, Jamie. "U.S. Drug Warriors Knock on Heaven's Door," *Insight Magazine*, April 21, 1997.

El Diario de Ciudad Juarez. "Muerto era padre de joven asesinada en Loma Blanca," July 18, 2006.

EFE. "Jane Fonda, Salma Hayek Seek Justice for Slain Juarez Women," May 12, 2006.

El Heraldo de Chihuahua. "Abogado de Victoria Loya se suicidó," October 25, 2005.

El Mexicano. "No desaparecemos mujeres, dice director de ECCO," April 9, 2002.

El Paso Herald-Post, "Kidnapping," 1995.

El Paso Times. "Death Stalks the Border," June 23-24, 2002.

El Paso Times. "Ex-Juarez police official shot to death," (Corral Barron) March 20, 2002.

El Paso Times. "Girl 16, is latest to disappear in Juarez," (ECCO), January 27, 2002.

El Paso Times. "Juarez murders inquiry turns to computer school,"

April 7, 2002.

El Paso Times. "Mexican law officials face corruption charges," (PGR), January 4, 2001.

El Paso Times. "Mexico's anti-drug officials visit Juarez," June 3, 1990.

El Paso Times. "U.N. investigator looks into murders," July 24, 1999.

El Paso Times. "U.N. investigates deaths of Juarez women," May 19, 2001. *El Paso Times.* "Woman wanted in 2000 slaying seen with man reported missing," July 30, 2005.

ElPueblo.com.mx. "Desaparece otra joven de Chihuahua," May 19, 2003.

El Universal and EFE online. "Expondrá Mexico en Europa feminicidios en Juarez," April 14, 2006.

El Universal. "Nazar: jamás torture ni asesine a nadie," February 21, 2004.

Esquivel, J. Jesús. "Revela ex jefe de la CIA secretos del régimen salinista,"

Proceso, reprinted in *El Diario de Juarez*, February 19, 2006.

ExtraTV Warner Brothers Studios. "Salma Seeks Help for Voiceless Women," June 23, 2006.

Flynn, Ken. "DEA mum on alleged role in raid," *El Paso Herald-Post*, May 6, 1995. Gootenberg, "The Birth of the Narcs: The First Illicit Cocaine Flows in the Americas, 1947-1964," draft, Stony Brook University, Summer-Winter 2003.

Halliburton News. "Halliburton Awarded $175 Million Contract By PEMEX," www.halliburton.com/news, May 6, 2004.

Hernandez, Margarita. "'Protege Fox a funcionario negligente,'" *Norte de Ciudad Juarez*, March 10, 2006.

Huerta, Carlos. "Identifican a banda 'Los Escajeda," *Norte de Ciudad Juarez*, March 10, 2006.

Huerta, Carlos. "Levantan y fichan a sexo servidoras," *Norte de Ciudad Juarez*, March 21, 2004.

Huerta, Carlos. "Libran contra violador serial orden de arresto en Juarez," *Norte de Ciudad Juarez*, March 9, 2006.

Huerta, Carlos. "Niega PGJE envió de expediente a Policía Municipal," *Norte de Ciudad Juarez*, April 6, 2002.

Huerta, Carlos. "Niega juez regresar el caso Escobedo," *Norte de Ciudad Juarez*, February 19, 2002.

Human Rights Watch News. "Dictamen judicial representa un retroceso," the Myrna Mack case in Guatemala, May 8, 2003.

Infosel Financiero. "Mi animal favorito es la mujer: Hank Rhon: Se queja PAN por comentario misógino del priista," www.terra.com.mx, June 16, 2004.

Jordan, Mary. "Former Spy Chief Arrested in Mexican 'Dirty War' Case," *Washington Post*, February 20, 2004.

Jordan, Mary. "Move Against Police Heartens Some," *Washington Post*, February 12, 2004.

Jordan, Sandra. "City of Lost Girls," Channel 4 of London, special television report, November 2003.

La Hora (Guatemala). "Trabajadores sindicalizados bajo amenazas de muerte," September 9, 2003.

Los Angeles Times. "Documents show prosecutors hid facts," October 29, 1997.

Los Angeles Times. "Mexican drug czar accused of human rights violations loses power with demotion," October 16, 1990.

Madigan, Tim. "A Monster Exposed," *Fort Worth Star Telegram*, August 8-10, 1999.

Martínez, Fernando. "Tomza y La Nueva Fiscalia del Caso Juarez," ad in *Norte de Ciudad Juarez*, 2004.

Martinez, Margarita. "Colombia sends man to face cocaine charges in U.S.," Associated Press, July 14, 2000.

Mejía, Fabrizio. "En el territorio del Tigre Blanco," *Proceso*, February 15, 2004.

McDonnell, Patrick. "FBI looks at alleged ties between traffickers and chief's former assistant," *El Paso Times*, June 28, 2000.

Mozingo, Joe. "New president of Honduras softens stance on street gangs," *Miami Herald*, reprinted in the *El Paso Times*, April 15, 2006.

New York Times. "Jorge Hank Rhon: un empresario sospechoso," April 14, 2004.

Norte de Ciudad Juarez. "Clausuran restaurante," April 24, 2004. Notimex. "Trasladaran a Durango cuerpo de Matutino," June 28, 2006.

Orme, William. "At pig farm, Vancouver Police Reap Grisly Clues," *Los Angeles Times*, March 26, 2002.

Paterson, Kent. "Crime of the Century," radio documentary aired by Radio Bilingue, California, 2004.

Paterson, Kent. "Globalization, Class Femicide and Human Rights Violations in Northern Mexico," presentation, 2004.

Pearson, Ryan. "Fugitive Max Factor Heir Caught in Mexico," Associated Press, June 18, 2003.

Pérez, Rosa Isela. "Desaparecidos: el drama de nuestras familias," *Norte de Ciudad Juarez*, special series, May 11-17, 2003.

Pérez, Rosa Isela. "Exhibe Morfin Impunidad," *Norte de Ciudad Juarez*, June 9, 2004.

Pérez, Rosa Isela. "Premian con altos puestos a impunes: Escalan con éxito en su carrera política servidores distinguidos por alterar evidencias en los feminicidios," *Norte de Ciudad Juarez*, May 8, 2004.

Pérez, Rosa Isela. "Ricos, los verdaderos asesinos," *Norte de Ciudad Juarez*, September 7, 2002.

Ponce de Leon, Alberto and Vélez, Armando. "El Patio de la Muerte," *Milenio Semanal*, February 2, 2004.

Prado, Edgar. "Cesan de Secretaria a policías homicidas," *Norte de Ciudad Juárez*, November 19, 2003.

Prado, Edgar. "Ignora el Estado a expertos de la ONU," *Norte de Ciudad Juarez*, May 3, 2004.

Prado, Edgar. "Manipulan el informe de la ONU," *Norte de Ciudad Juarez*, April 29, 2004.

Ramírez, Rodrigo. "Sigue libre la agente que sembró evidencia," *Norte de Ciudad Juarez*, April 6, 2002.

Ravelo, Patricia and Bonilla, Rafael. "Batalla de las Cruces," documentary, CIESAS, Mexico City, 2005.

Resendiz, Julian. "Police agree to back off from kidnapping case," *El Paso Herald-Post*, May 3, 1995.

Resendiz, Julian. "Prosecutors struggle to keep suspected killer in Juarez jail," *El Paso Herald-Post*, March 27, 1996.

Rodriguez, Armando. "Ejecutan a expolicía," *El Diario de Juarez*, February 14, 2002.

Rodriguez, Olga. "Hollywood Celebrities Join March to Protest Slayings in Ciudad Juarez," Associated Press, February 14, 2004.

Sánchez Orozco, Alejandra. "Ni Una Mas," 2002. Sánchez Orozco, Alejandra and Cordero, Jose Antonio. "Bajo Juarez," 2006. Documentary about the Juarez femicides; Mexico City.

Sánchez, Julián and Zarate, Arturo. "Niega Obispo versión sobre limosnas del narcotráfico," El Universal online, March 12, 2006.

Silva, Guadalupe. "Apology accepted: Mexico won't hold grudge in embarrassing arrest," *El Paso Times*, July 12, 1990.

Silva, Mario. "Relatora de la ONU para las mujeres asesinadas en Juarez," *El Financiero*, June 26, 1999.

Sosa, Luz del Carmen. "Denuncian presunto plagio de 2 paseños, Sospechan que ex conyuge de la mujer está implicado en el caso," *El Diario de Ciudad Juarez*, June 2, 2002.

Sosa, Luz del Carmen. "Recibi amenazas: Ruvalcaba," *El Diario de Ciudad Juarez*, March 21, 2003.

Stack, Megan. "Journalist, sister form rape center in Juarez," *El Paso Times*, September 24, 1998.

Telemundo. "Ciudad Sin Ley," documental sobre Ciudad Juarez, May 2003.

TV3 (Barcelona). "Crimenes sin Respuesta," Televisio de Catalunya, February 2, 2006.

V-Day News Alert. "Jane Fonda visits Guatemala to put spotlight of murders of women in Guatemala," V-Day bulletin, December 8, 2003.

Vélez, Armando and Ponce de Leon, Alberto. "Angelica Fuentes, la reina del gas,"

El Milenio Semanal, May 10, 2004.

Venegas, Juan. "Fox sobre el caso Juarez: A veces escasea la justicia en nuestro país; Familiares de desaparecidas afirman que no le darán al mandatario un cheque en blanco," *La Jornada*; and photograph of Norma Andrade with President Vicente Fox, November 26, 2003.

Villeda, Moises. "Pervertía Menores, Cae Jefe de Previas," *El Mexicano*, February 26, 2004.

Vulliamy, Ed. "Murder in Mexico," special report, *The (London) Observer*, March 9, 2003.

Washington Valdez, Diana. "2 Mexican generals suspected in 'mass graves' arrested," *El Paso Times*, September 2, 2000.

Washington Valdez, Diana. "Mysterious American kept files of Juarez trysts," *El Paso Times*, May 6, 2002.

Watson, Julie. "Mexican presidency linked to 'dirty war,'" Associated Press, February 28, 2006.

Zamarripa, Leticia. "El Paso detectives assist inquiry into Juarez slayings," *El Paso Times*, April 2, 1996.

Zamarripa, Leticia. "Gang paid to lure women, sources say," *El Paso Times*, April 17, 1996.

Appendix

Victims
(1993-2006)

Year, and when known, the victim's name, age and cause of death:

1993

Alma Mireya Chavarria Favila, 5; raped, strangled.

Angelica Luna Villalobos, 16; pregnant, strangled.

*Unidentified (*021793), 35, stabbed.

Jessica Lizalde de Leon, 30; shot to death.

Luz Ivonne de la O García, 20; sex-murder.

Yolanda Alvarez Esquihua, 28; strangled.

Elizabeth Ramos, 26; shot to death.

*Unidentified (*051293), 20-24 years old; raped, stabbed.

Veronica Huitron Quezada, 30; stabbed, incinerated.

Guadalupe I. Estrada Salas, 16; sex-murder.

*Unidentified (*08293), 28-30 years old; strangled.

Gabriela Domínguez Aguilar, 3; strangled.

Maria T. Contreras Hernandez, 40; shot to death.

Maria Esther Lopez de Ruiz, 43; stabbed.

Marcela Santos Vargas, 18; unknown.

Mireya Hernandez Mendez, 18-20 years old, strangled.

Maria de J. Barrón Rodriguez, 30.

Tomasa Salas Calderón; found seminude.

Esmeralda Leyva Rodriguez, 13; raped, strangled.

Rebeca E. Escobedo Sosa, 24; stabbed.

Gloria Yolanda Tapia Vega, 52; raped, stabbed.

Ana Maria Gil Bravo; 34; found seminude, strangled; shot to death.

1994

Unidentified (010294), 35; found seminude, strangled.

Esmeralda Andrade Gutierrez, 35; sex murder, shot to death.

Emilia García Hernandez (or Alicia Pulido Saraid Durón), 32; stabbed.

Maria del Roció Cordero Esquivel, 10; raped, strangled.

Patricia Alba ríos, 30; shot to death.

Lorenza I. Gonzalez Alamillo, 38; raped, mutilated, strangled.

Gladys Janeth Fierro Vargas, 10; raped, strangled.

Donna Maurine Striplin Boggs, 28; Albuquerque, New Mexico, stabbed.

Maria Agustina Hernandez, 33; strangled.

Maria Enfield de Martínez; shot to death.

Rosa Maria Lerma Hernandez, 23; stabbed.

Patricia "La Burra" (Maria del Rosario Lara Loya), 48; beaten to death.

Hilda Fierro Elias, 18; head injury.

Antonia Ramirez Calderon, 35; strangled.

Unidentified (102594), 25; strangled.

Viridiana Torres Moreno, 3; head injury.

Graciela Bueno de Hernandez, 26; shot to death.

Unidentified (110994); strangled.

Esmeralda Urias Saenz, 23; strangled.

Guillermina Hernandez Chavez, 15; sex-murder; suffocated.

1995

Unidentified (010195), 14-17 years old; sex-murder.

Maria Cristina Quezada Amador, 32; raped, strangled.

Graciela García Primero, 28; multiple wounds.

Leticia Reyes Benítez, 20; shot to death.

Carla Magdalena Contreras Lopez, 24; shot to death.

Miriam Arlem Velásquez Mendoza, 14; raped, stabbed.

Rosa Virginia. de Hernandez Cano; 31; stabbed.

Alejandra Viescas Castro, 13; shot to death with Ozuna Aguirre; double homicide.

Maria Inés Ozuna Aguirre, 18; shot to death; double homicide.

Rosario Aguayo; head injury.

Fabiola Zamudio, 35; found seminude at El Ranchito motel; police said drug overdose was cause of death.

Karina Daniela Gutierrez, 21; strangled.

Unidentified No.1 (050295); shot to death.

Unidentified No.2 (050295).

Silvia Elena Rivera Morales, 15; strangled.

Elizabeth Martinez Rodriguez, 26; shot to death.

"Garcia Aldaba;" serious wounds.

Rosalba Ortega Saucedo, 36; shot execution style.

Araceli Esmeralda Martinez Montañez, 20; raped, strangled.

Liliana Frayre Bustillos, 23; shot to death.

Erika García Moreno, 18; strangled.

Teodora de la Rosa Martínez, 53; stabbed.

Olivia Gloria. Morales de Ríos, 28; strangled.

Patricia Cortez Garza. 33; raped, strangled. Police reported it as a drug overdose.

Olga Alicia Carrillo Pérez, 20; sex murder; (Lote Bravo).

Elizabeth Castro García, 17; sex murder; strangled.

Gloria Elena Escobedo Piña, 20; raped, strangled.

Unidentified No. 1 (082295), 15; mutilated; sex-murder; (Lote Bravo).

Unidentified No.2 (082295); sex-murder; (Lote Bravo).

Maria de los Angeles Hernandez Deras, 28; shot to death.

Unidentified (090595); 20-24 years old; mutilated; sex murder; (Lote Bravo).

Maria Moreno Galaviz; crushed skull.

Rosa Isela Corona Santos, 16; shot to death.

Unidentified (081195/091095), 18; stabbed; sex murder.

Adriana Martinez Martinez; shot to death.

Adriana Torres Marquez, 15; mutilated; sex murder; (Lote Bravo).

Unidentified (110295), 18-20 years old; sex murder; (Lote Bravo).

Francisca Lucero Gallardo, 18; found in Guadalupe Distrito Bravos (east of Zaragoza); shot to death.

Cecilia Covarrubias Aguilar, 19; her infant daughter was kidnapped; shot to death.

Silvia Alcantar Enríquez; shot to death; triple homicide.

Claudia Escamilla Alcantar (2); shot to death; triple homicide.

Maria Maynez Sustaita (3); shot to death; triple homicide.

Francisca Lucero Gallardo; shot to death.

Ignacia (Morales) Rosales Soto, 22; stabbed, skull crushed.

Rosa Ivonne Paez Marquez, 14; shot to death.

Rosa Isela Tena Quintanilla, 14; stabbed and strangled; sex murder.

Laura Ana Inere, 27; shot to death.

Elizabeth Robles Gomez, 23; stabbed and shot.

1996

Unidentified (011496), infant; strangled; sex-murder.

Norma Mayela Palacios Lopez, 33; head wound.

Martha Arguijo Castañeda, 33; shot to death.

Francisca Epigmenia Hernandez, 36; raped and strangled.

Estefania Corral (Gonzalez) Martinez, 2; gunfire wound.

Silvia Valdez Martinez, 5; gunfire wound.*

Unidentified (031396); 10-12 years old; stabbed.

Unidentified (1295/031396), 19; sex murder.

Silvia Ocon Lopez, 17; shot to death.

Unidentified (022596/031896), 17; sex murder; (Lomas de Poleo).

"Lucy," (0296-0396/031896), 19; sex murder; (Lomas de Poleo).

"Tanya" (0296-0396/031896), 22; sex murder; (Lomas de Poleo).

Guadalupe Veronica Castro Pando (0296/0395/031896), 17; strangled; sex murder; (Lomas de Poleo).

Unidentified (031896); 16-18 years old; sex murder; Lomas de Poleo.

Unidentified (1195/032996), 14-16 years old; sex murder.

Rocío (Rosario) García Leal (1295/040796), 17; raped, stabbed; mutilated; (Lomas de Poleo).

Rosario de Fátima Martínez, 19; strangled.

Araceli Gallardo Rodriguez, 35; shot to death.

Unidentified (060996); 16-18 years old.

Silvia Rivera Salas (062096), 15-17 years old; stabbed.

Maria Cecilia de Jesus Navarrete Reyes, 14; head wound.

Unidentified (070896); 20-25 years old; stabbed.

Sandra Luz Juarez Vazquez (070796), 17; strangled.

Rocio Aguero Miranda, 30; unknown.

Sonia Ivette Sanchez Ramirez, 13; head wound.

Soledad Beltran Castillo, 30; shot to death.

Alma Leticia Palafox Zavala, 14; stabbed.

Unidentified (081896), 17; stabbed.

Luz Adriana Martinez Reyes, 17; shot to death.

Rita Parker Hopkins; 35; double homicide (1); shot in the head; lived in El Paso, Texas.

Victoria Parker Hopkins; 27; double homicide (2); shot in the head; lived in El Paso, Texas.

Hilda Sosa Jimenez, 29; shot to death in the Chulavista motel.

Luz M. Jimenez Aguilar; 18; shot to death; double homicide (1).

Maria Marisol Franco de Garcia; 47; shot to death;

double homicide (2).

Claudia Ramos Lopez, 8; shot to death.

Maria Domitila Torres Nava, 45; stabbed.

Antonia Hernandez Perez, 36; head wound.

Unidentified (100196); 19-25 years old; stabbed.

Leticia de la Cruz Bañuelos, 3; shot to death.

Leticia García Rosales, 37; head wound.

Maria S. Lujan Mendoza, 25; shot to death.

Police said it was a possible suicide.

Brenda Lizeth Najera Flores; 15; tortured and shot to death with her cousin; double homicide (1).

Susana Flores Flores; 13; tortured; shot to death; double homicide (2).

Rosario de Fátima Martínez Angel; strangled.

Alma Delia Lopez Guevara, strangled. * May be previous unidentified.

1997

Gloria Moreno Aviles, 33; head wound.

Maria de la Luz Murgado Larrea (Gutiérrez); 42; strangled.

Cinthya Rocío. Acosta Alvarado, 10; strangled; sex-murder.

Ana Maria Gardea Villalobos, 12; stabbed.

Maria Montes Lazcano, 27; shot to death; homicide-suicide.

Silvia Guadalupe Diaz, 19; strangled.

Maribel Palomino Arvizu, 17; stabbed; sex-murder.

Maria I. Haro Prado; shot to death.

Miriam Aguilar Rodríguez, 17; head wound; sex-murder.

Elvira Varela Perez, 38; head wound.

Karina Soto Diaz, 3; shot to death.

Amelia Lucio Borja, 18; stabbed.

Verónica Beltrán Manjarrez, 15; shot to death.

Apolonia Fierro Poblano, 66; stabbed.

Marcela Macias Hernandez, 35; strangled.

Roxana I. Veliz Madrid, 17; shot to death.

Unidentified (070897); 22-25 years old.

Maria de Lourdes Villaseñor, 32; strangled.

Elisa Rivera Rodriguez, 63; shot to death.

Teresa Helida Herrera Rey; 26; lived in El Paso; shot; double homicide (1).

Maria Eugenia Martinez Hoo; 27; shot; double homicide (2).

Unidentified (0897-0997); 55-60 years old; head wound.

Martha Yolanda Gutierrez Garcia, 28; strangled; sex-murder.

Maria Irma Plancarte Luna, 30; head wound.

Brenda Esther Alfaro Luna, 15-17; stabbed; sex-murder.

Virginia Rodriguez Beltran, 32; shot to death.

Juana Aguiñaga Mares, 25-30; strangled.

Hortensia Parra Chavez, 58-60; shot to death.

Sofia Gonzalez Vivar, 20; head wound; sex-murder.

Norma Julisa Ramos Muñoz, 21; shot to death.

Erendira Buendia Muñoz, 17; stabbed; strangled.

Maria Teresa. Renteria Salazar, 34; stabbed.

Araceli Nuñez Santos, 19-22; stabbed; sex-murder.

Amalia Saucedo Diaz de Leon, 33; broken neck; cervical trauma.

Karina Avila Ochoa, 29; beaten to death.

Rosa M. Arellanes García, 24; lived in El Paso, Texas; shot to death.

Julia Mauricio de Colorbio, 77; head wounds.

Unidentified (121997); 15-17 years old.

Rosa Linda Gardea Sandoval, 30; strangled.

Blanca Cecilia Rivas Lopez, 13; (20385/97); identified in 2006 PGR report. *May be previous unidentified.

1998

Jessica Martinez Morales, 13; strangled; sex-murder.

Paula Zepeda (Mena) Soto, 62; shot to death.

Martha E. Veloz Valdez, 20; stabbed; sex-murder.

Maria Isela Rivera (Herrera) Nuñez, 28; shot to death.

Silvia Gabriela Laguna Cruz, 16; stabbed; sex-murder.

Ana Hipólita Campos, 38; stabbed.

Maria Maura Carmona Zamora, 30; shot to death.

Clara Zapata Alvarez, 16; shot to death.

Raquel Lechuga Macias, 17; sex-murder.

Unidentified (021198); sex-murder.

Unidentified (021798); sex-murder.

Unidentified (021598); 14-17 years old; sex-murder.

Perla Patricia Sáenz Díaz, 22; stabbed.

Elizabeth Verónica Olivas, 17; stabbed.

Maria Rosa Leon Ramos, 23; stabbed.

Argelia Irene Salazar Crispin, 24; sex-murder.

Unidentified (031798); stabbed.

Laura Lourdes Cordero; sex-murder.

Maria Sagrario Gonzalez Flores, 17; stabbed and strangled; sex-murder.

Gabriela Edith Martínez Calvillo, 15; head wound.

Maria Rosa Leon Ramos, 23; stabbed.

Nora Elizabeth. Flores Flores, 18; strangled.

Brenda Patricia. Mendez Vazquez, 14; strangled; sex-murder.

Maria de Jesus Lechuga Meza, 56; 4 de julio; shot to death.

"Cervantes Avila;" a female minor; head wound.

Maria Lourdes Murillo Landeros; triple homicide; dismembered; revenge.

Aida Araceli Lozano Bolaños, 24; sex-murder; strangled.

Araceli Manríquez Gómez, 25; stabbed.

Emilia Ulloa Galván (Maria Elvira Ulloa Macias); 64; shot to death.

Aidee Osorio Rosales, 51; shot to death.

Olga Gonzalez Lopez, 23; shot to death.

Erendira Ivonne Ponce Hernandez, 17; head wound.

Rocio Barraza Gallegos, 23; shot to death.

Hester Susanne Van Nierop, 28; a citizen of the Netherlands; strangled; sex murder.

Maria Eugenia Mendoza Arias, 28; strangled; sex-murder; head wound.

Elizabeth Soto Flores, 26; strangled.

Zenayda Bermudez Campa; head wound.

Celia G. Gómez de la Cruz, 14; sex-murder.

Elba Reséndiz Rodriguez, 35; shot to death.

Alma Delia Lopez Guevara; remains identified (Federal Attorney General 2006 report).

1999

Maria Estela Martínez Valdez; 22; strangled.

Patricia Monroy Torres, 27; shot to death.

Unidentified (013199), 22; raped and strangled.

Rosalba Lopez Espinoza, 25; unknown.

Paulina Ibarra De Leon, 17; stabbed; homicide-suicide.

Elsa America Arrequin Mendoza, 22; shot to death.

Irma Angelica Rosales Lozano, 13; sex-murder.

"Selene;" 4; beaten to death.

Elena Garcia Alvarado, 35; raped and stabbed.

Gloria Martinez Delgado, 40; police said it was a possible drug overdose.

Gladys Lizeth Ramos (Escarcega) Esparza, 27; shot to death.

Unidentified (030198-031698), 16; raped, strangled and incinerated.

Maria Santos Ramirez Vega, 42; raped and strangled.

Irma Arellano Castillo, 63; stabbed.

Elizabeth Flores Sanchez, 20; beaten to death.

Rosa Maria Rivera Barajas, 36; strangled; sex-murder.

Berta Briones, 41; beaten and stabbed.

Margarita Gonzalez Hernandez, 38; run over by vehicle.

Unidentified (081099); possible drug overdose; stabbed.

Vanesa Horcasitas, 17; shot to death.

Unidentified (091599), 57.

Maria Ascension Aparicio Salazar; found tied with ax wounds.

Maria del Refugio Nuñez Lopez, 3; stabbed.

Blanca Estela Vázquez Valenzuela, 36; shot to death.

Nely America Gomez Holguin, 23; stabbed; sex-murder.

Maria de Lourdes Galvan Juarez, 26; shot to death; homicide-suicide.

Unidentified (111299); woman's skull; 19-22 years old.

Dora Sara Zamarripa, 48; dismembered.

2000

Maria Santos Rangel Flores, 42; head wound.

Juana Gonzalez Piñon, 37; stabbed.

Unidentified (011900), 42; strangled.

Maria Elena Salcedo Meraz, 36; shot to death.

Maria Isabel Nava Vasquez, 18; stabbed; sex-murder.

Ines Silva Merchant, 23; stabbed; sex-murder.

Unidentified (020300).

Laura Rocio Lara Amaro, 17; shot to death.

Alejandra del Castillo Holguin, 26; pregnant; strangled.

(Her sister Perla and a friend named "Graciela" were murdered, too, but their bodies were never found.

A state official said other murders and disappearances are part of the same crime.)

Berenice Ortiz Gomez, 22; shot to death.

Maria Diaz Diaz, 67; shot to death.

Amparo Guzmán Caixba, 17; sex-murder; cervical trauma.

Maria de los Angeles Alvarado Soto, 65; head wound.

Maritza Toribio Flores, 11; shot to death.

Alexis Guadalupe Ramirez, 24-27; strangled.

Yamileth G.; Mejia, 8 months; head wound.

Martha A.; Esquivel Garcia ; 30; shot in double homicide (1).

Sandra Herrings Monreal ; 38; shot in double homicide (2).

Liliana Holguin de Santiago, 15; head wound; sex-murder.

Flor Emilia Monrreal Melendez, 32; shot to death.

Aida Carrillo Rodriguez, 24; lived in El Paso, Texas.

Irma Márquez, 37; strangled.

Elodia Payan Nuñez, 45; strangled.

Leticia Armendáriz Chavira, 44; incinerated.

Sonia Yareli Torres Torres, 18; stabbed.

Maria E. Acosta Armendáriz, 43; shot to death.

Elba Hernandez Martínez, 40; shot to death.

Domitila Santos Trujillo Posada, 72; stabbed.

Adriana (Acevedo) Saucedo Juarez; 17; shot to death.

Maria Elena Chavez Caldera, 15; sex-murder; head wound.

Maria Veronica Santillanes Najera, 22; shot to death.

Fatima Vanesa Flores Diaz, 1; head wound.

Maria I. Chávez (Martínez) Gonzalez, 37; stabbed.

Karina Enríquez Amparan, 21; head wound.

Maria Gerarda (Rivas Triana) Ramírez, 44; stabbed.

Litzy Paola Ramirez, 8 months old; head wound.

Andrea M. Peña Espino, 1; trauma.

2001

Laura Georgina Vargas, 33; shot to death.

Susana Enríquez Enríquez, 29; unknown.

Elvira Carrillo de la Torre, 72; strangled.

Brizia Nevárez de Los Santos, 20; stabbed.

Sandra Corina Gutiérrez Estrada; 17; shot to death.

Reyna S. Lara Luciano, 3; multiple wounds.

Lilia Alejandra García Andrade, 17; strangled; sex-murder.

Maria Saturnina de Leon Calamaco, 50; shot to death.

Norma Leticia Quintero Moreno, 22; shot to death.

Maria Julia Luna Vera, 46; shot to death.

Laura A. Márquez Valenzuela; 18; double homicida (1).

Flor Márquez Valenzuela; 16; double homicida (2).

Irma Rebeca Siqueiros (Sifuentes) Castro, 18; strangled.

Maria Lourdes Gutiérrez Rosales, 34; strangled.

Antonia Valles Fuentes, 46; unknown.

Gema Nevárez García, 4; multiple wounds.

Nelidia Pedroza García, 68; head wound.

Rosa Maria Gonzalez Gutiérrez, 42; stabbed.

Leticia Vargas Flores, 48; shot to death.

Cinthia Paloma Villa Rodriguez, 17; shot to death with her stepfather; brother survived attack.

Consuelo Ortiz Contreras, 2; head wound.

Maria Victoria Arellano Zubiate, 55; stabbed.

Maria Cendejas Martínez (alias Graciela Hernandez), 46; unknown.

Unidentified (110501); sex-murder.

Claudia Ivette Gonzalez Banda, 20; sex-murder (cotton field).

Brenda Esmeralda Herrera Monreal, 15; sex-murder (cotton field).

Laura Berenice. Ramos Monarrez, 17; sex-murder (cotton field.)

Maria de los Angeles Acosta Ramírez, 19; sex-murder (cotton field).

Mayra Juliana Reyes Solis, 17; sex-murder (cotton field).

Maria Rocina Galicia Meraz, sex-murder (cotton field), added in 2006.

Merlin E. Rodriguez Saenz, 17, sex-murder (cotton field), added in 2006.

Martha C. Pizarro Velasquez, 23; sex-murder; found at the Motel Royal.

Alma Neli Osorio Bejarano, 21; strangled.

Unidentified (112501).

Francisca Torres Casillas, 80; head wound.

Natividad Monclova Moreno, 39; stabbed.

Rosa Martha Palacios Briones, 66; head wound.

Maria Luisa. Carzoli Berumen, 33 stabbed.

Susana Torres Valdiviezo, 20; shot to death.

Maria (Lorenza) Clara Mavie Torres Castillo, 27; body found in 2004.

2002

Maria Lopez Torres, 22; stabbed.

Lourdes I. Lucero Campos, 26; sex-murder; body had bite marks similar to earlier cases.

Alma García, 30.

Roberta G. Coronel Molina, 43; shot to death.

Merced Ramirez Morales, 35; head wound.

Kenia Rubi Estrada, 5.

Carmen Estrada Márquez, 26.

Clara Hernandez Salas (1), 32; suffocated.

Claudia G. Martínez Hernandez (2), 3; suffocated.

Leticia Alvidrez Caldera, 26; shot to death.

Elisa Carrera Laguna; 75; double homicide (1).

Carolina Carrera Aceves; 34; resident of El Paso, Texas; double homicide (2).

Miriam Sáenz (Rivera) Acosta, 14; resided in El Paso, Texas.

Gloria M. Escalante Rodriguez, 73; stabbed.

Miriam Soledad Saez Acosta, 14; shot to death.

Maria Luisa Cuellar Cereceres, 24; shot to death.

Cynthia Portillo de Gonzalez (De la Riva), 24; resided in El Paso, Texas; shot to death.

Rosa Inela de la Cruz Madrigal, 19; head wound.

Maria del Rosario Ríos, 40; shot to death.

Petra de la Rosa Moreno Meza, 55; shot to death.

Irma Valdez Sánchez, 35.

Zulema Olivia Alvarado Torres, 13; strangled.

Gloria Betance Rodriguez, 34.

Lucila Silva (Davalos) Salinas, 30; cervical trauma.

Manuela Hernandez (Hermosillo) Quezada, 55; stabbed.

Unidentified (061102); newborn; head wound.

Linda Sandoval (Sanchez) Sanders, 32; shot to death.

Cinthia Y. Armendariz (Moreno) Rodriguez, 16; shot to death.

Nancy G. Quintero Garcia, 20; shot to death.

Dora A. Martinez Mendoza, 34; stabbed.

Julieta Enríquez Rosales, 39; head trauma.

Erika Pérez Escobedo, 29; found seminude; ruled overdose.

Unidentified (092402).

Margarita Briceño Rendon, 36.

Unidentified (100702), 13; sex-murder.

Deissy Salcido Adame Rueda, 20; resided in El Paso, Texas; dismembered; double homicide.

Maria de Jesus Fong Valenzuela, 35; shot to death.

Sandra Maribel Frias Garcia, 22; shot to death.

Martha Elia Sosa Gallardo, 38; shot to death.

Maria de Jesus Gonzalez Apodaca, 32; shot to death.

Olivia Puentes Martínez, 60; unknown.

Gloria Rivas Martínez, 15; sex-murder (Cristo Negro).

Teresita De Jesus Gonzalez Mendoza, 17; case; sex-murder (Cristo Negro).

Mayra Yesenia Najera Larragoiti, 15; sex-murder (Cristo Negro).

2003

Claudia Ivette Tavares Rivera, 22; stabbed.

Brenda Berenice Delgado Rodriguez, 5; sex-murder; stabbed.

Amalia Morales Hernandez, 37; body showed wounds but police said she died of natural causes.

Lilia J. Reyes Espinosa, 26; throat slashed.

Violeta Mabel Alvidrez Barrios, 18; sex-murder (Cristo Negro).

Juana Sandoval Reyna, 17; sex murder (Cristo Negro).

Esmeralda Juarez Alarcón, 16; sex murder Cristo Negro).

Adriana Cecilia Adriano, 19; pregnant; shot to death.

Francilina Pereyra, 38; citizen of Brazil; police said human smugglers abandoned her.

Brenda L. Santos Gonzalez, 15; possible gunfire accident.

Anabel Mendoza Torres, 27; shot to death.

Diana M. Hernandez Vasquez, 14.

Antonia Ceniceros (Corral) Varela, 54; strangled; El Paso police assisted in solving case.

Maria Teresa Tullius, 22; lived in El Paso, Texas. She was found with hands and feet tied.

Olga Guadalupe Juarez Rodriguez, 39; stabbed.

Maria D. Quiñonez Corral, 43; stabbed; sex-murder.

Lorena Villalobos García, 34; unknown.

Maria Inez Estrada Mendoza, 42.

Aida A. Avila Hernandez, 18; shot to death.

Abigail Gonzalez Benitez, 42; stabbed.

Maribel Villa Santana, 31; shot to death.

Araceli Arreola Arreola, 38.

Emy Yamilet. Gaytan Nuñez, 2; multiple wounds.

Miriam Garcia Solorio, 22; shot to death; triple murder (1).

Karina C. Ramos Gonzalez, 22; shot to death; triple murder (2).

Mayra Alamillo Gonzalez, 20; shot to death; triple murder (3).

Miriam Garcia Solorio, 22; shot to death.

Gema Alicia Gamez Llamas, 5; stabbed.

Claudia Perez Serrato, 35; stabbed.

Melisa Montes Montes, 2; head wound.

Jennifer Carolina. Albino (Andino) Dueñas, 27; citizen of Honduras; head injury.

Ruth Micaela Felix Alvarado, 36; head injury.

Consuelo Valles Palacios, gunfire.

Maria de Jesús Hernandez Longinos, suffocated.

2004

Margarita Juarez Torres, 41; head crushed with rock.

Rebeca Contreras Mancha, 23; strangled.

Cristina Escobar Gonzalez, 25; strangled; head injury.

Lorenza Rodríguez Calderon, 32; strangled.

Rosina Solis Corral, 32; shot to death.

Irma Leticia Muller (Ledesma) de Contreras, 36; killed in crossfire.

Alma Delia Chávez Márquez, 37 (1); triple murder.
Killed with Vicente Leon and Laura Ivette Leon Chavez.

Laura Ivette Leon Chavez (2), 13; triple murder victim.

Guadalupe Santos Gomez, 26; strangled.

Alma Brisa Molina Baca, 34; sex-murder; strangled.

Lidia Elias Granados, 52; strangled; found in trash container.

Ana Maria Reyes Valverde, 35; strangled; victim of murder-suicide.

Maria L. Madrid, 78; unknown.

Unidentified (100604), 25; sex-murder.

Martha Lizbeth Hernandez Moreno, 16; sex-murder, strangled.

Barbara Franco Rivera (Leyva Hernandez), 4; unintended gunfire victim.

Unidentified (111304), 3; beaten to death.

Cinthia Irasema Ramos Quezada, 21; strangled; body left on sidewalk.

Flor Fabiola Farrer Rivera, 20; throat slashed.

Martha Cecilia Vargas Jimenez; strangled.

Unidentified (121304); body parts; woman's leg with shoe and sock

2005

Josefina Contreras Solis, 38; found seminude; head struck with a large rock.

Claudia Guillen Hinojosa, 28; pregnant; shot to death.

Maria Liliana Acosta Acosta, 19; shot to death.

Manuela Cano Luna, 50; shot to death.

M. Reyna Ruiz (Perez) Castillo, 55; found in a bag in El Sauzal; shot to death.

Patricia Montelongo De la O, 33; stabbed.

Rocio Paola Marin (Avila) Avalos, 19; stabbed; found in sewage canal.

Unidentified 012105; skull found in sports center and rest of remains inside a paint container.

L. Daniela Cruz Reyes, 6; bite marks and bruises on body; mother charged.

Alejandra Medrano Chavarria, 25; stabbed and strangled.

Coral Arrieta Medina, 17; CNCI computer school student; raped and strangled.

Unidentified (041505); found in Loma Blanca, whether bodies were found before.

Maria Estrella Cuevas Cuevas, 20; raped and stabbed.

Tomasa Chavarria Rangel, 54; beaten with a hammer.

Airis Estrella Enriquez Pando, 7; sex-murder; body found in drum container filled with cement.

Anai Orozco (Lorenzo) Lerma, 10; sex-murder, suffocated.

Martha Alicia Meraz Ramirez, 47; shot to death by stray bullets.

Estela Berenice Gomez Amezquita, 19; strangled.

Alejandra Diaz Sanchez, 13; sex-murder, stabbed, *Unidentified* (092605), 45; found seminude; stabbed.

Olga (Alicia) Brisia Acosta Diaz, 35; stabbed.

Dalila Noemi Diaz (Minjarrez) Moctezuma, 15; shot to death.

Micaela Quintero Quiroz Anguiano, 32; found dead in the Campesino hotel.

Carmen Patricia Ramírez Sánchez, 34; shot to death.

Angelica Isabel Pedroza Hernandez, 22; found seminude.

Alma Delia Moreno Cadena, 45; raped; double homicide (1) Diana Belén Ortega Moreno, 21; raped; double homicide (2).

Martha Granados Villegas, 37; stabbed.

Joseline Nicole Castro Aguilar; head wound.

Ana Miriam Chavira Chavira; ruled as overdose.

Martha Esther Valerio, 35; strangled.

Ingrid Dayana Jimenez Gallegos; infant; head wound.

Patricia Rodriguez Hernandez, 35; shot to death Rufina Verdugo Villalobos; strangled.

"Mague" or "Sonia" (121905), 30-35 years old; sex-murder, beaten.

Claudia Flores Javier; found seminude; stabbed; head injury.

2006

Zoraida Martínez Solís, 22.

Silvia Vela Hernandez, 31.

Margarita Cardoza Carrasco, 74.

Luisa Lorena Hernandez, 27; sex-murder.

Guadalupe Rodríguez Aguilera, 15; sex-murder.

Maria de la Luz Martínez García, 3; sex-murder.

Romelia Longoria Torres, 41.

Gloria Ivana Berumen Robles, 1.

Hilda Canela Rosario, 47.

Maria M. Milán Chacón, 46.

Petra Villalpando Candia, 46.

Elsa Aglae Jurado Torres, 23.

Rosalba Salinas Segura, 33.

Clarivel Ochoa Sánchez, 13.

Claudia Rodríguez Torres, 32.

Abigail Rodriguez Rincón, 25.

Cinthia Judith Zamora Zamora, 21; sex-murder.

Alicia Nava Barajas, 45.

Maria Magdalena Valenzuela Santillán, 16.

Maria Guadalupe Casas Olivas, 45.

Maria Dolores Jasso Arias, 65

Nora Norberto Carrasco, 31

Irma Hernandez Martínez, 51

Reported Missing in Juarez

The following were reported missing in Juarez between 1993 and 2003. Where provided, the missing person's report number is included. In 2004 federal Special Prosecutor Maria Lopez Urbina ordered her staff to assist in finding them. She said her office was able to account for several of the missing girls and women. The Inter-American Commission for Human Rights said in its 2003 report on Juarez that according to Chihuahua state officials about 260 girls and women were missing. The Federal Attorney General's 2006 report said 34 were missing.

Maria del Rosario Gomez Solis; 12/22/1993; 26456/93; located alive. She told a TV station in 2005 she was abducted and was a victim of sex trafficking for several years.

Verónica Montañés Monreal; 5/4/1995; 10659/93.

Abigail Esmeralda Reyes Jacobo, 15; 6/19/1995; 1426/93.

Maria Elena García Salas, 18; 12/5/1995; 2219/93; Gema.

Erica Ivonne Madrid Ríos; 1996; 168769/96.

Lidia Herrera Herrera; 1996; 6839/96.

Guadalupe Espinoza Boyso; 1/6/1996; 252/99.

Verónica Muñoz Andrade, 17; 1/25/1996; 1816/96.

Rosina Blanco Ramos, 26; 1/26/1996; 12905/96.

Maria Guadalupe del Rio Vásquez, 19; Feb. 27, 1996; 4011/96; Felipe Angeles.

Micaela Ríos Saldívar, 49; June 12, 1996; 13586/96; bus terminal.

Miriam Lizeth Bernal Hernández, 19; 6/6/1998 or 7/1/1996; 301/98.

Blanca Grisel Guzmán, 15; 10/10/1996 or 3/11/1996; 33/96.

Verónica Montañez Monreal, 29; 6/4/1996 Elena Guadian Simental, 19; 3/22/1997; 201/97.

Blanca Cecilia Rivas Lopez, 13; 10/1/1997.

Griselda Mares Mata, 23; 3/11/1998; 191/98; Pachangas.

Silvia Arce, 29; 3/12/1998; 5333/98; Pachangas.

Gabriela Holguín Griselda Reyes, 22; 4/2/1998; 7661/98; airport.

Maria del Rosario Palacios Moran, 18; 12/7/1998; 688/98.

Alma Delia Lopez Guerra, 26; 10/16/1998.

Ana Azucena Martínez Pérez, 9; 3/18/1999; 159/99;

Ejercito Nacional.

Carmen Cervantes Terrazas, 42; 5/1/1999; 354/99.

Rosa Velia Cordero Hernandez, 24; 5/1/1999; 368/99; downtown.

Elizabeth Rodriguez Pérez, 33; 11/18/1999; 557/99.

Celina Uribe Vásquez; 2/25/2000; 75/00.

Miriam Cristina Gallegos; 17; 5/4/2000; 17.

Blanca Estela Garza Aguirre; 5/20/2000; 242/00.

Nancy Edith Hernandez Chacón; 11/1/2000; 437/00.

Margarita Ruiz Chaparro, 37; 4/15/2001; 262/01; near Rio Grande.

Maria de los Angeles Acosta; 19; 4/25/2001; 118/01.

Maria de Jesus Sandoval Gonzalez, 33; 6/7/2001; 244/01.

Guadalupe Luna de la Rosa, 19; 9/30/2001; 398/00.

Verónica Martínez Hernandez, 20; 10/28/2001; 422/00.

Barbara A. Martínez Ramos, 20, 11/7/2001.

Sofia Torres, 15; 3/18/2002.

Alma M. Lopez Garza, 27; 2/25/2002; 40/02.

Claudia Noemi Romero; 3/10/2002; 47/02.

Karla P. Rodriguez Romero; 3/31/2002; 8513/03/999.

Maria Fátima Flores Ortiz, 16; 5/8-11/2002; 98/02.

Maria Isabel Mejía Sapien, 18; 5/10/2002; 103/02; downtown.

Teresa D. González Mendoza; 13; 7/6/2002; 139/02.

Beatriz Angelica Valera; 8/11/2002; 173/02.

Samantha Y. Carrasco Carrasco; 8/17/2002; 182/02.

San Juana E. Sifuentes Rivas; 11/16/2002; 243/02.

Rosa M. Mayela Ituarte Silva, 37; 11/21/2002; 252/02.

Erika Abigail Loera, 26; 12/20/2002.

Maria C. Torres Campos; 1/3/2003; 002/03.

Lizeth Sosa Mendoza, 1/6/2003; 006/03.

Estela Gardea Chávez, 32; 1/10/2003; 007/03; downtown.

Maria G. Segura Fernández, 1/11/2003; 008/03.

Luisa García Hernandez, 14; 1/20/2003; 017/03; Colonia Del Rey. Maricruz Leo Huerta; 1/23/2003; 019/03.

Maribel Parra Pérez; 3/2/2003; 044/03.

Maria D. Frank Martínez; 3/3/2003; 048/03.

Yohanna P. Miranda González, 3/9/2003; 056/03.

Sayra Luz Lujan Campa, 3/13/2003; 6642/03/999.

Victoria Paloma Holguín Varela; 3/17/2003; 062/03.

Blanca Estela Urrieta Colon; 3/23/2003; 065/03.

Adriana Morin Zugasti; 3/25/2003; 065/03.

Maria I. Rascón Fernández; 3/30/2003; 066/03.

Marisela González Vargas; 3/30/2003; 8513/03/999.

Cristal Palacios Rosales; 3/31/2003; 8513/03/999.

Perla de la Cruz Jacobo; 3/31/2003; 8513/03/999.

Ana Laura García Castrejón, 24; 7/21/2004; Ejercito Nacional.

Julia Hernandez Hernandez, 20; 8/11/2004.

Edith Aranda Longorio, 22; taught computer classes; 05/3/2005.

Irma Elizabeth Vargas, 16; 8/4/2005; downtown.

Chihuahua City Victims

Chihuahua City, the Chihuahua State capital, is about 250 miles south of Juarez. Young women began to disappear and were killed in ways similar to victims in Juarez, according to Justicia para Nuestras Hijas and Centro de los Derechos Humanos de las Mujeres.

Name, age and cause of death (when known):

Norma L. Luna Holguín, 16; sex-murder; 1999.

Jacqueline C. Sanchez Hernandez, 14; sex-murder; 2000.

Miriam C. Gallegos Venegas, 17; missing in 2000; sex-murder; identified in 2006 by Argentine forensic team.

Erika Ivonne Ruiz Zavala, 16; 2001.

Perla Chávez Rodriguez, 25; 2001.

Minerva Torres Alveldaño, 18; 2001.

Rosalba Pizarro Ortega, 16; 2001; sex-murder; identified in 2005 by Argentine forensic team.

Paloma A. Escobar Ledesma, 16; sex-murder; 2002.

Marcela V. Rayas Arellanes, 16; sex-murder; 2003.

Claudia Urias Berthaud, 14; sex-murder; missing in 2003; identified in 2006 by Argentine forensics team.

Maria Teresa Araiza Hernandez, 19; 2003.

Neyra Azucena Cervantes, 19; sex-murder; 2003.

Her cousin David Meza allegedly was tortured into confessing to the crime.

Charges against him were dismissed in 2006.

Diana Yazmin Garcia Medrano, 18; sex-murder; 2003.

Unidentified (032804), suspected of being a transient; 2004.

Teresa Torbellin Loya, 33; head wound; 2004(?).

Luisa R. Chávez Chávez, 14; 2004; sex-murder.

Unidentified (08/04).

Maria E. Cano Gutierrez, 21; 2004; double homicide victim found with 2-year-old daughter.

Denisse Perez Cano, 2; double homicide, 2004.

Sandra Rios Salmon, 15; sex-murder; 2004.

Brenda Daniela Garcia Anchondo, double homicide, 2005.

Missing in Chihuahua City

Erika Noemi Carrillo Enriquez, 20; 2000.

Miriam C. Gallegos Venegas, 17; 2000.

Yesenia C. Vega Márquez, 16; 2001.

Julieta Gonzalez Valenzuela, 17; 2001.

Bianca S. Quezada Pérez, 17; 2002.

Yesenia M. Barraza Quiñonez, 15; 2002.

About the Author

Diana Washington Valdez is an international journalist and author based in the United States. Her 2002 series about the Juarez women's murders "Death Stalks the Border" in the *El Paso Times* was nominated for a Pulitzer Prize. The series received a First Place Award from the Texas Associated Press Managing Editors. Some of her other recognitions include the Congressional Hispanic Caucus Institute Latina Leader in Literature Award, the National Association of Social Workers (Texas) Media Person of the Year Award for journalism that advances social justice, the Samuel L. Chavkin Award for Integrity in Latin American Journalism, and the National Association of Hispanic Journlists - Frank Del Olmo Print Journalist of the Year Award. Her book in English *The Killing Fields: Harvest of Women* was published by Peace at the Border and highlights eight years of investigation. Her book in Spanish *Cosecha de Mujeres* was published first by Oceano in Mexico and Spain. Over the years, Ms. Washington Valdez collaborated on various journalistic projects for print and online publications, radio programs, and documentaries in the United States, Mexico, Spain, the United Kingdom, Poland, Austria, Canada, Norway, and Germany. Her areas of reporting ranged from government corruption to drug-trafficking to the Gulf War Illness. She is the recipient of numerous awards and recognitions. She has a bachelor's degree in journalism and a master's degree in political science from the University of Texas at El Paso. She taught political science and served in the military.

About Peace at the Border

Peace at the Border Film Productions, LLC, is a media company based in the United States that focuses on issues of social importance. Company co-founder and executive producer Lorena Mendez-Quiroga produced "Border Echoes" ("Ecos de una Frontera"). The documentary highlights the work of investigative jouranalist Diana Washington Valdez, who exposed high-level corruption in the murders of women in Juarez, Mexico, in the book *The Killing Fields: Harvest of Women (Cosecha de Mujeres)*. A new digital edition of the book was published in 2020 in Spanish and English. Peace at the Border has produced such films as "Despues de la Tormenta" (After the Storm), which explores government corruption in Honduras during and after Hurricane Mitch; "Sarah's Journey" and "Orphans of Addiction." "The Jose Gutierrez Story," a forthcoming film, is about a Guatemalan immigrant in search of the American dream who was the first Latino Marine killed in the war in Iraq. Another film in development "Project Jumbo!" captures the everyday life of children in rural Kenya, Africa. While it exposes government corruption, it also demonstrates that the war against poverty can be won. See more at www.borderechoes.com.

INDEX

A

AFI. *See* Federal Investigative Agency (AFI)
Almaraz murder, 107–108
Amnesty International's 2003 report, 35
Anti-demonstrators, 79
Anti-drug officials, 85
Anti-insurgency campaign, 210
Anti-kidnapping unit, 99
Artifact, 24
Arvide's warning, 103
Atrocities
    business emperors, 36–37
    fear and relentless violence, 29
    homicide victims, 29
    Juarez violence, 34–36
    life on border, 31–34
Autopsy, 17, 223–224

B

Bandas civiles (CB radio), 75
Bandas civiles groups, 26
Barrio Aztecas, 169
Binational operation, 227
Black hole, 50
Blanco to fire, 151
Body's identity, 17–18
Border community, 9
Border echoes, 281
Border Industrialization Program 1965, 22
Border liaison mechanism, 145
Botched operation
    chain-link fence, 226
    Crawford leaves FBI, 228–229
    Crawford under fire, 229–230
    drug-induced comas, 227
    intolerable killings, 236
    joint border operation, 226
    journalist reprisal, 234–235
    killers protection, 234

Mexican official complains, 230–231
police chief quits, 232–233
sensitive file, 235–236
setback, 231–232
startling allegations, ex-chief, 233–234
Business class, 22–23
Business emperors, 36–37

C

Caballito (Little Horse) mountain, 28
Candlemas, 301
Cartel's bad girls, 105–106
Cartel wars
  allegations, 111–113
  conservative opposition party, 110
  corruption, 110
  explosive document, 111–112
  goal scored, 114–115
  intelligence sources, 111
  rumor, 115–116
  troubles, 116–117
Case surface flaws, 154–155
Center for Research and National Security (CISEN), 22
Cerillo death, 108–109
Chihuahua city
  California deputies, 272–273
  drug cartels, 271
  electric prods, 266
  femicides, 266, 269–270
  inconsistencies, 266
  investigations lacking, 273–274
  judicial system, 272
  near-asphyxiation, 266
  no interest in justice, 269
  planting evidence, 270–271
  protests against detentions, 267–269
  psychological abuse, 266
  victim's family skeptical, 267
Child sex, 279
Citizens/legal residents, 32
City's invisible victims, 48
Cocky drug dealer, 95–96
Colegio de la Frontera (COLEF), 45

Colombian accent, 140–141
Colombianization, 212
Community volunteers, 23
Confessions, 181
Corrupt system, 118
Cotton field murders
   announcement, 67
   blood residue, 72
   bloody month, 67–68
   Brazen killers, 68–69
   counting deaths, 69–70
   earth-moving equipment, 71
   evidence left behind, 72–73
   families reaction, 73–74
   massive candlelight vigil, 74
   workable evidence, 71
Crime organizations, 195, 208, 261
Crime-related shootings, 123
Crimes against humanity, 217–219
Crime scene
   border cargo (March 2002), 76–78
   border cross, 80–81
   company officials, 76
   DNA tests, 78
   marched for life, 78–79
   searchers, 75
   U.S. advocacy groups, 75
Crimes of passion, 95
Crimes of state, 163
Crime stoppers, 219
Cristo Negro
   body yields, 139–140
   cooperative, 52
   graveyards, 56–59
   handing out fliers, 53–54
   hitting bottom, 54–55
   land disputes, 56
   mysterious bodies, 55–56
   organized killers, 60
   planted bodies, 59
   state investigations, 53
   triangle on her back, 54
   victims, 53
   witness accounts, 51–52
   women's bodies, 51, 52
Cultural gap, 29

D

Death Stalks the Border, 144
Death threats, 11, 61, 254
Decomposition, 69
Delegate Zero, 296
Destabilization, 195–196
Dirty war, 130, 166, 187, 289, 310

activist encourages
mothers, 198–
199
artifact, 212
atrocities, 290
Chihuahua's victims,
211–212
dropkick operation,
205–206
FBI documents 600
deaths, 199–200
human rights activist,
197
Mexico receives file,
199
military implication,
206–207
mystery "Rambos,"
204–205
political dissidents,
198
political repression,
197, 201–202
prosecutor
appointment,
200–201
rape and kill training,
210–211
signed paychecks, 207–
208
training Argentine
style, 208
unsanitized report,
203–204

U.S. foreign policies,
202–203
victims, 209
witness, 198, 201
Downtown danger, 18–20
Drug addicts, 132
Drug cartel
corrupting influence
and terrorist
rule, 85
drug-trafficking
business, 86
excursion, 87
female victims, 88–90
friends circle, 87–88
Drug intoxication, 48
Drug possession, 155
Drug-trafficking, 32, 58,
86, 115, 191, 204,
205, 257, 262, 309

E

Easy Rider, 125
Economic development,
300
Economic dynamics, 31
Economic terrorism, 257
The Egyptian, 150–151
Ejido Lopez Mateos, 26
El Brujo (witch), 94
El Compadre, 100–101
El Mexicano newspaper,
47
El Paso Interreligious
Sponsoring

Organization (EPISO), 30
Empresarios, 36
Escajeda band, 124
Escaped killer
   devastating U.N. document, 179–180
   El Paso suspects, 177
   elusive suspect, 170–171
   experts detect corruption, 180–181
   Guatemalan serial rape suspect, 178
   judicial chaos, 181–183
   missing/on move, 172
   railway, 175–177
   raping and murdering, 170
   Richy letter, 178–179
   suspect's sketch, 169–170
   troubling account, 173–174
Espionage, 12–13
Evidence lacking, 152–153
Extermination of women, 282
Extrajudicial executions, 203

F
Family violence, 16
Federal Bureau of Investigation (FBI)
   cases with traits, 223–224
   chief on board, 216–217
   dangerous liaisons, 228
   drug gang involvement report, 221–222
   fear and loathing, 224–225
   personal altar, 222–223
   profilers, 214–215
   report leaked, 220–221
   serial killer at work, 215–216
   startling revelation, 265
   women's homicides, 228
Federal Investigative Agency (AFI), 210
Federal Preventive Police (PFP), 210
Federal security agencies, 255
Femicides, 70
   abductions, 278
   alarming, 277
   Americas, 283–284
   avoid incidents, 275

Canada's missing
women, 284–
285
cartel's corruption, 191
Chihuahua city, 269–
270
cocaine trail, 284
crimes across Mexico,
276–277
evidence, 277
evolution, 207
FBI, 213–225
Guatemala, 281–283
human-trafficking,
278–279
Mexican authorities,
298
myth, 202
police and judicial
procedures, 179
political agenda, 135
public shooting deaths,
110
Tijuana déjà vu, 279–
280
women's murders, 70
Ferrocarril Mexicano
(FERROMEX), 54
Fuero, 289

G
Graveyards, 56–59

H
Halcones, 210–211

High-profile
assassinations, 290
Homosexuals, 132
Human destruction, 285
Human sacrifices, 103–
104
Hydrofluoric acid plant,
39

I
Illegal drugs, 88
Impunity, 160
Injustice, 80
Insight, 58
Institutional
Revolutionary
Party (PRI), 27, 65,
110, 114, 232, 260,
289, 295
Intelligence agencies, 89
Intelligence network, 206
Inter-American
Commission of
Human Rights, 35,
66, 144
International Association
of Relatives and
Friends of
Disappeared
Persons, 132
Intolerable killings, 236,
271
Isla del Sacrificio (Island
of Sacrifice), 43

J

Jail sentence, 104
Juarez homicide investigations, 96
Judicial proceedings, 151
Juniors, 144, 256, 258–259

L

Labor organizations, 135
La Cueva, 15
Land disputes, 56
Laser visa, 32
Latin American Federation of Associations of Families of Detained/Disappeared Persons (AFADEM), 209
Law enforcement, 9, 25, 35, 91, 132
Lawyer death
  bond arrangements, 61
  bus driver suspection, 65–66
  death threats, 61
  police implication, 63–65
  truck crashing, 62
  witness account, 62
Legitimate businesspeople, 59
Loma Blanca, 40–41

M

Maquiladora murders, 15
Maras Salva Truchas, 281
Marijuana plantation, 291
Maxi proceso, 111
Melina's death, 92–94
Mexican authorities, 22
Mexican federal agent, 89
Mexican National Commission of Human Rights, 57
Mexican National Defense Secretariat (SEDENA), 211
Mexico's Integral Family Development Office (DIF), 279
Mexico's *machismo* culture, 16–17
Mexico's secret files
  death threats, 254
  double file, 255
  hellish flight, 259–260
  juniors, 258–259
  officials supplied women, 256
  protest NAFTA, 256–257
  serial killers, 254
  surveillance, 254
  untouchable killers, 260
Military's mission, 12
Modus operandi, 128, 190, 269

commission, 240–241
computer schools, 241–242
evidence lost, 239–240
Internet suspicions, 244–245
investigators, 237–238
report, 238–239
testimony, 242–243
victims, 237
Money laundering, 262
Muerte en Juarez (Death in Juarez), 99
Mujeres de Negro (women in black), 78
Mujeres por Juarez, 21
Multimillion-dollar cocaine transaction, 307–308
Mysterious bodies, 55–56

N
Narco corridos, 92
Narco democracies, 212
Narco terrorism, 88
Narco-violence, 291
National Action Party (PAN), 9, 11, 65, 110, 120, 127, 132, 135, 149, 159, 209, 290
National Security Archive (NSA), 203
Neutral international body, 265
New York Times Magazine, 279
Noches Juarenses, 196
Norte de Ciudad Juarez newspaper, 21, 48
North American Free Trade Agreement, 306

O
Odonatological forensics, 121
The Official Story, 209
Operation Casablanca, 90
Operation Hold the Line, 33
Operation Plaza Sweep, 188–189, 213
Operation Sagrario
  campaign's leadership style, 248
  crime and corruption, 247
  dangerous drug dealers, 252–253
  drug-related disappearances, 246
  informal basis, 246
  media blitz, 248–250

no response from
   Mexico, 250–
   251
officials ignore leads,
   251–252
Organized crime, 50, 53,
   88, 118, 129, 181,
   226, 227, 255, 258,
   284
Organ-trafficking, 163–
   164

P

Pachangas, 143
The Pact
   across border, 307–
      308
   Colombian drug dealer,
      308–309
   confidential sources,
      301
   crime lords, 304–305
   drug cartel, 306
   dust in desert, 309–
      310
   injustices, 301
   intelligence source,
      305
   president deal, 303–
      304
   ramifications, 304
   religion and drugs, 307
   unusual summit, 302–
      303
Pacts of power
   community of activists,
      261
   compulsion, 264
   experts, 262
   FBI's startling
      revelation, 265
   new officials, 264–265
   sexual disorder, 263
   sociopaths, 263
   violent sexual crimes,
      261
PAN. *See* National Action
   Party (PAN)
Pan American Health
   Organization
   (PAHO), 34–35
PAN's youth organization,
   11
Pattern of gender
   violence, 35
Paychecks, 207–208
Pesquisas en Linea
   (online searches),
   220
Petroleos Mexicanos
   (PEMEX), 22, 299
PFP. *See* Federal
   Preventive Police
   (PFP)
Plaza Sweep
   investigation, 16,
   124, 144, 163
   anti-crime summit, 294
   critics, 192–193

destabilize plans, 195–196
mass murders and disappearances, 187
media reports, 189–191
officials silent, 192
operation, 188–189
political dissidents, 195
polygraphs, 193–194
social and judicial decomposition, 187
systematic crimes, 187
transnational crime syndicates, 194
Police blotter
 captains, young woman disappear, 146–147
 Colombian accent, 140–141
 concerns, 134–135
 cops work for cartel, 136–137
 corrupt mayor protection, 147
 Cristo Negro yields, 139–140
 custody dispute, 133
 $100,000 bribe, 137–138
 drug-related conviction, 143
 fear killers, 135
 federal agents, 143
 jobs for sale, 145–146
 Juarez killer cops, 135–136
 killing/sexually assaulting women, 133
 Mexican federal police, 144–145
 narco cops, 141–142
 official's alleged sex ring, 138–139
 public comments, 132
 U.S. woman rape, 134
 violent deaths, 142
 women's murder investigations, 132
Police brotherhood, 129
Police cartel
 Lardizabal death, 118–119
 minor traffic offenses, 118
 mother seeks justice, 120–122
 prime suspect is murdered, 120
 women's murders, 118
Police cooperation, 213
Police death squad, 102
Political connections, 22

Political dissidents, 89
Political party, 9
Political repression, 201–202
Politicians
  allegations, 294
  convulsions, 289
  drug corruption, 289
  economic interests, 299–300
  help seeking, 297–299
  Mexico's next president, 295–296
  official offenses ignored, 290–291
  political insiders, 290
  political pacts, 292–293
  presidential female candidate, 296
  shocking video, 291–292
  Zapatistas campaign, 296–297
Ponte Viva (be alert), 74
Pornography, 279
Poverty, 41
PRI. *See* Institutional Revolutionary Party (PRI)
Proceso magazine, 295
Professional investigation, 76

Psychological exam, 156

R
Radio Magia Digital, 51
Railway killer, 175–177
Rebeldes, 27–28, 124, 125, 153, 158, 169, 179, 180, 182
Red Book, 45
Reforma newspaper, 242
Renteria gang, 176
Reprisals, 149–150
Residents, 21, 33, 57, 58
Revolutionary Democratic Party (PRD), 120
Richy's diary, 178–179
Rompope, 302

S
Sacrifices, 29
Sagrario's death
  cases grow cold, 44–45
  disappeared, 40–43
  esteem, 38
  fine, white dust, 39–40
  serial killers, 45–46
  trails of, 43–44
Santa Muerte (Holy Death) movement, 165
Satellite communications system, 189
Savage counterinsurgency campaign, 210

The Secret History of Drug-Trafficking, 111
Selena movie, 16
Sex offenders, 165–166
Sex ring, 138–139
Sex-traffickers, 25
Sexual assault, 10–11, 16, 43, 55, 70, 142
Sharif's patents, 156–157
Shocking desert deaths, 25–28
Shockwaves, 89
Shoddy investigation, 13–14
Shooting at Vertigo, 96
Smear campaign, 148
Smeltertown, 39
Social Democratic Party, 296
Social gatherings, 99
Socio-economic status, 21
Special Air Mobile Forces Group, 204–205
State police raid bars, 49–50
Strangulation, 26, 45

T
Tableau, 23–25
Terror with badge
  enigmatic commander, 130–131
  experts suspect police, 126
  family/political connections, 124
  former cop, Capo, 127
  high-profile cop, 124–125
  letter from Guadalajara, 127–130
  police under fire, 125
  state police task force, 123
  violent rape, 123
Threats against Arvide, 101
Toll-free hotline, 220
Toltecas, 155–156, 179, 180, 214
Torture techniques, 195, 208
Transnational corporations, 58
Trevi's imprisonment, 92
Trial investigations
  cotton field suspects 2001, 160–162
  death has saint, 164–166
  imprisonment, 158
  legislative commission, 159
  murder suspects, 158
  organ-trafficking, 163–164

proportional representation system, 159
security forces suspected, 166–167
sex, lies and videotapes, 162–163
Sharif's death, 160

U
Ultra-right wing, 260
United Nations Children's Fund (UNICEF), 279
United Nations Office Against Drugs and Crime (UNODC), 180
Urban growth, 57
U.S. and Mexico border wages, 30–31
U.S. foreign policies, 202–203
U.S. Immigration and Customs Enforcement (ICE), 135–136, 278

V
Violence
 communication system, 262
 crime-related, 32
 drug overdoses, 48
 evidence, 51
 family, 16
 fear and relentless, 29
 in Juarez, 34–36

W
White Brigade, 198, 202, 203, 209–211
Whores, 135
Women's crimes, 22

Z
Zapatistas campaign, 257, 296–297
Zetas, 205